vest, demographic determinants of British and American building cycles, and changes in the productivity of labor in the machine tool industry.

In a concluding section four authors discuss specifically the origins and development of the new economic history and show that, as a substantial supplement to work along more traditional lines, its methods and application are both desirable and possible.

Donald N. McCloskey is a member of the economics department at the University of Chicago. He is the author of *Economic Maturity and Entrepreneurial Decline: British Iron and Steel, 1870-1913*, awarded the David A. Wells Prize by Harvard University.

Quantitative Studies in History

QUANTITATIVE STUDIES IN HISTORY

Sponsored by the History Advisory Committee of the Mathematical Social Science Board, the series is designed to encourage the application of mathematical methods to historical analysis. Forthcoming volumes include *The Dimensions of Quantitative Research in History* (fall 1972), *An International Comparison of Systems of Slavery, Quantitative Studies of Legislative Behavior*, and *Social Mobility during the Nineteenth and Early Twentieth Centuries in Europe and America*. The series is being published by Princeton University Press.

Essays on a Mature Economy:
Britain after 1840

Essays on a Mature Economy: Britain after 1840

Edited by

Donald N. McCloskey

Princeton University Press

Princeton, New Jersey

1971

First published 1971
by Methuen & Co Ltd
11 New Fetter Lane, London EC4
© 1971 Methuen & Co Ltd
Printed in Great Britain

Published in the United States by
Princeton University Press

L.C. Card Number 73–170254
I.S.B.N. 0–691–05198–4

Contents

Contents vii

The Mathematical Social Science Board

This volume is one of a series sponsored by the History Advisory Committee of the Mathematical Social Science Board in order to encourage the application of mathematical methods to historical analysis. Other volumes planned in this series include: *An International Comparison of Systems of Slavery, Social Mobility during the Nineteenth and Early Twentieth Centuries in Europe and America*, and *Quantitative Studies of Legislative Behavior*.

The Mathematical Social Science Board (MSSB) was established in 1964 under the aegis of the Center for Advanced Studies in the Behavioral Sciences 'to foster advanced research and training in the application of mathematical methods in the social sciences.' The following fields are each represented on MSSB by one member: anthropology, economics, history, geography, linguistics, political science, psychology and sociology. The three methodological disciplines of mathematics, statistics and computer science are also represented. Members of MSSB are appointed, subject to the approval of the Board of Trustees of the Center, for a term of four years. At the present time the members of MSSB are:

Robert P. Abelson, Professor of Psychology, Yale University

Hayward R. Alker, Jr, Professor of Political Science, M.I.T. (Chairman)

Richard C. Atkinson, Professor of Psychology and Education, Stanford University

Hubert M. Blalock, Jr, Professor of Sociology, University of North Carolina

Preston Cutler, Center for Advanced Study in the Behavioral Sciences

Michael F. Dacey, Professor of Geography, Northwestern University

Robert W. Fogel, Professor of Economics and History, University of Chicago and University of Rochester

David G. Hays, Professor of Linguistics, State University of New York, Buffalo

Harold Kuhn, Professor of Economics and Mathematics, Princeton University

Roy Radner, Professor of Economics and Statistics, University of California, Berkeley

Howard Raiffa, Frank P. Ramsey Professor of Managerial Economics, Harvard University

A. Kimball Romney, Dean, School of Social Sciences, University of California, Irvine

MSSB has established advisory committees to plan its activities in the various substantive fields with which it is concerned. The current members of the History Advisory Committee are:

William O. Aydelotte, Professor of History, University of Iowa

Allen G. Bogue, Professor of History, University of Wisconsin

Albert Fishlow, Professor of Economics, University of California at Berkeley

Robert W. Fogel, Professor of Economics and History, University of Chicago and University of Rochester

Douglas Price, Professor of Government, Harvard University

Lawrence Stone, Professor of History, Princeton University

Charles Tilly, Professor of History and Sociology, University of Michigan

Supported by grants from the National Science Foundation, MSSB has organized five major classes of activities.

(1) *Training Programmes*, which last from two to eight weeks during the summer, are designed to provide young pre- and post-Ph.D.s with intensive training in some of the mathematics pertinent to their substantive field and with examples of applications to specific problems.

(2) *Research and Training Seminars*, which last from four to six weeks, are composed of both senior scientists and younger people who have already received some training in mathematical applications. The focus is on recent research, on the intensive exploration of new ideas, and on the generation of new research. The training is less formal than in (1); it has the apprentice nature of advanced graduate work.

(3) *Advanced Research Seminars*, last from four to six weeks, but they are almost exclusively restricted to senior scientists and are devoted to fostering advanced research. They afford the possibility of extensive and penetrating contact over a prolonged period, which would otherwise probably not be possible, of men deeply steeped in research.

(4) *Preparation of Teaching Materials,* In some areas, the absence

of effective teaching materials — even of suitable research papers — is a very limiting factor in the development of research and teaching activities within the university framework. The Board has, therefore, felt that it could accelerate the development of such materials, in part, by financial support and, in part, by help in organizing their preparation.

(5) *Special Conferences.* Short conferences, lasting a few days, are organized to explore the possibilities of the successful development of mathematical theory and training in some particular area that has not previously been represented in the programmes, or to review the progress of research in particular areas when such a review seems warranted.

Robert W. Fogel, *Chairman*
History Advisory Committee, MSSB

Chicago, Illinois
December 1970

Preface

This volume contains the papers and proceedings of a conference on the new economic history of Britain held at Eliot House, Harvard University on 1, 2 and 3 September 1970. Some forty scholars from the United States and abroad with an interest in the application of economic theory and statistical methods to British economic history participated. Fifteen papers, distributed in advance, were presented and discussed in morning and afternoon sessions over the three days. The papers treated a wide range of topics in British economic history from 1840 to 1930. Their unifying theme was their application of the tools of modern economics to economic history.

The discussion, which is published after the paper to which it refers, was both summarized by rapporteurs among the participants and taperecorded, and an account of it was compiled by me from these sources, guided by the revisions suggested by the participants. The account uses the participants' words where possible, but they are, of course, not responsible for the details of expression as they appear in the volume. To retain the flavour of the conference in the volume neither the papers nor the discussion of them have been revised substantially, apart from an additional note by Peter Lindert and Keith Trace on the discussion of their paper and a short summary essay and critique by Berrick Saul on the papers dealing with the performance of late Victorian entrepreneurs.

The conference was made possible by a generous grant from the Mathematical Social Science Board of the National Science Foundation. I should like to thank Preston Cutler and Robert Fogel, both members of the Board, for their help in formulating and administering the grant. The organizing committee under my chairmanship, consisting of Paul David, John H. Habakkuk and Barry Supple, was responsible for choosing the participants and the papers, and guided my inexperienced hand on many details of the work. I was helped in arranging the conference and in editing the volume by a great many other people. My secretary, Marilyn Gore, combined efficiency and good cheer in her inimitable way at every stage. Peter Mathias, performing an invaluable liaison function between Methuen in England and me in the United States, can be largely credited for the unusually short delay between the conference itself and the publication of the papers and proceedings. Brinley Thomas and the Cambridge University Press kindly permitted Thomas's essay, which is to be published in a new edition of his *Migration and Economic Growth*, to be published here as well. Alan Heimert, the Master of Eliot House, and the Eliot House staff were most generous in providing a congenial environment for the conference and G. S. Paulson of Beale Travel Service adjusted quickly and accurately to a continually shifting list of participants. Finally, the participants themselves deserve, of course, the major credit for any success the conference may have had. Their vigorous inquiry in the papers and discussion into the possibilities of applying economics to British economic history, as well as their wit and grace in the midst of considering these weighty matters, made the conference an unusually productive intellectual experience.

Chicago, Illinois   Donald N. McCloskey
December 1970

Participants of the Conference

D. H. Aldcroft, University of Leicester
P. A. David, Stanford University
P. Deane, Cambridge University
M. Edelstein, Columbia University
S. L. Engerman, University of Rochester
M. E. Falkus, London School of Economics and Political Science
C. H. Feinstein, Cambridge University
R. Floud, Cambridge University
P. Friedman, Massachusetts Institute of Technology
A. Gerschenkron, Harvard University
C. K. Harley, University of British Columbia
H. J. Habakkuk, Oxford University
R. M. Hartwell, Oxford University
G. Hawke, Victoria University of Wellington
J. R. T. Hughes, Northwestern University
E. H. Hunt, London School of Economics and Political Science
A. H. Imlah, Tufts University
D. S. Landes, Harvard University
P. H. Lindert, University of Wisconsin
C. Maier, Harvard University
P. Mathias, Oxford University
R. C. O. Matthews, Oxford University
D. N. McCloskey, University of Chicago
P. D. McClelland, Harvard University
D. E. Moggridge, Cambridge University
S. Pollard, University of Sheffield
J. B. Roth, Harvard University
L. Sandberg, Ohio State University
S. B. Saul, University of Edinburgh
B. Solow, Brandeis University
B. E. Supple, University of Sussex
P. Temin, Massachusetts Institute of Technology
B. Thomas, University of South Wales and Monmouthshire
K. Trace, University of Essex
J. Tyce, University of Manchester
W. Vamplew, University of Edinburgh
N. von Tunzelmann, Cambridge University
J. G. Williamson, University of Wisconsin

Editor's Introduction

The papers in this volume examine selected issues in the history of the British economy during the century following the Industrial Revolution from the perspective of economic theory and applied statistics. Nothing could be more natural than to apply the tools that have been used with some success in economics for two hundred years to economic history. It would be strange if the insights into the use of economic logic and economic fact that have been acquired since Adam Smith's day proved of little use in economic history, the more so considering that these insights were acquired by men studying economic issues that are now historical. Smith's theory of the division of labour, Ricardo's theory of rent, Marshall's theory of demand and supply, and Keynes's theory of employment were fashioned to make sense out of contemporary problems, as were the contributions of the economic statisticians, beginning with the political arithmeticians of the seventeenth and eighteenth centuries and running through Bowley and Stamp to the modern masters of national income accounting and econometrics. A historian looking at these problems, moreover, has at his disposal the end result of this long refinement of the study of economic behaviour. The intellectual tools used by Mill to examine the effect of the Corn Laws, for example, were improved by Marshall and Edgeworth and developed after them into a powerful engine of analysis, the theory of international trade, and it would be most surprising if that theory could not be made to yield insights into past as much as into present Corn Laws. The tools used by Marshall to examine Britain's relative economic decline at the end of the nineteenth century have been refined to the point where some of his beliefs and those of his contemporaries can be subjected to quantitative tests, as they are in fact in many of the papers in this volume.

To be sure, an economic historian has a wider purview than an economist, if only because he often deals with longer periods of time and, if he is to tell a coherent story, must sometimes deal with a larger number of varying factors. Yet this is hardly an argument against the use of economics in economic history. There is no reason to sacrifice the depth of insight into economic issues provided by modern economics in order to pursue breadth of insight: surely one would want both. Economics in any case provides a valuable framework within which to understand the ramifications of the large number of varying factors in economic history — tariffs, accounting practices, techniques of manufacture, movements of population, and the rest. And economists themselves, partly from their attempts to understand underdeveloped economies, have recently become more sensitive to factors traditionally outside the time-horizons of economics, as in the modern economic theories of growth, technological change, demography and property rights. If economics can offer some enlightenment on the economies of twentieth-century India, Greece and Brazil — and it would be hard to argue seriously that it does not — it is natural to suppose it could offer some on the economies of nineteenth-century Britain and America.

These noncontroversial notions provoked a good deal of controversy in the United States in the first few years after the inauguration there in the late 1950s of the 'new' economic history. The controversy has died down of late, partly no doubt because the main disputants have grown weary of *methodenstreit*, but more because the new economic history has compiled a solid record of achievement. When an approach to economic history has been able to accumulate such useful results as has the work on American slavery, industrial growth, railways, monetary history and national income (to name a handful of the topics that historians trained as economists have studied in the last fifteen years), it is not easy to mount counterattacks on it as impossible or useless. The sheer energy with which the new economic historians have rushed in accelerating waves over the ramparts of settled historical interpretation has been startling. A complete bibliography of the new approach would include several hundred articles and books, most of them written or published in the last five years. And this energy has won the new economic historians an important place in American academic life: they are to be found in every major American university, in growing numbers.

The phenomenon is puzzling on a number of counts. For one thing, it is not altogether clear why it did not happen before the late 1950s. There were foretastes, to be sure, in the thin, bright stream of economic analyses of history from men such as Heckscher, Ashton, Hamilton, Kuznets and Gerschenkron. The continuity of history is one of the easier themes to delineate in history and this part of intellectual history is no exception. But if the use of economics in economic history is natural, the puzzle is that the stream did not broaden into a river earlier. It must be admitted that economics has developed into a self-confident applied science only in the last twenty years or so, and this may account for part of the lag. Economic theory did not receive an injection of any fundamentally new ideas in these years — some economists are fond of pointing out that, if one reads carefully, the latest theoretical wrinkle can be found in Marshall, Ricardo or Smith — but it did experience a revolution in the mathematical and empirical expression of these ideas. The field achieved a measure of clarity and precision from the work of the mathematical economists and econometricians that broadened its usefulness, as in the refinements of national income analysis, the advances in the empirical estimation of demand and supply curves, and the development of measures of technological change. When economics had matured somewhat as an applied social science it was easier to apply it to economic history. Some of the remaining lag in application may be attributed to hostility to economic thinking in the literature of American economic history, imbued as it was with ideas from the American institutionalist and German historical schools, although the tolerant reception given to the new economic history by most of the men trained in the older tradition undercuts this argument. For the rest, the timing of the movement must be attributed to a miscellany of smaller factors, such as the new availability of money for support of research and conferences, the entrepreneurial skill of a few men in using the money, and a backlog of important topics in American economic history especially suited for the application of the new techniques.

A related puzzle is why the new economic history, developed now on a large scale in the United States, has not yet spread to other countries, especially the United Kingdom. The anti-theoretical bias of the German historical school is a much weaker tradition there than in America. Clapham, after all, was a student of Marshall, and Ashton drew on neoclassical economic ideas in all his work. Furthermore, before the advent of the new economic history in America there were proportionately more contributions to historical economics in Britain. Against the studies emanating from the American National Bureau of Economic Research and a handful of other works must be put the small but steady flow of British economic history informed by economics from Bowley, Stamp, Ashton, G. T. Jones, Cairncross, Jefferys, Rostow, Matthews, Sayers, Thomas, Phelps-Brown, Habakkuk, Hughes, Feinstein, and Deane and Cole — and this long list could easily be extended. Part of the explanation for the British lag in the broadening of the approach, as for the lag in the United States, may lie again in the way economics developed after the war. The economics profession in the United States expanded enormously and within this large group with advanced training in economics was a large enough subgroup interested in economic history to justify conferences, journals and other accoutrements of a specialized field. As Matthews suggests at one point in his contribution to the section of this volume on the future of the new economic history in Britain, the critical mass could for a long time be achieved only in the United States. Other factors in the explanation of the lag are suggested in the contributions by Hughes, Hartwell and Supple and in the discussion following. Whatever may have been the past obstacles in the way of a new British economic history, the consensus that emerged from these deliberations was that its future prospects are bright. The discussion was free, remarkably free in view of the way the new economic history was received in the United States, from fundamental doubts of the value of the new work. The remaining obstacles to the development of a more economic economic history in Britain were thought to lie mainly in matters of finance and in the structure of British graduate education, which is undergoing considerable change in any case, and certainly not in any resistance to the approach by the established figures in economic history. In short, it went without saying in the discussion at the conference that in terms of intellectual feasibility and merit, as a substantial supplement to work along other lines, there could and should be a new British economic history.

The papers in this volume should dispel any remaining doubts that this programme is in fact feasible. The writers of the papers reflect the composition of the conference as a whole in the roughly equal representation of Englishmen and Americans and economists and economic historians. It bodes well for the future that while the conference had a range of academic generations, and contributions to the stimulating and perceptive discussion came from all parts of that range, the papers themselves are for the most part by the younger men. The temporal limits of the contributions are the 1840s and the 1920s – that is, the earliest years of Britain's domination of the economic life of the world and the last years of the collapse of that position of domination. In this period Britain moved – or the rest of the world moved while Britain tarried, depending on one's point of view – from an environment in which British industrial technique and internal economic conditions determined what happened elsewhere (as in the American iron market in the 1840s described by Engerman) to one in which Britain, as Moggridge suggests in his paper on the ineffectiveness of direct controls of British investment abroad in the 1920s, was no longer master of its own economic fate. The bulk of the papers focus on the critical central period, 1870 to 1900, during which the balance tilted from dominance to dependence, if not in reality, at least in the opinion of many contemporaries. As Germany and America industrialized, Englishmen became increasingly aware of the shift in the balance of economic power and began measuring their own achievements against the standard of achievements abroad, with distressing results. The question of what standard is relevant for assessing British economic performance in these years, posed often in the discussion of the papers at the conference, was explicit in the papers by David on technology in agriculture and by McCloskey on technology in coal and steel, which both made direct comparisons of American with British performance, and it was implicit in the papers by Hawke on railways, Floud on machine tools, Harley on shipping, Edelstein on the capital market, and Lindert and Trace on chemicals. All these papers and the related discussion adopted the stringent standard of comparison with American and German successes against which late Victorians measured themselves, yet concluded on the whole that their gloomy self-assessment was not warranted.

This theme that British performance was better than has been commonly believed arose repeatedly in the conference. The theme was not planned, for the conference was designed to exhibit a new methodology applied to British economic history from 1840 to 1930 rather than to put forward any one interpretation of that history. Nonetheless the papers fall naturally into two groups supportive of this theme. The papers of Engerman and Moggridge, and those by Thomas on the role of internal and external migration in the cyclical interaction of the American and British economies in the late nineteenth century and by Hawke on the social saving of British railways on passenger traffic, set the scene of British economic development in the period as one of vigorous response to economic incentives. The other papers peopled that scene with industries characterized as more or less successful in their economic careers. The lietmotive of the villain of the play was entrepreneurial failure, and it was on this hypothesis that the papers, and still more explicitly the discussion, converged. The discussion of the hypothesis of failure occupied a long and stimulating hour begun by Hughes's remarks on the afternoon of the second day of the conference. The papers and related discussion on the issue are critically reviewed in Saul's contribution, printed here as an afterword to the first four sections of the volume.

The upshot of this intensive discussion was that at the very least the hypothesis of entrepreneurial failure has been put on the defensive. McCloskey, David and Edelstein attacked it directly in their papers: McCloskey found that around 1910 there was no difference between the total productivity of the British and American coal and steel industries, inferring that the alleged deficiencies of British entrepreneurs could not therefore have been very important; David admitted that there was a lag in the application of mechanical reapers in Britain compared with the United States, but was able to show that the lag can be fully accounted for by the unsuitability of the British landscape to the innovation; and Edelstein showed that the alleged irrational bias in the British capital market towards foreign investment, which besides serving as an example of late Victorian economic failure has served also as an explanation of the putative failure to invest enough at home, did not exist. Both Floud's measurement of productivity change for an important British machine tool firm from 1850 to 1900 and Harley's analysis over the same period of the relationship between productivity change in British shipping and the move from sail to steam found that British performance was creditable, though they did not explicitly draw the moral in their papers. The two other papers that treated the performance of the late Victorian economy directly, the examination of productivity change on Scottish railways by Vamplew and of Britain's slow move from the Leblanc to the Solvay soda processes by Lindert and Trace, reached less favourable verdicts on British performance, but the unfavourable verdicts were revised somewhat in the discussion of the papers. In Vamplew's analysis there was a hung jury: he felt unable to either affirm or deny the hypothesis of a failure of productivity growth on Scottish railways, as developed in Aldcroft and Richardson's work, given the fragility of the available statistics. In the discussion of the paper, however, it was pointed out that the statistics he did have implied substantial productivity growth. Only Lindert and Trace brought in a clear verdict of guilty, on the basis of substantial profits foregone by the British chemical industry in clinging to the Leblanc process after 1890. Again, however, the conclusion was modified in the discussion. In response to a point raised by Sandberg on fixed costs, Lindert and Trace recalculated the date when keeping the Leblanc process ceased to be rational, and found it to be 1897 rather than 1890. The revision is substantial, though it does still leave an important period of failure in this one branch of the industry.

The conference, then, reached a substantive conclusion, a rare enough event in academic meetings to be worthy of note. The British economy in the period of its dominance and relative decline performed as one would expect a competitive and prosperous economy to perform. Failures there were, but, as was pointed out several times in the discussion, there are isolated failures in any economy, the American and German no less than the British. The papers that were concerned directly with British entrepreneurs found them on the whole to have been responsive to the opportunities available. Even the papers that did not bear directly on this theme – Engerman's, Hawke's, Thomas's and Moggridge's – contributed indirectly, by their very use of the model of competitive economic actors responding quickly to the opportunities for profit in iron exports, railway development, building and migration, and the subtle evasion of direct government controls on capital flows, to the support of this view of British economic performance.

The route by which this and other conclusions of the papers and discussion were reached is perhaps even more significant for British economic historiography in the long run than the conclusions themselves. The hypothesis of entrepreneurial failure, for one, was already under attack from other quarters and there is nothing in the application of economics that by itself implies a negative finding on this hypothesis. Indeed, Lindert and Trace did uncover failures. What is most novel and important in the papers considered together is their methodology, or, better, 'methodologies', for the range of economic tools used was great. The theories ranged in scope from the theory of the firm's production processes used by Floud to measure productivity change in the machine tool firm of Greenwood & Batley to the aggregative economic theories used by Thomas to illuminate the effects of cycles in migration on economic activity in Britain and America and by Moggridge to analyse the effects of British restrictions on capital movements in the 1920s. Engerman used a model of supply and demand to separate the effects of tariffs, changes in foreign prices, technological advances, shifts in demand and variations in relative factor prices on the quantity of iron produced in Britain and America, expressing the model in a statistical form. Edelstein's use of the theory of the choice of investment portfolios was also given a statistical expression, and the two papers together were the most explicitly econometric of the contributions to the conference, if 'econometric' is understood in its usual meaning as the use of the statistical techniques of multiple regression analysis. These tools were appropriate because the variables being examined were confounded in the evidence with others and economic theory did not provide a simpler way of isolating one from another in quantitative terms: when Engerman wanted to measure the rate at which the demand curve for iron was moving out he had to hold constant the movement of supply, as Edelstein had to hold constant the risk and the scale of foreign and domestic issues of securities to isolate the effect of foreignness by itself.

The seven papers on technological change (that is, all except Thomas's, Moggridge's, Engerman's and Edelstein's) used for the most part non-econometric techniques. Statistical techniques were unnecessary in these studies because observations of the prices and qualities of inputs and outputs, supplemented in some cases by technical descriptions from the relevant engineering literature, gave the required measures of productivity. Although superficially different, the underlying logic of the measures was the same in all seven. Hawke's estimate of the social savings from passenger railway trains over alternative modes was the benefit half of-a study using the sort of cost-benefit analysis of an innovation used extensively in modern applied economics, in historical work most notably by Fogel and Fishlow in their studies of American railways. David's estimate of the profitability of the mechanical reaper in British conditions was a complete cost-benefit study of an innovation, as was Lindert and Trace's estimate of the profitability of the Solvay process. The mental experiment in Hawke's paper involved removing from the scene an innovation that was actually undertaken, whereas David's and Lindert and Trace's involved implanting an innovation that was not, in fact, undertaken. But clearly all three papers asked the same question: what would have been the social savings from an innovation in terms of more output for a given input (or in terms of more profit for the individual entrepreneur if he believed, as he would, that the benefit from the innovation would accrue in the first instance to him) had it been undertaken? The four papers using measures of productivity change directly asked an only slightly different question: what was in fact the social saving in terms of more output or profit for a given input from those innovations, whatever they were, that were actually undertaken? In Harley's paper the extent of social saving in steamships (or, what amounts to the same thing, productivity change in steamships) was used as one element in an analysis of why the shift from sail to steam proceeded as it did. Vamplew, McCloskey and Floud were concerned with the productivity change itself, for the light it throws on changes in technique and entrepreneurial performance. The measure of more output for the same input is essentially the same in the four papers and this measure involves in turn the same logic as the measures of social saving used in the first three. The difference in expression depends simply on what number is used to gauge the size of the cost saving of an innovation or a bundle of innovations. If the cost saving is expressed as a percentage of initial costs, the result is a productivity measure, as in the papers by Harley, Vamplew, McCloskey and Floud; if as a percentage of the capital required to be invested, the result is a measure of the rate of return, as in David's paper; and if as a dollar amount, the result is a measure of the social saving or the profits to be made by adopting the innovation in question, as in the papers by Hawke and Lindert and Trace.

The methodology of cost-benefit analysis underlying some of the papers given at the conference, then, is closely related to the methodology of productivity measurement used in others. The underlying unity in these papers is illustrative of a broader unity in all the papers. They all draw on what Joan Robinson called the economist's box of tools. The tools were fashioned to be used together in the economists work, to meet in a coordinated fashion one or another requirement of the description and analysis of economic events, and they have undergone improvements in the last two or three decades that have greatly increased their usefulness. They have become increasingly valuable for one who wishes to understand the complexities of economic life, past or present. The papers in this volume are cases in point. Certainly one could gain important insights into the topics treated here without drawing on the economist's elaborate tools of reasoning, embodied in the theory of income determination or relative price and in the statistical techniques for applying these bodies of theory, but much of the story, and often the critical element, would be overlooked. Without a measure of productivity change the historian would have to depend on vague, contradictory and often misleading contemporary testimony on the pace of technological advance in railways, iron, steel, coal, shipping, machine tools and the rest. Without an understanding of the logic of these measures, he would be tempted to rely on irrelevant quantitative evidence, such as labour productivity in an industry using little labour, to guide his assessment of the performance of the Victorian economy. Without the logic of cost-benefit analysis at his disposal he would have no cogent way of assessing the impact of the railways on British growth or the impact of the weight of the past on the performance of mid-Victorian agriculture or the late-Victorian chemical industry. Without the statistical techniques of regression analysis he would remain to a large extent ignorant of the relative importance of supply and demand factors in the explanation of the growth of the iron industry in the 1840s and 1850s or of the motivations of British investors in the 1890s and 1900s. Without a consistent model of the cyclical determination of national income and the role of capital markets in that determination he would be at a loss to delineate the impact of the free movement of capital before World War I or the impact of attempts to restrict its free movement after it. The inference is certainly not that the light the method of the economist casts covers the entire historical scene, even when the method is supported by careful and imaginative inquiry along more traditional lines, as it is in the papers here. The economist's perspective is not the only useful one in economic history. The papers and discussion in this volume, however, do suggest that there is much to be gained from that perspective, much narrowing of the necessary uncertainties in historical writing, and still more in the future.

I Britain and the Atlantic Economy

1

The American tariff, British exports and American iron production, 1840-1860

STANLEY ENGERMAN

The two decades preceding the American Civil War were years of significant changes in the iron producing sector in both the United States and Britain. To some extent these developments reflected the general pattern of economic change within the two economies, but there remain features unique to the industry. Developments in the two economies were related, by trade relations and factor flows, but in few industries were the trade relations so important and with such profound effect as in iron production. In this paper I shall describe the role of the American market in British iron production, as well as the effects of conditions in the British industry upon American output. The analysis of the latter effect will contain implications for one of the most heated of contemporary policy discussions, the role of the American tariff upon American production and imports of iron from Britain. In this study I shall be drawing upon a model used previously by Fogel and Engerman in explaining the expansion of the American iron industry in the period from 1842 to 1858 [1]. Before discussing the model I shall first describe the pattern of changes in iron output and consumption within the two economies.

I   IRON OUTPUT IN THE U.S. AND BRITAIN

The behaviour of the iron industry in the U.S. during the 1840s and 1850s attracted a great deal of attention at that time, an interest that has been subsequently carried forward by economic historians. It was a period of rapid change in the technology of blast furnaces. The almost exclusive use of charcoal for fuel at the beginning of the period was radically altered with the shift to mineral fuels, mainly anthracite, within the period before the Civil War [2]. This shift in the relative importance of fuels was accomplished not only by rapid introduction of furnaces utilizing the new fuels, but also by a high rate of abandonment of charcoal-using furnaces, particularly in those areas where charcoal was directly competitive with mineral fuels [3]. Other major technological developments within pig iron production were the

13

more extensive use of steam power and the hot blast, even within the charcoal-using sector. This was the period of the sharp increase in railroad construction, a source of demand for iron that has attracted much attention, and a time of rapid growth in other categories of investment as well [4]. Finally, and of most interest and importance to contemporaries, this was a period in which tariff changes appeared to dominate domestic activity [5]. There was a sharp increase in the tariff in 1842, an over two-thirds jump in the specific level, followed by a shift to an *ad valorem* rate of 30 per cent in the tariff of 1846. Whatever mild effect the shift to an *ad valorem* rate may have had when introduced, it did lead to a sharp decline in duty paid subsequently when the price of British iron fell [6]. There was a further reduction of the *ad valorem* rate to 24 per cent in the tariff of 1857.

It was these tariff changes, particularly those in the 1840s, that attracted most contemporary attention. For the years 1842-6 saw a very rapid expansion in domestic iron production (see Table 1). Part of this was a recovery from the cyclical trough reached in 1842, but the 1846 output was about double that of 1840, and in 1847 it was still higher. After 1847 there was a sharp reduction in domestic production, the 1851 output being less than 60 per cent that at the cyclical peak. This cyclical decline is almost unique to the iron industry, as the rest of the economy continued expanding. Growth was renewed after 1851 and continued through 1856, with, however, the 1856 peak being only slightly higher than the peak output of a decade earlier. There was then a decline to 1858, with recovery to an antebellum high in domestic output in 1860. While the pattern of the 1850s did not figure heavily in the tariff controversy, the very sharp discontinuity in the industry's fortunes in the 1840s could not fail to attract attention. While the expansion of the early 1850s was not so easily explained, what was more obvious than to attribute the varying fortunes of American production in the 1840s to the variation in the tariff?

This point was bolstered by the fact that it was obvious that the movements in American production did not reflect movements in the consumption of iron. The increased domestic consumption between 1847 and 1849, and the relatively minor decline from 1849 to 1851, contrasted sharply with the magnitude of reduced output in the U.S. [7]. In the 1840s there was a basically inverse movement between iron imports and iron production, which did not, however, impair the continuous expansion in iron consumption [8]. Although iron imports had risen slightly between 1842 and 1846, they did not recover the

TABLE 1
U.S. *production of pig iron and imports in pig iron
equivalents, 1840-1860* ('000 gross tons)*

	Production	Imports
1840	347	107
1841	278	125
1842	230	77
1843	358	55
1844	486	82
1845	574	85
1846	687	90
1847	765	142
1848	696	265
1849	627	379
1850	481	416
1851	413	467
1852	541	574
1853	723	619
1854	657	513
1855	700	409
1856	789	396
1857	713	310
1858	630	258
1859	751	327
1860	821	328

* Imports of pig and scrap plus pig iron equivalents (at 1.25 per ton) of rolled and hammered bar iron.
Source: Ref. (11), p. 316; ref. (10), p. 192;

levels reached in the late 1830s and the first two years of the decade. The post-1846 period saw a dramatic and prolonged increase in imports. Thus the relative importance of foreign iron rose sharply, at a time when the imports of rails were considerably less than those of pig and other rolled iron products, and at the very time when, by technological criteria, the American industry was at long last adopting the more modern methods [9]. In 1851 and 1852 imported iron satisfied more of the American demand for iron than did domestic production. In the ensuing expansion of iron consumption in the early 1850s imports first rose, peaking in 1853, then falling so that the 1855 level fell below that in 1850. The decline in imports continued until 1858, the 1856-8 decline occurring at a time of contraction in domestic production as well. Both domestic production and imports then rose to 1860. However, the sharp decline in imports after 1853 meant that at the end of the decade domestic production was more than twice as large as imports, a proportion higher than that in every year after 1849 save one. This ratio was nevertheless still considerably below that of the 1840s [10]. While the import pattern of the 1850s is difficult to fit into the tariff debate, there was an obvious chronological correlation between tariff levels and import movements in the 1840s.

Neither the technological changes nor the output movements in the British case were as dramatic as those in the U.S. [11]. Within the pig iron producing sector the shift to mineral fuels had been accomplished a half-century previously, while the replacement of water power by steam power had apparently similarly antedated the large scale American changes. The one seemingly major technological change, the introduction of the hot blast after 1828, did mean the growing importance of Scotland as an iron producer, relatively at the expense of South Wales [12]. However, while no one denied the existence of technical improvements within the sector, since there were obvious increases in furnace output and reductions in fuel usage, these changes were due to less dramatic factors than in the American case. Therefore, in contrast with the discussions of the American industry, technical changes in the British industry have not been the focus of historical attention.

While the British output statistics remain somewhat uncertain, particularly for the 1840s, it would appear that pig iron production grew more rapidly than in the United States, and without the extreme fluctuations that characterized the American industry (see Table 2). If the statistics can be accepted, there were no major declines in pig iron output between 1842 and 1860. There were two intervals of rapid expansion broken by a period of stagnation. The years of rapid growth were 1842 through 1846, and 1850 to 1856, both periods of expansion in the U.S. as well. In the years 1846 to 1850, however, whereas U.S. iron output fell sharply, British output remained relatively constant. There was, moreover, some shift from production for internal markets to production for an external market, with the U.S. absorbing almost the entire foreign increment [13]. This interval was unusual in that iron exports increased during a period of British cyclical contraction [14]. While there was a shift to export markets after 1846, the relative importance of exports was returning to its pre-1844 level after a period of internal boom. The pronounced, and permanent, increase in the role of the export market did not occur until the early 1850s, and this persisted even after the American market lost its dominance. Throughout the 1850s between 40 and 50 per cent of British pig iron was absorbed by export markets, a considerably higher ratio than for the first half of the nineteenth century [15]. Even in the 1840s, however, the export market was larger than the most discussed single internal market, the railroad, and railroad consumption in only two years equalled even one half that of other domestic uses [16].

TABLE 2
*U.K. production of pig iron and exports in pig iron
equivalents, 1840-1860* ('000 gross tons)*

	Production	Exports
1840	1396	323
1841	1388–1500	428
1842	1046–1348	438
1843	1215	524
1844	1575–2000	549
1845	1513–2200	420
1846	2214	501
1847	1999	644
1848	2094	739
1849		845
1850	2249–2500	943
1831		1099
1852	2701	1235
1853		1492
1854	3208	1423
1855	3201	1293
1856	3586	1697
1857	3658	1810
1858	3454	1597
1859	3709	1752
1860	3803	1718

* Exports of pig plus pig iron equivalents (at 1.25 per ton) of bar, railroad and other iron and steel exports.
Source: Ref. (3), pp. 124-5; ref (18), pp. 146-7.

Although cyclical conditions resulted in no major declines in British production, they did affect the behaviour of prices and capital formation [17]. From 1842 to 1845 prices rose, and they remained at a high level through 1847. This was a period of construction of new capacity at a rate substantially above that of preceding and subsequent quinquennia. In 1847 prices collapsed, and remained low until 1852. Thus the period of U.S. domination of the export market was one of low British prices and of declining capacity expansion. The years 1853 to

1857, a period of declining exports to the U.S., saw rising iron prices. Between 1858 and 1860, on the other hand, when exports to the U.S. rose, prices were falling. Throughout these decades, therefore, exports to the U.S. generally moved inversely to British prices. This was not true of total British iron exports, which were negatively correlated with iron prices in the 1840s and positively correlated in the 1850s. As noted above, the period of the middle and late 1850s saw a decline in the relative importance of the U.S. market, for while the U.S. still was usually the single largest market, the share of exports to European countries, particularly France, and to the British East Indies rose sharply. The years of major American importance were from 1848 to 1854, a period of first falling and then rising iron prices.

II   EXPLAINING THE GROWTH IN AMERICAN PRODUCTION, 1842-1858 [18]

In a recent article Robert W. Fogel and I have presented a model to be used in the explanation of industrial expansion, and have applied it to the analysis of the growth of U.S. pig iron production from 1842 to 1858. This model will be applied to the explanation of the cyclical fluctuations in output within this period, and will be further extended to the analysis of the variations in the level of American imports. Details of the model, and a technical description of problems of measurement, are to be found in that article, but it will be useful to present its basic framework here.

The model represents an attempt to use the economists' model of supply and demand to allocate the contribution of the different forces influencing the supply and demand schedules to the observed changes in output and prices. The basic model assumes constant elasticity supply and demand schedules, with γ the elasticity of supply and ϵ the elasticity of demand. These are presented as equations (1) and (2), where S and D represent the variables shifting the two curves, and Q and P are quantity and price, respectively.

(1) $Q^S = S \cdot P^\gamma$
(2) $Q^D = D \cdot P^{-\epsilon}$

These equations can be solved to obtain the equilibrium quantity and equilibrium price in terms of the shift terms and elasticities. Converting the equilibrium quantity equation into its rate-of-growth transformation, we obtain equation (3).

(3) $$\overset{*}{Q} = \frac{\epsilon}{\gamma + \epsilon} \overset{*}{S} + \frac{\gamma}{\gamma + \epsilon} \overset{*}{D}$$

The rate-of-growth of output is seen to be a weighted average of the rates-of-growth of the forces shifting the supply and demand curves, with the weights dependent upon the elasticities of supply and demand.

The shift variables included, and the actual computations, are described in the earlier article. In this article more attention will be paid to the cyclical behaviour of the iron industry, but it will be useful to present the calculated elasticities and to summarize the earlier findings pertaining to the period as a whole. The own-price elasticity (ϵ) was 1.57, the cross-elasticity with respect to the price of imports (ϵ_i) was 1.67, the elasticity with respect to investment (ψ) 0.61, and the elasticity of supply (γ) 4.18. These elasticity values will be used in the explanation of output changes.

From 1842 to 1858 the average rate of growth of iron output was 3.6 per cent per annum. The actual contribution of the demand components was negative. The impact of the falling price of imports offsets the contribution from the rapid expansion of U.S. investment. The decline in the price of imported iron reduced the demand for domestic production by an average of 5.7 per cent per annum. The decline in the price of imports (3.4 per cent per annum) was the result of a 2.5 per cent per annum decline in the net delivered price, and a 6.0 per cent per annum decline in the real tariff [19]. More than one half of the decline in imported prices resulted from that in the net price, and if there had been no change in the real tariff the rate of growth of domestic production would have been less than two percentage points per annum higher. Even at that higher rate of growth, iron production would have been growing less rapidly than manufacturing output as a whole. During this period the more rapid shift outward in supply than in demand (which actually declined) meant that there was a decline in the price of domestic iron, of approximately 2.5 per cent per annum.

III   THE CYCLICAL PATTERN OF DOMESTIC PRODUCTION

The elasticities computed in the earlier article will be used in this section to analyse the cycles in U.S. iron production. To highlight the fluctuations I shall discuss only the movements between terminal years, and the explanations will be based upon the levels of output predicted from the regression equation and not the observed levels. Thus there can be small discrepancies in magnitudes and in timing from the description of iron output presented in Section I.

The period can be subdivided into four specific cyclical phases. There was a rapid expansion from 1842 to 1846, a sharp decline from 1846 to 1851, another period of increase from 1851 to 1856, and then a decline from 1856 to 1858. Column (2) of Table 3 gives the percentage change (overall, not per annum) between the respective terminal years, while columns (3), (4) and (5) detail for each subperiod what would have been the percentage change in output if the only change had been in gross domestic investment, import prices and supply, respectively [20].

TABLE 3
Changes in U.S. iron production

(1)	(2)	(3)	(4)	(5)
		What change in output would have been if each item alone had changed		
Terminal years	*Change in production*	*Gross domestic investment*	*Price of imports*	*U.S. supply*
1842-46	+134%	+31%	+43%	+26%
1846-51	−41%	+19%	−59%	+22%
1851-56	+97%	+23%	+30%	+23%
1856-58	−14%	−8%	−9%	+3%

Source: See text.

In the 1840s the behaviour of investment and supply would, at unchanged import prices, have led to a continuous expansion of domestic output. Investment did grow less rapidly in the years after 1846, but still represented a positive contribution to demand. The important difference between the two phases of the cycle was in the behaviour of import prices. In the years preceding 1846 they were increasing at an annual rate in excess of 7.5 per cent per annum. The rising price of imported iron was the largest single contribution to the growth in domestic output. After 1846 import prices declined sharply, the 1849 level being only 55 per cent that of 1846, and that in 1851 less than one half the price at its peak. The declining price of imports offset the effects of expanding investment and increased supply upon the growth of output. So sharp was the fall in import prices that if investment and supply had remained unchanged the output level in 1851 would have been only 40 per cent that in 1846.

Thus the tariff controversy of the 1840s had properly emphasized the importance of the changing price of imported iron. However, whereas that debate implied the changes were to be attributed solely to the variations in the tariff level, the tariff changes were only part of the explanation. More attention should have been paid to the net of tariff price of British iron. In comparing the year 1842 with 1846, the tariff increase can explain only slightly more than one half the increase in the price of imported iron. The two-thirds decline in the real tariff between 1846 and 1851 can account for only 40 per cent of the decline in the price of imports between those years. Even if the tariff had remained unchanged in 1842 there still would have been a rapid growth in domestic production, and at the peak output would still have been about twice the 1842 level. Similarly continuation of the high specific tariff after 1846 would not have prevented some decline in domestic production, though the severity would have been reduced. An unchanged nominal tariff level would have limited the production decline between 1846 and 1851 to only 10 per cent, and cumulated output would have been about one third higher during this period.

Any interpretation of the tariff change as an independent component may, of course, be considered dubious. As described above, the basic change in 1846 was a shift from a specific tariff to an *ad valorem* tariff. Part of the decline in the size of the tariff was itself attributable to the decline in the price of imported iron. This further effect could have been avoided if the lowering had been of the specific amount alone. Since over 40 per cent of the real tariff reduction was due to the fall in the price of imported iron after the year of tariff revision, it is possible (for those preferring this particular alternative) to argue that the tariff reduction should have been considered to have been only the specific reduction in the initial year. The output decline in that case would then have been about one quarter, 1851 output being about 74 per cent that at the 1846 peak. Under either formulation the tariff changes in this period were less important in their impact upon domestic production than were the changes in the price of British iron.

The tariff features less importantly in the debates about the 1850s, because there was no change in the *ad valorem* rate until 1857. The expansion of output from 1851 to 1856, an expansion whose early years coincided with a continued increase in imports, can be attributed to increases in all three forces – an increase in investment, a rise (particularly sharp in 1853 and 1854) in the price of imported iron, and the shifting outward of the supply curve. The increased price of imported iron between 1851 and 1856 was the largest single contribution, accounting for about two-fifths of the increase. This again reflected the rising British price of this period. In the decline from 1856 to 1858 both investment and import prices fell, and now the latter decline was in large part due to the reduction in the rate of tariff. However, a maintenance of the earlier tariff rate would not have reversed the cyclical movement in production. Moreover, the 1856-8 decline, unlike that from 1846 to 1851, occurred at a time of falling imports, so the decline in production was concomitant with declining consumption. This differs from the decline in the late 1840s when there had been a substitution of imported iron for domestic production.

While changes in the tariff did, therefore, affect the magnitude of the cyclical movement in U.S. pig iron production, they were generally not as important in explaining the movements in production as were changes in the net of tariff price of British iron. To explain the cycle in U.S. production it is necessary to understand the movement in British iron prices. As will be seen in the discussion of U.S. imports of iron, the market-induced changes in British prices similarly had a greater impact upon the transatlantic iron market than did the legislated changes in the American tariff.

IV   THE VARIATIONS IN U.S. IMPORTS

There was a very rapid increase in American imports of British iron between 1842 and 1858, at a rate of approximately 11.7 per cent per annum. Three specific phases can be distinguished within this period. After a period of very slow growth in the high tariff years between 1842 and 1846, imports grew rapidly until a peak in 1853. After that imports declined, with a trough in 1858. Only over the years 1851-3 and 1856-8 were the movements in domestic production and imports similar. In most other years there was an inverse movement in these two forms of meeting domestic consumption. The frequency of the inverse relationship suggests the significance of British prices in the movements of U.S. production and imports. This relationship was, of course, noted in the tariff debates, and the changing tariffs of the 1840s had been the principal explanation proposed by Carey and others for the variations in the quantity of iron imported.

The model described in Section II can be extended to measure the importance of the tariff and the other forces in explaining the changing quantity of U.S. imports. This entails the estimation of the parameters of equation (4), the U.S. demand for imported iron.

(4) $M = [c \, I^\lambda P^\phi] \, P_i^{-\phi_i}$

The demand for imports (M) was influenced by the same determinants as was the demand for domestic production: investment (I), domestic price (P), and the gross-of-tariff price of imports (P_i). The import elasticities with respect to these variables are λ, ϕ and ϕ_i respectively. The U.S. faced an infinitely elastic supply of imported iron at world prices, while the price of domestic iron was determined endogenously. It is therefore necessary to substitute into equation (4) the equation giving the determination of domestic prices in terms of the exogenous variables. The reduced-form equation relates imports to the exogenous variables — investment, import prices and the supply shift. The import elasticities can then be computed from this reduced-form equation, given the values of ϵ, ϵ_i, ψ and γ determined previously. Equation (5) yields the following import elasticities: $\lambda = 1.06$, $\phi = 2.92$ and $\phi_i = 2.93$ [21].

(5) $\text{Log } M = 0.846 + 1.368 \text{ Log } I - 2.078 \text{ Log } P_i$
$$\qquad\qquad\quad (4.42) \qquad\quad (-4.02)$$

$$- 0.507 \text{ Log } (S + \nu)$$
$$(-2.36)$$

$$R^2 = 0.85$$

The rising price of imports between 1842 and 1846, when the shift outward in U.S. supply offset in part the increase in demand generated by the expansion in U.S. investment, helps account for the relatively small rise in imports between 1842 and 1846. If the low tariff level prevailing in 1842 had been continued, imports would have risen more rapidly. This would still have been at a rate considerably below that of the subsequent period since the changing price of British iron was as important as the increased tariff in explaining the raised price within the U.S. During the great expansion of imports the lowered price of imports was by far the major determinant. Although the increase in U.S. investment accounted for part of this expansion, the more than halving of the price of imports led to a more than three-and-a-half-fold increase in the demand for imports [22]. Even with the higher tariff of the mid-1840s there would have been a marked expansion of imports; a constant tariff at the 1846 nominal level would still have permitted a more than tripling of imports. Thus the most important factor in the growth of British iron exports to the United States in the late 1840s and early 1850s was the sharp decline in the price of British iron, and not the tariff change.

For the period of declining imports after 1853 the explanation is similar to that of the mild rise in the early 1840s. The expansionary effect of growing U.S. investment was again offset by the outward shifting supply schedule in the U.S. as well as by the increasing price of British iron. If the price of British iron had not increased after 1852, exports to the U.S. would have risen rather than declined between 1853 and 1857, although a constant price could not have prevented the decline in 1858. In 1858, a year in which the tariff decreased, the increased net British price offset the tariff rate decrease, so that the price of imports rose. This, in a year of declining investment, meant falling imports. A higher tariff would have meant a larger import decline, but since the 1857 decline in tariff rates was relatively small, the reduction would have been only marginally greater. However, in looking at the 1850s as a whole, the effects of the lowered tariff resulting from 1846 did not prevent imports from declining, although the tariff reductions did have some impact upon the magnitudes of both expansion and decline.

V   WHAT HAPPENED IN BRITAIN

The preceding sections have argued that to understand the behaviour of the Anglo-American iron market it is necessary to explain the behaviour of British iron prices in this period. Neither tariff changes nor developments within the American economy alone can explain the variations in U.S. imports of British iron, nor those in the U.S. production of iron. The explanation has been based upon the net price of British iron delivered within the U.S. Despite the charges of dumping made by American tariff advocates, the behaviour of the net of tariff price of iron in the U.S. reflected the movements of the internal price of iron in Britain [23]. The lowered net price received by British iron producers for these exports was matched for the most part by a decline in the price received for iron in the home markets.

As described in Section I, the cyclical characteristics of the British industry differed notably from those of the American. Whereas the American contractions were reflected in sharply falling output levels and large scale abandonment of furnaces, the British downturns were marked by sharply falling prices and lowered growth of capacity, but with only relatively short and minor declines in output, It is this curious behaviour of the British industry, particularly in the late 1840s, that must be explained.

From 1842 through 1845 (or 1846) there was a rapid increase in British iron output accompanied by sharply rising prices. This was the period of 'railroad mania', a factor that has attracted much of the attention in discussing this cyclical expansion [24]. However, although Mitchell's data imply that the railroad demand for iron had grown rapidly, the greater part of the increased output went into other domestic uses. Exports fluctuated about a constant trend in this period, peaking in 1844 and then declining. During the years of sharp price decline, 1846–51, output did not change dramatically. The declines in domestic consumption of iron, in both railroad and other uses, were offset by a sharp increase in exports, almost exclusively to the U.S. Since exports to the rest of the world did not increase, it would appear that in the absence of the U.S. import boom, the decline in the British iron industry would have been quite severe [25]. In this period, therefore, the expansion of British supply and the contraction of British demand provided the falling price which led to the U.S. import increase. While the expansion in investment in the U.S. would have increased iron imports from Britain, and the lowering of the tariff also raised demand, the British exports to the U.S. were generated more by the potential excess supply in Britain than by an increasing excess demand for iron in the U.S.

Could output really have fallen more dramatically after 1846 than the present statistics indicate? There are rather confusing hints in the literature. Gayer *et al.*, arguing in part from the statistics on the unemployment of iron-founders, claim that 'the estimate for 1848 . . . is almost certainly incorrect', presumably since it would have implied a rather substantial increase in per worker productivity [26]. Similarly the records of the Dowlais Iron Works, the largest in South Wales, show a decline of about one quarter in its pig iron production from an 1847 peak to the middle of 1848, a decrease more than twice that for South Wales indicated by the figures collected in Birch [27]. However, other data for these years suggest that no decline of major proportions need have occurred. Exports were rising, and the railroad demand for iron remained at relatively high levels. Scottish output was increasing, though mainly for export markets and inventory accumulation [28].

Thus it would seem that, even with the substantial price decline from the peak levels of the mid-1840s, the price received still exceeded variable costs of production, a development aided (at least in South Wales) by the apparent sharp fall in money wage rates within the industry and by the ability of firms to absorb reduced quasi-rents [29]. At this period within the U.S. there was apparently a lesser ability to reduce wages with declining prices, and, on the part of charcoal producers, a smaller margin of quasi-rents to buttress themselves against price falls. Why this apparent difference in the behaviour of the labour market between the two countries occurred is unclear, and it does not seem to fit comfortably within a sectoral variant of the labour-scarcity argument [30].

The course of British iron output and prices in the 1850s has been discussed in detail by John Hughes [31]. Briefly, both output and prices rose from 1852 to 1856 or 1857, which was a period of rapid expansion in British capacity. Prices declined after 1857 and remained low through 1860, while output fell only between 1857 and 1858 and then expanded. This was a period of increased importance of the export market, which now accounted for almost one half of pig iron production [32]. Britain had become more sensitive to export fluctuations, as seen in 1858 when despite an unchanged level of domestic consumption falling exports led to a 5 per cent decline in output. Although by this time the importance of the U.S. market had been reduced (it now absorbed only one quarter of British exports), the lowered level of U.S. imports in that year explains almost all the British export decline. When the U.S. market recovered after 1858, however, the other overseas markets declined so that no export boom resulted. The level of iron exports did not exceed the 1857 peak until after 1860. The price and output pattern of the 1850s, therefore, is quite different from that of the late 1840s. In the 1850s export quantities were generally positively correlated with prices, increasing during the period of rising prices and declining as prices were falling. Seemingly in the 1850s Britain benefited from a rising demand in Europe and the colonies for iron, whatever adverse effects these foreign demands may have had upon the one particular market represented by the U.S.

VI   SOME OTHER ISSUES

In this paper emphasis has been upon the aggregate amount of British iron exported to the U.S., and upon U.S. domestic iron production. It has been argued that these were generally inversely correlated. The price of imported iron affected domestic production and imports in opposite directions and by a sufficient amount to dominate their movements at times. While a rising price of imported iron explained only part of any increase in domestic production, the declines in the price of British iron were frequently large enough to offset the expansionary effects of investment and supply shifts and to cause output declines within the U.S. Similarly the movement in import prices dominated the behaviour of U.S. imports. Given the offsetting effects of investment and supply shifts, price declines generated increased imports so that an inverse pattern of U.S. production and imports resulted. What has been shown is that even in the 1840s the effects of the American tariff policy were relatively less important than other forces influencing the price of British iron. Washington could influence the movements in imports and production, but the ability to control these was limited by external forces influencing British producers.

There remain a number of issues relating to the Anglo-American iron market that bear more detailed examination. First is the obviously inadequate treatment of British production and price movements. Here, as in the U.S., more need be learned about the non-railroad uses of iron. There is no reliable data for this period with which to determine the relative importance of cast as opposed to wrought as a final use of domestic pig iron. While railroad demand has been the focus of attention, the other domestic uses generally absorbed anywhere from twice as much iron as did railroads to four or five times that amount. On the supply side little is known about the rate of technical progress within the iron industry. The short-run supply curve shifted outward (at what would be a rapid rate for any reasonable elasticity of supply) and at a rate probably in excess of that of new capacity. Moreover, this supply shift was probably more rapid than that in the U.S., but it is not yet possible to partition the increase among input prices, capital stock and technical progress. Thus nothing can be said about the relative rates of technical progress in the two countries. This would be of great interest because, while there were major changes in technology within the U.S., the only major change in Britain was the introduction of the hot blast. This type of comparison is useful for the debate on the nature of increases in productive efficiency and the relative importance of major improvements as opposed to the cumulated effects of minor changes. It is suggestive that the Dowlais Iron

Works had large increases in productive capacity throughout the first half of the nineteenth century with a few dramatic changes in the hardware utilized [33].

In considering the total iron traded in pig iron equivalents the possibility of examining the changing composition of the iron trade has been ignored. The justification for this grouping is that, for the U.S., imports of pig iron and of wrought iron moved together. This similarity of movement is also seen in British prices and in their exports to all countries. There was less variation in the relative prices of pig and bar iron than in the simultaneous changes in the absolute prices of each. Therefore no separate explanation for the development of rail production in the U.S. has been provided, although this has been frequently discussed. American rail production grew rapidly in the 1850s, and exceeded imported rails after 1858. The American market was heavily dependent on imported rails during the expansionary period of 1845 to 1854, and, conversely, in several years of the early 1850s more British rails were used in railroad construction in the U.S. than were used in Britain. The American production increase occurred during a period of declining rail demand, since total rail consumption, as well as the price of imported rails, was falling after the early 1850s [34]. The determinants of the expansion in rail-producing firms after 1852, and what may have been a relatively more rapid increase in productive efficiency in the U.S. than in Britain, are still unclear.

These represent only a few of the issues relating to the iron trade still to be answered. While they may appear, by themselves, to be of only narrow interest, they will have implications for many broader historical themes. For example, they can help shed light on the nature of international transfer of technology, the role of foreign markets in British economic growth, and, of course, the consequences of tariff policy for industrial development.

NOTES

This paper was written while visiting Nuffield College, Oxford, under a National Science Foundation Science Faculty Fellowship. Parts of this paper draw heavily upon work performed with Robert W. Fogel supported by the National Science Foundation under Grant NSF-GS-1454. G. N. von Tunzelmann and Robert Fogel have made useful comments upon an earlier draft.
    [1] See ref. (11).

[2] Charcoal furnaces represented 100 per cent of capacity in 1833 and about 86 per cent in 1840. The share fell to 44 per cent in 1858, with anthracite accounting for 45 per cent and bituminous fuel the remainder. The derivation of these capacity estimates is described in ref. (11), p. 315. For output, the 1858 shares were 41 per cent for charcoal, 51 per cent for anthracite, and 8 per cent for bituminous using furnaces (ref. 24, p. 268). Parenthetically, given the great debate concerning American backwardness in the adoption of mineral fuel, we should remember that in France, Belgium and Germany roughly the same lag behind the British technique was to be found (see ref. 20). Thus the expanded use of imported iron in Europe also occurred at a time of 'modernization' of production.

[3] Between 1841 and 1857, 191 charcoal-using blast furnaces were abandoned, 186 after 1846. These abandoned furnaces were disproportionately cold-blast and water-powered.

[4] For the importance (or unimportance) of railroad demands for iron see refs (9), pp. 132–49, and (10), pp. 147–206.

[5] See the literature cited in ref. (11), p. 315, most particularly ref. (22) and ref. (23), pp. 109–54.

[6] Compare ref. (23), p. 131, with ref. (9), p. 136.

[7] See ref. (10), p. 192.

[8] As often happens, the statistics of U.S. imports of British iron taken from American sources are not the same as those relating to British exports of iron to the U.S. taken from British sources. However, these series are quite similar in regards to timing and orders of magnitude. Unless otherwise noted, all subsequent comparisons of U.S. imports with U.S. production and consumption are based upon U.S. statistics, while comparisons with other British exports and production are based upon the British statistics Not all U.S. iron imports were from Britain in this period. There were small quantities of hammered iron imported from Sweden, but these had become quite unimportant quantitatively in this period. See ref. (1).

[9] Imports of rails did not exceed those of other rolled and hammered bars until 1850 (ref. 24, p. 281). Similarly the share of iron imported as pig, in contrast to wrought, was atypically high between 1844 and 1849.

[10] And, possibly, the 1830s as well (ref. 22, p. 379).

[11] On the British industry see ref. (3), Part I.

[12] See ref. (3), p. 128. The economic effects of this innovation have been widely debated. See refs (25), (13), among the many contemporary and historical sources. Truran pointed out the great increase in output per furnace and fuel savings before the hot blast, and it should be noted that the apparent royalty charged by Nielson was only 1s., hardly indicative of great benefits (ref. 13, p. 154). The reason for the conflicting opinions could be that while the hot blast was necessary for the use of Scottish anthracite, the cost curves in other areas were not so steeply rising that the hot blast was crucial for the British industry as a whole at this time. In the U.S. case it seems apparent that the hot blast was essential for the use of anthracite coal, but work by both Walsh and Fogel and Engerman suggests that the cost-saving output-increasing effects of the hot blast in charcoal furnaces were relatively minor. See ref. (27).

[13] The data on iron exports by country are from the annual Trade and Navigation Accounts found in the Parliamentary Papers. For a discussion of the 'Atlantic Economy' in the antebellum years, describing the mutual importance of the U.S. and Britain in international trade, see ref. (19).

[14] See ref. (12), p. 777.

[15] The time pattern of this export measure, based upon the ratio of the sum of pig iron exported plus the pig iron equivalents of other iron exports to domestic pig production, is similar to that in Deane and Cole although the absolute levels differ (ref. 7, p. 225). This difference in level is apparently due to their procedure of deriving a composite price of iron produced by dividing the value of all iron exports (including machinery and hardware) by the known tonnage of iron exported. This procedure should yield too high a composite price to be applied to domestic pig production even if the baskets of exports and domestic consumption were similar. Moreover, Deane and Cole purport to measure the share of exports in the output of the iron industry as a whole, whereas my measure is for allocation of pig iron alone.

[16] See ref. (17). I am indebted to Brian Mitchell for letting me use the annual estimates underlying his published statistics. At the time these estimates were prepared Mr Mitchell was at the Department of Applied Economics, Cambridge. These figures are not fully comparable with the export series I have presented, since the ratio used to convert rails into pig iron differs slightly from that used to determine the pig iron equivalent of exports. Data taken from the records of the Dowlais Iron Works and other sources suggest that the railroad demand may be overstated. The soon-to-appear estimates of Gary Hawke are generally lower than those of Mitchell, and their use would not affect this point.

For a similar argument, concerning the importance of the Scottish railroads for Scottish pig iron production, see ref. (26). In both cases what has been tested is the role of the domestic railroad demand upon domestic production. This is only a partial measure of the importance of the railroad as an invention, since rails were a major export product, and in several years in the early 1850s the Americans used more British rails than did the British themselves. As noted in refs (9) and (10) the major reason for a relatively small effect of American railroads upon American iron production in the antebellum period was this British connection.

Also it should be noted that the British consumption of iron at the very start of the railroad era exceeded American consumption of iron in almost every antebellum year.

[17] See ref. (3), pp. 124–5, for information on the number of furnaces. Price data are found in refs (18), pp. 492–3, and (2), among other sources, and can be compared, for years after 1848, with the unit export values derived from the Trade and Navigation Accounts.

[18] For a more detailed discussion of the material in this section see ref. (11).

[19] The component of the iron price attributed to the tariff deflated by the price index will be called the real tariff.

[20] The procedure used to allocate contributions, therefore, is slightly different from that described in Section II.

[21] The Durbin-Watson statistic for equation (5) indicated the presence of serial correlation in the disturbances. A first-order autoregressive scheme was applied, which then yielded an equation without significant serial correlation. The price elasticities computed from this transformation were not very different from those of equation (5), which will be used for the calculations described in the text. (A variant of the import equation using the alternative elasticities for domestic production calculated in ref. (11) gives elasticities here which provide a similar explanation of import changes.)

[22] To highlight the impact of import price changes, 1852 was used for the

cyclical peak in preference to 1853. No substantive changes in interpretation result. Between 1846 and 1852 imports had risen 542 per cent. If investment alone had increased imports would have risen 110 per cent. If the falling price of imports had been the only change the rise would have been 360 per cent.

[23] See, e.g., the Convention of Iron Masters Report summarized in *Hunt's Merchant Magazine*, 1851 (p. 577). Hidy claims that the reduction in commissions and the increased use of iron as ballast explain part of the increase in imports in the years 1848 to 1852. However, the reduction in commissions charged by 'the New York house (Grinnell, Minturn & Company) for selling and guaranteeing payment' was only 1-½ percentage points (ref. 14, p. 402). Freight reduction could have had a more substantial effect if the differential use of ballast increased in this period, since freight was generally quoted at about £1 per ton. One important explanation for the increase in imports, although widely cited, seems suspect. This is the acceptance of British rail producers of bonds of American railroads in part payment. This credit function was not, however, costless even if (as is not clear) the practice was widespread. Hidy comments that, in an 1849 sale, the 'ironmasters charged an extra £1 per ton . . . for taking bonds in partial payment' (ref. 14, p. 594). If bonds represented one half the payment, this would be equivalent to a 40-50 per cent surcharge for the provision of credit.

[24] For a discussion of the crisis of 1847 which does play down the direct role of the railroad sector upon industrial output see ref. (28). The collapse in pig and bar as well as rail prices suggests that all sources of iron demand were affected. Consistent with this is that the most pronounced decline in 1847 was in the Black Country area. However, any interpretation is made even more confusing by the fact that real investment increased less rapidly after 1846, but declined only in 1850 (ref. 6, p. 106).

[25] John states that 'in 1848 the political unrest [in Europe] was regarded by Welsh iron-makers as one of the main reasons for the depression they were then suffering' (ref. 16, p. 105). Exports to the major European powers declined by about one quarter in that particular year, with the decline restricted to the pig iron producing sector.

[26] Ref (12), pp. 320, 322.

[27] Ref. (3), p. 130. The figures for the Dowlais Iron Works were computed from the records of the company on deposit at the Glamorgan County Records Office.

[28] Ref. (4). The Carron Company accumulated inventory after 1848, at a time of sharp reduction in its profit rate (ref. 5, pp. 172, 333–4).

[29] See ref. (3), pp. 264, 265. The 25 per cent decline in money wages indicated between 1848 and 1851 (ref. 3, p. 265) followed an earlier reduction between 1847 and 1848 (ref. 3, p. 264). The decline in coal prices, if any did occur, was probably smaller (ref. 18, pp. 482, 483). There was a sharp decline in domestic prices between 1847 and 1851, of about 20 per cent (ref. 18, pp. 470, 472 and 474), but the decline in the price of iron in this period was about 40 per cent (ref. 18, p. 493). The fall in profits for those iron companies for which records exist indicates that the differential is not due to productivity increases.

[30] For a series of letters among ironmasters describing their collusive attempts to regulate wages, see ref. (8), pp. 33–57.

[31] Ref. (15), pp. 141–83.

[32] There were sharp rises in exports of pig iron to France (aided in part by the

sharp reduction in French tariffs in 1855: ref. (21), p. 201), Holland and
the German states, and of railroad iron to India and Spain, in particular.
[33] As emphasized by Truran (ref. 25), and seen quite clearly in the records of
the company. In response to adverse fortunes in the mid-1850s there were
changes in management methods and organization, which apparently raised
output per furnace sharply without any notable changes in hardware.
[34] The three recent studies of this problem (refs 9, 10 and 24) all point to
the importance of re-rolling in the growth of American rail production. The
greater part of the American rail mills built between the mid-1850s and the
mid-1860s were for re-rolling rather than the production of new rails.
Re-rolling would presumably have been heavily influenced by imports from
Britain during earlier years, and in this sense it became more difficult to
maintain the flow of rail exports to the U.S. There was a sharp increase in
new rails produced in the 1850s, however, as firms recovered from the
apparently sharp declines after 1848.

REFERENCES

(1) Adamson, R., 'Swedish iron exports to the United States, 1783-1860'.
Scandinavian Economic History Review, XVII (1969), 58–114.
(2) Barclay, J., *Statistics of the Scotch Iron Trade*. Glasgow, 1850.
(3) Birch, Alan, *The Economic History of the British Iron and Steel Industry,
1784-1879*. London, Frank Cass, 1967.
(4) Campbell, R. H., 'Developments in the Scottish pig iron trade, 1884-1848'.
Journal of Economic History, XV (September 1955), 209–226.
(5) Campbell, R. H., *Carron Company*. Edinburgh, Oliver and Boyd, 1961.
(6) Deane, Phyllis, 'New estimates of gross national product for the United
Kingdom, 1830-1914'. *Review of Income and Wealth*, Series 14 (June
1968), 95–112.
(7) Deane, Phyllis and Cole, W. A., *British Economic Growth, 1688-1959*.
Cambridge, University Press, 1962.
(8) Elsas, Madeline (ed.), *Iron in the Making*. Cardiff, Glamorgan Quarter
Sessions and County Council, 1960.
(9) Fishlow, Albert, *American Railroads and the Transformation of the Ante-
Bellum Economy*. Cambridge, Mass., Harvard University Press, 1965.
(10) Fogel, Robert William, *Railroads and American Economic Growth*.
Baltimore, Johns Hopkins Press, 1964.
(11) Fogel, Robert W. and Engerman, Stanley L., 'A model for the explanation
of industrial expansion during the nineteenth century; with an application
to the American iron industry'. *Journal of Political Economy*, 77 (May-June
1969), 306–28.
(12) Gayer, Arthur D., Rostow, W. W. and Schwartz, Anna Jacobson, *The
Growth and Fluctuation of the British Economy, 1790-1850*. Oxford,
Clarendon Press, 1953.
(13) Gibson, I. Forrester, *The Economic History of the Scottish Iron and Steel
Industry (with particular reference to the period 1830 to 1880)*. Unpublished Ph.D. dissertation, London, 1955.
(14) Hidy, Ralph W., *The House of Baring in American Trade and Finance*.
Cambridge, Mass., Harvard University Press, 1949.
(15) Hughes, J. R. T., *Fluctuations in Trade, Industry and Finance*. Oxford,
Clarendon Press, 1960.

(16) John, A. H., *The Industrial Development of South Wales, 1750-1850.* Cardiff, University of Wales Press, 1950.
(17) Mitchell, B. R., 'The coming of the railroad and United Kingdom economic growth'. *Journal of Economic History*, XXIV (September 1964), 315–36.
(18) Mitchell, B. R. with Deane, Phyllis, *Abstract of British Historical Statistics.* Cambridge, University Press, 1962.
(19) Potter, J., 'Atlantic economy, 1815-1860: the U.S.A. and the Industrial Revolution in Britain'. *In* L. S. Pressnell (ed.) *Studies in the Industrial Revolution.* London, Athlone Press, 1960, pp. 236–80.
(20) Pounds, Norman J. G. and Parker, William N., *Coal and Steel in Western Europe.* London, Faber & Faber, 1957.
(21) Scrivenor, Harry, *History of the Iron Trade.* London, Frank Cass, 1967.
(22) Taussig, Frank W., 'The tariff, 1830-1860'. *Quarterly Journal of Economics,* II (April 1888), 314–46, 379–84.
(23) Taussig, Frank W., *The Tariff History of the United States.* New York, Putnam's (6th ed.), 1914.
(24) Temin, Peter, *Iron and Steel in Nineteenth-Century America.* Cambridge, Mass., M.I.T. Press, 1964.
(25) Truran, William, *The Iron Manufacture of Great Britain.* London, E. F. N. Spon, 1855.
(26) Vamplew, Wray, 'The railways and the iron industry: a study of their relationship in Scotland'. *In* M. C. Reed (ed.), *Railways in the Victorian Economy.* Newton Abbot, David & Charles, 1969, pp. 33–75.
(27) Walsh, William D., *The Diffusion of Technological Change in the Pennsylvania Iron Industry, 1850-1870.* Unpublished Ph.D. dissertation, Yale University, 1967.
(28) Ward-Perkins, C. N., 'The commercial crisis of 1847', *Oxford Economic Papers,* II (New Series) (January 1950), 75–94.

DISCUSSION 1

Von Tunzelmann: He noted that Engerman's paper was an extension of his earlier and much discussed work done with R. W. Fogel on the antebellum American iron industry. That paper had set out regression equations explaining the American price and quantity demanded to establish among other things certain conclusions regarding the effect of tariff policy on American industrial development. The somewhat muted support for the role of the tariff in encouraging the development of the iron industry is borne out in the present study and extended by the addition of an econometric explanation of American import demand. The additional assumptions required for the particular specification of iron imports used here over and above those contained in the demand function (expressed similarly in the reduced forms) seem empirically plausible: for example, there was little possibility of substituting among alternative foreign iron producers for British iron within a reasonable range — although, of course, this would not necessarily be true in general. Here the assumptions are well validated by the resulting estimates of import elasticities.

The most suggestive and striking results from Engerman's paper bear upon Anglo-American trading relationships, as befits this morning's discussion, and particularly the powerful effect of British prices of iron on American demand for imports in the 1840s and 1850s. British economic historians, notably R. C. O. Matthews, have regarded the American trade as differing crucially from Britain's trade with other non-European markets. In the iron industry the differences are less apparent at first sight. Partly because of the underdeveloped state of other iron importing countries (especially their limited requirements of capital goods), and partly perhaps because of trade protection, in periods of slack domestic demand the British iron industry off-loaded especially freely on the American market. The situation was therefore rather like that of British cotton goods, at least until the inexpansible demands of other iron markets than the American had changed in the 1850s.

The situation in iron as Engerman describes it was similar to cotton in other respects as well. The evolution of leading industrial sectors with relatively high proportions of overhead to variable costs (judged, that is, by the standards of the time), constrained firms to maintain output irrespective of cyclical drops in demand. The cotton industry had attained this position at least as early as the 1820s and 1830s.

Cotton output, as measured by pounds of raw cotton imported, rose steadily during the long depression of prices and profits before the mid-1830s boom. Engerman demonstrates that similar price-quantity behaviour prevailed in the iron industry, with output maintained, surprisingly, during the depression of the late 1840s. If this was a new phenomenon in iron, it might be speculated that it was the diffusion of the hot blast that gave greater flexibility to the industry (or lessened its flexibility, which would provide a quite different explanation of the phenomenon). It does not seem to be product-specific, though more information would be useful on this issue. It would be useful as well to know what was happening to the total number of firms in the industry. One conjecture that such information would help to test is that the larger, more capital-intensive firms were expanding output to maintain total profits in the face of lower prices while smaller firms disappeared from production. But a partial refutation of this hypothesis is already suggested by Engerman's reference to the experience of the giant Dowlais company, which evidently did cut back production relatively sharply.

It is clear that existing knowledge on the structure of British industries in the first half of the nineteenth century is somewhat meagre. Engerman's addition of foreign trade as an element in the determination of output is therefore particularly welcome. The addition of an equation for American demand treating the price of imported British iron as exogenous, however, points to the difficulty of attempting a complete explanation of demand. The consistency of Engerman's estimates depends on there being no other functions interrelating prices of imports and quantities imported. Yet some sections of the paper suggest considerable sensitivity on the part of British iron producers to conditions of sale in the American markets, especially in the slump of the late 1840s. To quote a counterfactual proposition from the paper: 'Since exports to the rest of the world did not increase, it would appear that in the absence of the U.S. import boom the decline in the British iron industry would have been quite severe.' It seems doubtful that such a decline could have occurred without having an appreciable effect on British prices, unless the elasticity of supply were exceptionally high. Thus while the U.S. might have been quite a small proportion of the total market for British iron, it is likely to have been a particularly responsive one, at least for certain important spans of years. If the price of British iron exports was a function partly of the quantity the Americans demanded, then the estimates of the coefficients on these variables will in general be inconsistent. Biases might then be expected in the threefold apportioning of responsibility for import fluctuations.

The difficulties that econometricians have encountered in using simultaneous equation methods — the small-sample properties and even the predictive efficiency of the various estimating procedures still being in doubt — suggest that the hesitancy of economic historians to commit themselves to the construction and estimation of simultaneous equation models is more than justified. On the other hand, the biases from ignoring simultaneity are great and a good deal can be done in economic history with the statistical models developed to take account of it. In this, as well as in the substantive historical results, Engerman's paper stands out as a remarkable contribution.

BRIEF SUMMARY OF DISCUSSION*

Engerman was asked if he would comment on von Tunzelmann's last point on the possible existence of simultaneity. The question was: in the model of the American market is it legitimate to take the foreign (that is, British) price of iron as given, assuming no influence on it of American demand? If it is not legitimate, the methods of estimation in the paper may yield biased results. Engerman responded that iron exports to America were only one tenth to one fifth of total British output in the period, suggesting that this low share would reduce the impact of American demand on British prices. Supporting Engerman on this issue, someone pointed out that the elasticity of British excess supply (home supply minus home demand) implied by the supply and demand elasticities estimated in the paper is very high, on the order of 20: that is, a 20 per cent increase in the quantity of iron imported by Americans would raise British prices by only one per cent.

Another participant asked whether the fall in shipping costs in the 1840s and 1850s should be taken into account in the explanation of the American price that uses the variations in the price of iron imported from Britain. Engerman responded that ocean shipping costs across the Atlantic were only about 15 per cent of delivered prices and that iron came from Britain in ballast throughout the period, with little change in

---

* Due to a temporary failure of the arrangements for taking notes on the proceedings as they took place the account of the discussion for this paper is less complete than most. What follows is a very brief summary of the major points.

cost. Shipping costs could therefore play only a minor role in mediating the influence of British on American prices.

Other discussion concerned, among other matters, the question of how iron inventories (which would affect the lag structure of production responses) should fit into the analysis, how the re-estimation in the face of autocorrelation affected the significance levels of the estimated coefficients, how one could allow in the model for the spatially dispersed nature of the iron market in Britain and America, and whether there were substantial differences between the two countries in the rate of technological change experienced in iron making.

2

Demographic determinants of British and American building cycles, 1870-1913*

BRINLEY THOMAS

In the course of the debate on the working of the Atlantic economy no critic has been able to refute the existence of an inverse relation between long swings in construction in Britain and the United States and in British home and foreign investment, at least in the period 1870-1913. There has indeed been ample confirmation [1]. Where disagreement enters is in the interpretation of the nature of the mechanism by which the economies of the two countries reacted on each other. Contributors to the discussion can be divided into two broad schools — those who accept the reciprocal character of British and American long swings as systematic rather than fortuitous, and those who argue that the operative forces were in the domestic sphere and not in any interacting process. The line taken by this second group is seen in the work of H. J. Habakkuk and S. B. Saul [2].

Habakkuk is a sceptic not only about systematic influences in the alternation of British and American long swings, but even about the existence of a British building cycle, as the following quotation indicates.

There has recently been some suggestion that in England after the 1860s the trade cycle was not an independent phenomenon but simply the result of lack of synchronization between the long swings in foreign and domestic investment. [Footnote: *Matthews, A Study in Trade Cycle History.*] The view taken here is the reverse of this: it was the long swings which were the epiphenomena and the trade cycles the reality, in the sense that when the character of the individual cycles has been explained there is no residue which needs to be attributed to the behaviour of a long cycle. The appearance of alternation in British and American long swings is the result of the fact that British trade cycles no longer came to a violent end but the American ones often did [3].

* This paper is a sequel to Chapter XI of *Migration and Economic Growth: A Study of Great Britain and the Atlantic Economy* by Brinley Thomas (Cambridge University Press, 1954).

It is not easy to summarize Habakkuk's paper, but the essence of his thesis can be put as follows. Housebuilding in Britain before the 1860s did not exhibit long swings but fluctuated with the trade cycle. There were special reasons of domestic origin why the relation between building fluctuations and the trade cycle changed after the 1860s. For example, internal migration became more an affair of the middle classes and less connected with changing business conditions, and financial institutions became more stable so that building could be sustained after cyclical downturns. The increasing tendency for building booms to continue after cyclical downturns gave rise to regional long cycles which were not necessarily synchronized. The 1880s were an exception; even in that decade the volume of emigration was largely the result of domestic influences. 'The alternation of British and American housing activity in the eighties and nineties partly reflects the different rate at which electricity was applied to traction in the two countries. This was, in the present context, almost certainly fortuitous.' [4] With the exception of the later 1880s, the effect of emigration and foreign investment on British building fluctuations was 'of minor importance compared with domestic factors' [5]. This is a challenging argument deserving attention, although it rests mainly on speculations which are not subjected to rigorous testing. The issue can be decided only by an appeal to the empirical evidence.

S. B. Saul, in his study of local authority records for a large number of English towns in the period 1890-1914, has thrown light on matters such as the relation of building activity to the proportion of empty properties and the effect of changes in the availability of short term funds [6]. His general conclusion is as follows.

Migration, external and internal, was certainly an important matter and money-market conditions often helped to determine the timing of the upswing of the cycle. But the evidence for a complex interaction of the British and American economies, at least as far as investment in housing in Britain is concerned, is slender. The facts certainly seem to point to an industry whose fate was largely determined internally by the state of demand and by the nature of the operation of the trade itself. [7]

The two contributions referred to lay stress on so-called fortuitous domestic influences on the course of housebuilding in Britain: neither has paid enough attention to demographic factors. An adequate interpretation of building fluctuations must give a prominent place to the role of the population change.

In reappraising the conclusions of *Migration and Economic Growth* [8], I have re-examined the course of house building in England and Wales in the period 1870-1913 on the basis of new data yielding a more comprehensive record of regional cycles. The analysis seeks to attain a more accurate measurement of the demographic determinants of building cycles, regionally as well as in the aggregate. These results are then related to corresponding data on the demographic determinants of the building cycle in the United States in the same period.

I STATISTICAL SOURCES AND METHODS

The sources used are the Inland Revenue ledgers deposited in the Public Record Office. Inhabited House Duty statistics, available for each county, provide a basis for regional building estimates for the years 1875-1913 [9]. The ledgers also contain figures of profit income assessed under Schedule D. The characteristics of these sources and the method used are described in the Appendix.

We have information about the number of dwelling houses assessed and not assessed to house duty as well as 'messuages and tenements' not used as dwelling houses. Sir Josiah Stamp pointed out that the income tax Schedule A figures 'undoubtedly represent most closely the real facts but in revaluation years far more closely than at other times' [10]. To test the reliability of these data we expressed the annual change in the number of premises in Britain shown by the House Duty statistics as an index (1900-9 = 100) and compared it with Weber's estimates of housebuilding [11]. Figure 6 in the Appendix indicates clearly that the two series yield virtually the same long swing, and this justifies the use of the Record Office data for our purpose. It also reveals that the House Duty figures were affected by periodic revaluations and cannot be used for year-to-year changes. Both values and numbers were affected by revaluations. To overcome this difficulty we have averaged inter-revaluation years plus the revaluation year following them; this prevents any misleading impression that the series can be used for annual changes and at the same time provides an adequate indication of the time-shape.

The counties of England and Wales have been divided into two broad sectors, urban and rural. The urban counties form seven regions – the

Midlands, counties surrounding London, north-west of England, York-shire, northern England, South Wales and Monmouthshire, and London. The rural regions comprise the southern agricultural counties, those near the Midlands, and the south-west plus rural Wales. We shall deal mainly with the urban regions, defined as predominantly urban in that they contained the greater part of the population of England and Wales at the end of the nineteenth century.

The purpose of this analysis is to test the proposition that British building fluctuations in the period 1870-1913 are to be explained mainly by demographic variables and, in particular, by migration. Also, by relating this analysis to recent studies of population change and the building cycle in the United States since the middle of the nineteenth century, we can carry out a new test of the inverse relation between British and American building cycles and the process of interaction between the two economies.

To illuminate the connection between changes in building and changes in the house-seeking age group we have made estimates of the quinquennial change in the population aged 20–44 in each region, separating the effects of natural increase and migration. Figures on recorded deaths were obtained from the Registrar-General's annual reports and decennial supplements, and these were combined with census population figures in quinary age groups to estimate the quinquennial changes which would have occurred in the absence of migration.

The following demographic factors are relevant in explaining the volume of housebuilding in any region in a given period: (*a*) natural increase in the 20–44 age group, (*b*) internal migration, (*c*) external migration, (*d*) the headship rate (the ratio of heads of households to the total population in an age group). In this analysis we shall ignore changes in the headship rate: instead we shall refer to changes in the marriage rate. The age group 20–44 is taken as comprising the vast majority of the house-seeking section of the community. We shall concentrate on (*a*), (*b*) and (*c*) and examine the course of the demographic and building series quinquennially in each region and in the seven regions as a whole. Our method of obtaining regional estimates for both natural increase and migration is explained in the Appendix.

'Natural increase' in the 20–44 age group is an estimate of the population change which would have occurred in this age group in the two quinquennia following each census, if there had been no migration in either of these periods. Changes in natural increase reflect movements in the excess of births over deaths in previous periods. A five-year boom in the birth rate is followed twenty years later by a bulge in the 20–25 age group and after thirty years by a bulge in the 30–35 group and after thirty-five years by a bulge in the 35–40 group. In any given quinquennium the 20–44 age group is thus a composite of past influences. There is much to be explored under this heading, both nationally and regionally, but we cannot deal adequately here with echo effects [12] .

The other element to be taken into account is migration, internal and external, affecting the age group 20–44. The estimate is of course a balance of inward and outward movements. There is no means of distinguishing between 'immigrants' who come into a region from one of the other six regions and those who come from outside, i.e. from the rest of the United Kingdom or from abroad; and similarly with 'emigrants' from a region. Despite the limitations of the data, it is possible to make a reasonably firm estimate of the extent to which natural increase in the age group 20–44 in each region was augmented or reduced by migration. Parallel with our aggregate migration series for the seven regions we have plotted from an independent source the quinquennial emigration of occupied persons from England and Wales to the United States.

Having estimated natural increase and the balance of migration in the age group 20–44 in each quinquennium for each region, we derive an estimate of the change in the population in the house-seeking age group [13] . This series is then compared with the course of building in each region and in the seven regions as a whole.

2   REGIONAL BUILDING CYCLES, 1870-1910

Figures 1A-C show the course of the building cycle in each of the urban regions of England and Wales from 1875 to 1910. This series gives the average annual number of houses built in each quinquennium (years between revaluations plus the revaluation year following them being averaged). For brevity I shall refer to the Inhabited House Duty figures as the I.H.D. Index. With it we plot for each quinquennium from 1870 to 1910 the average annual increase in the population aged 20–44; this registers the net effect of natural increase and migration, which are also shown in the charts.

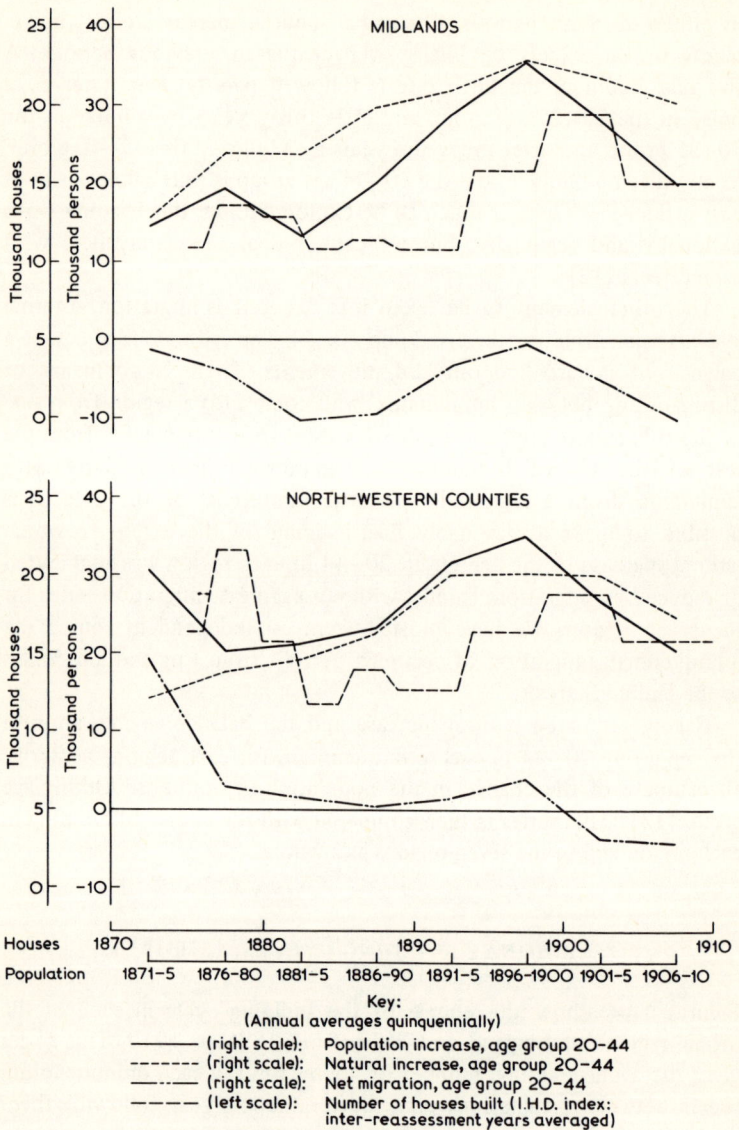

Figure 1A

Figure 1 Population and regional building cycles 1871-1910. *A* Midlands and north-west. *B* Yorkshire, north, and South Wales and Monmouthshire. *C* London and counties surrounding London. *Source*: Appendix.

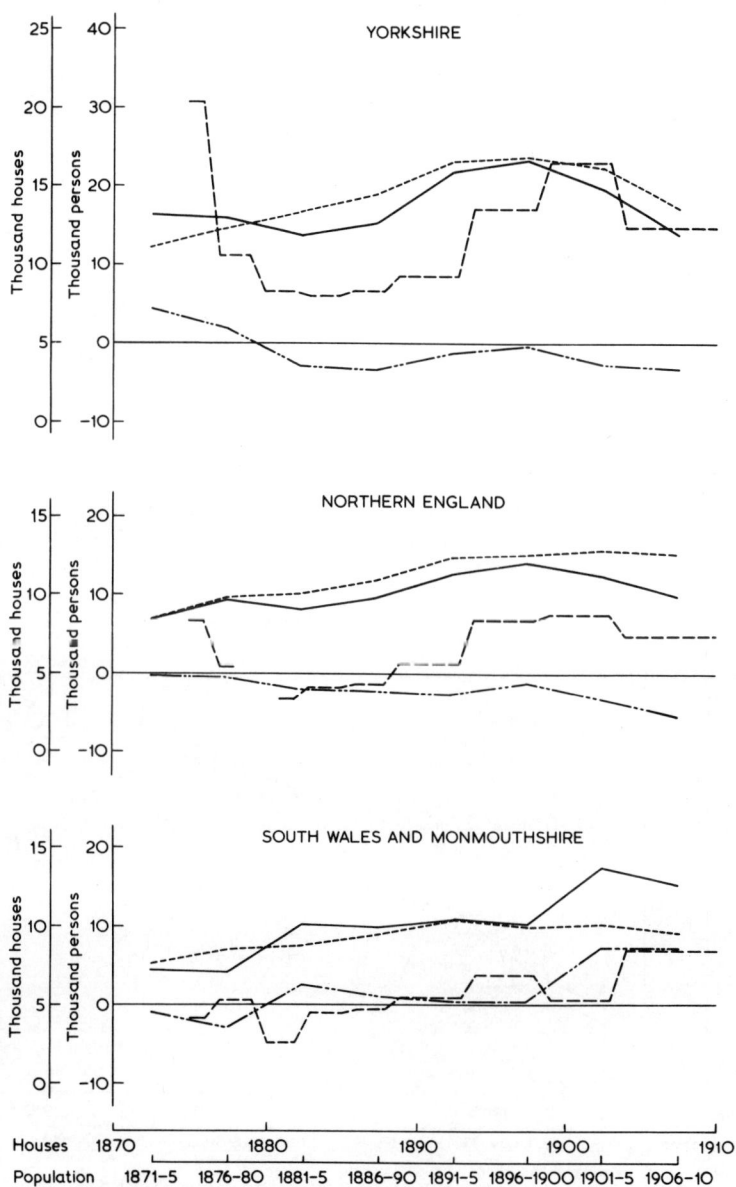

Figure 1B

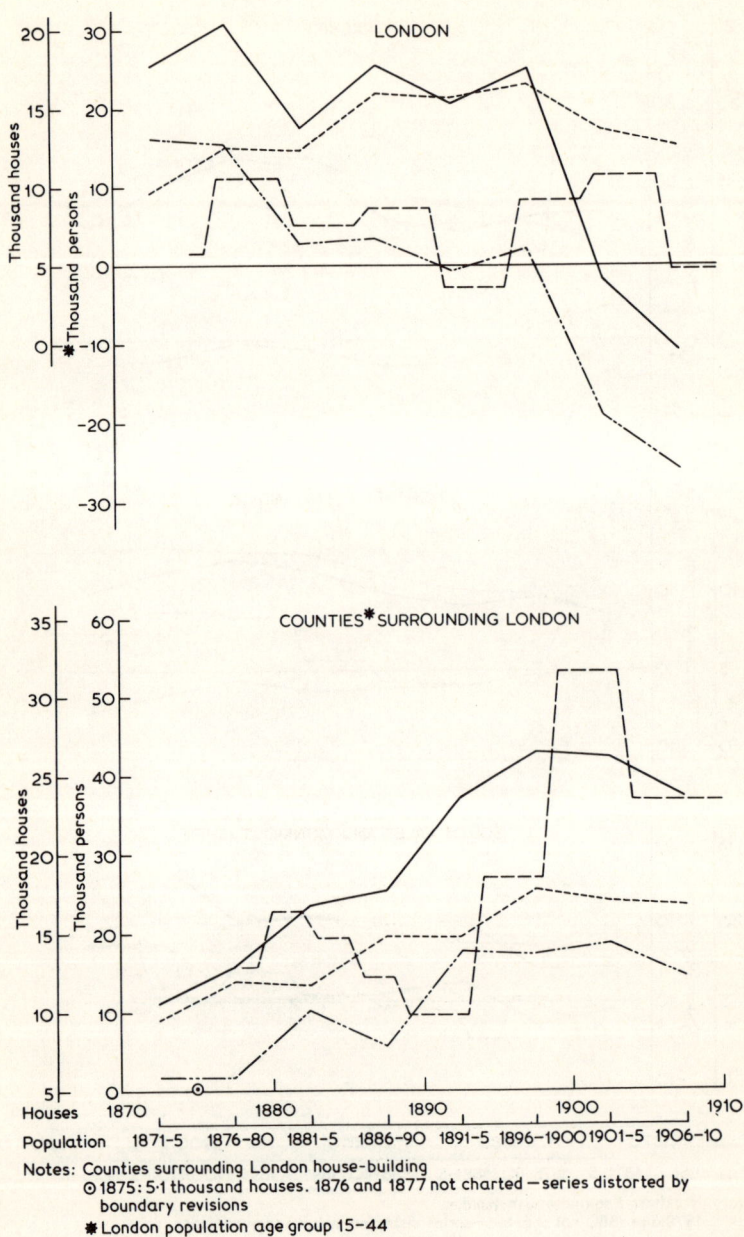

Figure 1C

The picture emerging from these charts dispels the uncertainty whether regional fluctuations were synchronized or were the result of diverse local circumstances. With the exception of London and South Wales there was a high degree of conformity between regional building swings, although the amplitude varied. London was particularly affected by outward shifts of population to the home counties; in the early part of the period, however, there was considerable net in-migration. The reason why South Wales is an exception is that its economy was entirely in the export sector [14].

It would be unreasonable to expect the peak of the building cycle to occur in the same year in every region: there is usually a cluster of individual peaks within a neighbourhood of three or four years. Our building series, beginning in 1875, reveals a high level of activity, though often declining, in the late 1870s in every region except the counties surrounding London where the peak came in the early years of the 1880s. The downswing lasted until the early 1890s in all regions except London and South Wales. Building activity was rising during the 1890s in all regions, with a peak at the turn of the century everywhere except in South Wales and London.

It might be argued that the averaging technique which has been used to overcome the difficulty of the reassessment years tends to blur the peaks and troughs of the cycle. In order to test the reliability of the new regional indexes, I shall look at the north-west (Lancashire and Cheshire) in more detail and partially disaggregate the I.H.D. index by plotting alongside it annual estimates of building in the Manchester conurbation and Liverpool, based on local authority data [15]. These are shown in Figure 2 together with the demographic series.

The peak of 1877-9 in our index coincides exactly with the peak in the number of houses erected by private enterprise in Liverpool. The peak in the Manchester conurbation index comes a year earlier, as one would expect, since these figures relate to houses for which planning permission had been obtained. The steep descent from the top to a very low trough in 1883-5 shown by the I.H.D. index corresponds exactly to what happened in the Manchester conurbation; in both series building then continues at a very low level until the upturn in 1892-4. The downswing in Liverpool is less steep and there is no early trough in 1883-5; the revival takes place at the same time as is indicated in the other two indices [16]. There is a close resemblance between the final peak and the subsequent decline in the I.H.D. series from 1899 to 1910 and the dominant Manchester component, again allowing for the fact

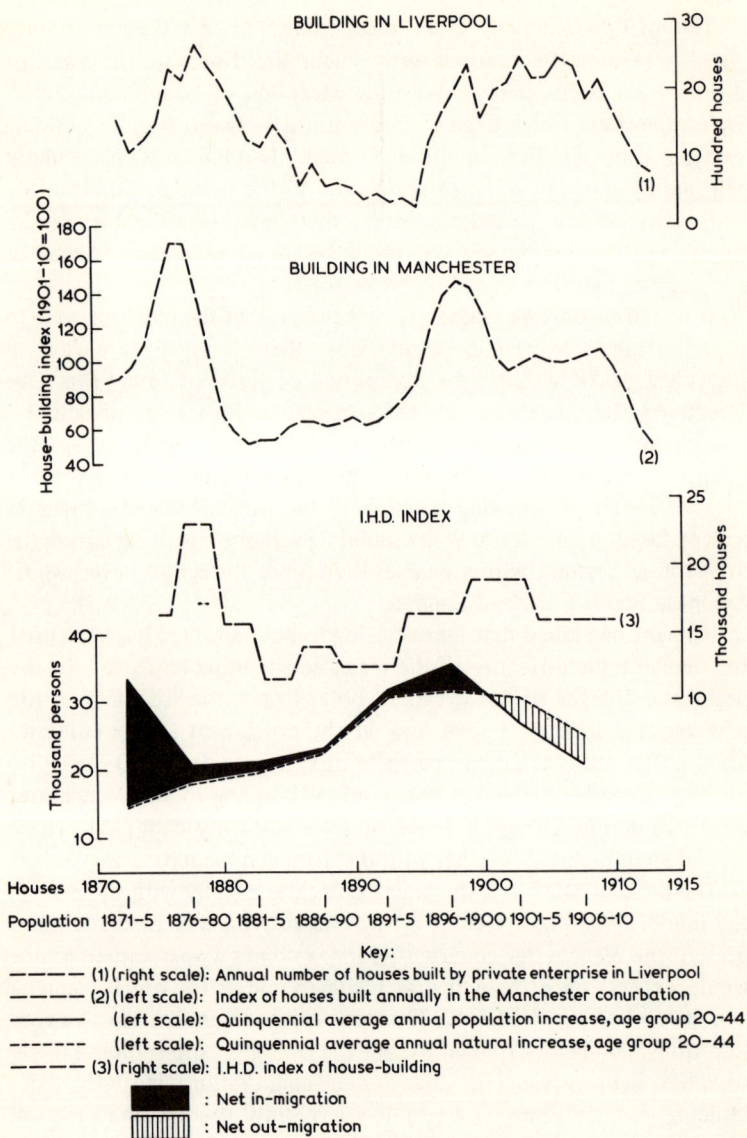

Figure 2 Migration, natural increase and housebuilding, north-west region, 1871-1913. *Sources*: (1) J. Parry Lewis, *Building Cycles and Britain's Growth*, pp. 335-6. (2) Ibid., p. 317.

that the latter registers building plans and not houses built. The high average level of activity in the region between 1899 and 1903 recorded by our index reflects a balance between the weakening boom in the Manchester conurbation and a continuation of buoyant conditions in Liverpool. A vigorous boom continued in Liverpool, with another high peak in 1906, whereas the level of activity in the conurbation was midway between the peak of the late 1870s and the trough of the 1880s. The sharp decline in 1909-13 is the same in both.

The I.H.D. index is the nearest one can get to full coverage of regional building in the period 1875-1910. The comparison with local authority data in two large component parts of the north-west region has been reassuring; the close fit with Weber's national index is reproduced regionally. Even before we bring in the population variable, the evidence points strongly against the argument that regional building was shaped largely by diverse local influences. S. B. Saul came near to the main explanation in the following sentence: 'Liverpool followed the national index to the recovery after the Boer War, but then building continued at a high level until as late as 1909, just as it did in South Wales and in the cotton towns' [17]. It is essential to distinguish between the Home Construction Sector and the Export Sector. Coal-exporting and cotton-exporting towns belong entirely to the export sector; building in such areas has a different time-shape from that of the home construction sector (areas other than purely export areas). There is always some building going on in the export sector; the regional as well as the national indices are composites of building activity in the two sectors. It is clear from the national index that the high phase of the long swing were the years when the ratio of building in the home construction sector to building in the export sector was high and vice versa in the low phase. The purest case of export sector building is South Wales; the index for that region was rising in the 1880s and in the late 1900s, contrary to the national swing. The same phenomenon was at work in parts of other regions but it was seldom strong enough to dominate the regional composite.

Saul presents a number of charts showing building in various towns in Cheshire between 1890 and 1913, and finds an upswing in a number of dormitory towns and in Stockport and a downswing in Crewe [18]. The more it becomes local history, the more variety we are going to see; but this is perfectly consistent with the presence of major ebbs and flows [19]. In the particular case of Cheshire, the boom in building in the dormitory towns was part of a universal tendency in the economic growth of large cities — the overspill (internal migration from the point of view of the region). This is part of the migration variable which, as we shall see, is the major determinant of the ebb and flow of building.

A glance at Figure 2 shows for the north-west region the quinquennial course of natural increase and population change in the age group 20—44 from 1871-5 to 1906-10. The excess of population change over natural increase (the shaded area) indicates the volume of net in-migration and the excess of natural increase over population change (the area with broken lines) indicates the volume of net out-migration. There is a close correspondence between the long swing in housebuilding and the curve of population change in the 20—44 age group, with the former lagging after the latter. The shape of the curve of population change is determined by the swing in the balance of migration.

The period begins with a very heavy net movement of migrants into the region in the years 1871-5, and this leads to a sharp rise in building activity which reaches a high peak in the years 1877-9. There was a marked contraction in in-migration in 1876-80, and it remained negligible through the 1880s and the beginning of the 1890s. This was accompanied by a sharp downswing and long trough in building activity. Meanwhile, beginning in 1885-90 the curve of natural increase rose sharply until it reached a record level in the 1890s. The quinquennium 1896-1900 saw the powerful echo effect of the sharp increase in the birth rate twenty-five to thirty years before and superimposed on this very high level of natural increase was a renewed rise in net migration into the region. There was also a considerable increase in the marriage rate in the 1890s. This time the lag relationship is between the natural increase build-up which attained its maximum in 1891-1900 plus the migration increase with peak marriage rate in 1896-1900 and the upswing in building which began about 1894-5 and went to a peak at the turn of the century and a few years afterwards. After 1900 net migration was negative until the end of the period and the level of natural increase was falling; this induced with a lag a downswing in the volume of building.

Now that we have taken a preliminary look at the pattern in the north-west region, with our I.H.D. index partially disaggregated, we shall examine the evidence for the other regions.

3   DEMOGRAPHIC DETERMINANTS: REGIONAL
    AND NATIONAL

The time-shape for the north-west is repeated in the north, Yorkshire, the Midlands and the counties surrounding London. The dominant influence of the course of migration is clearly brought out in all regions. It is interesting to compare the picture for London with that of the counties surrounding the capital. In the Home Counties building has a long swing corresponding to that of the rest of industrial England, with a very high peak in the early 1900s: in London, however, there is only a mild swing. The annual volume of building in the capital in 1902-6 was only slightly above the level of 1877-81, and the troughs in 1892-6 and 1907-10 were relatively shallow. Net migration into London, which was fairly high in the 1870s, fell to low levels in the 1880s and 1890s, and became a large net outflow in the 1900s. The gross outflows to the Home Counties were an important factor.

Some of these outflows went beyond the periphery of the capital, as can be seen from Figure 3, which gives the course of building in the predominantly rural areas of England and Wales. In the agricultural Midlands there was a steady low level of activity with hardly any fluctuation; in the southern counties movements were more erratic, and the south-west plus rural Wales showed mild peaks in the late 1870s and early 1900s. Putting the three together as a residual rural sector, we find a definite peak in the early 1900s, as in the Home Counties, the Midlands, the north-west and Yorkshire. This was chiefly the reflection of the demographic echo effect and the growth of residential and military towns in southern counties during the 1890s.

London displayed a unique pattern because it was a congested capital bursting at the seams. Behind the bare summary record of building and demographic change in Figure 1C is a fascinating story of population mobility, transport innovations and the expansion of suburbs. To do justice to it would need several volumes of the calibre of the admirable study of Camberwell by H. J. Dyos [20]. The following summary of Camberwell's demographic history is in miniature a faithful reflection of the course of population change in London shown in the chart.

Of the 75,000 persons by which the suburb had grown during its years of maximum development in the 1870s, about 52,000 represented the balance of migration into and out of the district, and

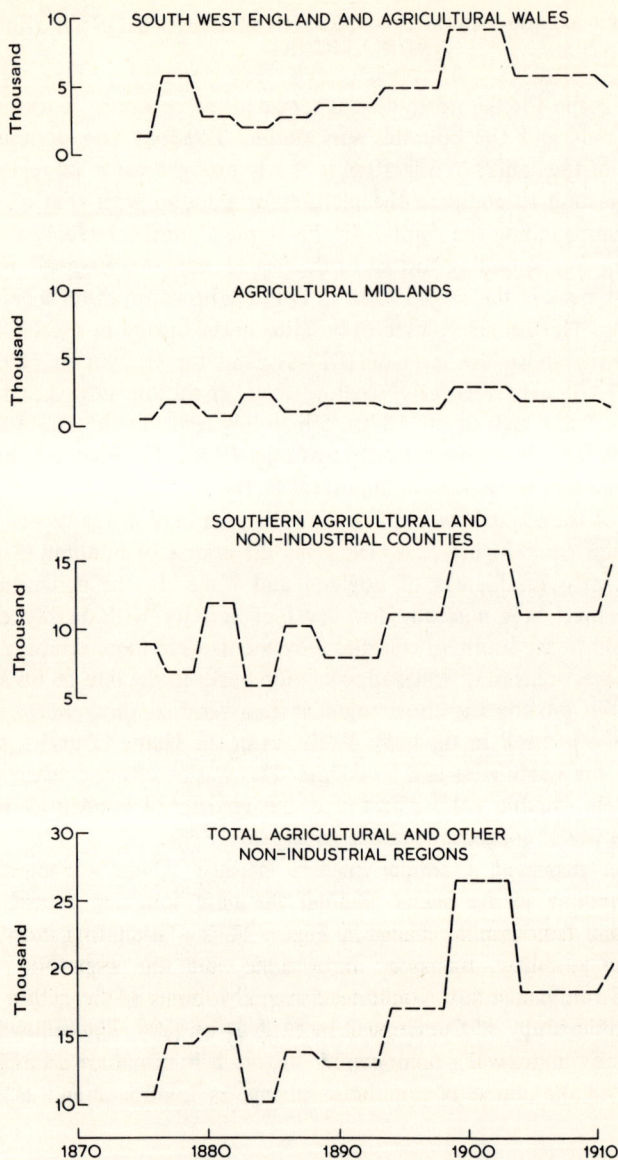

Figure 3   Housebuilding in agricultural and other non-industrial regions.
Source: Inland Revenue Inhabited House Duty records (see Appendix).

23,000 were the result of natural increase. But the stream of migrants which had been chiefly responsible for the growth of the suburb since the beginning of the century, and which was now in full flood, soon declined, and it had dried up all together by the end of the century. Of the increase of about 49,000 persons recorded between 1881 and 1891, only about 17,000 could be accounted for by net immigration, but in the last ten years of the century the increase of about 24,000 persons was wholly accounted for by natural increase, and would have been higher had not more people — over a thousand — left the suburb than came into it. By 1911, the balance of migration had detached a further 25,000 from Camberwell, and this attrition continued, despite the comparatively low average population density, in the post-war years. [21]

The natural increase component of the population curve rose everywhere to a peak in the late 1890s; this was the result of the high level of fertility a quarter of a century earlier (the number of births per 1000 women aged 15–44 in England and Wales rising from 150.7 in 1863 to 156.7 in 1876). In addition, the marriage rate was at a peak in 1896-1900, 16.1 per 1000 as against 14.7 per 1000 in 1886-90.

In all regions, except London and South Wales, population change in the age group 20–44 was at a maximum in the five-year period 1896-1900; there was a combination of a powerful echo effect on natural increase, a deep trough in emigration overseas, and heavy internal migration, particularly into the Home Counties and the north-west. In each of these five regions the peak in housebuilding came at the turn of the century and there can be no doubt that there was a common demographic determinant. South Wales, which was out of step, had relatively low building activity in 1899-1904 and then came a vigorous boom (in the wake of high in-migration) in the years 1905-10 when every other region was experiencing a decline in housebuilding.

The building cycle and the demographic variables for the seven regions as a whole (largely England and Wales) are shown in Figure 4. There is a very close similarity between the movements in our I.H.D. building index and those of the Parry Lewis weighted index. Population change in the age group 20–44 is the result of 'natural increase' and current migration. The charts show the quantitative significance of these two components. Figure 4 indicates the part played by migration in determining the *shape* of the curve of population change in the urban

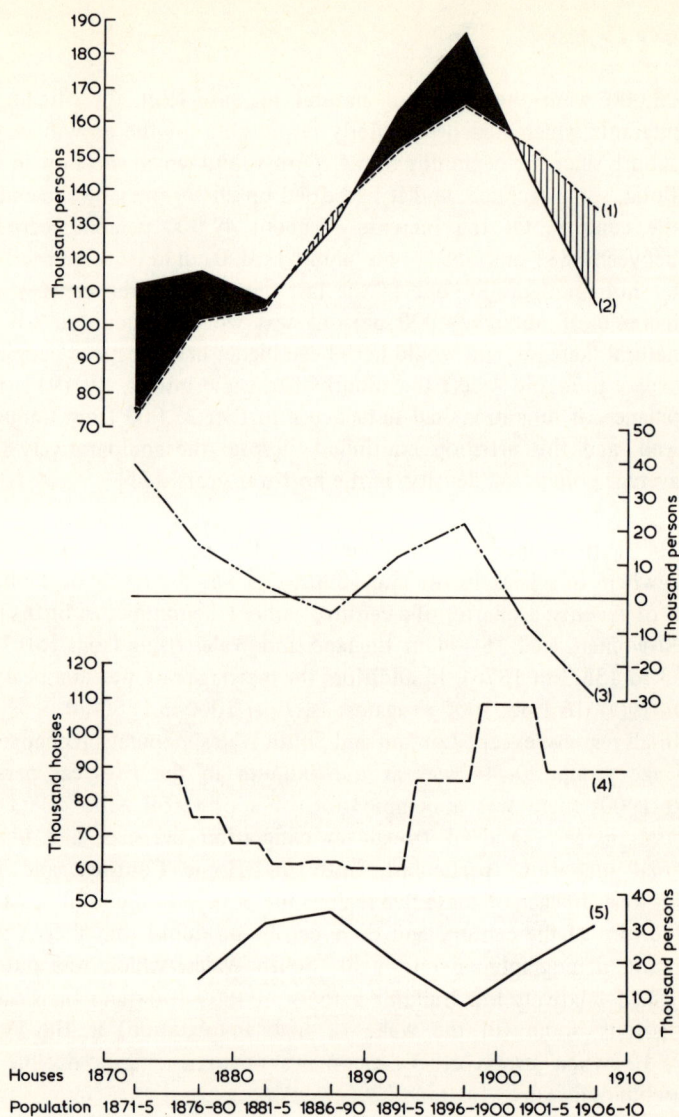

Key:

- - - - - - (1) (left scale): Quinquennial average annual natural increase, 20-44
———— (2) (left scale): Quinquennial average annual population increase, 20-44
—·——·— (3) (right scale): Quinquennial average annual net migration, 20-44
⬛ : Net in-migration
▥ : Net out-migration
- - - - (4) (left scale): Average annual number of houses built (I.H.D. index)
———— (5) (right scale): Quinquennial average annual number of occupied emigrants from England and Wales to the United States

regions of England and Wales taken together. The verdict of the analysis is that nationally and regionally the swing in housebuilding follows with a lag the swing in the population aged 20–44 as determined by migration. With regard to timing, the divergent fluctuations in London and South Wales did little to modify the major uniform swings in the other five regions that governed the aggregate. The inverse relation between internal and external migration is clearly shown. When internal migration was high, emigration was low; and it was in those years that building, with a lag, expanded; the opposite occurred when internal migration was low and emigration was high. The swings in house-building conform to the swings in the migration-dominated curve of population change. As Cairncross observed in his well-known analysis of fluctuations in the Glasgow building industry, 1860-1914, 'the building cycle was little more than a migration cycle in disguise' [22].

4   THE ALTERNATION OF BRITISH AND AMERICAN CYCLES

Since *Migration and Economic Growth* was written, much new work has been done on building fluctuations in the United States. To round off this reappraisal, I shall compare the British pattern with that of the United States in the period 1870-1910, drawing on the valuable researches of Burnham O. Campbell [23]. To take advantage of improvements in earlier building series, I shall use John R. Riggleman's index of the value of building permits as adjusted by Walter Isard and Clarence D. Long's index of the value of permits as adjusted by Miles L. Colean and Robinson Newcomb [24].

Burnham Campbell has conducted a detailed examination of the influence of demographic variables, particularly immigration, on the residential building cycle in the United States. By isolating movements in the headship rate, i.e. the ratio of households to total population in an age group, he has reached illuminating conclusions about the causation of the post-1945 building cycle. In the present context we shall be concerned only with his results for the period ending in 1913. He defines 'required additions' as the population change in each age

---

Figure 4   Population change and the building cycle, urban regions of England and Wales, 1871-1910. *Notes*: (i) London's population includes 15–20 age group. (ii) Method of averaging housebuilding is based on reassessment years for areas outside London. Different reassessment years for metropolitan areas are ignored. *Sources*: (1) to (4) Figure 1 (A-C). (5) *Migration and Economic Growth*, Tables 81 and 84.

56 Essays on a Mature Economy

group during a given period multiplied by the headship rate for the age
group at the beginning of the period. He has calculated for the United
States the change in population by age group in each quinquennium
from 1850-5 on, and he then estimates the change in required
additions by age group due to immigration in each quinquennium [25].
It is this latter series for the period 1870-5 to 1905-10 which I have
reproduced in Figure 5.

Campbell concludes that 'from the Civil War to the 1890s the rate of
change in required additions – and from the 1890s to the 1930s, the
direction of change – was controlled by the long swing in immigration.... Not only was the long swing in required additions greatly
influenced by immigration, but from the 1870s to the 1910s and again
in the 1930s there was a close connection between the long swing in
immigration and the long swing in household formations and housing
starts or residential capital formation.... The argument that fluctuations in immigration were the sources of those in residential building
can be stated most strongly in terms of quinquennial data. From the
1870s to the 1930s, residential building and required additions due to
immigration varied together in all but three half-decades, and the lagged
adjustment of residential construction to changes in housing demand
could explain all three exceptions. In summary, from the Civil War to
World War II the long swing in immigration was the dominant source of
the long swing in required additions and so of the residential building
cycle in the United States.' [26]

In Figure 5 we plot the British data for the period 1870-1910 with
the corresponding American quinquennial data on required additions in

---

Figure 5   Population change and building cycles, England and Wales and the
United States, 1871-1910. *Sources*: (2), (3), (4) and (5), see Figure 4. (1) J. Parry
Lewis, *Building Cycles and Britain's Growth*, p. 317, col. 7. (6) Burnham O.
Campbell, *Population Change and Building Cycles*, p. 194. (7) M. Abramovitz,
Evidence of Long Swings in Aggregate Construction since the Civil War, pp.
147–9. (8) and (9) Ibid.

Key:

(2),(3),(4) and (5):	As in Figure 4
———— (1) (left scale):	Weighted house-building index for towns in England and Wales, 1901–10=100 (Parry Lewis)
———·— (6) (left scale):	Quinquennial changes in required additions (in thousands of dwelling units) due to immigration, age group 20–44, U.S.A.
———— (7)(right scale):	Riggleman's index of value of building permits per capita in U.S.A. as adjusted by Isard (1920–29=100)
———— (8)(right scale):	Long's index of the value of residential permits in U.S.A. (1920–30=100)
———— (9)(right scale):	Long's index of the value of all permits in U.S.A. as adjusted by Colean and Newcomb

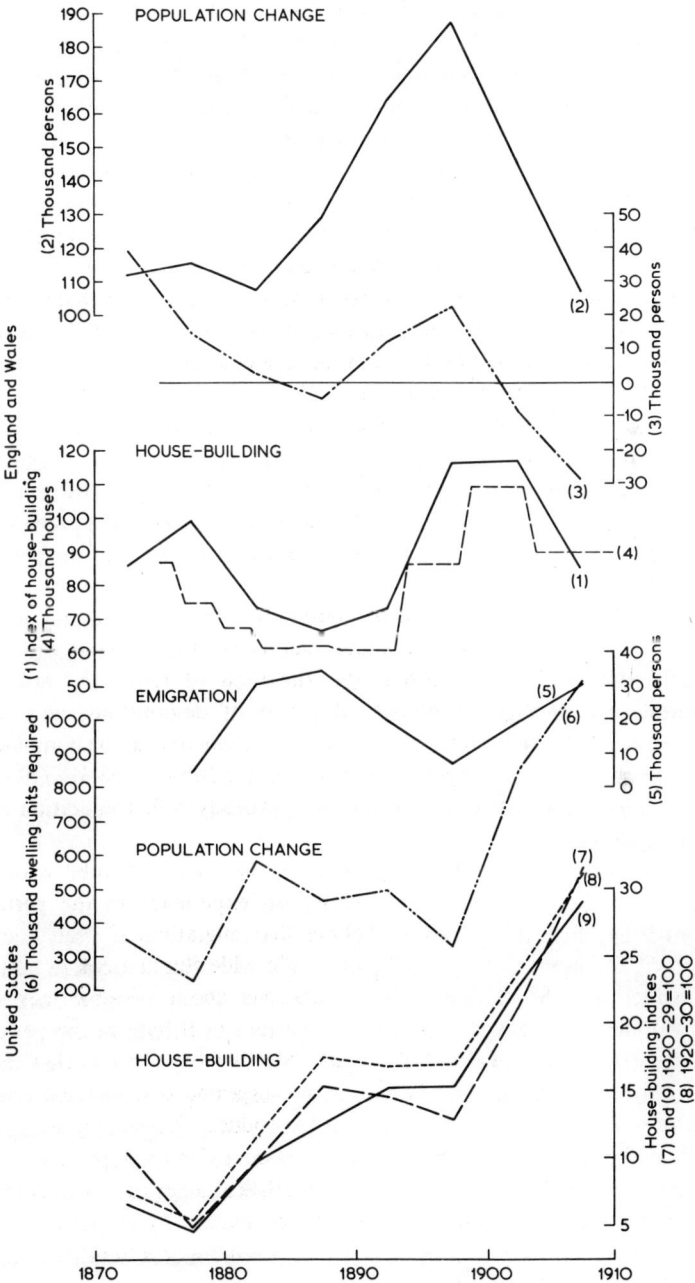

the age group 20–44 due to immigration, and three indices of building activity. There is an impressive inverse relation between the quinquennial increase in population in the age group 20–44 in Britain and the quinquennial change in required additions due to immigration in the age group 20–44 in the United States. The building cycles are inverse and the time-shape of each is governed by the course of migration. If it were possible to produce quinquennial estimates of internal migration for the United States, this would complete the picture. Kuznets has shown, on the basis of decadal estimates, that changes in internal migration of native born in the United States were synchronous with changes in additions to total population and that the volume of internal migration in any decade was probably at least equal to the total additions to population [27].

Figure 5 amply confirms the conclusions of *Migration and Economic Growth*. The crux of the problem is the mechanism of the migration cycle. Housebuilding is an important part of population-sensitive capital formation, and the fluctuations in the latter are crucial in the process of interaction between the British and American economies in the period under review.

The demographic factor is, of course, not the sole determinant of the building cycle: there are other factors on the demand and the supply side, e.g. income levels, the stickiness of rents, the rate of interest, the quality of houses, the rate of demolitions, and the organization of the building trades. Various elements can be combined to form a satisfactory explanation based on the cobweb theorem. What the empirical evidence demonstrates unequivocally is that migration is a major determinant.

Our analysis refutes the assertions of the writers quoted earlier, e.g. S. B. Saul's statement about British experience in the period 1890-1914, that it is 'hard to believe that migration of itself could account for more than a small part of the wide fluctuations in house construction' [28]. Habakkuk's speculations about possible lack of synchronization between regional fluctuations in Britain in the period 1870-1914 are also wide of the mark. Starting from the notion that the only real cycle is the trade cycle, he suggested that regional trade cycles were behaving in such a way as to produce a bogus long swing in aggregate building, which became more moderate in its amplitude. The evidence contradicts any such notion. Statistical analysis confirms that there was a real building cycle determined mainly by migration. The degree of synchronization or lack of it between regional building cycles has very little to do with the trade cycle [29]. Moreover, instead of moderating, the amplitude of the aggregate long swing increased, the high peak of the early 1900s reflecting the force of the demographic determinants in the late 1890s.

So far as the United States is concerned, Habakkuk says that 'an increase in immigration did not *initiate* a revival of building; the revival was started by changes in migration within the United States which preceded changes in immigration' [30]. There is no statistical support for this assertion; the figures for internal migration cannot be used for this purpose. What we do know about annual time series for immigration and building in the United States refutes the assertion. Lag analysis has demonstrated that throughout the period 1845-1913, except for the years 1869-70, immigration consistently preceded American building activity [31].

According to Habakkuk, 'the problem posed by the hypothesis of the Atlantic economy is the balance between domestic – and in this context fortuitous – influences on the one hand, and foreign and systematic influences on the other' [32], and he comes down heavily on the side of the former. The empirical evidence presented in this paper strongly confirms the proposition that migration, internal and external, played a major role in the housebuilding cycles in Britain and the United States in the period 1870-1913. To those who contemplate the tides of building activity and are impressed only by what seem to be accidental, wayward or local influences, I commend the well-known lines of Arthur Hugh Clough:

> For while the tired waves, vainly breaking,
> Seem here no painful inch to gain,
> Far back, through creeks and inlets making,
> Comes silent, flooding in, the main.

5   OUTLINES OF AN INTERACTION MODEL

Any interpretation of the interaction between the British and American economies in the pre-1913 period must also account for the fact that all the oversea developing countries, e.g. U.S.A., Canada, Argentina and Australia, had their investment upswings and downswings at the same time. Those who have attempted a one-sided explanation of the long swing in terms of variations in American aggregate demand see supporting evidence in the fact that there were simultaneous swings in migration from a number of European countries to the United States [33] : they never pose the question why there were simultaneous investment and immigration swings in a number of countries of new settlement. This latter phenomenon, which can hardly be due to variations in American demand, is an important part of the problem of inverse long swings.

The answer is to be sought in two basic features of the period. First, the opening up of new sources of food and raw materials required flows of population and loanable funds to be invested in infrastructure overseas, and there was necessarily a long lag between the input phase and the output phase. Secondly, the countries were linked together by the gold standard dominated by London, the financial centre of the world. When an infrastructure upswing became intense, there was a serious problem of undereffected transfer; and drastic action by the Bank of England to protect its reserve had powerful repercussions on the supply of money in all oversea borrowing countries.

This is not the place to spell out the mechanism of interaction, but the basis of it can be very briefly indicated. On the one hand, we have Great Britain, the creditor country (C) and, on the other, the factor-importing 'country' (D) representing the whole periphery of oversea developing countries.

(*a*)   Each is divided into two sectors, home construction and export.

(*b*)   C exports capital goods and D food and raw materials.

(*c*)   Migration depends on the difference in real wages which can be approximated by the difference in real incomes.

(*d*)   Export capacity is generated through population-sensitive capital formation, i.e. the building of infrastructure – railways, roads, land-clearing, ports, houses, public utilities, etc. – and this investment has a relatively long gestation period. There is an intertemporal relation between a country's infrastructure investment in one period and its export capacity in the next period.

(*e*)   The level of activity of a country's export sector depends on the marginal efficiency of investment in the construction sector of the other country in the same period.

(*f*)   A major fraction of total capital formation is population-sensitive, i.e. varying with the rate of change in population growth and internal migration.

(*g*)   The population growth rate is a function of the external migration balance and the population structure (i.e. a vector showing proportions of population in various age groups).

(*h*)   The countries are linked by a gold standard with specie currency.

These assumptions imply a complicated see-saw movement in which both 'real' and monetary factors are at work. The task is to take the basic relationships and build up an econometric model. An important constraint on the form of the functions is the long infrastructure gestation period. Another crucial factor is that population structure in each country has a cyclical element in it and that at any moment population structure is a function of an earlier population structure and of intervening migration. The ability of the model to generate long swings would seem to depend very much on population structure and the infrastructure lag. What is required is an experimental simulation of a complete model, to try out various types of functions with different numerical values of the parameters and different lags in order to discover what effects these different functions have upon the simulated values of the endogenous variables.

The see-saw movement seems to arise fundamentally out of the alternation of infrastructure and export upsurges, and the whole thing is played according to the rules of the gold standard game, with the creditor country as referee. This mechanism of interaction may offer an explanation of the fact that the oversea countries of new settlement experienced *simultaneous* long swings in capital formation which were inverse to those of the United Kingdom.

NOTES

[1]   An outstanding work is J. Parry Lewis, *Building Cycles and Britain's Growth* (London, Macmillan, 1965). This thorough study confirms the inverse relation between home construction cycles from the 1850s to 1913 in Chapter 7, pp. 164–85. See also Arthur I. Bloomfield, *Patterns of Fluctuations in International Investment before 1914* (Princeton, N.J., International Finance Section, Department of Economics, Princeton University, Princeton Studies in International Finance No. 21, 1968). Bloomfield points out that not only did British home and foreign investment move inversely over the long swing between 1870 and 1913, but they also tended to move inversely *in the short run*:'The correlation coefficient of the first differences of net capital exports and gross domestic fixed-capital formation from 1860 to 1913 was −0.32, significant at the 5 percent level. Compare this result with Cairncross's assertion (*Home and Foreign Investment 1870-1913*, pp. 187–8) that in the short run home and foreign investment generally moved together.' (Bloomfield, op. cit., p. 22).

[2]   H. J. Habakkuk, 'Fluctuations in house-building in Britain and the United States in the nineteenth century', *The Journal of Economic History*, XXII (2), 1962, reprinted in A. R. Hall (ed.), *The Export of Capital from Britain*

1870-1914 (London, Methuen, 1968), pp. 103–42. The references here are to the latter. S. B. Saul, 'House building in England 1890-1914', *The Economic History Review*, 2nd ser., XV (1), August 1962, pp. 119–37.

[3] H. J. Habakkuk, op. cit., p. 120. The footnote reference must be an error: it should be 'Matthews, *The Trade Cycle'.*

[4] Ibid., p. 137.

[5] Ibid., p. 141.

[6] S. B. Saul, op. cit.

[7] Ibid., p. 136. For a critique of Saul's analysis, see J. Parry Lewis, op. cit., pp. 203–5.

[8] Brinley Thomas, *Migration and Economic Growth: A Study of Great Britain and the Atlantic Economy* (Cambridge University Press, 1954).

[9] The series for England and Wales, Scotland, and Britain, are given in B. R. Mitchell and Phyllis Deane, *Abstract of British Historical Statistics* (Cambridge University Press, 1962), pp. 236–7.

[10] J. C. Stamp, *British Incomes and Property* (London, King, 1916), p. 31.

[11] B. Weber, 'A new index of residential construction, 1838-1950', *Scottish Journal of Political Economy*, II (2), June 1955, pp. 104–32.

[12] Comprehensive studies of echo effects for the United States are to be found in Richard A. Easterlin, *Population, Labor Force and Long Swings in Economic Growth: The American Experience* (National Bureau of Economic Research, Columbia University Press, 1968), and Burnham O. Campbell, *Population Change and Building Cycles* (Urbana, Ill., Bureau of Economic and Business Research, University of Illinois, 1966).

[13] A similar analysis of the potential demand for houses from population aged 20–44 in Great Britain as a whole quinquennially from 1871-5 to 1906-10 was carried out by C. H. Feinstein in his unpublished Ph.D. dissertation, *Home and Foreign Investment 1870-1913* (University of Cambridge, 1959), pp. 291–6. The methods used here, as explained in the Appendix, are different from those of Feinstein.

[14] See Brinley Thomas, 'Wales and the Atlantic economy', *Scottish Journal of Political Economy*, November 1959, pp. 169–92.

[15] The figures for the towns in the Manchester conurbation are the number of houses on approved building plans. For Manchester itself there is a gap from 1871 to 1890 and values for these years were estimated from other sources. See J. Parry Lewis, op. cit, pp. 307–17. The Liverpool series are the number of houses erected by private enterprise. They were supplied to B. Weber by the Town Clerk of Liverpool. See J. Parry Lewis, op. cit., pp. 335–6.

[16] The kink and sharp rise in the Liverpool index in 1895 is explained by the extension of the boundaries of the city in November of that year, adding 23,263 dwelling houses to the original stock of 106,962. See J. Parry Lewis, op. cit., p. 335.

[17] S. B. Saul, op. cit., p. 122.

[18] Ibid., p. 124.

[19] Analysis is concerned with phenomena which exhibit statistical uniformities. In the words of Sir John Hicks, 'Every historical event has some aspect in which it is unique; but nearly always there are other aspects in which it is a member of a group, often of quite a large group. If it is one of the latter aspects in which we are interested, it will be the group, not the individual, on which we shall fix our attention; it will be the average, or norm, of the group which is what we shall be trying to explain. We shall be able to allow that the individual may diverge from the norm without being deterred from

the recognition of a statistical uniformity.' (Sir John Hicks, *A Theory of Economic History* (Oxford University Press, 1969), p. 3).

[20] H. J. Dyos, *Victorian Suburb: A Study of the Growth of Camberwell* (Leicester University Press, 1961). See also Thomas A. Welton, *England's Recent Progress* (London, Chapman & Hall, 1911), pp. 188–206; *The New Survey of London Life and Labour*, vol. I, *Forty Years of Change* (London, King, 1930), Chapter II 'Area and population' by A. L. Bowley, pp. 58–83, and Chapter VI 'Travel and mobility' by G. Ponsonby and S. K. Ruck, pp. 171–99; A. K. Cairncross, 'Internal migration in Victorian England', in *Home and Foreign Investment 1870-1913* (Cambridge University Press, 1953), pp. 65–83.

[21] H. J. Dyos, op. cit., p. 56.

[22] A. K. Cairncross, op. cit., p. 25.

[23] Burnham O. Campbell, op. cit.

[24] For an account of the characteristics of these indices, see M. Abramovitz, *Evidences of Long Swings in Aggregate Construction since the Civil War* (New York, National Bureau of Economic Research, Columbia University Press, 1964), pp. 206–20.

[25] For details of the statistical treatment of immigration, see Burnham O. Campbell, op. cit., Appendix C, pp. 189–94.

[26] Campbell, op. cit., p. 110.

[27] S. Kuznets, *Capital in the American Economy* (Princeton, N.J. National Bureau of Economic Research, Princeton University Press, 1961), pp. 325–7.

[28] S. B. Saul, op. cit., p. 131.

[29] The whole question of housebuilding and the trade cycle was thoroughly examined by B. Weber. He concluded that 'taking the period from 1842 to 1913 as a whole, neither an emphatic anti-cyclical movement in building nor the reverse can be established unequivocally.' See J. Parry Lewis, op. cit., p. 359.

[30] H. J. Habakkuk, op. cit., p. 121. Italics in the original.

[31] See Brinley Thomas, *Migration and Economic Growth*, pp. 159–63.

[32] Ibid., p. 133.

[33] e.g. Kuznets, Abramovitz and Easterlin.

POPULATION CHANGE AND REGIONAL BUILDING CYCLES IN
ENGLAND AND WALES 1870-1910: SOURCES AND METHODS

The sources used are Inland Revenue ledgers deposited at the Public
Record Office, Ashbridge, Hertfordshire [1]. They comprise revenue
raised from the Inhabited House Duty and profits assessed under
Schedule D. The data are available for each county.

1 Inhabited House Duty Statistics

The Inhabited House Duty was introduced in 1851 and was levied on
dwelling houses of £20 annual value and over. There is information
about dwelling houses assessed and not assessed to duty as well as
'messuages and tenements' not used as dwelling houses. We took the
series showing the total number of houses assessed and not assessed to
duty from 1875 to 1910, and obtained a measure of housebuilding
activity from the change in the numbers recorded.

It is important to be clear about the limitations of these data and
how we have sought to overcome them. The first difficulty is the effect
of the periodic reassessments of properties. In England and Wales, with
the exception of London, reassessment took place in 1876, 1879, 1882,
1885, 1888, 1893, 1898, 1903 and 1910; the revaluation years for
London were 1876, 1881, 1886, 1891, 1896, 1901, 1906 and 1911.
Josiah Stamp, in his authoritative work, stated that 'the income tax,
Schedule A, figures undoubtedly represent most closely the real facts,
but in revaluation years far more closely than at other times' [2]. In
years between revaluations the series tend to be below the true figures.
'The reason is that while effect is given in practice to all *bona fide
reductions* in rent wherever they occur, no effect is, or can be, given to
increases in rents, and the totals are only maintained by new properties
and structural alterations. There is a continuous drag downwards, and
the "slack" is not taken up until the next revaluation year.' [3] In
some areas the figures for revaluation years showed a decline rather
than an upward revision; this was likely to happen where a large
number of houses were becoming empty or where there was a general
fall in rents and the revaluation provided an opportunity for a general
revision of assessments. The numbers of houses as well as the values
were affected by the reassessments. Another awkward fact about these
data is pointed out by B. R. Mitchell and Phyllis Deane, namely, that
'the figures are of net quantities, offsetting much demolition against

new building, and it seems probable that demolition was nothing like constant from year to year' [4].

For the above reasons the Inhabited House Duty figures are not an accurate guide to *year-to-year* changes in housebuilding, but this does not necessarily rule them out as an indication of the time-shape of housebuilding. Their reliability for this purpose can be tested by comparing them with Weber's building index. From the House Duty records we have taken the annual change in the number of premises in Great Britain [5] and produced an index for the years 1875-1910 (1900-9 = 100). This is shown together with Weber's index of residential construction in Figure 6.

Figure 6 Housebuilding in Great Britain. *Source:* B. R. Mitchell and Phyllis Deane, *Abstract of British Historical Statistics* (Cambridge University Press, 1962), pp. 236-9.

The chart brings out clearly the effect of the periodic revaluations and the impossibility of using the series for *annual* changes. On the other hand, it also demonstrates that the long swing in building revealed by the Inhabited House Duty statistics follows closely that of the Weber index. It was therefore decided to overcome the reassessment difficulty by averaging the years between revaluations plus the revaluation year following them. The year is the financial year ending on 4 April; thus, for example, the difference between the number of houses in existence at 4 April 1876 and 4 April 1875 is taken as an estimate of housebuilding in 1875.

The counties of England and Wales are divided into two sectors, roughly urban and rural. The urban sector has seven regions — Midlands, counties surrounding London, north-west England, Yorkshire, northern England, South Wales and Monmouthshire, and London. The three rural regions are the southern agricultural counties, Midlands agricultural counties, and the south-west plus rural Wales.

In compiling these regional estimates we had to consider the effects of the frequent changes in income tax districts. Since our classification splits the country into large sections, most of the district revisions fell within (and not between) regions and can therefore be ignored. Where major revisions distort our series we have noted these on the tables as boundary revisions and left breaks in our charts for the years affected.

For the years 1893 and 1894 two volumes were missing from the Ashbridge ledgers. Counties are entered alphabetically, and the missing ledgers contained those beginning S-W (including Wales) for 1893 and B-R for 1894. Our table notes the method used to produce estimates. In most regions we had records for one or more counties and we applied the percentage change for available counties in the region to the missing counties. Where figures for all the counties in a region were missing, we used the percentage change in ledger section totals as a guide. The sections were alphabetical and we took the most appropriate ledger section in two cases; Section 4 containing Lancashire, Leicester and Lincoln was used for the north-west; Section 9 containing Wiltshire, Worcester and Yorkshire was used for Yorkshire. A third method seemed preferable for Wales. In view of the slow rate of increase in numbers of houses for rural Wales, we assumed there was no change here between 1892 and 1893, and allocated the whole increase for Wales to the urban section — South Wales and Monmouthshire.

The counties composing the regions are as follows.

MIDLANDS
Derby
Leicester
Northampton
Nottingham
Staffordshire
Warwick
Worcester

NORTH-WESTERN COUNTIES
Lancashire
Cheshire

NORTHERN ENGLAND
Cumberland
Durham
Northumberland
Westmorland

LONDON

SOUTHERN AGRICULTURAL
Bedfordshire
Berkshire
Buckinghamshire

SOUTHERN AGRICULTURAL
(CONTINUED)

Cambridge
Gloucestershire
Hereford
Norfolk
Oxford
Suffolk
Sussex
Wiltshire
Hampshire

COUNTIES SURROUNDING
LONDON

Essex
Hertford
Kent (extra-metropolitan)
Middlesex (extra-metropolitan)
Surrey (extra-metropolitan)

YORKSHIRE

Yorkshire

SOUTH WALES AND
MONMOUTHSHIRE

Breconshire
Cardigan

Carmarthen
Glamorgan
Monmouth
Pembroke
Radnor

MIDLAND AGRICULTURAL

Huntingdon
Lincolnshire
Rutland
Shropshire

SOUTH-WESTERN ENGLAND
AND RURAL WALES

Cornwall
Devon
Dorset
Somerset
Anglesey
Caernarvon
Denbigh
Flint
Merioneth
Montgomery

A grouping of this kind is bound to be arbitrary and parts of regions classified as urban are rural; but the seven regions are urban in the sense that they contained the greater part of the population of England and Wales in the last quarter of the nineteenth century. A great advantage of the Inhabited House Duty data is that they give even coverage of all parts of the country, so that a comprehensive picture of regional cycles can be obtained.

2   Profits assessed to Schedule D

The Inland Revenue ledgers contain a great deal of information on profit income assessed to Schedule D. They show gross and net profits, with allowances for wear and tear and life assurances, and a table is given of profits arising from foreign and colonial securities and possessions. Stamp approved the use of Schedule D profits as a guide to trade prosperity. 'This test is generally regarded as one of the most reliable and it has been made by many writers. There is no doubt a close correspondence between the assessments and trade.' [6] Breaks affect the gross assessment series in 1876 and 1894, i.e. the financial years ending 5 April 1867 and 5 April 1895, and Stamp presents six alternative methods of allowing for these. We have applied a form of the second method (using abatements) described in his Appendix I [7], and the series are linked accordingly.

There is one more break in 1874. From 1866 to 1874 the profit figures described as gross were actually net of life assurance allowances [8], and to make them comparable with later series some adjustment for this should be made. Also from 1866 to 1873 we have not deducted profits arising from foreign securities and possessions. If we take the north-western counties, for example, we find that in 1874 the allowances for life assurance amounted to £57.9 thousand and the profits from foreign securities were very small, certainly never more than £100 thousand and were probably in the region of £50 thousand annually. Therefore the two adjustments required would seem to be almost entirely offsetting.

The records contain two sets of figures separating 'Trades, Manufactures, Professions and Employments' from 'Public Companies, Societies, etc.' Since there would have been transfers over time from one group to the other with the extension of limited liability, we have taken the two groups together, and have used gross profit figures to avoid breaks caused by statutory changes in allowances and abatements. From this total profit income we have deducted (except in 1866-73) profits earned from foreign securities and possessions. We should also have deducted profits on railways outside the United Kingdom, which are listed separately, in order to get a more accurate figure for domestic profits. However, they were negligible in relation to total profit income, so that they were ignored, except for London for which they were deducted.

Before 1874 abatements were not included in profit income but given separately, so that they had to be added to the figures for profits to make them comparable with subsequent years. With regard to London, before 1875, separate figures are not given for the metropolitan and extra-metropolitan parts of the counties of Kent, Middlesex and Surrey. Therefore an assumption is made that the proportionate distribution of profits between the two areas was the same before 1875 as in the years immediately following. For each of the years 1875-8, 94 per cent of the profits were assessed in the metropolis and so this figure forms the basis for our metropolitan estimates of profit income in 1867-74.

Some of the ledgers are missing in the years 1892 (i.e. the year ended 4 April 1893) and 1893. An estimate has had to be made for profit income (as well as building) for those years. Summary totals in ten sections are available and the percentage change in profits recorded in the relevant year in these section totals is applied to the particular county which forms part of the section.

Space does not allow an analysis of these data on profits, but the figures have been used as part of the method of handling the demographic data, as explained below.

3 Demographic data

We have concentrated on population change as reflected in the 20–44 age group and have made quinquennial estimates for each region, separating the effect of natural increase and migration. Data on recorded deaths for each region were collected from the Registrar-General's Annual Reports and Decennial Supplements, and these were used with census population figures in quinary age groups to estimate the quinquennial changes which would have occurred in the absence of migration.

The method was as follows. We took the population in quinary age groups at each census date, and allocated recorded deaths for the next five years to these groups, thus obtaining an estimate of the survivors from each group (now five years older) at a mid-census point. In the allocation we assumed that the deaths, say, of persons aged 15–19 during the five years could be allocated on a 50:50 basis between the persons aged 10–14 at the census date (moving up into the 15–19 group) and those aged 15–19 at the census date (moving up into the 20–24 group). From these estimated mid-census survivors we then deducted deaths for the following five years in a similar way to produce an estimate of survivors from the previous census population at the subsequent census date. The difference between actual census population and estimated survivors from the previous census indicates the decade's migratory flows.

Where population is flowing into an area, some of the persons dying would be migrants, and to adjust for this we assume that migrant deaths bear the same proportion to total deaths in their age groups as these migrants' life years in the decade bear to total life years of all persons in the area within the relevant ages for the same decade. That is, we applied the following equation:

$$x = d \frac{C(m-x)}{10(i+x)} + C(m-x)$$

Where

  x is migrants' deaths
  d is total deaths in relevant age groups
  c is life-year coefficient for migrants
  m is migratory flow before adjusting for migrant deaths
  i is our estimate of survivors from the previous census population at the subsequent census date (i.e. natural increase component of population) before adjusting for migrant deaths (the life year coefficient for i is, of course, 10).

The figure for x thus obtained was deducted from m and added to i, producing final estimates of migration and natural increase which take account of migrant deaths.

Our 'natural increase' in population aged 20–44 is the change in the number of persons within these age groups shown by the survivor estimates five and ten years later. It should be noted that the increase is based in *both* quinquennia on the population of the preceding census. For the second quinquennium it would have been preferable to calculate from a mid-census population. In order to obtain a mid-census population in quinary age groups, however, we must be able to allocate migration quinquennially for each group of persons as they move up through two succeeding age groups. As we cannot do this with the information available, the base for the second quinquennium has been left as the population of the census taken five years earlier. The definition of natural increase in this context must therefore be carefully noted. The natural increase figures are estimates of the population changes which would have occurred in the two quinquennia following each census if there had been no migration in either of these periods. At each census date the population base is changed, but between census reports it remains the same.

Although it was not possible to split the migration figures quinquennially within each age group, we have used the domestic profit income series as the criterion for allocating the total migration. We have already noted that there is a close correspondence between assessments and trade, and it seems reasonable to assume that migration into an area is likely to occur mainly during times of rising local business activity and that this local activity will also influence the amount of any outflow, with perhaps, in each case, a short lag before the effects are transmitted.

We have taken the years of rising profit income assessed as the probable years of migratory inflow, and the Inland Revenue's use of a

preceding year basis of assessment has the effect of introducing a short
lag. The next step was to compare the number of probable years of
inflow in each interdecadal quinquennium, and split the decade's
migration in the proportions indicated by this comparison. For
example, if migration probably occurred in five years of the first
quinquennium of a decade and in one year of the second, the decade's
migration would be split between the quinquennia in the proportions of
5:1.

Since we wish to compare the demographic features with the other
long swing series, it would have been more satisfactory to use some
independent indication of migration. Where population is flowing out
of an area we have brought in external factors by looking at the Board
of Trade figures for external migration, taking an average of the
proportions indicated by internal and overseas criteria. Where net
decennial flows were very small, we have not attempted any division of
numbers, but merely divided the migrants equally between the two
periods. A low decennial total could be misleading where a flow in one
direction during one quinquennium is offset by a flow in the opposite
direction during the next.

We compare our decadal migration figures with those obtained from
the census reports, having first adjusted our totals to take account of
any boundary changes which occurred. The best way of doing this was
to compare, say, the total population in 1901, of a region, with area of
1891, with population in 1901, with area of 1901 — the difference
being actually due to a change in boundary. Assuming that 35 per cent
of the total population is contained in the age groups 20–44, we reduce
or increase migration figures by an amount corresponding to 35 per
cent of the numbers spuriously gained or lost by a change in boundary.
In some areas it was found that migration in our age group was of
opposite sign to total migration, implying that the flow of migrants
under 20 and over 44 was greater and in the opposite direction.

A special note needs to be added about London. As already
mentioned, our method produced estimates of natural increase based,
in each interdecadal quinquennium, on the population at the preceding
census date. This did not allow for the effects of migration during the
first quinquennium on the natural increase in the second quinquennium. In certain circumstances, this could give misleading results,
as in London where the heavy inward movement of young women
(under 20) made the method inappropriate. Since we could find no way
of arriving at a reasonably accurate mid-census population, we took the

age group 15–44 for the analysis of London. This avoids the distorting effect which a swollen age group can have on the results shown by our usual method.

STATISTICAL DATA
Inhabited House Duty statistics
Total number of houses assessed and not assessed to duty (thousands)

Year ended 5 April	North-Western counties	Northern England	Midlands	London	Counties surrounding London	South Wales & Mon.	Yorkshire
1875	766.4	266.3	677.9	479.1	370.4	113.1	567.4
1876	788.5	276.3	690.9	485.4	375.5	117.9	584.0
1877	798.9	282.8	¡699.7	490.9	412.5	121.0	607.8
1878	824.7	289.4	720.6	501.1	385.1	125.9	616.0
1879	849.5	293.5	734.8	513.6	394.2	128.1	630.7
1880	868.1	322.6	740.4	520.7	410.8	132.3	639.2
1881	888.5	315.2	753.1	535.9	424.2	134.3	652.3
1882	905.1	316.8	762.1	543.4	438.2	137.4	660.8
1883	915.1	322.1	778.7	556.6	459.9	139.0	664.2
1884	931.8	326.7	790.6	569.2	475.8	141.8	674.6
1885	945.8	330.9	800.1	572.8	489.5	145.1	681.8
1886	950.1	334.5	811.1	579.9	504.0	150.1	688.1
1887	966.4	339.4	821.7	581.5	515.7	154.5	696.4
1888	979.1	343.3	834.8	591.3	526.4	158.2	706.3
1889	992.2	347.3	844.9	600.8	540.4	162.1	713.7
1890	1010.5	351.9	855.5	613.3	550.2	165.8	725.5
1891	1025.2	356.6	866.6	612.7	559.8	170.0	736.8
1892	1038.8	363.1	878.6	625.0	569.9	175.0	748.8
1893	1053.1			630.4			
1894				636.7			760.5
1895	1066.0	380.4	912.0	635.8	600.8	192.4	771.5
1896	1083.5	388.2	927.7	641.7	616.7	199.5	783.6
1897	1104.9	396.8	946.9	643.4	635.4	206.0	798.5
1898	1124.1	403.9	962.5	652.1	650.7	210.7	809.6
1899	1137.8	417.7	977.9	669.0	682.6	217.4	828.1
1900	1170.5	428.5	1004.2	673.0	713.9	221.9	845.6
1901	1193.3	438.5	1024.2	681.9	745.0	225.4	865.0
1902	1211.3	450.2	1044.1	689.4	776.0	229.0	881.2
1903	1224.4	459.7	1060.4	700.3	803.5	234.5	892.4
1904	1232.3	461.5	1074.8	711.3	840.5	239.2	910.4
1905	1251.5	471.2	1093.4	725.9	868.4	245.0	925.9
1906	1271.2	480.0	1119.0	738.4	900.7	254.9	941.8
1907	1289.0	489.3	1134.7	742.8	923.0	259.9	955.6
1908	1291.4	495.8	1143.2	744.4	935.9	265.9	957.9
1909	1322.0	505.2	1164.2	751.4	964.4	275.3	974.3
1910	1338.8	516.1	1179.8	755.9	984.2	283.9	992.1
1911	1343.6	513.5	1180.1	759.0	1003.8	289.8	996.4
1912	1359.2	524.2	1194.9	766.8	1022.5	299.4	1009.2

Source: Inland Revenue Ledgers.

Natural increase and migration, population aged 20–44
Seven urban areas of England and Wales 1870-1910 (thousands)

	1871-5	1876-80	1881-5	1886-90	1891-5	1896-1900	1901-5	1906-10
Natural increase								
North-western England	70.3	88.7	96.1	113.2	150.5	156.6	152.4	123.0
Northern England	35.1	48.1	50.5	59.9	74.6	77.1	79.7	76.4
Midlands	78.1	117.5	117.0	147.2	158.8	179.2	166.6	151.0
London (ages 15—44)	46.4	75.3	73.7	109.7	106.3	115.0	86.5	77.1
Counties surrounding London	46.1	69.4	66.5	98.0	97.2	128.2	119.9	116.6
South Wales and Mon.	26.4	35.2	37.5	44.5	53.1	49.2	50.8	45.0
Yorkshire	60.3	71.1	82.0	94.6	115.9	118.8	111.2	86.3
	362.7	505.3	523.7	667.1	756.4	824.1	767.1	675.4
Migration								
North-western England	+96.6	+14.5	+ 9.5	+ 2.1	+ 8.0	+20.0	-18.9	− 20.8
Northern England	− 0.3	− 0.9	-10.0	-11.2	-11.8	− 6.4	-16.9	− 27.6
Midlands	− 7.0	-20.5	-51.4	-47.5	-16.9	− 1.9	-27.0	− 51.9
London (ages 15—44)	+80.7	+78.3	+15.0	+17.7	− 2.9	+10.8	-96.0	-130.1
Counties surrounding London	+ 9.7	+ 9.2	+50.5	+28.8	+88.7	+86.6	+92.4	+ 71.6
South Wales and Mon.	− 5.0	-14.6	+13.1	+ 4.8	+ 1.4	+ 1.4	+36.6	+ 35.7
Yorkshire	+20.9	+ 8.5	-14.2	-18.2	− 6.3	− 1.6	-13.1	− 17.8
	195.6	74.5	12.9	-23.5	60.2	108.9	-42.9	-140.9
Natural increase and migration								
North-western England	+166.9	+103.2	+105.6	+115.3	+158.5	+176.6	+133.5	+102.2
Northern England	+ 34.8	+ 47.2	+ 40.5	+ 48.7	+ 62.8	+ 70.7	+ 62.8	+ 48.8
Midlands	+ 71.1	+ 97.0	+ 65.6	+ 99.7	+141.9	+177.3	+139.6	+ 99.1
London (ages 15—44)	+127.1	+153.6	+ 88.7	+127.4	+103.4	+125.8	− 9.5	− 53.0
Counties surrounding London	+ 55.8	+ 78.6	+117.8	+126.8	+185.9	+214.8	+212.3	+188.2
South Wales and Mon.	+ 21.4	+ 20.6	+ 50.5	+ 49.3	+ 54.5	+ 50.6	+ 87.4	+ 80.7
Yorkshire	+ 81.2	+ 79.6	+ 67.8	+ 76.4	+109.6	+117.2	+ 98.1	+ 68.5
	558.3	579.8	536.6	643.6	816.6	933.0	724.2	534.5

NOTES

[1] Thanks are due to the authorities at the Public Record Office at Ashbridge for their courtesy and cooperation in granting facilities for this research. The work was carried out by Mrs Margaret Evans and Mr Kenneth Richards when they were Research Assistants in the Department of Economics at University College, Cardiff. I wish to pay tribute to the substantial contribution which they made in collecting and analysing these data. I am particularly indebted to Mrs Evans for preparing the material for this Appendix and for drawing the charts.

[2] Josiah Stamp, *British Incomes and Property* (London, King, 1916), p. 31.

[3] Ibid. Italics in the original.

[4] B. R. Mitchell and Phyllis Deane, *Abstract of British Historical Statistics* (Cambridge University Press, 1962), p. 233.

[5] This series is given in Mitchell and Deane, op. cit., pp. 236–7.

[6] Josiah Stamp, op. cit., p. 257.

[7] Ibid., pp. 473–90.

[8] Ibid., p. 207.

Chairman: S. Pollard

Prepared Comments: A. Imlah, J. Williamson

Imlah: No critical comment was offered on that part of Thomas's story he knew best – namely, the English. Doubts, however, were expressed about the demographic argument for America. Surely *internal* migration in America was significant, perhaps more significant than migration from abroad, in influencing the housing cycle there, as in England and Wales. The very high percentage of the American population residing outside their state of birth during 1890-1910, for example, suggests that internal migration was a potent force in the housing market. In other words, a regional breakdown such as the one Thomas provides for England and Wales is needed for America as well, to find out how important internal migration was and to make sure that the cycles of immigration and building do in fact coincide within each region. Until this is done the American half of the argument must be considered unproven. The English half, though, is quite convincing.

Thomas:* He noted that Imlah has doubts about the demographic argument for America, and his reason seems to be that internal migration was very important. The role of internal migration is dealt with in the paper, where it is pointed out, on the basis of Kuznets's work, that changes in internal migration of native born in the United States were synchronous with changes in additions to total population and that the volume of internal migration was at least equal to the total additions to population. An immense amount of research has been done on this subject, e.g. the monumental study, *Population Redistribution and Economic Growth, United States, 1870-1950*, vols. I and II (American Philosophical Society, Philadelphia, 1957 and 1960), prepared under the direction of Simon Kuznets and Dorothy S. Thomas. Imlah is ignoring this work when he says that a regional breakdown is required for America to find out how important regional migration was. This job has been done in the most thorough manner.

Imlah is not justified in saying that the American half of the argument is unproven. On the contrary, the voluminous evidence summarized in Kuznets's *Capital in the American Economy* (National Bureau of Economic Research, 1961, pp. 324–7) and the work of Campbell used in the paper demonstrate conclusively that the building cycle in the United States was propelled by demographic determinants,

* These remarks were contributed by Professor Thomas after the conference.

i.e. the simultaneous long swings in immigration and internal migration. It was precisely because so much more is known about this for the United States that it was desirable to do a regional breakdown for Britain.

Williamson: Thomas's work has been an important part of the impressive concentration of professional resources in the last two decades documenting the interaction between population changes and residential construction. However, if Thomas and the others were to counter the sceptical resistance that the notion of a population-related long swing has generated, they would have to move towards formal model-building and simulation. This road would be difficult, but the turns are well marked. First, one must establish econometrically the proper theory of investment demand in the housing sector. Second, the theory must be embedded in a complete, even if simple, model of the economy. Third, the model must be tested to see how well it predicts the economic history of the period. Fourth, the significance of the population variable alone for generating long swings should be examined. Fifth and finally, if population is found to have a significant independent influence, the population variable should itself be brought into the system as an internally determined variable. The data for such a product on Britain before 1913 are not good. For the United States between the wars, however, four of the five steps have been completed recently in studies by Bolch, Pilgrim, Fels and McMahon, and a similar approach might prove fruitful for British studies of the long swing. Bolch and Pilgrim fitted the following equation, embedded in a system of equations, to explain the key variable, residential construction:

$$I_t^R = a + b\,[CC/R]_{t-1} + c[y^P]_{t-1} + d[F/H]_{t-10} + e[i^L]_{t-1}$$

where I_t^R is residential construction in some year t, $[CC/R]_{t-1}$ is the ratio in the previous year of construction costs to rents, $[Y^P]_{t-1}$ is a measure of the previous year's permanent income, $[F/H]_{t-10}$ is the ratio of non-farm families to the existing stock of non-farm housing ten years previously, and $[i^L]_{t-1}$ is the yield in the previous year on high-grade corporate bonds. In the context of the debate over the explanation of the long cycle in Britain from 1870 to 1913, Thomas would emphasize the $[F/H]_{t-10}$ variable in this equation, whereas Saul and Habakkuk would emphasize $[Y^P]$ and $[i^L]$ and point also to components of investment other than housing. In the American case the fit of this equation was good. If it was good in the British case as well, the opposing conjectures of Thomas on the one hand and Habakkuk and Saul on the other could be tested.

McCloskey: Serious redundancies existed in the Bolch-Pilgrim equation presented by Williamson. For one thing, in equilibrium the interest rate $[i^L]$ and the ratio of rents to construction costs $[R/CC]$ would be the same: landlords would earn the rate of interest on their investment in housing. For another, population enters twice, in both the aggregate income variable and in the non-farm families variable.

Williamson: One could argue over what precise form was appropriate, but the main point would remain: the issue of long swings can only be resolved by formal model building. In any case, the model worked fairly well in the period 1919-38 in the United States and gave a most interesting result. When the demographic influence $[F/H]_{t-10}$ was allowed to assume its actual historical values, varying from year to year, while all the other exogenous variables in the entire ten-equation model were set constant at their *mean* values over the period, the model as a whole traces out the variations in national income quite accurately. In other words, migration behaviour and the 'echo effects' of internal demographic cycles are sufficient *by themselves* to reproduce the outlines of long cycle movements during the 1920s and 1930s.

David: The simulation described by Williamson held all exogenous variables except $[F/H]_{t-10}$ constant. Williamson regards the finding that the variable found to have the greatest explanatory power in rationalizing the wave of investment in residential building during the 1920s was the ratio of non-farm families to the stock of housing at time y-10 as providing support for the hypothesis that demographic influences, operating upon the demand for housing, were generating building cycles. There is a different interpretation of the findings, one in which waves in demographic variables play no casual role. Because it made current values of net investment dependent upon some past value of H, the housing capital stock, the model described by Williamson could be regarded as a recursive equation in which current investment was a function of past investment. Then if one posited the existence of a previous cycle of (I), investment in housing, for reasons yet to be explained, it would be found that despite the absence of any cyclical behaviour in the number of non-farm families (F), the ratio (F/H) would fluctuate. Moreover, the fluctuation of (F/H) would tend to lag behind the initial wave in (I), and thus would appear as anticipating the next residential investment cycle. In any case, the relevance of these results on the United States for the Thomas problem was questionable. The period 1919-38 in the United States, with all the innovations in monetary policy and other shifts in the structure within which the economy operated, does not appear relevant to the British case before 1913.

Williamson: His object in mentioning the American work was not direct generalization from the American to the British experience. The structure of the two economies, to be sure, was very different. But the American work was still a promising approach to the problem in general.

Thomas: He agreed with Williamson that while the American results were not directly applicable to Britain, the approach leading to them may be applicable, perhaps in limited form, to Britain and the periphery of new nations. In other words, the results that Williamson reports are technically important. Unfortunately, the approach requires quarterly data, which is available for Britain only in scattered cases from the 1890s on. The emphasis on the population variables – the headship rate, for example – can be overdone. It is important only when it shifts drastically, as was shown by Easterlin.

Mathias: Thomas's analysis did not mention income conditions, which would mediate between demographic variables and housing demand. For example, the relative prosperity of the population over the business cycle affects the intensity of use of the existing housing stock, independent of demographic factors.

McCloskey: He agreed with Mathias. The point involved was similar to the one concerning the equation presented by Williamson, in which population enters both by itself and through the income variable. It is income, not population by itself, that is the operative factor. More people have more income and demand more housing, whether the income change is regional or national.

Thomas: The intensity of use of housing was not left out of his analysis, as Mathias suggested, but he agreed that there may have been some effect of income irrespective of demography. In particular, the monetary factor is important. Most American researchers into the long swing deal exclusively with the American experience, overlooking the fact that the *entire* 'periphery' (that is, the new countries: America, Australia, Canada, Argentina, and so on) swung inversely with Britain. Migration plays a large part in this inverse relation, but the monetary factor is important, too. In the gold standard framework the key variable was the extent of under-effected transfer, that is, the difference between *ex ante* loans abroad (measured by issues of securities) and *ex post* capital exports (measured from Imlah's balance of payments figures). At the end of each upswing, more *ex ante* lending occurs than is effected as capital exports. Bank rates go up as this gap widens, affecting the supply of money in the periphery. He confessed that he was a Milton Friedmanite at this point of the story. But we still do not have an adequate theory of the monetary aspects of the long swing.

II The Functioning of the Capital Market

3

Rigidity and bias in the British capital market, 1870-1913

MICHAEL EDELSTEIN

Like similar structures in other advanced economies of western Europe and North America in the late nineteenth and early twentieth centuries, the organized institutions of the British capital market conducted two types of transactions. First, claims to ownership of domestic and overseas capital goods were traded in the equity market. Second, claims to future amounts of domestic and foreign monies were traded for current liquid assets in the debenture and preference securities market. In so far as its operation facilitated the accumulation of capital goods by, on the one hand, making the traded assets more attractive than alternative forms of wealth through easier revision by exchange, and, on the other hand, providing a cheaper long term financing service than available elsewhere, the capital market may be said to have aided in the efficient allocation of resources in the British economy. Through more precise knowledge of alternative allocations of financial resources, a relatively centralized market for trading assets from many sectors of the economy increases the opportunity for more efficient decisions by all borrowers and lenders, whether participants in the organized capital market or not.

Considerable controversy surrounds the role of the British capital market in the years between 1870 and 1913, and, while often not identified as such, in essence the central issue is the efficiency with which the market delivered its financial services. In large part, the heat of the debate derives from another, broader issue – the question of Britain's economic growth during this period. Britain is said to have faltered because, among other reasons, her capital market failed to effect a proper distribution of financial resources among the competing needs of her multiple activities at home and abroad.

Between 1870 and 1913, the nominal value of the stock of outstanding home and foreign long term securities held in the United Kingdom increased by almost 350 per cent [1]. In the same period, the proportion of non-domestic securities increased from 37 per cent to 48 per cent. At the mid-point of the nineteenth century, the same statistic had stood at 25 per cent [2] . Having never before nor since seen such a large proportion of a nation's long term assets committed abroad, it is not surprising that contemporaries and historians have speculated on the possibility of bias in the workings of the British capital market. The same sources, however, also reveal that long term securities of domestic, non-railway enterprises rose from around 4 per cent of the total in 1870, to 19 per cent in 1913. These, then, are the pivotal magnitudes. Did there exist a set of biases that restricted the flow of funds to domestic securities to a fivefold increase in their share of domestically held, long term negotiable securities?

Two factors are given serious consideration as impediments to a more efficient allocation of the nation's financial resources. First, it is suggested that the facilities available to satisfy the expanding needs of domestic industry in Britain's largest centre of financial activity, London, were quite slow in developing and grossly inadequate relative to the facilities available to governments and public utilities, home and foreign. Thus, Saville writes,

> The increase in the size of the industrial unit, with its corresponding increased demand for capital, was met in part by the introduction of limited liability in the 1850s; but the development of a new institutional framework for long term investment was markedly slow. This tardiness in the emergence of new types of institutions in the English capital market was the product of many factors. . . . The first is the long establishment of the London capital market as the source of capital for overseas investors, and by the second half of the 19th century investment institutions of first class repute were concerned almost exclusively with the world demand for capital outside of the United Kingdom. . . . As the scale of capital requirements increased the individualistic traditions of self-financing no longer sufficed, but the absence of powerful . . . (domestic) . . . finance houses as well as what has been called the 'entrepreneur' spirit in banking meant that the gap between individual resources, admittedly considerable, and the capital requirements of industry must have been growing before 1914. [3]

The fact that the costs of company promotion and expansion through public issue of securities were relatively high — particularly for small firms — is taken as a sign of this tardy and inadequate institutional development [4]. International comparisons of facilities available in other advanced economies also raise a number of doubts about British methods [5].

Second, investors are suspected of bias towards certain types of assets, notably the large issues of governments and public utilities, home and overseas [6]. The purpose of this paper is to examine and test these hypotheses as closely as possible.

I

Turning to the first hypothesis, it is well to begin with the often cited remarks of Henry Lowenfeld on the issuing services of London in the first decade of the twentieth century. Lowenfeld was a financial journalist who wrote several introductory volumes on financial and stock exchange affairs.

The cost of issue depends entirely upon the number of prospectuses sent out, the amount spent on advertising, the fees paid to the bank which receives the applications, to the brokers, solicitors and accountants whose names appear on the prospectus, and the cost of the underwriting fee. These expenses are very heavy in any case, and hardly ever amount to less than 2000 pounds, even on a modest issue. But as there are some firms of brokers and solicitors who consider themselves but poorly remunerated by a fee of 1000 guineas for merely giving the promoters the right to print their name on a prospectus, their work and out-of-pocket expenses being paid extra, and as it is quite easy to spend 5000 pounds on advertising a prospectus, the cost of launching some issues very considerably exceeds the smallest sum which can be expressed in five figures. Whenever the issue is large this does matter, as even 25,000 pounds is only 2½% of 1,000,000 pounds; but on small issues 50,000 pounds or 100,000 pounds the expense is proportionately burdensome. [7]

In sum, the charges for public floatation fall into four categories: fees for registration and other legal matters; fees for the various professionals and public figures required by law, custom or necessity to attest to the issue's respectability; fees for increasing the public's awareness of the firm and its new issue; and lastly, fees to insure against failure, i.e. underwriting fees. The last three types of charges were directly related to the degree of risk and, more importantly, the degree to which the amount of risk was uncertain. The higher the uncertainty, the more which had to be spent to overcome the public's ignorance or suspicion, to purchase reputable names, and to pay the underwriters.

> The underwriter is paid a percentage which varies from 1% on the amount underwritten, up to 6% or even more in the case of issues of new companies which are speculative. [8]

Lowenfeld makes it quite clear that the unit costs of a large issue were lower than for a small one, but the reasons for this phenomenon are not immediately obvious. It may have been that issuing houses tended to more quickly reject risky large issues that they would not have rejected if the issue in question was somewhat smaller. In this case, the resulting price schedule for issuing service might still show falling unit costs as issue size rose but the schedule would be misleading in so far as it was not pricing a homogeneous good. On the other hand, over the size range cited by Lowenfeld there was probably a vaguely defined level of advertising expenditure beyond which word-of-mouth and newspaper stories began to do an increasing part of the advertising job, thereby reducing the incremental advertising cost of attracting more buyers. Such external economies would be directly related to the breadth and depth of the demand for negotiable securities in London and the surrounding counties, as well as the size and vigour of London's financial press. Furthermore, the incremental research fee for a larger issue probably declined over the range of issue sizes mentioned by Lowenfeld. This, in turn, would cause the schedule of unit charges for underwriters and some of the other professional services to fall across issue size, again, given the size of demand. The view that Lowenfeld's data support the presence of economies for larger issues, holding risk and uncertainty constant, seems to be confirmed on closer inspection of Lowenfeld's cost schedules. Importantly, the lowest unit costs for small and large issues are lower for large issues by 50 per cent, if not more.

It follows from this analysis that there were probably sound technological reasons for specialization within the security issuing industry. Rather than being the result of illogical habit or some ill-defined distaste for domestic industrial affairs, the technology of issuing securities seems to explain the specialization of the City's first class merchant banking houses in the business of floating the large issues of governments and railways, home and foreign. Why should a business, based on producing long runs of an item with the afore-mentioned economies, be particularly efficient at producing small batches of specialized items? Since a high proportion of the limited companies in need of the services of professional issuing houses were relatively untried enterprises, it is probable that there were even diseconomies in the joint production of small and large size security issues. House stability was absolutely essential for effective public marketing of large issues. In this connection, it is important to note that the first class merchant bankers ignored small and medium sized issues from overseas no less than they did domestic issues of the same size.

Very little is known about those who specialized in floating modest sized issues. It is fairly certain that there were always individuals and firms engaged in arranging long term financing for the relatively moderate needs of domestic firms, but their average business life was quite short. Between 1866 and 1883, 243 of the newly registered limited companies were interested in promoting domestic industrial and commercial enterprise; 45 per cent were immediately abortive and 84 per cent of the remaining public limiteds were dead within ten years [9]. The involvement of investment trusts in underwriting domestic industrial and commercial issues from the 1880s onward is well known but it is likely that somewhat more informal and ephemeral under-writing facilities were usually the case for small scale borrowers in London and elsewhere [10].

If little is directly known about the behaviour of those engaged in domestic issuing activities, perhaps something can be inferred from other data. Concentrating on the facilities available in London, for the moment, it seems plausible to assume that for firms of similar size, expected return, risk and uncertainty, the costs of London issue were higher for provincial firms than they were for firms from the London region. Familiar with local business through the newspapers, consumption and work activities, the London investor was probably more easily, and therefore more cheaply, convinced of the worthiness of an investment in a local enterprise. This hypothesis helps to explain the fact that securities of London limiteds appear on the official list of the London Stock Exchange with a frequency that is well out of proportion to the region's share in the nation's industrial and commercial output or capital stock. A second aspect of the funding of small and medium sized issues in London is also explained by the hypothesized differential cost of issue for London and provincial firms. The first security issues of many provincial firms listed on the London exchange were not floated (publicly or privately) in London [11]. Having raised their initial capital elsewhere, these companies acquired an official listing on the London exchange after doing business for a number of years. Subsequently, London issuing facilities were used to float supplemental amounts of equity and fixed-interest securities. If funding was unavailable elsewhere, London costs of floatation for a relatively moderate sized issue of a *new* provincial venture could easily have been so high as to either constrain the firm's initial scale of operations or to abort the venture completely.

Most of the nation's industrial and commercial capital stock was located in the provinces, and for most of the period between 1870 and 1913 the vast majority of Britain's enterprises in these sectors had capital requirements below the level that Lowenfeld terms 'moderate'. It has been argued so far that location and moderate size of issue would lead to plausible differentials in the costs of issue through their effects on the costs of information. Thus, the question of rigidity or bias in the institutional arrangements of the British capital market becomes a matter of finding out (*a*) whether institutional developments to minimize costs attributable to these and other 'technical' factors were slow or inadequate, and (*b*) whether some form of imperfect competition was operating to significantly misdirect capital market behaviour. It was just noted that London issue costs might have been sufficiently high to reduce initial scale or abort new provincial ventures. In fact, to view the costs of London issue as a matter of major importance for most provincial industrial and commercial firms is to misconstrue the locus of most of the nation's long term external financing decisions in these sectors.

The vast majority of provincial public limiteds were floated locally, without use of the full complement of professional issuing services available in London. A frequent procedure was to place securities privately among the former partners, the directors (if the firm was already a limited) and wealthy friends and contacts. At a minimum the services of a local solicitor, banker, professional stock broker or London company promoter would be purchased to handle the legal formalities and the cash transactions. If the new issue was either large, or offered at a time when the local capital market was highly active, or floated for a new, relatively untried, type of venture, their services would be further utilized to reach a wider group of local investors.

Importantly, competition was quite high among those performing these functions. One must not be misled by the frequently mentioned career of the London-based company promoter, H. Osbourne O'Hagan

[12]. As with any new industry, in this case the promotion of domestic limited liability companies, the returns to the highly responsive and innovative entrepreneur are quite high. O'Hagan was often among the first to begin the conversion of an old industry to limited liability or to promote a new industry, but throughout his career from the 1870s to the 1920s he was invariably and quickly followed by a host of local solicitors, bankers and professional stock brokers, as well as other London-based company promoters, all eager to reap the rumoured high profits [13]. And, as might be expected, the competition and publicity rapidly lowered the cost of issuing services and raised the offer price of the new securities [14]. Nor should one place undue emphasis on the initiating role of London-based promoters. The Oldham cotton spinning limiteds were easily floated in the 1860s and 1870s by the local professions mentioned above [15].

Integral to long term external finance in the provinces was the availability and adaptability of the provincial stock exchanges and professional stock brokers. In 1873 eleven provincial towns, all major centres of the nation's industrial and commercial activity, had active stock exchanges, meeting several times weekly, if not daily [16]. By 1912 the number of towns with stock exchanges had nearly doubled and it seems a fair guess that over the same period the growth in the number of formally associated brokers was almost as rapid as the growth in the London Stock Exchange membership (see Table 1).

Up to the 1870s provincial stock exchanges were primarily concerned with a trade in the securities of local railway and other social overhead enterprise [17]. From the peaks of turnover in the late 1840s, provincial trading slackened fairly strongly in the late 1850s and 1860s. The depth of the London market and the relative advantage of the City's specialized services for large issues shifted the locus of ownership and trading to the metropolis and attracted the vendors of new public issues. As the conversion of British enterprise to limited liability accelerated in the late 1860s and 1870s, and more and more firms made immediate use of the new form of business organization, the character of the securities traded on the provincial stock exchanges changed accordingly. Killick and Thomas have recently argued that up to the home company boom of the 1890s the activity on the provincial stock exchanges remained fairly low and, second, brokers acted mainly as shunters of provincial securities to London [18]. This latter point is quite important, for, combined with the fact that the nation's stock exchanges were in constant telegraphic contact by the late 1870s [19], it suggests the existence of a competitive national market in a large number of outstanding securities, as well as a fairly low transactions cost to surmount before inter-regional trade took place.

With regard to the first point of Killick and Thomas, the fact that the total volume of business slackened in the late 1850s and 1860s is not necessarily a sign that local trading in non-social overhead investments was also slack. First of all, it would be quite surprising if the new opportunities for non-social overhead investment, made possible by the general limited liability legislation of the late 1850s and early 1860s, were able to fill the place left by the very large trading volumes in railway securities. Second, it is highly probable that the bulk of the securities listed on the provincial stock exchanges from the

TABLE 1
Great Britain's stock exchanges, 1873-1912

		1873-4	1881-2	1892-3	1902-3	1912-3
Provincial stock exchanges						
Aberdeen	F[a]	8	10	14	11	11
	M	–	–	(15)	(13)	(14)
Birmingham	F	14	12	15	27	36
	M	–	–	(22)	(46)	(61)
Bradford	F	–	–	–	12	8
	M	–	–	–	(17)	(12)
Bristol	F	20	12	18	20	20
	M	–	–	(26)	(29)	(30)
Cardiff	F	–	–	–	19	14
	M	–	–	–	(28)	(20)
Dundee	F	–	8	10	14	16
	M	–	–	(12)	(15)	(17)
Edinburgh	F	16	30	36	39	38
	M	–	–	(52)	(67)	(69)
Glasgow	F	30	81	92	123	147
	M	–	–	(142)	(207)	(260)
Greenock	F	–	–	6	6	6
	M	–	–	(10)	(13)	(11)
Halifax	F	–	–	–	10	5
	M	–	–	–	(12)	(8)
Huddersfield	F	–	–	–	6	9
	M	–	–	–	(9)	(15)
Hull	F	7	–	–	–	–
	M	–	–	–	–	–
Lancashire (Oldham)	F	–	–	–	–	–
	M	–	–	(35)	(26)	(27)
Leeds	F	12	8	8	8	15
	M	–	–	(13)	(17)	(31)

TABLE 1 (continued)
Great Britain's stock exchanges, 1873-1912

		1873-4	1881-2	1892-3	1902-3	1912-3
Provincial stock exchanges						
Liverpool	F	87	127	119	–	–
	M	–	–	(158)	(142)	(176)
Manchester	F	55	50	52	66	63
	M	–	–	(82)	(115)	(103)
Newcastle upon Tyne	F	4	7	8	11	15
	M	–	–	(10)	(14)	(22)
Nottingham	F	–	–	–	–	14
	M	–	–	–	–	(16)
Sheffield	F	18	18	15	16	16
	M	–	–	(26)	(40)	(40)
Southport	F	–	–	–	8	6
	M	–	–	–	(8)	(6)
Swansea	F	–	–	–	–	6
	M	–	–	–	–	(7)
Total Provincial	F	271	363	393[b]	396[c]	445[c]
	M	–	–	(603)	(818)	(945)
London Stock Exchange	F	–	–	–	–	–
	M	(1500)	(2200)	(3377)	(4776)	(5010)

Notes:
[a]F = Firms, M = Members.
[b]The number of Oldham firms is unavailable and not included.
[c]The number of Oldham and Liverpool firms is unavailable and not included.
Source: Trade directories.

1870s to World War I were never traded in London. For each Oldham limited listed on both the Oldham and London exchanges in the late 1870s, there was another firm quoted in the Oldham lists that had yet to be quoted in London by 1913 [20]. Similarly, most of the issues on the Birmingham exchange were never listed in London [21]. Finally, O'Hagan leaves little doubt that private and public placement of new issues from local enterprises was a substantial part of the activity of all provincial brokers, including those who were members of the local stock exchanges [22].

In any case, for most of the period, the majority of new and old provincial limiteds would never have thought of offering securities to investors in distant regions of the country. Local investors were automatically involved in any thoughts on the subject, their superior knowledge, interest and loyalty simply assumed. For a new venture, short term financing from local banks and merchants was probably far easier and cheaper if local men were known to be intimately involved in the affair. If one's credit was good enough, bank overdrafts and commercial credit notes were automatically renewed. Throughout the nineteenth century this was one of the most important methods of long term external finance, though its importance for the larger industrial and commercial firms diminished with the development of local debenture markets in the 1880s [23]. As evidenced by the large numbers of provincial businesses listed in *Burdett's* but not quoted in London, the expense of local provincial issue must have been fairly cheap. In any event, the cost of increasing investor awareness sufficiently to achieve a successful floatation was much less for most businesses than what London enterprises probably paid in London, and usually less than what was necessary to convince more distant investors [24]. In effect, the local brokers, solicitors and bankers and the visiting London promoters were the professional issuing houses of the provinces. The fact that the lawyers and bankers did not change their occupational designations while practising a broker's or a promoter's business, or that the average cost of the less extensive issuing services in the provinces was lower than average London charges for similar firms, should not have led Lavington, an early and careful researcher in this area, to ignore their essential, highly organized role in provincial financial affairs [25].

On the whole, it was the leading firms that went limited and whose equity and debentures were traded on the local and, perhaps, the London exchange [26]. Thus the liquidity of provincial investors was significantly enhanced; first, the volume of local assets with a regular market increased, and second, the assets were generally those of the leading, local enterprises.

All the same, a number of provincial firms still found it necessary to turn to London's facilities for public issue and her market for outstanding issues for help with their financial needs. In the 1860s, 1870s and 1880s a number of industries, including cotton spinning, iron and steel, and some sections of the engineering sector, experienced several waves of conversions to limited liability. Concentrated in relatively few locations, local capital markets must have been severly strained by the size of the total demand on local resources. If conversion had proceeded slowly, local wealth might have been able to absorb the large number of new issues. The individual size of industrial equity and fixed-interest issues, catalogued in the annual volumes of *Burdett's* in the 1870s and 1880s but not mentioned in the new issues lists of the *Investors Monthly Manual* or quoted on the official list of the London Stock Exchange, indicate the provinces could absorb what London called a modest sized issue under some circumstances. Perhaps it was here, during the conversion booms, that provincial brokers began to make their fees as shunters, unloading issues in London to help finance the next new issue in a provincial city. Some iron and steel companies used the domestic issuing houses of London (e.g. Chadwicks) to market part of their initial equity issues but this was unusual [27]. As noted earlier, in these years and afterwards, the new issue facilities of London were employed primarily for supplemental funding, usually subsequent to a period of London quotation of an outstanding issue of the given firm. With the London region somewhat more familiar with the securities of the firms, and perhaps other firms in the same industry as well, the cost of a supplemental issue in London was undoubtedly more favourable. At this point the aged provincial firm with 'modest' borrowing needs probably paid issue costs not far from those paid by slightly younger London firms and provincial firms with national reputations were probably able to place their securities privately or publicly on terms entirely comparable with London enterprise of similar size.

It was mentioned earlier, that in the 1870s and 1880s the locus of individual demands on London by industrial and commercial firms was well within the size of issue that Lowenfeld termed 'modest'. The vast majority of individual issues from industrial and commercial long term borrowers were significantly less than a million pounds per issue. In the mid-1880s, however, a new class of borrowers began to appear, floating issues of £0.5–2.0 million or larger. Firms in brewing, cotton textiles, chemicals and iron and steel were most prominent among those forming the new class.

Starting with the floatations of Guinness and Ind Coope in 1886, the size of brewing firms expanded rapidly, largely the result of newly discovered economies of scale in distribution and a very high degree of competition in the industry [28]. The movement reached a peak in the late 1890s when Watney amalgamated with Combe & Reids, floating £15 million in equity and fixed-interest securities. In chemicals and cotton textiles, firms amalgamated in the 1890s for defensive purposes. Stiff competition in the face of unstable but secularly rising demand seems to have led to excess capacity and the first task of the new, larger structures was to try to organize production and investment to eliminate this source of reduced profitability. In iron and steel, two factors were operating to encourage increases in the size of issues. Changing technology involved a fairly steady secular increase in the size of the efficient plant and, second, there seemed to have been sufficient savings in the combination of various stages of production to encourage vertical integration. From the mid-1890s to the turn of the century amalgamations to achieve the latter objective were quite widespread.

In the face of these enlarged demands, the evidence suggests that London responded fairly quickly. Investment trusts first became involved in underwriting industrial securities in the late 1880s and it is certain they were involved in a number of the amalgamation issues at the turn of the century [29]. Barings was involved in the Guinness issue of 1886 and leading joint-stock banks such as Westminster participated in other major issues of the period [30]. On the question of what these industrial and commercial giants paid for issuing services, relative to what was paid by the older large scale borrowers, there is very little direct evidence. In so far as yields on outstanding issues give some indication of the relative level of risk entering into issue costs, it seems likely that the relative costs of London's new issue facilities fell for large scale domestic industrial borrowers starting in the mid-1880s. From that point to the outbreak of World War I, the gap closed between the yields on domestic industrial debentures on the one hand, and home and overseas social overhead investments on the other [31]. Since domestic railways and other social overhead investments were probably far less risky than domestic industrial and commercial investments in this period, it is not surprising that yields on industrial issues did not fall below home social overhead yields. Importantly, however, home industrial yields fell below the yields on a large proportion of overseas railway debentures in the 1890s and 1900s.

Britain, of course, was not alone among the advanced economies of the late nineteenth century that experienced a jump in the scale of industrial and commercial firm size. But the fact that Britain's giants were relatively modest by U.S. and German standards raises the question of whether Britain's financial institutions lacked something that inhibited the growth of firm size to the fullest extent [32]. L. Davis argues that rapidly growing advanced capitalist economies of the late nineteenth century were subject to three types of shock: growth that involved a shift in the location of industry, growth that involved significant shifts of resources to new industries, and, third, technological developments that involved large economies of scale [33]. With respect to attendant financial needs, the most important aspect of these shocks was their timing in relation to the currently available set of services for external finance. Davis concluded that Great Britain was much less subject to such shocks; there were few changes in the location of production, the older industries remained profitable and dominant, and substantial economies of scale were not found in the technologies profitable with Great Britain's natural resources. Second, he found that British industry and commerce could rely on a much superior system for external financing, when and if shocks appeared. Regional banking facilities, mortgage markets and commercial credit facilities were much older and better developed in Great Britain. It is well to point out again the important role of the automatically renewed short term credit instrument among the methods available for long term external financing. Finally, as it has been argued above, not only were the metropolitan and provincial capital markets older and more highly developed initially, but they were also capable of adapting fairly rapidly to changing circumstance. The American response to inadequacies in its financial structure was enlarged firm size, making possible internal financing through expanded net income. In sum, it appears it was the very adequacy of Britain's long term external financing institutions for both modest and large scale borrowers that helped to yield the relatively smaller scale of its enterprises, not the hypothesized rigidities [34].

II

Economic theory has long postulated the existence of a relationship between asset risk and return. The risk attaching to a particular asset may be viewed as the probability distributions of possible rewards accruing to the asset's owner at future points in time. Uncertainty refers to the degree of confidence the investor places in his perception of these distributions. The usual hypothesis is that in the absence of barriers to competition in the capital market (including an unequal distribution of knowledge), differences between the returns to various assets depend on the relative degrees of risk and uncertainty associated with each asset. Recently, a fully articulated theory of the relationship between relative degree of risk and return has appeared [35], an outgrowth of the mean-standard deviation models of portfolio choice first evolved by Markowitz and Tobin [36]. Importantly, the new model of capital asset pricing makes possible a test of the propositions that certain regional and scale of issue effects biased the allocations of financial resources passing through the British capital market. There are two hypotheses concerning the bias of the British capital market: (*a*) British investors and capital market institutions, and particularly the issuing houses, were biased in favour of overseas assets; (*b*) these same individuals and institutions were biased in favour of large borrowers. In both cases, given the high degree of competition in the market for outstanding securities, the implication of these hypotheses is that some factor or factors impinged on the British capital market's perception of risk and its effect on return.

This section is devoted to a test of the existence of such factors in the market for equity shares. While the equity market does not include the substantial amounts of government debt instruments found in the debenture market, it has the advantage of a much broader coverage in manufacturing and commerce than found in the debenture market. Furthermore, most hypotheses lump the behaviour of the capital market towards government debt instruments with that of the railways, a sector well represented in the equity market. Finally, since the hypothesized investor biases and phobias are more likely to evince themselves in relation to assets with the highest levels of uncertainty, a test that concentrates on equity assets has implications about behaviour towards less uncertain and risky types of assets. A test of bias performed with debenture data could not be said to carry over to equity behaviour with as much strength.

Let us assume that (1) the British capital market consisted of risk averters who maximized their expected utility from end-of-period wealth, and (2) these investors made their optimal portfolio decisions solely on the basis of expected return and standard deviation of returns with the various available portfolios [37]. In other words, investors always chose the portfolio with a lower risk (standard deviation) for a given level of return and, given the level of risk, they always chose the portfolio with the highest return. Further, let us assume that (3) all investors had similar decision horizons, (4) all investors had similar attitudes toward expected returns and their standard deviations, (5) the capital market was perfect in the sense that there were many buyers and sellers with the best information, and (6) investors could borrow and lend at the same rate of interest, having equal access to the same portfolio opportunities.

With these assumptions it is possible to build a pricing model for

capital assets that gives the equilibrium relationship between risk and
expected return. In this relationship the expected return on an asset is a
linear function of the asset's risk *vis-à-vis* other assets and the return on
a riskless asset. Thus,

$$(1) \quad E(R_j) = R_f + \lambda Cov(R_j, R_M)$$

where $E(R_j)$ = the expected return on the *j*th equity instrument,

R_f = the return to a riskless asset,

$Cov(R_j, R_M)$ = the covariance of R_j, the return to the *j*th
equity instrument, and R_M, the rate of return
to the nation's portfolio of all assets (including,
of course, the *j*th asset).

Another way of stating (1) is

$$(2) \quad \frac{E(R_j) - R_f}{Cov(R_j, R_M)} = \lambda.$$

$E(R_j) - R_f$ is the return to the *j*th asset over and above the return to
the riskless asset, that is, what is commonly called the 'risk premium'.
$Cov(R_j, R_M)$ is the asset risk variable in the Sharpe-Lintner model. Risk
on the individual asset is thus measured by its contribution to the risk
of the national (or market) portfolio, or more simply, the asset's risk
vis-à-vis other assets.

Equation (2) states that the relationship between an asset's expected
return and its risk is proportional and the numerical value of the
proportion is constant across all assets. It is implicit in assumption (2)
that all assets were close substitutes, given expected return and risk.
With numerous investors operating in many sectors of the capital
market, differences in λ due to these two factors were probably
reduced to a minimum through arbitrage [38]. However, if, for any
reason, assets of differing region and scale of issue were construed to be
somewhat differing commodities, λ need not be constant across all
assets.

In order to test this hypothesis two further assumptions must be
made: (1) λ is not deterministic but stochastic, and (2) expectations
were realized. The latter assumption is tantamount to assuming the
default rate was roughly similar across region and scale of issue. In this
regard, it is usually alleged that overseas securities had high default
rates, with the implication that home investments were relatively free

of such behaviour. Shannon's work on the limited companies makes it quite clear that default was certainly not unknown to domestic enterprise but precisely how much, relative to overseas rates, can not be settled with available data [39].

The statistical tests were carried out by fitting a least squares regression line to

$$(3) \quad \frac{(R_j - R_c)}{Cov(R_j, r_m^i)} = a_1 + a_2 X + a_3 Sc + e$$

where
$R_j = R^{t \to T}$, the compound annual rate of growth of equity wealth in the jth industry, invested at time t and sold at time T,

R_c = the compound annual rate of growth of wealth of a fixed sum placed in Consols at time t and sold at time T,

$Cov(R_j, r_m^i)$ = the covariance over time from t to T of R_j and r_m^i, a proxy for a national or market rate of return [40],

X = (0 if the jth industry was domestic, 1 if the jth industry was non-domestic),

Sc = (0 if the firms in the jth industry generally made issues of significantly less than a million pounds, 1 if the jth industry's issues were around a million pounds or more).

With regard to the direction of bias, if the capital market was biased in favour of non-domestic assets, a_2 should be negative in sign. This would mean that in the act of bidding for non-domestic assets, the risk premium was bid down, relative to a unit of risk.

If the British capital market was biased in favour of large scale issues, a_3 should have a negative sign. It is not clear, however, that all scale effects will be registered. If investors were biased towards large scale issues because of a disproportionate belief in their marketability, the sign of a_3 could be negative for the same reasons presented above in connection with the bias for non-domestic issues — investors were willing to pay more per unit of risk, thus lowering the risk premium, $R_j - R_c$. On the other hand, if the scale effects were the result of economies of scale in the issuing procedures, the market price of the asset should not be affected. Assuming that large and small borrowers' assets have the same level of risk (inclusive of marketability) and the same expected income stream per share, the issue price of the assets of the two borrowers should be the same if the issuing house has properly forecasted the effect of risk on each asset's price. In a competitive environment the large borrower would probably derive a part of the benefits from the lower cost of issue with the issuing house, at least in the short run, making somewhat higher profits. Obviously, once put out on the market, the costs of issue are irrelevant.

Equation (3) was estimated using returns over two periods, 1870-89 and 1890-1913. Not all thirty-nine industries listed in Table 2 were included in each regression. Industries with returns that did not span most of the given period were dropped. Two proxies for a market rate of return were tested: r_m^1, an equiproportional weighting of returns to all groupings in Table 2 except 'Oldham cotton spinners' (sampled in all textiles) and the non-domestic 'Social overhead: regional groupings' (included in non-domestic 'Social overhead: industrial groupings'), and r_m^2, utilizing the same groupings as r_m^1, but weighted according to a rough estimate of the market value of each industry's equity during the first decade of the twentieth century [41].

In the light of the changes in the scale of issue for industrial and commercial companies in the London capital market beginning in the mid-1880s, a different definition of scale of issue (Sc) was adopted for each regression. For the 1870-89 test, only railway and social overhead industries were treated as large scale issuers (ScA). In the 1890-1913 regression, the textile, food, drink, chemical, and iron, coal and steel industries were added (ScB).

The results of the regression tests may be found in Table 3. On the whole, they offer little encouragement for the scale of issue or regional bias hypotheses. The R^2 values that measure the fit of the entire equation were uniformly terrible. With regard to the coefficients on individual variables, none pass t-test criteria. The usual upper bound for statistical significance is a probability level of 0.05, or, in terms of the t-test statistic given in Table 3, a t value of about 2.04 or higher [42].

Although none of the coefficients pass muster on t-test criteria, the signs on the coefficients are suggestive. The sign of the scale bias is uniformly negative, confirming the direction of bias, albeit weak, implied by the scale of issue hypothesis. Investors appear to have had a persistent but weak tendency to bid up the price of large scale issues, thereby yielding lower risk premiums per unit of risk.

Turning to the regional bias hypothesis, the sign on the regional variable's coefficient is negative in the 1870-89 regression test, but turns positive in the 1890-1913 test. British investors appear to have switched from a highly unstable and weak preference for non-domestic issues, 1870-89, to a somewhat less unstable preference for domestic issues, 1890-1913. In the earlier period, investors showed a tendency to raise (lower) the risk premium on domestic (non-domestic) assets relative to a unit of domestic (non-domestic) risk. Later the market showed a disproportionate preference for domestic issues which led to a lower (higher) price per unit of domestic (non-domestic) risk, a higher (lower) price on domestic (non-domestic) issues and a lower (higher) risk premium.

In conclusion, hypothesized scale of issue and regional biases in the British capital market do not appear to have significantly affected the

TABLE 2
The time composition of the equity data base

	1869	1879	1889	1899	1909	1913
A Domestic						
1 Railways (19)[a]	16	16	16	15	15	15
2 Finance						
a banks (19)	16	18	17	16	15	14
b insurance (14)	12	14	14	14	13	12
3 Light industry and commerce						
a all textiles (14)	3	6	6	11	13	14
b. Oldham cotton spinners (11)	–	10	8	11	11	11
c. food (9)	–	–	3	6	8	8
d drink (7)	1	1	5	7	7	7
e retail stores (5)	–	–	–	4	5	5
4 Heavy industry						
a iron, coal, steel & heavy fab. (25)	8	13	15	21	25	25
b mechanical equipment (14)	6	8	9	11	10	11
c electrical equipment (3)	1	1	1	3	3	3
d bldg. & construction materials (4)	–	2	3	2	3	3
e chemicals	2	2	5	4	6	6
5 Social overhead						
a electricity (3)	–	–	1	2	3	3
b gas (5)	3	5	5	5	5	5
c water (7)	6	7	7	7	–	–
d canals and docks (8)	5	7	7	6	4	4
e shipping	8	8	10	10	8	7
f telephone and telegraph (4)	1	2	2	3	2	1
g tramways and omnibuses (3)	1	3	3	2	2	1
Subtotal (196)	90	126	141	165	162	159

TABLE 2 (*continued*)
The time composition of the equity data base

	1869	1879	1889	1899	1909	1913
B *Non-domestic*						
1 Railways						
a India (11)	6	7	7	8	8	8
b western Europe (11)	9	11	9	6	4	2
c eastern Europe (4)	2	3	4	2	2	2
d United States (10)	3	4	6	9	9	9
e Latin America (11)	6	7	8	9	9	9
2 Banks						
a Asia and Australasia (13)	12	13	12	7	7	7
b South Africa (1)	1	1	1	1	1	1
c Canada (1)	1	1	1	1	1	1
d eastern Mediterranean (4)	4	4	4	4	4	4
e Latin America (3)	2	2	2	3	3	3
3 Social overhead: indus. groupings						
a electricity (6)	–	–	–	–	6	5
b gas (14)	6	10	10	11	11	10
c telegraph and telephone (15)	–	10	13	12	13	13
d tramways (10)	1	4	7	5	6	4
4 Social overhead: regional groupings [b]						
a India and China (8)	3	4	6	6	8	8
b western Europe (10)	2	6	8	8	8	7
c North America (5)	–	2	2	2	4	4
d Latin America (19)	3	11	12	10	13	14
5 Tea and coffee (16)2	2	5	7	15	14	14
Subtotal (130)	55	82	91	93	98	92
Grand total equity securities (326)	145	208	232	258	260	251

Notes:

[a] The figures in parentheses represent the total number of securities used.

[b] The securities in the Social overhead: regional groupings category are not included in the subtotals for non-domestic equities or the grand total for equity instruments. To include them would involve double counting the securities already enumerated in the Social overhead: industrial grouping category.

long run pricing of equity assets, 1870-1913. It would be misleading, however, to deny the presence of bias, even though the biases were not sufficiently stable to influence capital asset pricing in the long run. British investors evinced a weak and unstable preference for large and non-domestic issues in the 1870-89 period. In the following twenty-four years, a somewhat less unstable bias for domestic issues appeared with the very weak bias for large issues continuing.

TABLE 3
Capital market biases: regression tests

Estimated equation:

$$(R_j - R_c)/Cov(R_j, r_m^i) = a_1 + a_2 X + a_3 Sc + e$$

Index of market returns Utilized	X	Coefficient t-values for ScA	ScB	R^2	#obs.
1970-1889:					
r_m^1	−.74	insig.		.02	35
r_m^2	−1.22	−.61		.05	35
1890-1913:					
r_m^1	1.68		−.46	.08	37
r_m^2	1.24		−.77	.10	37

III

Between 1870 and 1913, limited liability became the major framework for private industrial and commercial enterprise in the United Kingdom [43]. In the process, something like £1400 million in domestic industrial and commercial securities were successfully issued, raising the share of such assets in the total of all long term securities held in the United Kingdom from around 4 to 19 per cent. The number of provincial brokers rose fourfold and the number in London increased by almost as much [44]. Rapid expansion of other occupations concerned with provincial and London services is also evident. Given the analysis of the technology of issuing services and the role of location, the rapid growth of specialized services in both the provinces and London does not seem to suggest institutional rigidity. Rather, it points towards an increased extent of market yielding a more complete division of function. Direct evidence on increased liquidity and diminished relative costs of borrowing is slim but the materials available are highly suggestive. Regular trading of a greatly enlarged proportion of Britain's industrial and commercial property could not help but increase liquidity [45], especially in the provinces, if not lower the cost of borrowing.

Evidence has not been offered to substantiate the possible gains to Britain's productivity from the increase in the quantity and quality of information concerning her industrial and commercial sector, let alone the multiple overseas activities that sought and received funding from British wealth in this period. Nor has the question of externalities been raised [46]. A market that brings together private investors and borrowers will offer signals for the allocation of financial resources based on private, not social rates of return. Any external economies or diseconomies from overseas railway investment, domestic urban agglomerations, or overseas investment in the presence of domestic unemployment, will not be fully registered, if at all. However, it does seem likely that two hypothesized biases that were alleged to have significantly altered the private signals of the market, regional and size of issue biases, were fairly weak in the long run.

NOTES

[1] These estimates are a reworking of A. R. Hall, *The London Capital Market and Australia, 1870-1914* (Canberra, Australian National University, 1963), pp. 4, 16, based on Hall's critique, pp. 5–19. Major changes involve an increase in the share of domestic railways and a drastic reduction in the share of foreign governments in 1870. The principal changes for the 1913 estimate were again a large decrease in foreign governments, and a similar shift in American and foreign railways. For details, see M. Edelstein, *The Rate of Return on Home and Foreign Capital, 1870-1913* (unpub. MS., 1970), available on request from the author.

[2] L. H. Jenks, *The Migration of British Capital to 1875* (London, Nelson, 1963), p. 413.

[3] J. Saville, 'Some retarding factors in the British economy before 1914', *Yorkshire Bulletin of Economic and Social Research*, 1965, p. 57.

[4] Ibid.; see also A. K. Cairncross, *Home and Foreign Investment 1870-1914* (Cambridge, Cambridge University Press, 1953), p. 101.

[5] D. Landes, *The Unbound Prometheus* (Cambridge, Cambridge University Press, 1969), pp. 349–50; Saville, op. cit., p. 57.

[6] Hall, op. cit., pp. 56–7.

[7] H. Lowenfeld, *All About Investment* (London, Financial Review of Reviews, 1909), pp. 174–5.

[8] Ibid., p. 172.

[9] 33 per cent of all companies registered were immediately abortive; 60 per cent of all remaining public limiteds dissolved within ten years. H. A. Shannon, 'The limited companies of 1866-1883', *Economic History Review*, 1933, pp. 306–9.

[10] Hall, op. cit., pp. 78–83; F. Lavington, *The English Capital Market* (London, Methuen, 1921), p. 208.

[11] Hall, op. cit., p. 28.

[12] See Henry Osbourne O'Hagan, *Leaves from my Lives*, 2 vols (London, Lane, 1929).

[13] Ibid., vol. 1, pp. 150–1, 255–6.

[14] Ibid., vol. 1, pp. 256–7.

[15] Lavington, op. cit, p. 208.

[16] See Great Britain, *Royal Commission on the London Stock Exchange*, Parl. Papers, 1878, vol. XIX.

[17] See J. R. Killick and W. A. Thomas, 'The provincial stock exchanges, 1830–1870', *Economic History Review*, 2nd series, 1970, pp. 96–111.

[18] Ibid., p. 110.
[19] Great Britain, op. cit., Q. 7894, 7907, 7952–4, 8141–61.
[20] Various Oldham newspapers and *The Investors Monthly Manual.*
[21] G. H. Phillips, *Phillip's Investors Annual* (London, Effingham Wilson, 1887), pp. 309–11.
[22] O'Hagan, op. cit., vol. 1, pp. 150–1, 255–6.
[23] On debenture markets, see J. B. Jefferys, *Trends in Business Organization in Great Britain since 1856* (unpub. Ph.D. dissertation, London School of Economics, 1938), pp. 249 ff.
[24] Lavington, op. cit., p. 208.
[25] Ibid.
[26] For the generally leading position of the public limiteds in their respective industries, see J. H. Clapham, *An Economic History of Modern Britain*, vol. 2 (Cambridge, Cambridge University Press, 1932), pp. 138–42.
[27] Jefferys, op. cit., pp. 295–8.
[28] P. Mathias, *The First Industrial Nation* (London, Methuen, 1969), pp. 393 ff.
[29] U.S. Securities and Exchange Commission, *Investment Trusts and Investment Companies: Report of the S.E.C. Pursuant to Sec. 30 of the Public Utility Holding Company Act of 1935, Supplementary Report: Investment Trusts in Great Britain* (1939).
[30] J. H. Clapham, *An Economic History of Modern Britain: Machines and National Rivalries (1887-1914), with an Epilogue (1914-1929)* (Cambridge, Cambridge University Press, 1938), p. 210.
[31] Edelstein, op. cit. The spread between home social overhead debentures narrowed by about 20 per cent into the 1890s and widened slightly after interest rates generally turned up in the decade or so before the war. With regard to the overseas railway yields, only Indian railway yields remained below the yield on industrial debentures. The yield on industrial debentures fell below western European, United States, Canadian and Latin American railway debentures. There was a reversal of this trend in the years immediately preceding World War I, but here, too, the relative positions did not fall back to those prevailing in the 1880s.
[32] For a comparison of British and U.S. firm size, see P. L. Payne, 'The emergence of the large scale company in Great Britain, 1870-1914', *Economic History Review*, 2nd series, 1967, pp. 519-42.
[33] L. E. Davis, 'The capital markets and industrial concentration: the U.S. and UK., a comparative study', *Economic History Review*, 2nd series, 1966, pp. 255–72.
[34] For discussion of this point in the framework of European economic development, see A. Gerschenkron, *Economic Backwardness in Historical Perspective* (Cambridge, Mass., Harvard University Press, 1962), pp. 11–16.
[35] John Lintner, 'Security prices, risk and maximal gains from diversification', *Journal of Finance*, 1965, pp. 587–615; and 'The valuation of risk assets and the selection of risk investments in stock portfolios and capital budgets', *Review of Economics and Statistics*, 1965, pp. 13–37. William F. Sharpe, 'Capital asset prices; a theory of market equilibrium under conditions of risk', *Journal of Finance*, 1964, pp. 425–42.
[36] Harry Markowitz, *Portfolio Selection: Efficient Diversification of Investments* (New York, John Wiley, 1959). James Tobin, 'Liquidity preference as behavior towards risk', *Review of Economic Studies*, 1958, pp. 65–86.
[37] The model of capital asset pricing used in this essay comes from an excellent article, which clarified the earlier work of Sharpe and Lintner. See

Eugene Fama, 'Risk, return and general equilibrium: some clarifying comments', *Journal of Finance*, 1968, pp. 29–40.

[38] Insurance companies and the financial trusts operated in both home and overseas markets; see Hall, op. cit., pp. 47–56. The holdings of industrial companies reveal a regional and industrial diversity; see E. M. Sigsworth, *Black Dyke Mills* (Liverpool, Liverpool University Press, 1958), p. 229; F. E. Hyde, *Blue Funnel* (Liverpool, Liverpool University Press, 1956), pp. 144–7; R. Smith, *The Lancashire Cotton Industry and the Great Depression, 1873-1896* (unpub. Ph.D. dissertation, Birmingham University, 1954), pp. 130–203.

[39] Shannon, op. cit, pp. 306–9.

[40] It is possible to show that if r_m, a common underlying market factor affecting all assets, is used instead of R_M^m, the return to all assets, equation (3) may still be used to test propositions concerning equation (2), for both sides of (3) are off by the same constant. See Fama, op. cit, pp. 39–40.

[41] Insufficient data exist to construct an index incorporating annual changes in the level of each industry's equity. Hall, op. cit., is the basis of the rough estimates for the weights, 1900-10.

[42] A dummy variable for security denomination was also tested in order to investigate the possibilities of asymmetry in 'entry' costs; the variable proved even less significant than those discussed in the text.

[43] Corporate profits from non-railway limited jumped from, at most, 8 per cent of non-agricultural profits, 1870-9, to 49 per cent, 1910-14. See C. H. Feinstein, 'Changes in the distribution of the national income in the United Kingdom since 1860', ch. 4 in J. Marchal and B. Ducros (eds.), *The Distribution of National Income* (London, Macmillan, 1968), p. 116, for estimates of domestic profits from non-agricultural enterprise, 1870-9, 1910-14, and corporate income 1910-14. Estimates of railway profits are those of A. K. Cairncross, op. cit., p. 138. The estimate of non-railway profits, 1870-9, is £30 million, an upper bound estimate that assumes a rate of return of 13 per cent (E. H. Phelps Brown, *A Century of Pay* (London, Macmillan, 1968), p. 412) on an average stock of long term securities from domestic, non-railway, limited companies, 1870-9, of £230 million.

[44] The figure for provincial brokers is a rough estimate based on trade directories for the entire United Kingdom. In addition to the approximate levels implied by the figures for provincial member brokers in Table 1, the estimate above involves the small number of Irish brokers and the much larger numbers of provincial brokers who were not members of any stock exchange.

[45] Little is known about the types of collateral acceptable by British banks in this period. The only mention of the subject in the secondary literature suggests use of industrial securities as collateral as early as the 1860s, and this in London. See R. S. Sayers, *Lloyds Bank in the History of English Banking* (Oxford, Oxford University Press, 1957), pp. 107, 184.

[46] For an excellent introduction to the role of externalities in the growth of Britain, 1870-1913, see C. P. Kindleberger, *Economic Growth in France and Britain, 1850-1950* (Cambridge, Mass., Harvard University Press, 1964), chs. 3 and 7.

Chairman: J. G. Williamson
Prepared Comments: S. Pollard, J. Tyce

S. Pollard: Edelstein's paper was quite valuable, saying something new about an issue that has inspired a long debate in the British literature by using a mathematical approach. This general feature of the paper raises a few interesting methodological questions. For example, the issue turns in part on an alleged irrationality of behaviour: were British investors irrational in preferring foreign securities? In testing for irrational behaviour, it is hazardous to use a rational model, as Edelstein does. The return on the issues that were actually made may not show any lack of enterprise on the part of investors, but it does not follow that some issues that were *not* made might not have been better. It may be, for example, that the returns to investing in British steel, railways and other well-funded sectors are found to have been about the same, as the rational model demands, but the wool industry, say, may have needed the capital, may never have obtained it, and may not have appeared in the figures of investment returns at all. This problem of a counterfactual is particularly important when the very thesis to be tested is whether people were rational.

The other point is that of dynamics. The approach in the paper does not really deal with the question of where initiative comes from. The speed of German growth in this period, for example, was due partly to the pressure exerted by the banks, or by industrialists through the banks, to organize combines and encourage industrial expansion. The argument that the British capital market was efficient because people acted in a rational way does not, then, take account of this counterfactual on the German model: if British businessmen had had the incentive to act as the Germans did, possibly *all* the returns on *all* British investments might have been lifted up.

There are two minor points as well. The discussion of the cost of issue is most valuable, suggesting that because the difference in the charges on large and small issues reflected real cost differences the Macmillan gap did not in fact exist. But the question in a small or medium issue is not so much a higher or lower cost but whether the issue is made at all. The availability of capital, in other words, is as important as its cost. The other point is that the length of the issue should affect the risk premium. A foreign investment of five years is a very different investment than one of ten or twenty years and this is not reflected in the argument of the paper.

Edelstein: Pollard's point on the availability of capital suggests the concession that rejection of borrowers did occur sometimes, but the significance of the rejections for the whole market is difficult to judge. One piece of evidence is that in the volume of studies edited by Aldcroft on *The Development of British Industry and Foreign Competition, 1875-1914* there are few references to capital as a limiting factor, but this and similar evidence is hardly conclusive. On irrationality in general, the first half of the paper attempts to paint a picture of competition and growth in the finance industry, partly to make it plausible that the industry contained vigorous and rational men who would be forced by competition to abandon any residual irrationalities they might have had.

J. Tyce: There is a lingering suspicion in the profession that Britain's large export of capital in the late nineteenth century may have played an important part in explaining her economic retardation somewhere between 1870 and 1913. In 1911-13, for example, about 9 per cent of national income was invested abroad and about 3 per cent at home, barely adequate to maintain the capital-labour ratio. It has been argued by some that if there had been a substantial reduction in British capital exports, there would have been a more rapid accumulation of domestic capital and that this accumulation, with a generous measure of endogenous technical progress, would have raised productivity, output and income by more than enough to compensate for the loss of foreign investment income.

Given these hypothetical gains waiting to be grasped by Britain, why did the British portfolio contain such a large element of foreign securities? Was the capital market functioning perfectly, though possibly distributing resources in a way that was at odds with the socially desirable distribution; or was the market operating imperfectly, showing a preference for foreign and large issues? Edelstein sets out to discover whether any imperfections of the second sort account for the high proportion of foreign securities in the British portfolio. By the ingenious use of the mean-standard deviation model of portfolio selection, he is able to consider the investor as a purchaser of a unit of risk; if he pays different prices for risks otherwise identical, then he shows a bias to some forms of risk. Edelstein uses the price per unit of risk (λ) for each industry as the dependent variable, which is then explained in terms of two dummy variables representing foreign and scale factors. It is not clear, however, that this is the best way of assessing the biases in lending, for three reasons.

First, the price per unit of risk is, of course, determined by a whole host of factors aside from the two singled out for examination, and this may well account for the poor 'explanation' his equations provide for (λ). As the purpose of the test is to identify whether differences in (λ) correspond to foreign and scale biases, a more discriminating test would be to explain the *difference* in the price of risk on foreign as opposed to domestic issues and in large as opposed to small issues. An appropriate specification might be:

$$\lambda^j_{for} - \lambda^j_{dom} = a + bD + C \frac{S_{for^j}}{S_{dom^j}}$$

where D is a dummy variable taking the value 1 for foreign securities, 0 for domestic; $\frac{S_{for^j}}{S_{dom^j}}$ is the ratio of the average size of foreign issues to the average size of domestic issues in the jth industry. The coefficient b will be negative if there is a bias to foreign securities and the coefficient c will be negative when foreign issues are typically larger than domestic issues and lenders prefer large issues. To test the hypothesis of a bias towards scale in a more general sense, a similar test could be devised:

$$\lambda^i_j - \lambda^n_j = a + b \frac{S^i_j}{S^n_j}$$

The difference between the price of risk on the ith security and the average price, λ^n, in that jth industry should be positively related to the size of the issue. Such a test would be useful, because by concentrating on an intra-industry difference explained in terms of the scale dummy, it would be possible to establish the limiting price per unit of risk for small domestic issues.

The second objection is that the study is confined to equity, thus excluding the important element of debenture and preference shares from British portfolios. J. B. Jeffreys has suggested that domestic issuers were constrained after the 1880s to imitate the type of security offered by large public utilities, on which, so to speak, so many investors had been brought up. A separate assessment of bias should be made for each type of asset, not only because each asset type has different risk-yield characteristics, but also because such a large proportion of foreign lending was in preference shares and debentures issued by public utilities.

The final difficulty is that it may be true, as many people claim, that the market was biased against small issuers because the issuing houses simply would not handle them. This implies that discrimination against such issues would leave no evidence because they would never have gone to the market. The mean-variance framework used by Edelstein applies only to that part of capital market that was able to trade freely in existing issues at market prices.

Edelstein: His data were equities, not debenture and preference shares, and it may well be that the price of risk on these was different from the other. But if the market was approximately perfect and if both home and foreign industries could issue both kinds, it would not make a difference for the case to be made if debenture and preference shares were included. On Tyce's other points, the alternative procedure of explaining the difference in the prices of risk would not improve his own equation. Indeed, there would be a grave problem in finding foreign equivalents of British industries, as required by Tyce's test for bias.

Friedman: The mean-variance framework that Edelstein used depends on the assumptions of a normal distribution of returns for the assets and a quadratic utility function in the mean and variance alone of the asset.

Edelstein: This problem does exist and it is a difficult one. Some crude tests of the underlying assumptions of the model had turned out well enough to justify the degree of approximation required.

Engerman: It is uncertain whether the results implied that the capital market was truly rational or that it was merely confused. If the market were fully rational, the price of risk, λ, should be constant across every variation of the character of assets, in which case the low significance level would be a result of λ itself having no variation. The other possibility is that λ varies a great deal, but unsystematically, in which case the low significance level is evidence of a confused and disorganized market, not of a rational one.

Edelstein: λ did, in fact, vary, indicating that there was a slight bias towards one security or another, but the bias was unstable. Hall's characterization of the London market as being enthusiastic about Australian securities for two or three years, enthusiastic about Canadian securities for the next two or three years, and so on, was accurate. All that his results indicate is that the enthusiasms evened out on balance: at some point they were enthusiastic about various types of *domestic* securities for a span of years.

Harley: Could the variation in λ among industries be explained?

Engerman: Extending Harley's query, the hypothesis to be affirmed was that the variation in λ among industries was zero, that is, that there was one price of risk for the entire market. The low significance levels on the coefficients of the two variables included imply merely that λ is not explained by the two variables included, not that the variation in λ itself is zero.

Temin: Turning to another issue, that of Pollard's and Tyce's point that there may have been perfect allocation of capital among those issues that were in fact floated in the market, but that certain issues were barred from being floated at all: this argument is predicated on a very peculiar assumption about the structure of the market, in which there is a sharp threshold between acceptable and unacceptable issues. It seems more plausible that while some issues would not be floated at all, others would be floated, but under more difficult circumstances than the better ones, making inefficiency observable if it was there. Unless there was some institutional feature of the market that makes the threshold model more appropriate, then, there is nothing wrong with looking at the securities actually issued to uncover or to fail to uncover inefficiency.

Pollard: This point could be rephrased. The argument, a longstanding one, was that if British businesses had been forced to amalgamate, Britain would have done better. Is this the hypothesis being tested implicitly by Edelstein?

Edelstein: No. Pollard's point is that the private and social return to various projects differed, as Kindleberger suggests in his book. Had the social returns been internalized in larger firms or combines, Britain might indeed have done better. But this is not the issue treated in the paper.

Mathias: The point Pollard raises is nonetheless the key one. The chief difficulty with Edelstein's argument is that it focuses on the one particular part of the capital market and the one set of institutions for mobilizing capital for which the data happen to be suitable for the sophisticated tests employed, and then attempts to generalize to the larger questions of capital and industrial growth. This procedure ignores the relationship between the banking system and entrepreneurship. In the United Kingdom, in contrast to the Continent, the mobilization of capital was separated from entrepreneurial functions. It is this fact, not the degree of perfection of the capital market, that is most relevant to the impact on growth of Britain's way of mobilizing capital.

Edelstein: It is probably incorrect to characterize British banking as unhelpful to industry. Moreover, and this point is relevant to Pollard's argument as well, the financial market was much broader than it seems at first. Formal banking was supplemented by private investors and by the investments, neglected in the literature, of one limited company in another.

4

*British controls on long term capital movements, 1924-1931**

D. E. MOGGRIDGE

Peacetime controls on long term international capital movements undertaken primarily for balance-of-payments reasons are relatively modern phenomena. In Great Britain they date from the period of the inter-war gold standard. This paper concerns itself with the origins, operation and effectiveness of these British inter-war controls in an attempt to add to our understanding of the operation, from Britain's point of view, of the inter-war gold standard.

By returning to gold at $4.86 in 1925, the British authorities saddled themselves with an overvalued exchange rate [1]. Given their policy goals [2] — pre-war levels of unemployment, free trade, unrestricted foreign lending and international economic stabilization — and given that a deliberate devaluation of sterling was 'unthinkable' [3], the overvaluation of sterling presented the authorities with the prospect of a series of difficult policy choices. To restore something approaching balance-of-payments 'equilibrium' the authorities could:

(i)   Reduce income and employment by an amount sufficient to reduce imports to a level more compatible with the reduced export potential and higher underlying volume of imports resulting from the overvaluation.

(ii)   Hope that rises in overseas costs relative to British costs would, through their effects on relative prices, increase exports and reduce imports.

(iii)   Hope that the increased unemployment generated in (i) would reduce U.K. money wages (or hold them stable while foreign money wages rose) and that this (plus divergent rates of productivity growth) might reduce sterling wage costs per unit of output relative to such costs abroad, thus making U.K. exports and import-competing goods cheaper relative to foreign goods and allowing (ii) to operate.

* I should like to thank Professors Lord Kahn, Joan Robinson and Sir Ralph Hawtrey for comments on earlier drafts of this paper.

(iv)   Hope that the terms of trade would turn in the U.K.'s favour through a decline in the price of non-competing imports, which, if demand were price inelastic, would reduce the import bill.

(v)   Reduce overseas lending by intensifying informal controls [4] on lending abroad by U.K. residents.

(vi)   Expand the range of protective duties.

(vii)   Hope that a rise in world import demand for goods and services would raise U.K. exports despite their high relative cost.

(viii)   So alter the structure of relative interest rates that, with a given level of Bank Rate, a larger volume of short term funds would be attracted to London and, over time, a larger proportion of increases in wealth would be so attracted [5].

This list is by no means exhaustively taxonomic, but it provides some indication of the options open to the authorities in 1925 and succeeding years. At the time of the return to gold, they had expected, often implicitly, that, in so far as they had detected signs of overvaluation, (ii) would be the operative mechanism with (i) and (iii) remaining in reserve [6]. However, events after 1925 did not evolve in accordance with their expectations.

In the first place, devaluations plus divergent wage-price-productivity movements abroad meant that Britain, if anything, became even less competitive internationally in the years following 1925 [7]. This meant that alternative (ii) was not available. In the second place, although up to 1929 British exports were carried upwards by rising world demand, the increased exports did not offset the increased volume of imports resulting from rises in British incomes and Britain's weakening competitive position, despite the favourable combined impact of falling prices and slightly improved terms of trade on Britain's overall international position. In fact, only an improvement in the net invisibles position, particularly in investment income and government transactions, meant that Britain's balance of payments on current account improved at all in the years up to 1929. After 1929, of course, the international slump put severe pressure on the invisibles position, so that, even though the trade position's deterioration up to September 1931 was minimal, Britain faced the prospect of a large current account deficit [8]. Finally, it proved extraordinarily difficult to resort to alternative (i) beyond the impulses provided by the initial act of appreciation to an overvalued exchange rate. Throughout the years after 1925, the Bank of England faced heavy political pressure to keep interest rates down. In fact, every bank rate increase from 1925 to 1929 was opposed by the Chancellor, often violently so [9]. In addition, there are grounds for believing that the Bank of England's asset position was such that it would have proved almost impossible for the Bank to engineer a significant measure of deflation through open-market operations, even if the Chancellor and his advisers had been willing to see interest rates rise [10], and even if Governor Norman had, within his limited frame of reference, believed such a deflation necessary on technical grounds [11].

Given that aggregate policy measures were substantially immobilized as weapons for short term balance-of-payments defence or long term adjustment, the authorities were forced to search for supplementary means. In theory such supplements could take a variety of forms and work on almost any sector of Britain's international accounts [12]. However, in the inter-war gold standard period policy preferences and traditions of thought eliminated many possible courses of action. The tradition of free trade, which in some respects was even stronger than that of the gold standard, made further direct intervention on the trade account to reduce imports politically impossible [13]. The same tradition, plus desires to keep expenditure down and administrative complexities, ruled out intervention to increase the surplus on private invisibles account, while operations on the government account, loaded as it was with imperial commitments and debt agreements and almost immune from direct analysis, was also never seriously considered. Thus almost by default, in an operational sense, the authorities were left only with the possibility of influencing the capital and official settlements accounts of the balance of payments.

From the point of view of the Bank of England, which carried operational responsibility for balance-of-payments matters, and from that of the Treasury and the government, which directly or indirectly carried ultimate political responsibility, intervention in these areas carried with it several distinct advantages. First, intervention by the Bank removed the government from any formal responsibility in a world where official intervention was *a priori* unpopular [14]. The Treasury could encourage intervention by the Bank privately — and even publicly set guidelines for such intervention [15] — if it so desired, but if challenged by hostile public reaction it could say that legally it had nothing to do with the intervention in question [16]. Second, intervention in these areas was possible without legislation, for in the City — and to a lesser extent among sister central banks — the

Bank might make its wishes felt effectively without fuss and publicity. Third, as the Bank carried ultimate legal responsibility for the maintenance of sterling's exchange value and was constrained in other areas of operation, it had the maximum incentive to innovate and to ease its way along the golden path for which it had fought so effectively in 1924-5. Thus within limits, the time was ripe for the exercise of moral suasion by the Bank.

Moral suasion as an instrument of economic policy represents an 'attempt to coerce private economic activity via . . . exhortation in directions not already defined by *existing* statutes' [17]. Such exhortation may take qualitative or quantitative form, but it basically involves an encouragement to private businesses to undertake action that is unprofitable or relatively less profitable than that which it would normally take. The success of such suasion depends on several factors. The numbers of firms to be persuaded normally must be small [18]. The requests and the consequences of non-compliance must be clear and credible. Here small numbers are an advantage in that deviations from the requests can be easily identified and the costs of compliance for any one firm as compared with its competitors can be kept down. The consequences of non-compliance ultimately depend on the powers of the authorities concerned with this 'polite blackmail' [19]. for although they may be increased by threats of legislation, these threats may backfire and force the authorities into legislation they hoped to avoid [20]. The occasions on which such suasion finds use are also important. In a national emergency or when the national interest or the interests of those subject to suasion are clearly involved, suasion may become more effective as public support for its ends increases the scope for private altruism and the group penalties for non-compliance. Similarly, suasion's projected period of operation is of considerable importance, for pressures for its termination will increase as the unprofitability of compliance becomes cumulative and self-restraint becomes onerous. Finally, because suasion's ultimate success depends on contact between individuals or groups of individuals, the personal relationships and beliefs of those involved become most important. In the former respect, Montagu Norman's dominant position in the City of the 1920s and his usefulness to its members were of great importance [21], as in the latter respect were the City's almost uniform belief that *laissez-faire* was the best policy and its almost universal anti-intellectualism in matters of a broad economic nature, which blurred any ends-means considerations beyond the very simple and the very short term [22].

These considerations provide the background for the efforts of the authorities to control various types of transactions on Britain's long term capital account [23]. During World War I the authorities had attempted to limit the export of capital in all forms through controls which grew more pervasive as the war progressed [24]. However, the end of the war brought pressures for the relaxation of controls, to which the authorities deferred to a considerable extent. Nevertheless, as there were pressures favouring loans to capital-starved Europe and to the Empire and as the capital market faced domestic demands for industrial reconstruction and for such officially encouraged programmes as local authority housebuilding, the authorities, with their own needs for continuous debt refinancing, maintained some measure of control over overseas issues, especially during the boom of 1919-20. However, by January 1924, they had removed all restrictions on overseas lending other than loans to governments in default and governments that had not funded their war debts [25].

At this point it is best to examine the Bank's suasion position. In any possible future attempts to control overseas issues, the Bank had several advantages. Just before 1914, the issuing houses (of which six did the bulk of the foreign issues) had started to consult the Bank about forthcoming new overseas issues and during the war consultations had occurred for all issues [26]. After the war, consultations continued and firms normally took all big foreign issues to the Governor to obtain his views, big issues being those over £1 million [27]. This process, almost inevitably, also brought some small issues to the attention of the Bank at an early stage. When consultations occurred, the Governor had an opportunity to express his views on both the soundness and general advisability of the issue concerned. The consultations gave him valuable information concerning forthcoming demands on the London market and allowed him to influence their timing [28]. Clay's biography of Norman provides several examples of the Governor's diary notes on such occasions [29]. On some occasions, his advice might be unambiguous and his wishes generally followed [30], but more frequently his advice was more ambiguous and became just another factor in the merchant banker's decision to undertake an issue [31]. In periods when the Bank might wish to restrict new overseas issues, this consultative process provided a basis for restriction. However, the Governor could reinforce its effects in several ways. Speeches by politicians such as the Chancellor of the Exchequer might be used to enlist public support and to provide a justification for certain courses of action by the Bank. The government of the day could approach potential borrowers, particularly within the Empire, and ask them to rephase their borrowing, or, using the Bank's good offices, go elsewhere. Action of this kind would remove pressure at its source, the borrower, and could usefully supplement action taken in London. Finally, the Bank could issue general directives to bodies such as the Bankers' Clearing House or the Committee of the Stock Exchange to favour or bar certain broad classes of issue such as loans to countries with unfunded war debts or loans under twenty years [32].

All of these avenues of suasion could be backed by sanctions of various types. The ultimate sanction was a refusal of permission to deal in the offending issue on the Stock Exchange, for this would largely destroy the marketability of the issue concerned [33]. Pressures to limit clearing bank participation in the issue would be almost as effective, as would well timed press leaks as to the Bank's opposition. In addition, as the largest issuing houses combined an acceptance business with their issuing activities, they were dependent upon the willingness of the Bank to rediscount or take as collateral the bills they had accepted. If they incurred the Bank's displeasure, such facilities for their bills might disappear or be somewhat restricted, thus weakening one foundation of their business. Beyond that, the Bank and the Treasury both suggested agents to local authorities and other issuers of trustee securities and could use this influence to direct business away from the offending houses [34]. Thus the authorities had several channels of influence to keep offenders in line. These channels were only useful on an individual basis: any show of strength by the issuing houses as a group would break the system of sanctions as their use on a large scale would damage the London market in a long term sense. However, such a mass revolt would probably end in a rise in bank rate, which, although it represented the policy step the authorities had attempted to avoid through the use of suasion and was, therefore, counterproductive, would affect the issuing houses by reducing the volume of business and imposing capital losses on portfolios of unsold securities [35]. Nevertheless, the rise in bank rate represented less a sanction than an admission of failure.

Given the channels of influence and sanctions available to the authorities, how and when did the controls work. For this purpose one needs a fairly detailed breakdown of such aggregate figures as exist for the period. Table 1 presents a summary of all new issues for overseas issues extracted from worksheets prepared by Dr J. Atkin, formerly of the London School of Economics [36]. The summary includes all

TABLE 1
New overseas issues by type of borrower, 1923-31

TYPE

	Empire						Foreign						Total (£'000)	Midland Bank estimate Total (£'000)
	Government		Municipal		Company		Government		Municipal		Company			
Year	(£'000)	No. of issues	(£'000)	No. of issues	(£'000)	No. of issues	(£'000)	No. of issues	(£'000)	No. of issues	(£'000)	No. of issues		
1923	64 406	16	4788	10	18 430	72	26 461	7	–	–	18 491	30	137 376	136 176
1924	50 080	10	6085	9	16 014	66	40 615	6	2412	1	9 350	20	124 560	134 223
1925	30 648	10	2625	11	27 262	142	–	–	1350	1	14 970	30	77 055	87 798
1926	31 866	8	1222	4	20 227	81	23 817	8	6235	2	18 361	36	101 728	112 404
1927	55 697	13	5135	7	38 851	77	11 027	6	7186	6	30 546	34	148 422	138 671
1928	40 222	11	7304	9	15 344	61	15 937	8	4331	4	22 204	34	105 342	143 384
1929	26 366	5	3859	3	30 881	70	3 650	2	472	1	22 469	35	81 697	94 347
1930	49 080	11	3031	44	9 207	28	21 330	3	–	–	14 387	21	97 035	108 803
1931	30 571	5	–	–	7 983	26	1 740	1	–	–	5 658	11	45 952	46 078

Sources: J. Atkin, Worksheets compiled from The Economist. Midland Bank Monthly Review.

issues to the public, except private placings and introductions, the key to inclusion being mention in *The Economist*'s weekly list of new issues. The totals for such issues are rather lower than those of the Midland Bank present in column 14 of Table 1, but they provide a useful indication of the trends and Dr Atkin's worksheets listing every issue in the series have eased the job of analysis.

From the totals in Table 1, both for the amounts and numbers of issues in each class, certain indications of policy possibilities clearly arise. First, the only loans which, on average, exceeded £1 million, the consultation limit mentioned by R. H. Brand, were those of governments – the company issues, even with large railway issues included, averaged under one half that amount or just over £434,000 between 1923 and 1931. Second, the relative stability of company issues is also extremely noticeable during most of the period before 1929, after which the depression made such borrowing less likely. Third, the volatility of foreign official issues, both in number and in value, is immediately apparent, as are the sharp swings in the annual figures for 1925 and 1929-31 (the figures are even more depressed for these years and for 1924 if the large, officially 'approved' League of Nations and Reparations loans are excluded). From these figures alone, a rough guide to the timing and the direction of official capital market intervention is immediately available. However, understanding of what occurred and its problems is increased by a combination of the new issue figures with material from documentary sources.

Although the authorities had removed most restrictions on new overseas issues in January 1924, the development of overseas lending in the early part of the year soon gave cause for alarm. By April, Governor Norman was recording in his diary, 'Foreign loans [are] too frequent, too cheap and poor reasons', and noting his agreement with Reginald McKenna's view that 'our only remedy [is] a 5 per cent rate if such loans continue on a large scale' [37]. Given that a rise in bank rate at the time would have raised a political storm [38], the Governor seems to have turned to increasingly forceful negative advice in consultations on further new issues, for after 24 May there were no non-League-of-Nations, non-Reparations loans for foreign governments of municipalities until January 1926. At the time the controls were intensified, loans, to foreign governments totalled £16,015,000, implying a rate of lending above that of 1923. Thus it would seem that the Bank became much more strict in its treatment of applications for foreign government new issues from mid-1924, a date which aggrees with the Royal Institute of International Affairs informed estimate [39].

However, the early stages of the intensification of controls were not widely noticed and there was still considerable discussion as to whether controls on foreign issues might be necessary as a part of the package of measures surrounding the return to gold [40]. Thus the Chamberlain-Bradbury Committee from its Third Draft Report onwards made specific references to the need to prevent foreign lending. In this regard, it is interesting that the Committee made reference only to foreign lending rather than Empire and foreign lending, a distinction common at the time. The authorities were advised that 'any tendency to weakness in the exchanges should be treated as a ground for discouraging foreign loans upon the London market and even for a general restriction of credit *in the event of other methods of discouragement not being effective*' (italics added) [41]. Thus, before the return to gold, some of those influential in the formulation of official policy believed that informal or formal restrictions on overseas, and particularly on foreign, lending were preferable, in the first instance, to credit restrictions.

By the autumn of 1924, 'the Governor's polite blackmail against foreign issues' [42] was in full operation, and after the Dawes Loan of October 1924 [43] and the Greek Government League loan of December, all foreign government issues, except a small League loan to Danzig of April 1925, were kept from the market. The Governor also appears to have attempted to prevent some company issues in cases where the company was foreign rather than British owned, but the results here were probably of less importance in the overall outcome [44].

There matters stood until after the return to gold. From 28 April onwards the Governor pressed further restrictions, this time on Empire issues [45]. At first the Treasury was 'not disposed to be over alarmed' and hoped to 'trust such persuasion as the Governor can use in the City and the repercussions of that persuasion', even though it realized that Colonial and Dominion loans would be more difficult to restrict owing to sentiment and the attractions of their trustee status [46]. However, although the failure of four badly priced large loans effectively closed the market in the ensuing weeks, the pressure for Treasury in addition to Bank action continued and the Treasury prepared a draft telegram to Dominion Governors-General, which expressed concern at the volume of their London borrowing and asked for official action at the borrowing end to limit demand to essential loans and to allow the British authorities to coordinate future demands with British policy [47]. However, the Colonial Office opposed any attempts to restrict Empire borrowing and threatened to take the matter to the

Cabinet [48] The Treasury believed that this attitude was unreasonable and urged Churchill to settle the matter privately and orally, which, spurred on by further warnings from Norman, Churchill appears to have done successfully as the telegrams went off as drafted [49]. However, possibly as a *quid pro quo* for Colonial Office agreement to the telegrams, the Committee of Civil Research on 18 June set up a subcommittee to investigate the issue of overseas lending [50].

The request to the Dominions had its effects and their borrowing in London fell off, partially because the authorities encouraged them to meet their needs through joint issues through a British house in London and New York [51]. However, in the course of the summer, the restrictions became increasingly unpopular in London, where they were regarded as 'a distinct "off-side" ' in the gold standard game and there was a 'unanimous feeling' that they should go as soon as possible [52]. The Treasury at the time still foresaw the market remaining closed until well into 1926 and favoured non-discriminatory controls on all overseas government issues to preserve London's reputation [53]. The controls were unpopular because City firms were losing income and because the controls were easy to evade through the purchase of foreign securities issued abroad and through issues for British concerns operating abroad [54]. Moreover, the Bank of England was also finding that the embargo had unfortunate side effects, for with the expectation that the embargo would not last forever, potential lenders built up liquid balances that inundated the short term market and complicated the Bank's task of short interest rate management [55]. In these circumstances, Norman was under pressure from his directors to raise the embargo, let gold go and, if necessary, raise the bank rate [56]. It was in these circumstances that the Overseas Loans Sub-Committee of the Committee of Civil Research finished its deliberations and signed its Report on 16 October.

The Report recommended that the embargo be lifted on 9 November 1925 [57]. It noted that evasion was becoming more frequent, that evasion increased the unpopularity of a measure that was already regarded as being harmful from a national point of view, and that in its present form the embargo was becoming unworkable. However, the Sub-Committee saw the alternative of making the embargo statutory as 'undesirable in itself' and subject to such 'insuperable' practical difficulties as to be 'utterly unworkable' in peacetime. It thus accepted the other alternative, removal of the embargo, as being 'consistent . . . with our traditions' and the policy of the return to gold. It accepted that there was a margin for overseas lending in the balance of payments and national savings, that 'the normal operation of the gold standard will supply a speedy, although perhaps drastic, corrective' to any future overlending and that 'whatever inconvenience may arise must be faced as part of the price which has to be paid for restoring normal conditions'.

The Report then went on to reject any tying of loans to U.K. purchases because of formidable administrative difficulties. It recommended that the trustee status of Dominion and Colonial issues be maintained but not extended. Finally, it expressed its approval of attempts to issue securities jointly in London and New York and its hope that, if New York lending rates developed so as to make such issues attractive, Dominions and Colonies would resort to such issues rather than sever their London connections completely.

There matters stood, except for the advancing of the embargo's removal to 3 November [58], when the Chancellor announced that 'the old full freedom of the market will be restored' in a speech at Sheffield [59]. The 'old full freedom' excluded countries that had not funded war debts or were in default, but these exceptions remained private and in the Governor's hands for interpretation and enforcement. The only public limitation, or guideline, for future consultations attached to the restoration came in Churchill's comment that:

I trust with confidence to the corporate good sense of the City to manage its affairs with discretion; to pay regard not only to the capacities of the market but to the position towards this country of would-be borrowers, and I hope that so far as possible, without impairing the freedom of the market, that preference will be given in the matter of credit to those issues which bring a high proportion of orders for goods immediately to the trade of this country.

The removal of the embargo did not lead to a rush for loans, if only because a badly priced Colonial loan failed, leaving 97.5 per cent with the underwriters, and because the ensuing bank rate uncertainties made issuing houses, borrowers and potential investors wary. However, five Colonial issues found their way to market before the end of the year. Foreign issues waited until 1926.

Given the tone of the Report of the Overseas Loans Sub-Committee and given its signatories, who included Norman, Niemeyer and Bradbury, one would have thought that, for the moment, efforts to control new overseas issues by suasion were over. During 1926 and

1927 this appears to have been the case, for I can detect only one indication [60] that there were any new restrictions on overseas lending in London beyond the informal consultations. During that period interest rates made London more expensive then New York, or even many borrowing countries [61], and helped to keep foreign issues from London, particularly when one adds the 2 per cent stamp duty on bearer bonds, the type most commonly issued by foreign governments, and the decline in issuing costs in the United States that resulted from competition between issuing houses [62]. This reduction in London's cost advantage, which had partially offset higher interest rates in the early 1920s, brought representations to the Treasury for the reduction or removal of the 2 per cent duty [63]. This reduction in new issues resulting from cost considerations did not mean a fall in the net outflow of funds of a comparable amount, for British investors purchased securities issued in lower cost foreign markets, often holding them abroad to escape payment of any duty. One firm of brokers reported doing £7 million of such business in New York in the period 1924-7 [64], and on many occasions new foreign issues in New York reserved large blocks of securities for European sales of this type. However, the duty, in so far as market imperfections existed, did keep foreign lending below what it otherwise might have been during the period after 1925 and it lessened the need for further controls. The authorities realized that the 2 per cent duty was 'a serious obstacle to the issue of foreign loans', but they were at first, and to some extent always, unwilling to sacrifice the revenue, unwilling to make the 1929 pre-election budget too long and too complex and believed that 'some slight check such as the stamp duty imposes on issues for abroad is rather useful at the present moment . . . apart from revenue considerations' [65]

From mid-1928, the rise in American interest rates, the increasing attractiveness of shares in New York *vis-à-vis* bonds and a shift in American asset preferences towards shares combined to make London more attractive to foreign borrowers than previously. The authorities appear to have allowed the 1928 pattern to develop without too much interference, as they just kept their watching brief on new issues and even lifted the embargo on loans to countries that had not funded war debts [66], but after loans in February and March 1929 there were no foreign government loans for the rest of the year. There were no overseas government issues of any kind after 27 July. Clay argues that Norman imposed no ban on foreign lending [67], but the absence of overseas issue, Snowden's Mansion House Speech in which he hoped that a rise in bank rate could be avoided by restrictions on overseas lending [68], and the efforts of the Governor to keep bank rate down, at least until the Hague Conference was over, all made restrictions likely [69]. Moreover, in 1933, both the Treasury and the Governor of the Bank admitted that they had discouraged foreign lending in 1929 and after [70].

Certainly in 1930 and 1931 there were few foreign loans, particularly when one excludes the Young and Austrian Government Loans of 1930, none of the proceeds of which were transferred abroad. The two remaining loans were for coffee valorization in Brazil (March 1930) and for Greece (March 1931). Empire lending appears to have remained buoyant and unrestricted, except in so far as the growing international economic crisis made investors unwilling to subscribe new money. Both the Bank and the Treasury continued to exercise general scrutiny over such issues, but there is no recorded attempt to block such loans after 1925, although, of course, Colonial lending could be more easily controlled. Company borrowing also fell off, but here again economic conditions rather than controls appear to have been the prime reason.

Now how effective were these efforts to control overseas lending in its various forms? In answering this question, one must first emphasize that the controls were never extended to cover more than a few possible potential avenues for British overseas investment during the period. Thus, in so far as other avenues remained open, British residents could increase their holdings of foreign assets by, for example, purchasing bonds in foreign markets and even holding them abroad to escape the 2 per cent duty. Moreover, if these other avenues offered securities with characteristics similar to those that might have been offered in London, the only impediments to investment might be higher transactions costs, reduced information and some element of exchange risk. Given that the use of moral suasion did not extend to the large institutional potential holders of foreign securities, such as insurance companies and investment trusts, the existence of these alternative avenues plus reasonably large supplies of securities that were reasonable substitutes for new London issues in their portfolios, the controls may not have stopped that much overseas investment. Instead, the controls may have merely changed the forms overseas investment took so as to reduce the incomes of City firms. Certainly City firms frequently opposed the controls for this very reason and their opposition made even the achievement of limited suasion more difficult.

To see whether these alternative avenues, particularly for fixed interest securities, existed, ideally one would like to have a fairly detailed knowledge of Britain's international capital transactions on a gross basis. However, Britain's international payments statistics are so inadequate for this period [71] that one must rely on very rough, largely non-quantitative evidence. Certainly the possibilities for evading such controls as existed were so great that Governor Norman remarked that the embargo on loans to France resulting from her non-payment and non-funding of war debts meant 'that London has pro tanto found the capital and other countries have earned the commission and the profit', for French securities issued in Holland and Switzerland rapidly found their way to London [72]. In addition, in cases of joint London-New York issues, such as the Australian issue of July 1925, a large portion of the New York *tranche* normally found its way almost immediately to London. The reverse rarely, if ever, happened [73]. Moreover, the fact that almost £500 million of securities issued in London were held by foreigners meant that purchases of outstanding issues from foreigners might offset some of the balance of payments effects of an embargo on new issues of similar type [74]. The 'regular army of bond sellers' catering to the demand of the insurance and trust company markets for foreign-issued securities also pointed to the existence of a large and profitable business in channels outside the controls [75], as did the large volume of American transactions in securities with European markets including London [76]. Moreover, as British residents' portfolios of non-sterling, particularly dollar, securities were relatively low in 1925, given wartime vesting and official sales and the unattractiveness of American securities for other than short term speculation during the years 1919-25 when sterling was expected to rise in value, a reduction in new supplies of foreign issues in London might have induced a more rapid rebuilding of American portfolios. If, in addition, there were changes in tastes as between domestic and overseas issues or between types of overseas issues during the period, the controls might have proved even less effective [77]. The existence of a variety of channels for investment in overseas securities and the internationalization of the inter-war security market thus probably meant that controls on one segment of the market did not necessarily lead to an equivalent improvement in the balance of payments, excluding for the moment possibilities of any repercussions on such items as exports or interest and dividends.

However, in so far as the controls did reduce overseas lending, they probably reduced short term pressure on the exchange rate and/or the official gold and foreign exchange reserves. Any foreign loan initially resulted in a deterioration in London's short term international financial position as domestic assets passed into the hands of foreigners. Thereafter, the effect depended on the use of these assets by the foreigners concerned (and on the sources of these assets in Britain). Assuming, for simplicity's sake that the assets were not transferred from London until the foreigners involved actually spent them on goods and services, and assuming that the act of borrowing increased foreign demands for resources, let us concentrate on the effects of this increased foreign expenditure. If the loan was spent entirely in Britain on British goods at the outset, the transfer was easily effected. However, if the proceeds were spent in third countries or initially were used to finance domestic expenditure in the borrowing country, the process would be more roundabout and the initial weakening of the exchange rate and/or the loss of reserves caused by the financial transfer would not be offset by the repercussions of the increased expenditures abroad except after a considerable time lag. If the balance-of-payments position of the lending country was weak, the resulting loss of reserves might have necessitated official short-run deflationary measures [78]. Moreover, in an uncompetitive economy such as Britain's in the 1920s, it was highly unlikely that the secondary expansive effects on Britain resulting from the expenditure of the loan abroad would be anything but slight, particularly in the short period.

In addition, it was highly unlikely that British foreign lending in the 1920s actually increased British exports above the levels that they would have reached if some other financial centre had done the lending [79]. As recent research has suggested, direct overseas investment by U.K. (and U.S.) companies (which occurred to a limited extent in the 1920s) would probably not have led in the short term to a substantial offsetting of the initial effects of the financial transfer through increased exports and remitted profits [80]. Portfolio investment, despite its contribution to invisible earnings through commissions and issuing expenses, would have been even less likely to do so, for a 'buy British' bias would have been unlikely to be operative simply because the loan came from London [81]. However, in so far as potential borrowers might have been unable to substitute foreign for British loans, which might certainly have been the case after 1928 and which was the case for such schemes as Brazilian coffee valorization, [82], British foreign lending might have been necessary to increase the volume of British exports. But in these cases, the export stimulation could have been increased by tying the loans that would have reduced, or eliminated, the initial financial deterioration and ensured that the increased demand for goods came to Britain. However, the Bank of England rejected tying as an alternative, as did City firms, who, lacking the intimate connections with industry characteristic of other financial centres, saw reduced earnings as the outcome [83].

To sort out the full effects of restrictions on foreign lending, not only must we know the disposition of the funds involved and the alternatives, as outlined above, but we must also know the sources of the funds borrowed by foreigners. If the funds involved came initially from domestic dis-saving or credit creation, the act of lending itself had no effects on the level of domestic activity and the process of effecting the transfer would result – in conditions of unemployment such as those that characterized Britain in the 1920s – in an increase in exports and a rise in domestic income, the savings from which would equal the increase in exports. If, on the other hand, the funds involved were diverted from domestic investment as a result of the operation of the capital market, effecting the transfer would only tend to restore the *status quo ante* and, in so far as the transfer was undereffected, would leave Britain with a lower level of income than before. Thus, in conditions of unemployment, if the latter mechanism was operative, restrictions on overseas lending that resulted in other countries providing the necessary funds would enable Britain both to have a higher level of income and to avoid any additional deflationary pressures that might result from the financial transfer. If the former mechanism was operative, restrictions on British overseas lending merely avoided only the short term deflationary effects of the financial transfer.

In the discussions of the 1920s, the Treasury knights concerned tended to make a different set of assumptions. They assumed that the mechanism involved was classical (i.e. that the loan increased foreign expenditure and reduced domestic expenditure while leaving the level of income unchanged), that if London did not make the loan no one else would, and that the transfer was perfectly effected in such a short period as to rule the financial deterioration out of court. Working from these assumptions, they could see no improvement in the balance of payments or domestic employment as resulting from restrictions and no *a priori* reason for interfering with overseas lending. Thus R. G. Hawtrey could suggest: 'I think I *would* go so far as to say that in practice "no measures to restrict overseas issues would have any effect" [in improving the balance of payments] '; and 'It is hardly going too far to say that (except when it is desired to facilitate Government borrowing in time of war) measures should *never* be taken to check external capital issues' (italics in original) [84]. Similarly, the Treasury's 1929 White Paper on the Liberal Party's election proposals could conclude that 'one would naturally expect that a great decline in the exports of British capital must ultimately result in a decrease in our exports and an increase of imports' [85], and believed that this argument, among others, made the Liberal proposals unworkable.

However, it is unlikely that this was an accurate description of the forces at work during the 1920s, for several reasons. First, it seems highly unlikely that the transfer mechanism worked as efficiently as the Treasury suggested. Second, it seems unlikely that foreign investment took place at the expense of home investment in the short to medium term. The capital market in which the process of bidding funds away from domestic uses would have to occur was not that important as a means of financing home investment and, moreover, much overseas lending was, through the Trustee Acts, hardly competitive with domestic lending [86]. Third, as the economy was well below full capacity and full employment, it is highly unlikely that foreign lending, if it did not bid resources away from domestic uses in the capital market, bid resources away through other means. Finally, it is not entirely clear that if controls had been effective and London had been unable to lend, even indirectly, that other centres would not have provided most of the funds. Where they did not, tying the loans might have raised British incomes and employment.

However, much of the above discussion is somewhat beside the point, as the authorities' control over overseas lending in the 1920s probably only reduced the level of lending slightly, if at all. But, in certain periods, such slight overall reductions may have represented a significant proportion of the overseas lending for that short period and thus the restrictions may have helped get the authorities over particular 'humps'. Thus, for example, in 1924-5 the controls on lending may have assisted the appreciation of sterling, for so long as sterling was expected to rise against the dollar and such continental currencies as were stable, many of the routes for avoidance were closed both for new issues and outstanding securities. Similarly, after 1929 with alternative sources of funds closed, with many outstanding securities of uncertain prospect, and with American financial problems so obvious and so pressing, the controls on new issues may have had more impact. However, in this case, tying new issues would have increased the effectiveness of the controls, for it would have allowed new issues that would have increased British incomes and employment. But in the remaining periods of their operation, the existence and size of the available loopholes probably made the controls ineffective and only served to reduce the City's invisible earnings. Moreover, the authorities were loath to undertake further intervention to close the available loopholes – they only began to restrict the freedom of financial intermediaries to invest abroad and to reduce transactions in outstanding securities in the 1930s, and even the first year of World War II saw them trying to slowly complete their controls over the latter type of transactions [87]. Nevertheless, the experience of the 1920s did prepare the way for later extensions, represented a marked change in British international financial policy, and suggested the direction of future evolution in Bank of England-Treasury-City relations

NOTES

[1] The exact extent of the overvaluation is difficult to assess, but at least 10 per cent would seem an appropriate estimate. On the whole issue, see D. E. Moggridge, *The Return to Gold 1925: The Formulation of Economic Policy and its Critics* (Cambridge, 1969), pp. 71–6, 91 ff., and bibliography.
[2] Ibid., pp. 69–70.
[3] On this point, see Keynes Papers, Macmillan Committee, Notes of Discussions, 7 November 1930, p. 19.
[4] At the time of the return to gold such informal controls did exist for part of Britain's overseas lending. See below, p. 121.
[5] This might also favourably affect long term capital movements. See p. 124.
[6] Moggridge, op. cit., ch. 2.
[7] See Appendix Table 1 for some indication of the changes involved.
[8] See Appendix Table 2 for details of Britain's balance of payments between 1924 and 1931.
[9] See P.R.O. T176/13 (Niemeyer Papers), Bank Rate, 1923-30; Sir F. W. Leith-Ross, *Money Talks: Fifty Years of International Finance* (London, 1968), pp. 95–6; Sir Henry Clay, *Lord Norman* (London, 1957), pp. 230–1, 293, 297; P. J. Grigg, *Prejudice and Judgement* (London, 1948), p. 193.
[10] To provide a dividend of 12 per cent per annum on its capital, the Bank would have to hold £35 million of War Loan 1929-47 or a similar security yielding 5 per cent. One would expect this dividend-producing holding to be fairly firmly held. Such a holding would immobilize a considerable part of the Banking Department's assets. In addition, the Bank would need to cover such running expenses as were not covered by Treasury grants. Moreover, before 1928, the Issue Department's potential for holding Treasury bills was limited as the bulk of the note issue was covered by securities in the Currency Note Account, which does not appear to have

been a vehicle for day-to-day money market operations. See P.R.O. T176/13, note by Niemeyer, undated but position in file suggests November 1925.

[11] See D. Williams, 'Montagu Norman and banking policy in the nineteen twenties', *Yorkshire Bulletin of Social and Economic Research,* XI (1), July 1959.

[12] For a relatively exhaustive outline of the possibilities, see F. Machlup, 'Real adjustment, compensatory corrections and foreign financing of imbalances in international payments', *in* R. E. Caves, H. G. Johnson and P. B. Kenen, *Trade, Growth and the Balance of Payments* (Amsterdam, 1965).

[13] See, for example, K. Middlemas and J. Barnes, *Baldwin: A Biography* (London, 1969), pp. 310 ff.; Keynes Papers, Macmillan Committee, Notes of Discussions, 7 November 1930, p. 29.

[14] In this connection, see Committee on Industry and Trade, *Final Report,* Cmd. 3282 (London, 1929), pp. 49–50.

[15] See, for example, the speeches of the Chancellor of the Exchequer noted below on pp. 123 and 125

[16] See, for example, P.R.O. T175/4 (Hopkins Papers), Leith-Ross to Churchill, 6 October 1928.

[17] J. T. Romans, 'Moral suasion as an instrument of economic policy', *American Economic Review,* LVI (5), December 1966, p. 1221.

[18] However, the number to be persuaded need not always be small. Thus, since 1965, the Chancellor of the Exchequer's requests for voluntary restraint on investment, both direct and portfolio, in the four developed sterling area countries have in the Chancellor's words been quite successful as 'United Kingdom companies and institutions ... under growing pressuure have continued to give loyal co-operation' (799 H.C. Deb. 5s Column 1227). See also 'The U.K. exchange control: a short history', *Bank of England Quarterly Bulletin,* VII (3), September 1967, pp. 258–60.

[19] P.R.O. T175/4, Niemeyer to Churchill, 5 March 1925.

[20] See, for example, the negotiations between the Treasury and the clearing banks concerning gold holdings between 1925 and 1928 (P.R.O. T176/22).

[21] Clay, op. cit., pp. 278–9.

[22] L. E. Jones, *Georgian Afternoon* (London, 1958), pp. 111–28; R. H. Brand, 'A banker's reflections on economic trends', *Economic Journal,* LXIII (252), December 1953, pp. 763–4; P. Einzing, *In the Centre of Things* (London, 1960), pp. 54–5.

[23] During the period under consideration, the Bank of England, in order to increase its freedom of action, also undertook operations on its own account in gold and foreign exchange markets, worked hard for central bank cooperation and used moral suasion in the London gold and short term capital markets. For some discussion of these, see S. V. O. Clarke, *Central Bank Cooperation 1924-31* (New York, 1967); R. S. Sayers, *Gilletts in the London Money Market 1867-1967* (Oxford, 1968), ch. 5. A full discussion in these terms will appear in my forthcoming volume tentatively entitled *Studies in British International Monetary Policy 1924-1931.*

[24] E. V. Morgan, *Studies in British Financial Policy 1914-1925* (London, 1952), pp. 261–6. Before 1914, Bank of England efforts to control overseas investment informally appear to have been minimal. However, see H. Feis, *Europe: The World's Banker 1870-1914* (New York, 1965), pp. 86–7.

[25] Previously controls had existed as to the terms of overseas loans and, to a diminishing extent after 1920, their destination.

[26] Keynes Papers, Macmillan Committee, Notes of Discussions, 28 November 1930, p. 20.

[27] Ibid., p. 21.
[28] Ibid., pp. 20–2; Committee on Finance and Industry (Macmillan Committee), *Minutes of Evidence* (London, 1931), Q391–5, 1352–68, 1584.
[29] Clay, op. cit., pp. 144–5, 239–40.
[30] Macmillan Committee, *Evidence,* Q392, 395.
[31] Keynes Papers, Macmillan Committee, Notes of Discussions, 28 November 1930, p. 21.
[32] See, for example, P.R.O. T160/111/F4319/1, Norman to Chairman of Bankers' Clearing House, 1 February 1922 and 14 January 1924.
[33] C. Iversen, *Aspects of the Theory of International Capital Movements* (London, 1935), p. 85.
[34] Royal Institute of International Affairs, *The Problem of International Investment* (London, 1937), p. 77.
[35] However, whether it would reduce the volume of business to the same extent as the suasive controls is another matter. If it did not, and if the increase in business (ex controls) increased profits by more than the capital losses resulting from the rise in bank rate, the issuing houses might prefer it.
[36] J. M. Atkin, *British Overseas Investment, 1918-31,* unpub. Ph.D. dissertation, University of London (1968), presents the results of his research using the worksheets.
[37] Clay, op. cit., p. 145.
[38] As indicated by the reactions to Walter Leaf's 'trial balloon' of the early summer. On this, see Moggridge, op. cit., pp. 31, 36.
[39] Royal Institute of International Affairs, op. cit., p. 134.
[40] See, for example, Moggridge, op. cit. pp. 33–4.
[41] P.R.O. T160/197/F752 ,01/2, Committee on the Currency and Bank of England Note Issues, Third Draft Report, para. 30.
[42] P.R.O. T175/4, Niemeyer to Chancellor, 5 March 1925; Niemeyer, Memorandum, 29 November 1924.
[43] The proceeds of this loan were kept in London, presumably by agreement, until well after the return to gold. See Clarke, op. cit., p. 113.
[44] Clay, op. cit., p. 145.
[45] P.R.O. T176/17, Norman to Niemeyer, 11 May 1925.
[46] P.R.O. T176/17, Niemeyer to Churchill, 13 May 1925.
[47] P.R.O. T176/17, Niemeyer to Churchill, 27 May 1925; Niemeyer to Lambert, 30 May 1925.
[48] P.R.O. T176/17, Lambert to Leith-Ross, 5 June 1925.
[49] P.R.O. T176/17, Leith-Ross to Fergusson, 8 June 1925; Norman to Churchill, 9 June 1925.
[50] P.R.O. Cab. 58/1, Meeting of 18 June 1925, Conclusion 4.
[51] Thus Australia, for example, instead of borrowing £20 million in London, placed only £5 million of its July 1925 issue in London and raised the balance in New York. P.R.O. T176/17, Niemeyer to Churchill, 21 July 1925.
[52] *The Nation and Athenaeum,* 26 September 1925, p. 774; *The Bankers' Magazine,* CXX (980), November 1925, p. 641; P.R.O. T176/17, Churchill to Niemeyer, 21 July 1925.
[53] P.R.O. T176/17, Niemeyer to Churchill, 21 July 1925.
[54] P.R.O. Cab. 58/9, Committee of Civil Research, Overseas Loans Sub-Committee, *Report,* para. 24; Macmillan Committee, *Evidence,* Q7597.
[55] Federal Reserve Bank of New York Archives, Norman to Strong, No. 56, 15 October 1925.
[56] Federal Reserve Bank of New York Archives, Strong to Norman, No. 93, 22

October 1925. This cable was written to Sir Charles Addis, a director of the Bank.

[57] P.R.O. Cab. 58/9, Overseas Loans Sub-Committee, *Report*. The recommended date for the removal of the embargo was omitted 'in view of the exceptional need for secrecy' from para. 41, but it appeared in the second draft of 12 October in P.R.O. T176/17, Niemeyer Papers.

[58] Both dates were under consideration in late October. Federal Reserve Bank of New York Archives, Norman to Strong, No. 80, 30 October 1925.

[59] The speech appears in *The Times*, 5 November 1925.

[60] The one suggestion I have found occurred in an unsigned note in *The Nation and Athenaeum* of 13 November 1926 (p. 205), which the marked copy of that issue in the Keynes Papers reveals to have been by Keynes, which ran as follows:

> The view, which we have expressed strongly in The Nation that there had better be no more Foreign Government Loans for the present has, we understand, been accepted in responsible City circles. An exception will be made in favour of the Bulgarian Loan, which is to appear shortly under the League of Nations. But other applicants will be quite definitely discouraged. Thus, in effect, probably by agreement rather than by open compulsion, the old semi-official embargo has been largely restored.

[61] This occurred also in the case of Empire loans. See Atkin, op. cit., pp. 172-4.

[62] Royal Institute of International Affairs, op. cit., p. 173.

[63] P.R.O. T160/470/F10549/1, Vansittart to the Secretary of the Treasury, 28 November 1927; Revelstoke to Churchill, 26 March 1928, and enclosed Memorandum. The Colwyn Committee had recommended that the tax go if it hindered foreign issues. Committee on National Debt and Taxation, *Report*, Cmd. 2800 (London, 1927), para. 562–5. At the time of writing the *Report*, 1926, the Committee did not believe that the tax was impairing London's competitive position.

[64] P.R.O. T160/470/F10549/1, Revelstoke Memorandum, 26 March 1928, pp. 4, 6.

[65] P.R.O. T160/470/F10549/1–2, Hopkins to Grigg, 23 April 1928; Churchill to Hopkins and Gowers, 4 July 1928; Hopkins to Financial Secretary, 27 November 1928; Phillips to Hopkins, 9 January 1929; Phillips to Hopkins, 9 July 1929; Hopkins to Grigg, 10 July 1929; Phillips to Hopkins, 6 February 1930; Leith-Ross to Hopkins, 24 March 1930.

[66] P.R.O. T175/4, Leith-Ross to Churchill, 6 October 1928; Hopkins to Norman, 10 October 1928.

[67] Clay, op. cit, p. 238. However, in 1930 Clay refers to a tightening of controls (op. cit., p. 368).

[68] The speech appears in full in *The Bankers' Magazine*, CXXVIII (1026), September 1929, pp. 411–19, esp. p. 416. For the Bank's reaction, see P.R.O. T176/13, Harvey to Hopkins, 26 July 1929.

[69] P.R.O. T176/13, Hopkins to Grigg, 13 August 1929; Clay, op. cit., p. 253.

[70] P.R.O. T160/533/F13296/1–2, Hopkins, Foreign Issues – Discussion with the Governor, 9 February 1933; Warren Fisher to Chancellor, 30 November 1933.

[71] Appendix Table 2 summarizes what we do know.

[72] P.R.O. T175/4, Norman to Warren Fisher, 2 October 1928. See also T175/4, Norman to Niemeyer, 21 February 1927; Middlemas and Barnes, op. cit., p. 182.

[73] R. Kindersley, 'British foreign investments in 1928', *Economic Journal*, XL
      (158), June 1930, p. 176. As R. H. Brand, a director of Lazards, put it:

      When the Bank of England does agree and an international issue is made
      partly in London, partly in New York, and partly in Amsterdam, it is ten
      to one within six months London and Amsterdam have bought back
      nearly all the New York issue. The Americans do not hold it. They take
      the commission and make the issue, but they do not place it really like
      [sic] we do. They have a selling syndicate which holds it until they can
      sell it abroad very largely. (Keynes Papers, Macmillan Committee, Notes
      of Discussions, 28 November 1930, p. 21)

[74] R. Kindersley, 'British foreign investments in 1930', *Economic Journal*,
      XLII (166), June 1932, p. 193.
[75] Macmillan Committee, *Evidence*, Q1352, 1358, 6821–2.
[76] H. B. Lary and Associates, *The United States in the World Economy*,
      (Washington, 1943), p. 107, table 10; A. E. Kahn, *Great Britain in the
      World Economy* (New York, 1946), p. 163, esp. footnote 15.
[77] During the 1920s, for example, life insurance companies, with the National
      Mutual in the vanguard, became more adventurous in their portfolio
      management and in some respects 'discovered' the New York Market. The
      aggregate statistics for all companies give little indication of this change, for
      it occurred outside the area of government issue, the only one even broadly
      classified as to origin, and largely in the area of debentures, preference
      shares and, occasionally, ordinary shares. For the American and other
      overseas interests of the National Mutual, whose overseas securities rose
      from 10.07 to 34.59 per cent of its security portfolio (rather than from 8.4
      to 11.0 per cent, as one might gather from the published balance sheet)
      between 1926 and 1929, see Keynes Papers, Files NM/1$_4$, 1$_5$, 3$_1$, 3$_2$,
      P.C./1$_1$.
[78] Of course, these deflationary measures might have only a small effect on
      domestic incomes and employment as the rise in interest rates needed to
      attract increased foreign balances might be very small.
[79] Assuming, of course, that the centre that made the loan actually held the
      securities after issuing them. See above, p. 126.
[80] W. B. Reddaway *et al., The Effects of U.K. Direct Investment Overseas,
      Interim and Final Reports* (Cambridge, 1967 and 1968); G. C. Hufbauer
      and F. M. Adler, 'Overseas manufacturing investment and the balance of
      payments', *Tax Policy Research Study Number One* (Washington, n.d.).
[81] Thus the fact that 95 per cent of Indian Loans raised in the U.K. in the year
      ending 1 March 1923 were spent in the U.K. is not relevant in this context,
      for in so far as India would have spent the proceeds of, say, American loans
      in the U.K. the additional British exports to India would have occurred in
      any case. As it was the Colonial authorities who were borrowing, it would
      seem likely that the proportion spent in the U.K. would have been almost
      as large as if the funds had come from the U.S. R. B. Stewart, 'Great
      Britain's foreign loan policy', *Economica*, N.S. V (17), February 1938, p.
      53.
[82] See J. W. F. Rowe, 'Studies in the artificial control of raw material supplies,
      No. 3, Brazilian coffee', London and Cambridge Economic Service, *Special
      Memorandum No. 35*, January 1932, pp. 36, 37, 52, 56-7; H, Feis, *The
      Diplomacy of the Dollar 1919-1932* (New York, 1966), pp. 31-2.
[83] P.R.O. T160/394/F11324, Harvey to Leith-Ross, 16 April 1931; D. C. M.

Platt, *Finance, Trade and Politics in British Foreign Policy 1815-1914* (Oxford, 1968), p. 27.

[84] P.R.O. T160/470/F10549/1, Hawtrey to Leith-Ross, 1 December and 26 November 1927.

[85] *Memoranda on Certain Proposals Relating to Unemployment*, Cmd. 3331 (London, 1929), p. 51. See also pp. 48–9. Here it must be noted that the Liberal proposals were not at all clear on the mechanism involved; J. M. Keynes and H. D. Henderson, *Can Lloyd George Do It? The Pledge Examined* (London, 1929), pp. 37–8.

[86] The favouritism granted to certain classes of overseas lending by these Acts, along with a belief that there was a divergence between private and social returns in overseas investment, lay at the root of Keynes's early suggestions for restriction. Later the grounds upon which he based his case for restrictions changed considerably, and became one of the safeguards to a programme of domestic expansion. J. M. Keynes, 'Foreign investment and the national advantage', *Nation and Athenaeum*, 9 August 1924, p. 586; 'Home versus foreign investment: further suggestions for revision of the trustee list', *Manchester Guardian Commercial*, 21 August 1924; Committee on National Debt and Taxation, *Minutes of Evidence* (London, 1927), esp. Q4013–14; Keynes Papers, Macmillan Committee, Notes of Discussions, 6 March 1930, pp. 8 ff., and 28 November 1930, pp. 20 ff.; J. M. Keynes, *A Treatise on Money* (London, 1930), II, pp. 311–15, 374–7. On the role of the capital market in industrial finance, see A. T. K. Grant, *A Study of the Capital Market in Britain from 1919-1936* (London, 1967), esp. part 3; T. Balogh, *Studies in Financial Organisation* (Cambridge, 1947), pp. 274 ff.; H. Clay, 'The financing of industrial enterprise', *Transactions of the Manchester Statistical Society, 1932.*

[87] For developments in the 1930s, see Stewart, op. cit.; Balogh, op. cit., pp. 268–72. For wartime problems, plus a brief review of the 1930s, see R. S. Sayers, *Financial Policy 1939-1945* (London, 1956), ch. 8.

APPENDIX

TABLE 1

(a) Unit wage costs in industry in four countries, 1925-31

1925 = 100

Country	1925	1926	1927	1928	1929	1930	1931
U.K.	100	100	97	97	95	92	90
Germany	100	102	101	106	112	113	108
U.S.	100	98	96	93	90	88	79
Sweden	100	90	87	88	80	72	70

(b) Indices of export unit values (incurrent dollars), 1925-31

U.K. = 100

U.K.	100	100	100	100	100	100	100
Belgium	72	69	65	69	72	72	75
France	73	63	67	64	64	64	63
Germany	73	77	81	83	83	82	86
Netherlands	83	81	82	83	84	80	79
Sweden	91	99	96	97	97	95	94
Switzerland	90	88	90	94	95	95	102
U.S.	84	82	81	84	84	79	74
Competitors' Average	81	80	80	82	83	81	82

Note: German unit wage costs in 1925 were approximately 87 per cent of British costs in 1924-5 while French unit wage costs remained below Britain's throughout the period (see source (a), pp. 224–9).

Sources: (a) E. H. Phelps Brown and M. H. Browne, *A Century of Pay* (London, 1968), appendix III.

(b) A Maddison, 'Growth and fluctuations in the world economy, 1870-1960', *Banca Nazionale del Lavoro Quarterly Review*, June 1962, table 29.

TABLE 2

Balance of payments of the United Kingdom, 1924-1931 (£ million)

	1924	1925	1926	1927	1928	1929	1930	1931
CURRENT ACCOUNT								
Visible Trade								
Retained imports (c.i.f.)	1137	1167	1116	1095	1075	1111	958	797
Exports of U.K. produce (f.o.b.)	801	773	653	709	724	729	571	391
Net	−336	−394	−463	−386	−351	−382	−387	−406
Invisibles								
Shipping (net)	+140	+124	+120	+140	+130	+130	+105	+ 80
Investment income (net)	+220	+250	+250	+250	+250	+250	+220	+170
Short Interest and commissions (net)	+ 60	+ 60	+ 60	+ 60	+ 65	+ 65	+ 55	+ 30
Other invisibles (net)	+ 15	+ 15	+ 15	+ 15	+ 15	+ 15	+ 15	+ 10
Government transactions (net)	− 25	− 11	− 4	+ 4	+ 15	+ 24	+ 19	+ 14
Net	+410	+438	+449	+467	+475	+484	+414	+304
Current Balance	+ 74	+ 44	− 14	+ 81	+124	+102	+ 27	−102
LONG-TERM CAPITAL ACCOUNT								
New issues	−134	− 88	−112	−139	−143	− 96	− 98	− 41
Repayments	n.a.	n.a.	+ 27	+ 34	+ 35	+ 49	+ 39	+ 27
Other long term movements	n.a.	n.a.	n.a.	n.a.	n.a.	n.a.	+ 40	+ 15
Balance of long term capital	−134	− 88	− 85	−105	−108	− 47	− 19	+ 1
Balance of current and long term capital transactions	− 60	− 44	− 99	− 24	+ 16	+ 55	+ 8	−101

TABLE 2 (continued)

Balance of payments of the United Kingdom, 1924-1931 (£ million)

	1924	1825	1926	1927	1928	1929	1930	1931
MONETARY MOVEMENTS								
Change in short term liabilities	n.a.	n.a.	n.a.	n.a.	+136	− 84	− 26	−293
Change in acceptances on foreign account	n.a.	n.a.	n.a.	n.a.	− 61	+ 25	+ 15	+ 35
Change in gold and foreign exchange reserves	+ 15	+ 10	− 23	− 22	+ 19	+ 8	− 7	− 36
Change in central bank and other assistance							+ 7	+102
Balance of monetary movements	+ 15	+ 10	− 23	− 22	+ 94	− 51	− 11	−192
Balancing Item	+ 45	+ 34	+122	+ 46	−110	− 4	+ 3	+293

Note: n.a. = not available

Sources:

Current account – Board of Trade Journal.

Long term capital account – A. E. Kahn, *Great Britain in the World Economy*, table 13.

Monetary Movements –
Short-term liabilities – 1930-1, D. Williams, 'London and the 1931 financial crisis', *Economic History Review*, 2nd Ser., XV (3), April 1963, p. 528.
– Pre 1930, Committee on Finance and Industry, *Report*, Cmd. 3897 (London, 1931), appendix 1, table 11, adjusted on the assumption that the Committee's Figures for Deposits Bills and Advances understated the true figure by the same proportion as the 1930 figure understates Williams's estimate.

Acceptances – Ibid., appendix I, table 11.

Gold and foreign exchange reserves – Bank of England, *Quarterly Bulletin*, X(1), March 1970, Supplement, adjusted for appreciation of sterling 1923-5, depreciation of sterling 1931, and Currency Note Account gold.

Central bank and other assistance – Federal Reserve Bank of New York Archives, File C261 – Bank of England, P.R.O., T160/444/F12901, Lefeaux to Hopkins, 4 March 1932.

DISCUSSION 4

Chairman: J. Williamson
Prepared Comments: P. Temin

Temin: The paper deals essentially with two questions. The first is to what extent there were in fact effective informal restrictions on overseas lending. The conclusion of the paper on this point is that aside from a transitional period in 1924-5 there were very few effective restrictions. The second, raised in the last few pages, is what the effect was on the British economy of the foreign lending that did take place. This second question is broken into two parts: the effect on exports, and the effect on national income. The discussion on exports is quite cogent and convincing, but that on national income less so. Moggridge criticizes the Treasury for adopting a simple classical model in which regulation is always and inevitably futile, and apparently has a Keynesian model in his own mind, but he never specifies which model he thinks was in fact operating. The Keynesian model is surely a reasonable one to apply to the inter-war period, in which case the argument of the paper should perhaps be directed away from the effect of capital market controls on the institutional details of the sources of finance and towards their effect on the determinants of investment and, possibly, on the consumption function.

Aldcroft: The statistical difficulties, prior to the theoretical difficulties mentioned by Temin, are great. Estimating the effect of controls on capital flows, especially short term, given the data limitations before 1928 and even after, was no easy task. One would have to entirely rework the balance of payment figures.

Moggridge: He agreed with Aldcroft that the figures would need to be reworked, but was fairly optimistic that the bulk of the investments could be uncovered in the records of limited insurance companies and unit trusts, especially for long term flows, but also some short term flows. It was fortunate for the purposes of this paper that the insurance company records were usable. He had discovered them in the course of other research.

Edelstein: He wanted to ask a question on the impact of the capital redirection one can in fact measure for John Atkin, who has recently done a good deal of work on British investments between the wars. Contrary to Moggridge, Atkin believes there was a strong link between British investments abroad and British exports in this period, as, for example, with the borrowing and importing by Argentine railways, the colonial refunding of previous short term borrowing for the purpose of importation from Britain, and the borrowings by the French railways. *Moggridge*: He had explicitly assumed that if London had not done the lending someone else would. This assumption, which is especially appropriate for the period up to mid-1928, meant that in all probability the additional exports resulting from the fact that London did the lending would be relatively small. The borrowings by the French railways were *indirect* because direct lending to France was controlled (France had not funded her war debts to Britain). Moreover, the limited effectiveness of the direct controls illustrates the point that the link between exports and direct lending in the 1920s was largely irrelevant. There were several Australian issues floated in New York between 1925 and 1928, but it is very probable that the securities ended up in London. The selective controls had little effect unless, as in 1924-5, attempts to get around them were foolish. The expected appreciation of sterling probably limited evasion, for it was uneconomic in that case to buy dollar-denominated securities. However, on the whole the controls had so little effect that, in short, the connection with exports is irrelevant.

Saul: In any case the connection between investments and exports, except for dependent colonies such as India, was slight. Australia and New Zealand were buying where they pleased. And much of the investment went to pay workers in the borrowing country, not to buy machines from the lending countries. On another matter, how important over the long run did Moggridge think the meetings were between Montagu Norman and Governor Strong, in which they developed methods whereby Strong was able to relieve the pressure on the London market temporarily; or were they offset by the difficulty with the Bank of France − that is, the constant fear that funds frozen by France in London would be unfrozen?

Moggridge: He thought the meetings with Strong served only as palliatives. Moreover, these well documented meetings tended to obscure the very real cooperation Norman received from both France and Germany, apparently by agreement, at crucial junctures. The fear on the part of Norman concerning France was that any unfriendly British act might result in Britain being driven off gold. However, Britain's position was so precarious that Norman feared for the gold standard on many other occasions as well, the French affair of 1927 being just one. The American pressure of 1928-9 was another.

Engerman: How was the calculation in the first footnote on the effect of depreciating the pound by 10 per cent done?

Moggridge: It was a rough, back-of-the-envelope calculation, using pessimistic estimates of the elasticities, to estimate the effect on the level of demand and employment. The estimate of the elasticity of demand for exports, which was greater than one, was taken from Maizels, Zelder, Harberger and Brown.

Hughes: Balogh at one point used an elasticity less than one. In that case, the problem was not that the pound was pegged too high in the 1920s, but that it was not pegged high enough: it should have been at seven or eight dollars!

Moggridge: Hughes's argument was only plausible in periods such as that immediately after World War II, when some of Britain's competitors were out of the picture.

Falkus: He wondered about three points. First, by the criterion now used, the current balance, Britain was in fact undervalued, not overvalued in the 1920s. Second, as Richard Sayers has put it, it is arguable that unemployment was a problem of regions concentrating on industries for which there just was no demand at any reasonable exchange rate, and, consequently, a 10 per cent devaluation would have been ineffective in curing unemployment. Finally, a devaluation would not have changed the exchange rate with the colonies which, after all, were very important trading partners of Britain.

Moggridge: Although the current account balance was in surplus, a strong case can be made that the surplus was not large enough to allow the authorities to achieve their policy goals regarding overseas lending, trade, employment and the like. Of course, if the authorities had *different* goals, which did not require the earning of as much foreign exchange, sterling could well have been regarded as undervalued. Admittedly, a 10 per cent devaluation might not have restored export demand in the traditional industries sufficient to allow employment approaching full employment levels in *these* industries. However, a lower exchange rate for sterling would have allowed, through a reduction in import competition and some rise in export competitiveness, an expansion in the level of demand in the U.K. as a whole, drawing off the unemployed in the traditional industries. That the external sector acted as a depressing influence on the level of domestic activity in every year after 1923 except two was not unconnected with exchange rate policy. A devaluation would not have changed Britain's exchange rate with the colonies and thus would not have changed Britain's competitive position *vis-à-vis* colonial domestic producers of manufactures, but it would have changed the position *vis-à-vis* other exporters to the colonies, an indirect effect of possibly greater importance for Britain.

III *Economic Efficiency and the Choice of Technique*

5

The landscape and the machine: technical interrelatedness, land tenure and the mechanization of the corn harvest in Victorian Britain

PAUL A. DAVID

The observation that the mid-nineteenth-century farming landscape in Britain was not congenial to the introduction of agricultural machinery forms the point of departure in this inquiry. Certainly there is little novelty attached to this observation. Contemporary writers in the agricultural press frequently discussed the problems of using horse-drawn and steam-powered equipment in field operations where terrain conditions were 'unsuitable', and references to these difficulties dot the major scholarly works on the modernization of British agriculture. The admirable account of the 1846-1914 era provided by Christabel S. Orwin and Edith H. Whetham is, perhaps, rather unusual in going beyond mere mention of the subject to suggest that terrain conditions exerted a powerful influence upon the extent and the spatial pattern of farm mechanization. In reference to the situation that existed in Britain during the period immediately following repeal of the Corn Laws, Orwin and Whetham have written [1] :

> Broadcast sowing, hand weeding, the sickle and the scythe were still generally used on many farms, especially where rough or stony soils shook to pieces the new-fangled inventions of the agricultural engineers. . . . To be effective and economic, the new implements required a new system of farming — large level fields with straight hedges and wide gateways, and with no boggy patches and land-fast stones. It is not surprising therefore that the new implements and the new type of farming were to be found mainly on the eastern side of the country, from Lincolnshire through Northumberland and the Lothians to Aberdeenshire, on the big fields newly created from marsh and stones, and farmed in large units.

Yet it must be agreed that the influence of the landscape inherited from long periods of agricultural settlement has still to be acknowledged as one of the dominant themes in the agrarian history of nineteenth-century Europe. Indeed, the point that the physical state of the land and the arrangement of existing fields, fences and buildings

145

may have been of some consequence to the reception farmers accorded the new techniques of production, generally fails to be properly understood and appreciated. For one thing, it has tended to be all but submerged in the flow of words currently lavished upon the putative role of rural 'labour abundance' as the crucial condition inhibiting farm mechanization throughout western Europe. This prevailing theme, which could be illustrated with innumerable passages from the recent literature dealing specifically with the British experience, is concisely conveyed in Folke Dovring's comments on the slow European adoption of agricultural machinery [2]:

> Machinery primarily designed to save labour could not be expected to spread very much until labour could be said to be scarce in one sense or another. Such was the case in America through most of the nineteenth century; but in fully settled western Europe, farm labour could become scarce only after the agricultural population had ceased to increase in absolute numbers and, to a higher degree, after it had begun to fall.

A re-evaluation of the validity of the 'American labour scarcity thesis' — and that of its obverse, the hoary 'British labour abundance doctrine' — as it has been applied to agricultural technology, is certainly long overdue [3]. But I must beg leave to defer treatment of this larger subject to another occasion. It is not my purpose here to adduce arguments and detailed evidence controverting the oft-stated, but sometimes only implicit proposition that comparative labour abundance *vis-à-vis* the United States bore principal responsibility for delaying or retarding the adoption of mechanized techniques in British (and western European) farming during the nineteenth century. I do mean, nevertheless, to advance the independent claim for considering the state of the farming landscape of mid-Victorian Britain as a significant impediment in the way of rapid and widespread mechanization of field operations during the second half of the century. Although I shall not be able to refrain from remarking upon the differences separating Britain and American in this respect, and in others closely related to it, the focus of the discussion must remain almost exclusively upon the British side of the story; an explicit assessment and explanation of Anglo-American differences in the extent and rate of diffusion of agricultural innovations would pose complications demanding treatment at much greater length.

Even so, from the study of one such innovation — the mechanical reaper — it will become apparent that the substitution of horse-powered machines for manual labour on Britain's farms was a more complex affair than naive neo-classical models of factor substitution allow; it transcends the overly simplified general theoretical terms in which the choice of techniques in Britain versus that in America has lately come to be discussed; it forces an encounter with technical and institutional conditions whose significance has for too long passed without adequate consideration from either economists or historians. Limited as the case of the reaping machine is, the complexities it raises do seem well worth confronting and trying to analyse in rigorous fashion [4]. For they are far from being peculiar to the diffusion of mechanical innovations in agriculture, and turn out to have a direct bearing upon at least one major line of explanation that has been advanced for Britain's loss of her position of technological leadership in the course of the nineteenth century.

THE LANDSCAPE AND THE REAPING MACHINE

When the Crystal Palace was opened in 1851, the reaping of grain crops with machines as a practical matter was essentially unknown anywhere in the British Isles, and the appearance of the 'American Reapers' sent by Obed Hussey and Cyrus H. McCormick to the Great Exhibition created a considerable stir of interest. Given the prevailing structure of harvest wage rates, the overdraft rate of interest at which equipment purchases might be financed, and the prices at which these machines could be purchased in the years around 1851, manual sheaf-delivery reapers like those exhibited at Hyde Park would have represented a quite profitable investment for a British farmer whose acreage under cereals matched the average of the farms situated on 'the corn side of the island' — provided his fields offered suitable conditions under which to operate the device [5]. Such field conditions were to be found in the Lothians, for example; and it is notable that by the early 1860s virtually the whole of the corn harvest of that region was being cut by machine. The progressive Lothians formed a British topographical counterpart to the American Midwest, but — unlike the latter region — carried little quantitative weight on the national farming scene. Although the corn harvest of this lowland district might have been entirely mechanized, my estimates indicate that by 1863 rather less than 6 per cent of Great Britain's wheat, oats, rye and barley acreage was being cut with reaping machines. The corresponding measure of the extent of the mechanical reaper's adoption in the United States had already passed the 15 per cent mark on the eve of the Civil War, and climbed above 78 per cent by 1870, whereas in 1874 probably more than 53 per cent of the British corn harvest was still being cut by the sickle and the scythe [6].

One cannot hope to understand this divergence between British and American experience during the third quarter of the nineteenth century without observing that the landscape of Britain's principal grain-producing districts — especially if viewed in juxaposition to the United States setting — was on balance inimical to the immediate successful introduction of the mechanical innovation that had been suddenly brought to the attention of her farmers through the medium of the Great Exhibition. While it has recently become less than fashionable to notice them, the nineteenth century offered significant contrasts between Britain and America in dimensions other than that of the relative prices of the factors of production. In the United States the broad, level and stone-free prairies of the Midwest, where grain production was becoming increasingly concentrated even before the Civil War, provided extensive regions whose topography was singularly well suited to the operation of horse-drawn machines in field work. And it was, of course, in precisely that physical setting that the cumbersome reapers designed by Hussey and McCormick and their followers first gained popular acceptance. As I have elsewhere shown [7], so technically hospitable an environment in itself was not sufficient to induce the farmers of the American Midwest to abandon hand methods of harvesting the small grains prior to the 1850s. At the halfway point in the century, American grain farming was actually not so much further down the road towards harvest mechanization than British agriculture: less than 1 per cent of the acreage under wheat, oats, rye and barley in the United States appears to have been cut by reaping machines in 1849-50. On the other hand, the favourable physical conditions did mean that during the 1850s — when an alteration of the structure of Midwestern factor prices combined with a rise in average farm acreage devoted to small grain crops, providing a stronger inducement to substitute machinery for labour on the region's farms — the mechanization of the harvest could proceed without the limitations that terrain problems would have imposed, and actually did impose in sections of the Northeast and the seaboard South.

Two features of the farming landscape in Britain must be considered as having obstructed the progress of mechanical reaping: the character of the terrain – which is to say, the nature of the field surfaces across which the implements would have to be drawn; and secondly, the size, shape and arrangement of the fields – or more generally speaking, the layout of farms' cereal acreage.

From the outset terrain problems were recognized. They occasioned the single note of caution Phillip Pusey felt obliged to sound in reporting to the Royal Agricultural Society on the results of his trial of the McCormick reaper in 1851 [8]:

> This trial was witnessed by many farmers, and no fault was found with the work. The land, I should say, however, being stock land is even; where ridges and water-furrows exist, some difficulties seem to arise.

The exact nature of the manifold 'difficulties' on ridge-and-furrow land soon became evident, and can be adumbrated from scattered reports of the performance of British, as well as of American machine designs, under trial and practical field conditions during the 1850s and 1860s.

The larger, heavier models – like Croskill's resurrection of the Bell reaper dating from 1826-8, and the Burgess and Key swath-delivery adaptation of McCormick's machine – were especially likely to be found 'now and then sticking fast into the uneven ground, especially when the off wheels descended into the furrow; . . .' [9] Secondly, where the ground was not level, and particularly where high-ridge ploughing had left a pronounced corduroy field profile, the reaping machines' draft might prove too great: a normal, easily managed two-horse team could not maintain a steady rate of forward motion sufficiently rapid to prevent the reciprocating knives of the cutter bar from clogging [10]. The larger the swath taken, the more serious was the problem of draft, and hence the poorer the performance of the machine was likely to be over uneven terrain. Smaller models, by cutting a swath narrower than the 5 ft 3 in standard, 'were certainly enabled to do their work rather better; but, on the whole, not so thoroughly satisfactorily as we could have wished to witness' [11]. Thus, among the early machines that cut the standard width swath, manual delivery reapers on Hussey's pattern won considerable favour in many parts of Britain for reasons other than their low costs [12]:

> They are lighter of draft, less liable to derangement, . . . more easily managed, and thus more to be depended upon for the regular performance of a fair amount of daily work than their heavier rivals.

And when sturdy but lighter, more compact and more efficiently geared reaping machines became available in the 1860s, they alone would be considered by farmers in hilly districts, or in areas like the North Riding of Yorkshire where the old ridge-and-furrow system remained [13]. Finally, the pronounced undulations in such terrain also adversely affected the quality of the work. For, if the machine's cutter bar was set to take the grain properly at the crown of the ridge, it left the stubble too high in the furrows, causing losses of straw and troubles for the binders and stookers who would have to cope with the sheaves of varying lengths.

Elsewhere on the island the progress of wheeled implements like reaping and mowing machines was obstructed by the presence of open irrigation trenches and deep drainage furrows, or 'water-cuts' [14]. This source of difficulty was especially noticed in Essex and Suffolk, where fields customarily were ploughed in long 'stetches' of varying width, each stetch being limited on its two sides by deep furrows that served as gutters to carry off the surface water [15]. On heavy lands, as in the Suffolk strong loam belt, close spacing of water-cuts of this kind were required and dictated stetches as narrow as 2 yards across. Narrow stetches, in addition, were usually ridged up slightly to further improve the drainage. Such fields proved notoriously inhospitable to the early reaping machines, and at later dates to self-binders and combine harvesters, for, 'the continual jolting over deep furrows soon put the most robust machine out of action' [16].

Of course, in the absence of effective subsurface drainage, grain fields adequately drained by high-ridge ploughing or water-cuts would at least have been freer from the hazards encountered in negotiating soggy ground with a horse-drawn reaping machine weighing upwards of half a ton. Additional horses could be used to overcome the greater friction on wet fields, although withal, as one farmer despairingly reported, 'at the turns the [reaping machine's] wheels sunk so deeply into the soft ground, that care and the occasional aid of a lever were required' [17]. In some districts these problems were especially serious. The fen arable in Huntingdon was said to be 'mostly too soft to carry reaping machines' [18], while on Lincolnshire's heavy clays — even after underdrainage was installed — in wet weather the horses' hooves sank deeply into the soil [19]. Such considerations had led to the double furrows separating Suffolk's stetches being used 'in every operation, either in sowing the seed or after the seed was in the ground, as a trackway for the horses, which are thus never permitted to trample or injure the tender soil' [20]. The fact that the water-cuts formed impassable barriers to wheeled implements had contributed to this practice, by forcing cultivation to be done along the length of the stetch. Yet, where the movement of horses and machines was so constrained, the breadth of the swath cut by the generally available makes of reaping machines often turned out to be ill matched to the width of the cultivated tracts. Indeed, as Caird observed in 1850-1, this was a more general problem and Suffolk farmers had overcome it only by providing themselves with drills and harrows designed to fit the dimensions of their particular stetches [21]. But the reaping machine, not being similarly built up from modular components, proved more difficult to adapt.

The lessons learned at the expense of those who purchased the new machines without heed to the state of their farm's terrain were succinctly communicated to the membership of the Highland and Agricultural Society by Jacob Wilson in 1864 [22]:

Too much, therefore *ought* not to be expected from the reaping machine; and where it *is* employed, care should be taken that the previous preparation and treatment of the land be such as will *allow* it to work to the greatest advantage. Such preparation should consist in the thorough drainage of the land and subsequent levelling of the surface, in the abolition of water-cuts and furrows, as well as of large stones, and in properly finishing the process of cultivation by rolling, &c. By careful observance of these few points, the chief obstacles to reaping by machinery will thus be removed.

Farm layout was another matter. Alderman J. J. Mechi, that irrepressible lay apostle of High Farming, in a speech before the Coggleshall Institute in 1850, gave it as his opinion that a farm of 600 acres [23]

should represent a square mile with a farmery in its centre, having half a mile diverging roads to its extremities; whereas now, under the system of old custom and inalterability, a farm of that size generally involved the intricate threading of miles of almost impassible green and muddy lanes, with fields of every form except the right one.

Reaping machines did not require rectangular, or preferably square, fields as did the steam-ploughing rigs that were being tried in Britain — notably in the Lothians and Northumberland — during these decades. Nevertheless, small and irregularly shaped fields did cause losses of time in turning, particularly when the lie of the grain called for the cutting to proceed in a direction orthogonal to the principle axis of an oblong enclosure. And where very small fields were common — such as those of the 160 acre Devonshire farm visited by Caird shortly after its average field size had been increased to 10 acres by the removal of 7 miles of hedgerows — the early reaping machines would have had to be set to work in two or more enclosures during the course of a single day. Devon was, of course, quite notorious for the smallness of its farms' enclosures, but was not so exceptional as is sometimes thought. In the parts of Durham that had been longest enclosed, average field sizes ran from 2 to 6 acres during the 1850s [24]. Considerable time might thus be spent leaving ancillary harvest labourers less than fully occupied whilst the machine was being resituated. For it was complained that the reaping machines' form was 'unwieldy, and requires much time and labour in taking to pieces for removal from field to field or from farm to farm' [25].

Additional, albeit only marginal, wastage of time was likely to be incurred in moving equipment between adjacent enclosures, due to the separation of fields by hedges through which only a single gate had been let. But the grain ripe for harvesting did not necessarily lie in adjacent enclosures on the farm. Hence, when small dispersed fields required a number of moves during the day, carefully taking the reaping machine along miserable lanes that wound their way through the least well drained portions of the farm, the overall expenditure of time might amount to a significant reduction of the acreage that could actually be harvested by the cumbersome early models.

Still, in comparison with the problems encountered on farms whose fields remained unimproved by subsurface draining and levelling, the non-optimal aspects of typical farm layouts in mid-Victorian Britain posed rather subsidiary impediments to the efficient use of reaping machines. Certainly such was the implicit judgement of contemporaries, who fastened quickly upon drainage as the key to the matter. In 1852, James Slight — whose efforts to restore injured Scottish pride, in the aftermath of the American reapers' triumphant appearance, succeeded in retrieving Patrick Bell's swath-delivery machine from its long initial career of obscurity — thought he saw clearly the cause for the workable reaping machines invented in Britain during the first of the century having 'fallen so much into disuse'. They had simply appeared 'before their time' [26];

... that is to say, before the subject on which they were to act had
been prepared for their reception. In the first quarter of the present
century, furrow-draining, levelling high ridges, and filling up the old
deep intervening furrows, were only beginning to assume their due
prominence in the practice of agriculture; and so long as these
improvements remained in abeyance, the surface of the land was
very ill suited for such operations as that of a reaping machine.

Actually, the truth of the matter [27] seems to have been that prior
to the late 1840s the high purchase cost of the Bell reaper, relative to
the wage of the harvest labour it could displace, would have prevented
widespread adoption of the device on the large farms in the Scottish
lowlands, as well as south of the Tweed, even if the land improvements
described by Slight had not remained largely in abeyance. John Wilson's
formulation, offered a decade later, comes closer to the position one is
now inclined to maintain, in suggesting that changes in both the state of
the terrain *and* rural labour markets explain the curious re-emergence of
the neglected Bell reaper, which began to take its place alongside the
American-style machines in Britain's grain fields during the 1850s [28]:

Not only was manual labour then abundant and cheap ...; but
thorough draining had made little progress, and the land was
everywhere laid into high ridges, presenting a surface particularly
unfavourable for the successful working of a reaping machine. Now
[1862] conditions are reversed.

Wilson rather exaggerated the historical contrast in making his point.
Although contemporaries might properly be impressed with the
progress of drainage and kindred improvements since the second
quarter of the century, the physical transformation of Britain's
farmlands was far from complete twenty years after the Great
Exhibition opened. It is true that between 1846 and 1876 something
on the order of £24 million was spent on drainage and related works,
one third of it having been financed with public funds under the terms
of the programme of government loans for thorough drainage schemes
that had been set up by parliament in 1846-8. Yet Caird thought that
more than four-fifths of the farmland in England and Wales that ought
to have been drained still stood in need of that treatment in 1873. And
on the greater part of the 4 or 5 million acres that had been thus
improved by the mid-1870s the work was executed outside the
somewhat exacting conditions laid down by the Inclosure Commis-

sioners as qualification for public loans [29]. Drainage, moreover, was a necessary but not sufficient preparation for the mechanization of field operations. The layout of the existing stetches often conflicted with the desirable arrangment of runs for a more carefully calculated system of subsurface drains, which might well traverse both stetches and furrows, resulting in an awkward variation in the depth of soil above the installed pipes. Rather then taking the additional time and trouble to then plough out the ridges and level the field, the conflict could be resolved in favour of retaining the existing stetches:

> Field drains were therefore sometimes run down the old furrows, leaving the ridges to plague another generation of farmers whose drills and reapers were not adapted to undulating surfaces [30].

Thus, a quarter century after the advent of the American reaping machines, there remained much to be done even in Britain's corn counties if the landscape was to be thoroughly cleared of those vestiges of an older system of husbandry, which obstructed the harvesting of grain and the mowing of rotation grasses by horse-power.

And yet this cannot be the whole of the story. While the extent of the mechanical reaper's diffusion in Britain in the period after 1851 may have been *at any given moment of time* effectively circumscribed by the serious difficulties encountered in seeking to operate it on 'unimproved' arable, the pace at which farm improvement – and specifically land improvements – proceeded cannot legitimately be taken as an exogenously determined feature of the British environment. It might be admissible to argue that the lack of technical advances in the design and manufacture of suitable drainage materials in the period before the repeal of the Corn Laws had held up extensive land improvement. But clearly, from the early 1850s onward, this technical barrier had been removed by the successful machine production of cylindrical agricultural pipe, which offered drains that were cheap, durable and available in standard sizes for ready installations [31].

If, as appears to have been the case, mechanization of the corn harvest would have been a profitable undertaking on a great part of Britain's cereal acreage even at the beginning of the 1850s, supposing only that the more serious among the terrain problems surveyed here could have been first removed, the logic of the argument demands a reason why this significant profit opportunity could have remained only partially exploited for want of the indicated modifications. Putting the matter another way, the proposed explanation of the comparatively limited diffusion of mechanical reaping in Britain during the 1850s and 1860s may be correct so far as it goes; but it is unsatisfyingly incomplete until we also know why the farming community did not more generally heed the advice of Jacob Wilson, and instead suffered the land to remain in a condition that did not permit the machine to be employed to advantage in place of harvesters wielding the sickle and the scythe.

TECHNICAL INTERRELATEDNESS AND FARM MECHANIZATION – RECASTING THE PROBLEM

In seeking an answer to the question just posed, it is illuminating to begin with the perception of most of the physical obstructions to mechanical reaping surveyed by the preceding section as having been man-made, rather than of 'natural' origins. They represented the legacy of past capital formation directed towards improvement of the British farm. Some of these 'improvements', such as the drainage afforded by ridge-and-furrow contours, were, to be sure, the durable by-products of cultivation activities extending over a very long span of time. Conceived of in this way, the topography of British agriculture at the mid-point of the nineteenth century bears an immediate resemblance to the structure of industrial plant, which – at any given moment – remains as the heritage of investments in specific kinds of durable capital. The latter structure, in its turn, has sometimes been likened to the accumulation of strata deposited by historic geological action [32] ; in the agricultural context, however, it proves instructive to reverse the usual direction of the analogy.

For, by drawing attention to the features of the British farm landscape that appear to have obstructed ubiquitous application of the novel harvesting technique, we are in effect acknowledging the importance of compatibility between the various capital goods available for employment in agriculture. The problem of the landscape is one of the 'interrelatedness' of the techniques of grain harvesting on the one hand, and, on the other, the techniques used for drainage, wind damage control, the management of livestock, and on-farm transportation of field equipment. These being mutually complementary activities of the Victorian arable farm, any capital goods embodying techniques for their execution within this general system of husbandry must have been, at least, mutually compatible [33] .

To recast the farmer's problem in this formal way may seem strained and too unfamiliar; it is nonetheless useful in calling forcibly to mind the existence of parallel situations in other, non-agricultural branches of production. For it is widely recognized that attempts to introduce modern machinery into a plant composed of older equipment preforming complementary functions may be utterly frustrated by the technical incompatibility of the new with the old [34]. The inadequacy of the floor layout, pillar spacing and lighting arrangements in existing factory buildings appears to have hampered the installation of new, more automatic equipment in the British cotton textile industry – providing an oft-cited illustration of simple, yet frequently encountered problems of technical interrelatedness and incompatibility in the manufacturing sector [35]. Perhaps still better known is the instance cited by Veblen as illustrative of the penalties of Britain's having an early start: the impossibility of replacing the inefficiently small 10 ton railway coal wagons without also modifying the coal screens, weigh-bridges and sidings in the collieries, and altering the hoists and tips at the ports, to enable these facilities to accommodate the larger wagons [36].

Now, in the case at hand the difficulty posed by the presence of interrelatedness is essentially one of cost: the newly available type of capital equipment, the reaping machine, would have higher unit costs of operation when used in the environment of an outmoded physical 'plant', i.e. on a farm whose fields had not been rationally laid out, thoroughly underdrained and levelled. The implication this carried for the choice of harvest technique by the operator of such a farm is quite straightforward. Translated into the terms I have used in an earlier analysis of the adoption of mechanical reaping [37], operation of the machine in small enclosures and under terrain conditions causing it to stick in furrows or bog down at the turns obviously would reduce the acreage of grain it could cut in a normal working day. Since the crew responsible for the machine and the horses, and possibly also the labourers needed to bind up the sheaves and set them up in stooks, would remain on hand throughout the day, the number of man-days of labour saved through mechanization would be reduced – *per acre cut*. Time lost in frequent moves between enclosures would have the same consequence. Because sub-optimal farm conditions would thereby lower the realized per acre savings on labour costs that the farmer could set against the fixed capital charge he incurred for the use of the machine, a larger acreage would have to be harvested in an average season before the break-even point was reached for the conversion from hand to machine harvesting. Rough terrain might also take a toll by increasing normal maintenance expenses, or by actually shortening the expected service life of the machine and, hence, raising the (imputed) annual rental cost of the equipment. Other things being equal, this too would serve directly to raise the scale of the annual harvest operation required to just cover the interest and amortization charges entailed by the more capital-intensive technique. Of course, once the higher break-even scale – which I have called the 'threshold acreage' – thus established for sub-optimal operating conditions was reached, for farms further and further up in size distribution the adoption of mechanical reaping would be increasingly profitable [38].

Comparing Britain's 'unimproved' farms with farms of equal extent existing in an already 'improved' state – improved either as a result of remedial outlays made in the past, or because, as on the prairies of Illinois in the 1850s, durable capital formation of a kind incompatible with subsequent mechanization had never been undertaken – the higher costs of harvesting with machinery on the former would effectively have raised the threshold acreage and thereby reduced the profitability of abandoning the old, hand method of reaping grain. The distinction here between improved and unimproved farms does not turn on whether or not the land was in a virgin state; we may designate as 'unimproved' all farmlands that either in their original condition, or as a result of past investments that had become outmoded, possessed features incompatible with the efficient operation of reaping machines. Functionally, an unimproved farm in this context is one on which additional capital outlays would be required to remove existing incompatible elements, and 'install' wheeled implements like the early generations of mechanical reapers and mowers in technically optimal operating condition [39].

Of course it is possible that without some improvements being made to the land the new technique simply could not be introduced; in the limiting case incompatibility with the terrain might push the threshold acreage for adoption of the mechanical reaper upward beyond the seasonal capacity of a single machine, thus restricting the commercial feasibility of harvest mechanization to the class of 'improved' farms. On undrained heavy clays, for instance, horse-drawn machinery might bog down so repeatedly that under no circumstances would it be worthwhile to rely upon them. More generally, however, the unsuitability of the terrain and farm layout did not constitute an absolute barrier to mechanizing the corn harvest. For the purposes of explaining Britain's incomplete conversion to mechanical reaping during the third quarter of the century, it is quite enough that the efficiency of the machines was sufficiently impaired to render their use more costly than the hand techniques on all but very large farms in many of the country's principal grain-producing districts.

One cannot deny the aesthetic appeal of the argument that in British agriculture the rapid adoption of new, mechanical methods being taken up in America was blocked by problems of technical interrelatedness akin to those perceived by Veblen in 1915. At very least, it offers a restoration of some measure of symmetry to discussions of developments in the industrial and non-industrial sectors of the British economy during the latter part of the nineteenth century. There is no *a priori* reason why the durable legacies of an 'early start' should impose obstacles in subsequent phases of the race for technological leadership in manufacturing, or in transportation, but not do so in agriculture. But by the same token, the argument raises the same questions irrespective of the sector to which it is applied: if old plants could not accommodate new machines, why were they not modified, or scrapped and replaced with new structures? Why did the use of antiquated labour-intensive methods on unimproved farms persist alongside progressive husbandry? Are we ultimately led to an explanation cast in terms of entrepreneurial poverty? Or can it be shown that rational profitability considerations — as well as the elements of ignorance, stupidity, inertia and economic irrationality, all of which undoubtedly were present in some degree — could have been responsible for the failure to modernize the physical overhead facilities and operations of existing high-cost farms?

According to the hypothesis advanced by W. E. G. Salter [40], the continuing use of outmoded capital equipment is an indication not of inefficiency and entrepreneurial failure, but of relatively cheap labour, and/or high interest rates. The one — in Salter's model — keeps variable costs low in the old, ostensibly more labour-intensive production methods; the other makes for high fixed costs, and hence high full costs with the new and comparatively capital-intensive techniques that might otherwise displace them. It is, then, just conceivable that outmoded farms and farming methods persisted in Britain because in relation to the prevailing cost of capital rural wage rates remained too low to warrant these facilities being 'scrapped', or modified to accommodate labour-saving machinery. And, were that the essence of the matter, would one not be compelled to acknowledge that the state of the British farming landscape — rather than furnishing a separate, quite independent reason for the restricted extent of the reaping machine's diffusion — is nothing but a less familiar incarnation of the 'relative labour abundance' explanation? Evidently there is much we may hope to learn by asking whether Jacob Wilson's admonition to prepare the land before undertaking to mechanize the corn harvest — in addition to making obvious technical sense — represented sound economic advice for farmers in Victorian Britain.

INTERRELATEDNESS, TENANCY AND INTERDEPENDENT DECISION-MAKING

Physical improvements such as the draining and levelling of fields entailed capital expenditures. These outlays, it has already been suggested, could simply be regarded as installation costs required to assure efficient operation of a reaping machine. Thus, for the project to be at all worthwhile to the farmer, the sum of his annual fixed expenses arising from the purchase and installation of mechanical reaping equipment would have to be covered by the difference between the cost of harvesting his (unimproved) grain acreage by hand methods, on the one hand, and, on the other, the labour costs of harvesting his grain with the aid of the reaping machine once the unsuitable features of the terrain had been removed.

Quite obviously the addition of a capital charge for 'installation' would reduce the rate of return on the farmer's investment in mechanization; the threshold adoption acreage for the reaping machine would be raised above the level applicable in the case of farms on which the existing state of the terrain required no further improvement. Indeed, it is entirely conceivable that 'mechanization-cum-improvement' would be an attractive proposition only for very extensive grain farms, holdings even larger than those on which it would pay to leave the fields unimproved and use mechanical reapers in a less than fully effective manner [41]. Hence, the mere fact that terrain obstructions could be removed to permit efficient operation of mechanical reapers gives us no reason to presuppose it must have been sensible for farmers in general to have done so.

This is, however, an overly simplified formulation of the mechanization-cum-improvement problem. If it is not to prove misleading, it must be immediately amended in two important details. First, one would be wrong to depict investment in land improvements as literally nothing more than installation outlays facilitating the introduction of reaping machinery. Levelling and enlarging the size of fields allowed lower costs in cultivation and other field operations apart from the grain harvest, while subsoil drainage – in addition to permitting the elimination of ridges and water-cuts – directly increased grain yields per acre and facilitated heavier stocking of the land. Regarded from this perspective, which is certainly the way contemporaries thought about it, the expense of removing physical concomitants of the old system of husbandry was only incidentally chargeable to the introduction of machinery in grain harvesting operations, and in its own right would yield economic benefits to the farmer. The cost savings afforded by mechanical reapers on an improved, rationally laid out farm must be seen to have constituted an *additional* incentive for the agricultural community to 'thoroughly reform the hedge-and-ditch-row-ism and topography of this kingdom' [42]. The question at issue is whether this *further* incentive was actually sufficient to induce a significant acceleration in the pace of such reform.

If we are then to consider the inducements to convert to a system of farming with which mechanical reaping was compatible, it is surely pertinent to specify who was to be induced. The need for a second emendation becomes evident at this point. For, no sooner is the question phrased in terms of the way the availability of reaping machines affect farmers' decisions about land improvements, we must acknowledge that the land was typically not the farmer's to improve. Unlike the situation in American agriculture where owner-occupancy was the norm, nineteenth-century British grain farming was typically conducted by tenants [43]. The form of land tenure greatly diminished not only the incentive, but also the financial ability of Britain's farmers to undertake substantial improvements of any sort. Admittedly, where custom and mutual trust had been firmly established, English annual tenancies were not necessarily less secure than the long leaseholds characteristic of Scottish farming; moreover, tenants might well prefer not to be bound to rent schedules and crop and grazing patterns by the terms of restrictive leases [44].

But the issue here is not long leases *v.* tenancy at will; it is tenancy *v.* owner-occupancy. Contemporaries, like Caird, may have been prone to overstate the case for granting long leases, and too quick to ascribe the rapid pace of agricultural improvement taking place in Scotland during the 1840s and the 1850s to the fact that a large proportion of Scottish farmers held 19 or 21 year leases [45]. It is nonetheless true that before compensation for unexhausted improvements was made compulsory, in 1883, tenants were understandably loath to sink money into extremely durable improvements, the full benefits of which they would not capture should their occupancy of the farm be terminated, either voluntarily or at the landlord's insistence [46]. Furthermore, whereas owner-occupants were in a position to mortgage their land to secure funds needed in carrying out costly improvements, Britain's tenant farmers (having no comparable asset to hypothecate) would be obliged to seek the money, and pay the same overdraft rates, in the same quarters that provided their working capital: the country bank parlour.

Considerations of security and finance would have mattered less were the contemplated capital expenditures trifling in relation to the farmer's current outlays. But in the case of an improvement such as the laying of pipe drains, which was less disruptive to the routine of the farm and productive of more beneficial results when done all at once instead of piecemeal, very substantial sums would be required at the outset. Thus, in the event, it was left to the landowners to decide upon major estate improvements and arrange for their financing. Of course, this scarcely meant that tenants could expect landlords to bear the entire cost without recompense; improved farms would be expected to fetch higher rental incomes and, ultimately, higher market prices. Moreover, in the important instance of drainage projects it was usual for tenants to be required to pay a specific annual charge in addition to the agreed rent – normally a fixed percentage of the improvement outlay – to defray the interest and amortization costs of his landlord's investment [47]. For the landlord to profit under such an arrangement without otherwise increasing the rent of the farm, the annual improvement levies would have to be more than sufficient (over the amortization period) to recoup the principal and the actual or foregone interest. Caird, however, was to be found condemning such practice as extortionate – in the instance of those Yorkshire landowners who, after 1846, took government drainage loans repayable in twenty-two equal instalments of 6.5 per cent of the principal, but charged their tenants 7.5 per cent of the initial improvement outlay [48]. Apparently, it would have been deemed more sporting for the landlord to assume the entire risk by trying to take his improvement profit in the form of non-specific increases in the farm's rents. Implicitly, however, many landowners might still have done so whilst maintaining the fixed improvement charges: offsetting rent abatements frequently were granted when agricultural prices declined markedly [49].

The implications of these institutional arrangements are worth pursuing. Apparently mechanization-cum-improvement was not, in actuality, a subject for unilateral decision. It required, instead, a collaborative decision by two parties who normally would not be united by mutually shared hopes and fears. The problem was a recurring one, and would arise at later points, in connection with the introduction of tractors, for example. Field gates, and entrances to cattle yards and cow sheds, were designed for horse work, and, as E. H. Whetham has recently observed, British landlords were not quick in volunteering new buildings merely to suit the tractor. While owner-occupiers might feel free to rip out hedges and knock larger holes in their walls, tenants were constrained to work with the existing buildings and gateways: 'Farmers will continue to ask their landlords to repair their old buildings and give them new ones, and landlords will continue to promise to do something next year.' [50]

Looking at the present problem from the viewpoint of the tenant, were his landlord to agree to make improvements that would increase a mechanical reaper's effectiveness, he could anticipate that he would in one way or another be asked to bear the associated interest and amortization costs. Yet, could he be sure that the improvements would not occasion a readjustment in the farm's rent, which would effectively absorb whatever pure profit he might otherwise derive from his own investment in a reaping machine? Unless he secured a lease, which might be fraught with other dangers, what was to stop the landlord from leaving him no better off than he had been before he had gone to the trouble and fixed expense of changing his production methods? From the landowner's vantage point, sober consideration of the proposition would disclose parallel risks. Should he initiate improvements permitting a reaping machine to be employed to greatest advantage, was there any assurance that his tenants would in fact seize that opportunity, prosper by it, and thus permit some profit to be extracted on the capital sunk into improvements? Were the landowner to contemplate setting a farm rent and improvement levy that would compel the occupant to offset the incremental burden by reducing harvesting costs through mechanization, such a coercive strategy might only end in his having to look for a new tenant. And, unless his fellow landowners could be depended upon to adopt the same stance, a suitable tenant might prove very hard to find.

On farms that would have to be physically improved before a reaping machine could become a paying proposition, the normal risks attending the adoption of a technical innovation were thus compounded with the uncertainties created by the characteristic system of land tenure in Britain. In the absence of owner-occupancy, a feature that, it must be stressed, differentiated the American from the British agrarian scene, the problem of technical interrelatedness (between agricultural machinery and farm topography) necessitated joint decision-making by *at least* two parties who would have to reach some tacit or explicit understanding about the division of the prospective gains [51]. Reluctance on the part of landlords to grant long leases, and the disadvantages to tenants of restrictive leases, further complicated matters by casting doubt upon the reliability of such understandings.

The serious problems of investment coordination to which the system of tenancy gave rise have tended to go insufficiently noticed and analysed. This oversight is not wholly surprising, in view of British agrarian historians' absorption with the (circumstantial) association between the growth of tenancy and the economic benefits derived from the advance of larger scale, commercial farming. When the alternative is taken to be the inefficiently small, imperfectly commercialized owner-occupied holding, 'large tenancies' become a 'good thing'. The preceding corrective observations have sought to shift attention from well recognized issues of security of tenure and compensation for permanent improvements, to the less familiar difficulties that arose because the tenancy prevented automatic 'internalization' of the returns from complementary investments.

Though the import of these difficulties for the receptivity of British agriculture to technical innovations forms the present focus of concern, the basic point might be expanded into a more comprehensive argument concerning the change-inhibiting effects of the system of land tenure that had become so firmly established by the second quarter of the nineteenth century. 'In Britain', as C. P. Kindleberger has remarked, 'it is appropriate to regard owner, wheat-producing tenant, and other potential tenant or tenants as separate firms, and to observe that the gains from the change may involve economies that are external to a particular firm from which investment is required.' [52] Having in mind the inadequately thorough conversion from grain farming to dairying during the final quarter of the century, Kindleberger suggests that this failure to fully respond to profit opportunities was due in major part to the uncertainties created by the 'disarticulated' structure of British agriculture. Lack of an unambiguous relationship between respective efforts and gains diluted the incentives for each of the various parties who would have to have collaborated in the transformation. The parallel is apparent between this suggestion and the line of argument Kindleberger advances in explaining the failure of British mining companies to replace their coal wagons with larger vehicles, which would have resulted in lower operating costs to the railways.

One must be careful, however, not to misapprehend the nature of this sort of argument and to ask too much of it. It is not suggested here that the problems of coordinating complementary investments were inherently insuperable. Far from it. If reciprocal externalities existed it remained entirely possible for the parties involved to 'internalize' the benefits flowing from their joint efforts, by entering a formal or informal 'profit-sharing' arrangement [53]. If within such arrangements, as we have pointed out, uncertainties remained concerning the precise compensation that each participant was going to receive, the problem boils down simply to the fact that the venture held some (perhaps appreciable) risks for the investors.

But neither in principle nor in practice can it be asserted that such uncertainties *alone* would have blocked the extension of mechanical reaping into areas where preparatory terrain modifications were indicated. Tenants and landowners were no strangers to risk-taking. Much would depend upon the magnitude of the expected gains that would be available to be shared among the investing parties. For, when great uncertainties cloud the future division of the pie, petty collaborative baking ventures are much more likely to be abandoned than are large ones.

To properly assess the significance that should be attached to the uncertainty created by land tenure arrangements in Britain, one must, therefore, return to the original question of the profitability of investment in mechanization-cum-improvement. We should, in other words, first establish whether or not the whole of this particular pie was really big enough to make worth baking under the most certain of conditions.

Providing a rigorous answer to this question would be no mean undertaking. That much should be clear from the first of the two emendations set out above. For, to ensure that due allowance was made for interdependence among the myriad activities comprising an agricultural enterprise, and for the multiple elements of technical interrelatedness and joint production cost to which that interdependence gave rise, it would first be necessary to explore the full range of the choice of technique problems confronting farmers in the period under consideration. The aim would be to arrive at a cost comparison between the best mode of grain farming in Britain and the most economically efficient among those combinations of techniques, which would, nonetheless, restrict farmers to harvesting their grain by hand methods. The comparison would, moreover, have to be made for farms of varying sizes. More precisely: we should consider the difference between the unit operating costs (including interest on working capital) of (1) an existing unimproved farm restricted to using outmoded methods, including hand harvesting of grain at very least, and (2) a thoroughly improved farm using the most superior techniques available, including mechanical reaping. Assuming the *natural* fertility of the soil to be the same in both cases, the difference in unit operating costs should be compared with the unit rental charges – i.e. annual interest and amortization costs per unit of output – for all the additional fixed reproducible capital, the livestock inventory being more conveniently treated as part of the farmer's working capital. Since less land would undoubtedly be needed to produce a given volume of output on an improved farm, it would be appropriate to subtract the land rents on the unnecessary acreage (at the pre-improvement rental rate) from the additional fixed capital costs [54].

It is, indeed, a daunting prospect, one that would vastly extend the scope of the present inquiry and turn it into a full scale study of mid-Victorian agricultural technology. Humbled before so imposing a task, it is permissible to ask if the relevant empirical point may not be established by pursuing a less ambitious course and focusing attention upon the core of the problem, the connection between land improvements and harvest mechanization. The choice between machine methods and hand methods of cutting grain was surely bound up with decisions regarding drainage and, consequently, the terrain profile. But to suppose it was equally entangled with decisions about the application of fertilizers, or the conduct of non-field operations such as grain threshing and the preparation of livestock fodder, does seem to be stretching the point. Similarly, while better drainage did *permit* a shift to mixed farming, and large additional outlays for 'elaborate new dairy parlours, cattle houses, pig-sties and barns' often did accompany land improvement projects [55], these were hardly necessary concomitants in a technical sense. In fact, there are grounds for the suspicion that the incremental advantages derived by grain farmers from stall-feeding of livestock and greater recovery of animal manure failed, in the event, to justify the associated capital expenditures that were made for buildings and yards [56]. It is certainly clear that during the period 1847-79 as a whole, English landowners received miserably low returns from their investments in new farm buildings – as distinct from land improvements – and that the former thus served only to depress the overall rate of return on expenditures for comprehensive estate improvement schemes [57'

THE RATE OF RETURN: A QUANTITATIVE EXERCISE

There is, then, some reasonable ground for narrowing the focus to consider only complementary improvements made upon the land itself. Doing so makes it feasible to try to gauge the profitability of mechanization-cum-improvement by examining the following illustrative investment project: (*a*) installing pipe drainage, (*b*) spreading the subsoil removed from the drainage trenches, (*c*) levelling the tillage and (*d*) purchasing a manual sheaf-delivery reaping machine. We shall posit that the land improvements specified offered a direct gain in the form of increased yields on the farm's total cereal acreage without any additional application of fertilizers. Further, it will be supposed they assured optimal terrain conditions, thereby guaranteeing the full saving on harvest labour costs obtainable by employing the reaping machine in place of scythesmen to harvest the crops of wheat and oats – and what little rye might be grown.

From a purely technical standpoint there was no reason why the cutting apparatus of the manual sheaf-delivery (or, in simpler contemporary American parlance, the 'hand-rake') reaper could not cope perfectly well with barley, as with the other small grains. But in the case of barley crop – which in Britain vied with oats in terms of the extent of acreage sown – a complication arose due to the common practice in handling the grain once it was cut. In the era with which we are concerned, English farmers most frequently regarded it as not worthwhile to bind barley into sheaves. Instead, they left it to dry lying in swathe in the mown fields – before carting and stacking it in much the same way as hay or straw [58]. This practice, however, would not have been feasible where a rear-delivery machine of the American (Hussey-McCormick) type was employed: the gavels, swept from the platform by the raker who rode the machine, had to be quickly bound up and removed from the horses' path before the contraption came round on its next pass. It is therefore supposed that a farmer purchasing one of the comparatively small and moderately priced machines in this design class would not contemplate using it to harvest his barley [59].

In reckoning the per acre saving of harvest labour costs (wL_S^*) for the representative acre cut by machine, one must take into account the differential advantage the mechanical reaper offered in wheat compared with oats; this may be done simply enough, by weighting the unit labour savings coefficient ($L_S^*[j]$) for each jth crop in proportion to the relative acreage devoted to the two grains in the country at large [60]. To the unit saving in labour cost, it is then necessary to add – for each acre of wheat and oats harvested – the per acre value of the incremental cereal yield. The latter ($p\dot{y}G'$) depends upon the absolute increase in the number of bushels per acre sown with cereal crops ($\dot{y}$), the market price per bushel (p), and (G') the number of acres annually devoted to cereals of all kinds per acre sown with wheat and oats. Now it would be just profitable to undertake the complete investment project if, at the combined wheat and oats acreage being contemplated (S_T^{**}), the total monetary benefits ($[wL_S^* + p\dot{y}G'] S_T^{**}$) began to exceed the sum of the fixed rental cost of the land improvements and the yearly interest and amortization cost of the reaping machine. Denoting the latter as the product of the machine rental rate and purchase cost, $R_m C_m$, the imputed annual charge for the land improvements may be analogously represented as $R_I [C_I A' S_T^{**}]$; for each of the S_T^{**} acres of grain harvested with the machine during the year, it would be necessary to allow for continuing crop rotation by draining and levelling A acres of the arable, at a capital cost of C_I per acre of land thus improved. The interest rate at which finance could be obtained (r_I), and the conventional amortization period for such improvements (D_I), between them, determine the appropriate annual rental rate expressed as (R_I) a fraction of the initial capital expenditures [61]. Setting out the problem in this way facilitates arranging the pertinent quantitative information in an augmented threshold function – from which it is a simple matter to calculate the wheat and oats acreage (S_T^{**}) beyond which this particular project, considered as a package, would be economically rational.

While the purpose of calculating the level of the 'mechanization-cum-improvement threshold' thus determined must be regarded as primarily illustrative, it will be seen from Appendix B that a serious effort has been made to arrive at appropriate magnitudes for the parameters and variables that have thus been explicitly introduced into the discussion. The general expression defining the threshold, and the parameter estimates, are arrayed in summary form in the upper panel of Table 1. The lower panel of the same table carries the values assumed

TABLE 1
Determinants of the threshold acreage for harvest
mechanization under illustrative conditions of interrelatedness

Implicit threshold function for mechanization-cum-improvement:

$$R_m C_m - (p\dot{y}G' + wL_s^* - R_I C_I A')S_T^{**} = 0$$

Fixed technical coefficients and parameters:

L_s^* = 1.096   for hand-rake machine v. scythes, per acre of wheat and oats cut, bound and stooked;

$\dot{y}$ = 4.0,   the additional wheat yield in bushels per acre;

ϵ = 0.70,   the wage share in improvement costs;

G' = 1.60,   the ratio of cereal acreage to wheat and oats acreage;

A' = 2.85,   the ratio of arable to wheat and oats acreage;

R_m = 0.127,   the machine rental rate, for r_m = .05 and D_m = 10 years.

D_I = 22,   the land improvement amortization period, in years.

Variables subject to change over time (all prices expressed in shillings):

Price	c. 1851 = t_0	c 1861	c. 1871
$w(t)$	3	1.30(w_0)	1.50(w_0)
$p(t)$	5	1.25(p_0)	1.25(p_0)
$C_m(t)$	660	1.00(C_{m0})	0.76(C_{m0})
$C_I(t)$	180	[1 +.30ϵ] (C_{I_0})	[1 +.50ϵ] (C_{I_0})

Source: See Appendix B for estimates of technical coefficients and price-variables; see Paragraph 3 of Technical Notes in Appendix A for the relationship between rental rates (R) and parameters (r) and (D).

by the four price variables of the analysis – w, C_m, C_I, p – at the beginning, middle and end of the period 1851-71.

The proximate results of this exercise in quantification are displayed by the main portion of Table 2 and are subject to interpretation in either of two ways. The first is quite straightforward: each column in the body of the table shows how the mechanization-cum-improvement threshold would be altered by changes in (R_I) the yearly rental rate for the land improvements, given the structure of other input costs and output benefits prevailing at the date in question. As expected, one may see that if lower annual rental rates were charged for the land improvements, *ceteris paribus*, it would become worth-

TABLE 2
The mechanization-cum-improvement threshold acreage
and the landlord's rate of return

Land improvement investments		Threshold wheat and oats acreage for investment in mechanization cum improvement, S_T^{**}:		
Net per annum rate of return	Gross annual rental rate			
r_I	R_I	c. 1851	c. 1861	c. 1871
.020	.0559	12.7	8.7	10.1
.030	.0620	24.1	14.4	31.2
.035	.0650	43.0	21.1	0
.040	.0684	$> S_{max}$	45.0	0
.045	.0716	0	0	0

Threshold wheat and oats acreage for simple mechanization:

$S_T^* = (R_m C_m)/(L_s^* w)$		25.5	19.6	12.9

Source: See Table 1 for underlying parameters and variables.

while for tenants with smaller acreage in wheat and oats to apply to their landlord to have these improvements made, and then to invest in the purchase of a reaping machine [62].

An alternative interpretation of the same data, this time from the viewpoint of the landowner, is perhaps more illuminating. Given the prevailing price of grain, the level of agricultural wages, the fixed annual (imputed) rental cost of a reaping machine, the per acre cost of improvements, and a farm on which the combined wheat and oats acreage is that shown in the body of the table, the corresponding (r_I) entry in the left-most column reveals the 'maximum compatible rate of return' on the associated improvement outlay. This is the highest average annual rate of return, net of amortization charges over a twenty-two year period, which a landlord could extract on the land improvement expenditures without actually making it unprofitable for his tenant to purchase a handrake reaping machine on the date in question [63]. An improving landlord who was thus prepared to skim off any pure profits from mechanization – that is, any savings in harvest labour costs over and above the imputed rental costs of the reaping machine used by his tenant – as well as the entire incremental cereal yield on the improved arable, could obviously secure higher rates of return on (larger) outlays made to improve the land of larger individual farms. Here we have a nice concrete illustration, should one be needed, of the potential economic advantages that larger scale tenant farming offered to the nineteenth-century landowner [64].

The blessings of scale were not, however, boundless. In this case an approximate upper limit to the maximum compatible rate of return would be reached on farms whose area under wheat and oats equalled the 100 or so acres that represented the normal yearly limit on the cutting capacity of a single reaping machine (S_{max}). At still higher rental rates (R_I) designed to secure an even greater net rate of return on the landowner's improvement outlay, the tenant would not be left with enough to meet the yearly interest and depreciation costs of his reaper — no matter what the extent of his grain acreage [65].

The low level of the maximum rates of return on improvement expenditures compatible with mechanization, in both the technical and the economic senses, constitutes a striking general feature of the findings presented by Table 2. It deserves further comment and amplification.

Under the terms of the government's drainage loan programme initiated by Peel immediately following the Repeal Act, landowners were able to finance this class of improvements over a twenty-two year repayment period at an annual interest rate of 3.5 per cent — the annual interest and amortization charges worked out at 6.5 per cent of the principal. Perhaps for this reason, it seems that 3.5 per cent became accepted as a notional interest rate applicable to estate improvements of all descriptions, and not exclusively to drainage projects [66]. In the case of drainage loans, however, this rate did reflect an element of public subsidy. According to evidence given in the early 1870s, the interest rate at which the private land improvement companies had been accustomed to lending was 4.5 per cent; the sinking fund typically was calculated to repay the loan in twenty-five years, but when these companies were finished adding in interest and amortization of the 'preliminary expenses' of the loans, the average yearly payment on the 'effective outlay' was brought up 'to a little more than 7 per cent' [67]. Over a twenty-five year period the latter annual rental rate would in reality be generating a compound interest yield of 5 per cent per annum on the company's principal.

It is to be noted, then, that in the years immediately surrounding 1851 a yearly rental rate of 6.5 per cent, when applied to the expenditure required to drain, spread the subsoil and level the arable of an average British farm, would apparently have imposed improvement rental costs upon the occupant exceeding the estimated value of the increase in cereal crop yields [68]. In these circumstances, for which the abnormally low price of wheat during 1849-52 was in large part responsible, investments in this particular set of land improvements could provide a yield matching the 3.5 per cent interest rate only if other, indirect gains were captured – namely, the margin of super-normal profit derived by harvesting 43.0 acres of wheat and oats with a reaping machine instead of scythes [69]. Mechanizing the harvest of as much as 80 acres of wheat and oats – in the standard 57 : 43 proportions assumed throughout these calculations – would merely offer the landlord the prospect of extracting a 3.75 per annum net rate of return; for this, according to the present estimates, he would be obliged to expend more than £2000 on the improvement of some 228 acres of tillage [70]. And the very most a landowner could hope for, with conditions as they were *c.* 1851, appears to have been an annual pure profit rate less than one half a percentage point above the (3.5 per cent) rate of interest on government improvement loans; unless, of course, his tenant was to be made worse off than he had been without the improvements and the reaping machine.

A 'maximum compatible rate of return' as high as 4.5 per cent per annum was not only unattainable when the Crystal Palace opened: Table 2 indicates that rates of that magnitude eluded the improving landlord's grasp over the course of the ensuing two decades. Moreover, the size distribution of existing agricultural holdings [71] would not have permitted even these terribly modest maximum feasible rates of return to be obtained on outlays for land improvements compatible with harvest mechanization. In England and Wales as a whole the average farm in 1851 was only 111 acres in extent, of which perhaps 23 acres were devoted to wheat, oats and rye – the latter counting for little in the total. Over the next twenty years the size distribution of holdings remained much the same. Fully half of the agricultural acreage in England and Wales lay in holdings smaller than 200-250 acres, and it is quite likely that rather more than half of the country's acreage under wheat, oats (and rye) was being farmed in units of under 40-50 acres. Looking then at the rate of return that Table 2 indicates a landlord could hope to extract on his investment in improving a farm with 45 acres of these grain crops, we may therein observe the very highest rate attainable on the half of the country's grain acreage being farmed in holdings below that size class. It rose from a shade under 3.5 per cent

172

Essays on a Mature Economy

c. 1851 to 4.0 per cent a decade later, and then retreated to the neighbourhood of 3.1 per cent *c*. 1871, more or less paralleling the movement of the maximum feasible rate for acreage in the upper half of the farm size distribution – which remained under 4.0, 4.5 and 3.5 per cent per annum, respectively, on the same three dates. Giving equal weight to these two sets of maximum rates, in accord with the relative shares of the nation's grain acreage to which each refers, it appears appropriate to conclude that for England and Wales as a whole the maximum expected rate of return to a landlord's investment in the type of mechanization-cum-improvement project described here could not have been as high as 4 per cent on any of the three occasions in the period 1851-71.

Now these findings should not really provoke surprise. For, in this, the line of the present argument converges with other, more familiar conclusions about developments in mid-Victorian agriculture. The £24 million spent on drainage and land improvements during the years 1846-76 notwithstanding, it was the rare and extremely lucky (or judicious) landowner who managed to secure an average annual rate of return as high as 4.5 per cent from land improvement outlays. Those wicked Yorkshire landlords, whose greed (in charging their tenants more than the rate implied by the government drainage loans) had drawn down upon them James Caird's wrath, were only aiming to extract a 5 per cent per annum rate of return. To most, the capital poured into their estates after the repeal of the Corn Laws brought disappointingly meagre financial rewards – well below those being earned from equally risky industrial investments [72]. The estate improvement expenditure of the great landowners recently studied by F. M. L. Thompson yielded – at maximum – a gross annual return of 3.6 per cent, and in many instances this high a rate appears to have been enjoyed only for a few years toward the close of the period 1847-79 [73]. Less fortunate still were those who had begun improvements too late to clear off their debts before the rent reductions of the 1880s fell upon them [74]. Had the money thus deployed simply been left in Consols, it would have brought in a steady 3.2 per cent per annum – without the worry [75].

In the light of the illustrative calculations presented here, one can well understand why in 1873 the House of Lords' Select Committee on Land Improvement believed that those who borrowed to finance drainage projects – let alone construction of new farm buildings and labourers' cottages – might readily find themselves out of pocket, despite the indirect pay-offs to facilitating the mechanization of field operations. Even were no allowance to be made for the uncertainty surrounding both the size of the total return and, owing to the prevailing system of tenure, its division between improving landlord and progressive tenant, the Committee's *Report* appears fully justified in its opinion 'that the improvement of land . . . as an investment is not sufficiently lucrative to offer much attraction to capital' [76].

RICARDO EFFECTS, WICKSELL EFFECTS, AND THE PENALTIES OF AN EARLY START

A second broad facet of the findings reported by Table 2 concerns the way in which the profitability of mechanization-cum-improvement was affected by trends in grain prices and agricultural wages during the interval separating the opening of the Crystal Palace from the House of Lords' inquest on the nation's investment in land improvements. These movements, like the general absolute level of the rate of return, merit closer attention.

Previously, in discussing the determination of the profitability threshold for 'simple mechanization' – the introduction of mechanical reaping on a farm whose terrain already offered suitable operating conditions – it was proper to be exclusively concerned with the influence exerted by the level of agricultural wage rates relative to the rental cost, or (in the absence of interest rate and service life alterations) the purchase costs of the reaping machine itself. Now, however, it is important to recognize that through their influence upon the profitability of complementary land improvements, changes in the price of grain (p) also must have played a significant role governing the diffusion of the mechanical reaper in Britain. Moreover, it must be appreciated that although the profitability of 'simple mechanization' was enhanced by increases in the relative price of farm labour, paradoxically, the same upward drift of rural wage rates relative to the price of reaping machines *and grain* could simultaneously diminish the profitability of investment in harvest mechanization-cum-land-improvement [77].

One might be led instinctively to doubt the validity of the last contention, at least on the basis of some general acquaintance with W. E. G. Salter's notable theoretical work on the economics of scrapping and replacement decision [78]. It is certainly more usual to find economists maintaining that, on the contrary, a rising real wage rate tends not only to hasten the scrapping of old machinery, but also works to insure that the introduction of new, more advanced labour saving techniques will not be long obstructed by the existence of outmoded but extremely durable industrial plants. In the limit, 'interrelatedness' simply means that scrapping and replacement decisions must be taken with reference to complete plants, rather than individual pieces of equipment. But the 'Salter model' suggests that when wage rates rise relative to the price of an industry's product, the real costs of new capital goods available to the industry will have fallen in relation to the real savings in operating (labour) costs, which their use would permit. Replacing outmoded plant and equipment with capital embodying superior techniques would, therefore, tend to be made more profitable; whatever 'penalty' had been imposed by the industry's 'early start' in accumulating durable capital would be sloughed off as soon as it grew burdensome. Clearly, to adopt such a position in the present connection would be tantamount to reviving the germ of an all-embracing 'British labour abundance' explanation for the restricted diffusion of mechanical reaping: had the real wage of farm labour been higher in Britain, capital expenditure for reaping machines and complementary land improvements would have been more attractive.

I must confess to having brought this proposition forward only to reject it now the more firmly. It is not difficult to see why precisely the opposite result could emerge from a rise in harvest wage rates relative to grain prices, when – as in the case at hand – the assumptions underlying the Salter model were not fulfilled.

As one might expect, if the fixed cost of reaping machines did not increase as rapidly as the level of wage rates facing the farmer, harvest mechanization *per se* would become a more attractive proposition on any given holding – whether otherwise improved or not. But concurrently, higher rural wage rates would also tend to force up the per acre costs of carrying our land improvements. The more labour-intensive this kind of capital formation was, and the more sluggish was the pace of productivity advance in such activities as trench digging, the stronger the upward wage pressure upon the unit price of the improvements. Both conditions are especially pertinent here and, it might be added, also seem germane to the construction trades in general during the nineteenth century [79]. Nearly 60 per cent of the per acre cost of pipe drainage installations was accounted for by direct wage costs, materials making up the balance. Spreading the subsoil and levelling the tillage, the two operations following the drainage work, were usually conducted in a manner that made wages the only significant cost item; thus, it is estimated that *c*. 1851 labour's share comprised 70 per cent of the total unit price of this particular set of land improvements [80]. Moreover, there is little reason to think that the period under review saw any notable increase of productivity in on-farm capital formation activities of this nature. Note, however, that the degree of labour-intensity of improvements only affects the *sensitivity* of their price to changes in the level of agricultural wages; 'labour-intensity' itself – the description of the situation in which the wage share (strictly, the elasticity of output with respect to labour inputs) exceeds one half – is not a necessary condition for a real wage increase to issue in a decline in the profitability of mechanization-cum-improvement [81].

As improvement costs per acre rose in relation to the price of grain, and consequently in relation to the value of the direct benefits in the form of greater grain yields per acre improved, investment in land improvement *per se* would become less and less profitable. Ignoring for the moment the possibility of a change in the grain price of the reaping machine, when the resulting addition to the cost of improvements reckoned in terms of grain turned out to exceed the incremental grain value of the wage savings due to mechanization, the higher real wage rate would have the perverse effect of depressing the overall rate of return on the joint investment project. Restating the situation more concisely: although increasing real wage rates in agriculture produce the familiar 'Ricardo effect' as far as simple mechanization is concerned, in regard to the complementary land improvements the same wage movements result in an opposing 'Wicksell effect'. The latter could easily be strong enough to dominate the *net* influence exerted upon the rate of return to investment in the whole project [82].

There is more to this than mere theoretical speculation. Looking at the influence of agricultural wage and price changes during the 1850s and 1860s, the situation just envisioned may be seen to have actually materialized well before the close of the 'Golden Age' of British farming. The upward course of grain prices had supplied vital impetus to the high farming movement of the 1850s, which through its emphasis on land improvement – if in no other way – was conducive to the more widespread diffusion of reaping machines [83]. Although with the cessation of hostilities in the Crimea grain prices dropped quickly from the heights touched in 1854-6, they remained well above the levels that prevailed when the decade opened. The rise of approximately 25 per cent registered by the *Gazette* price of wheat between

1849-52 and 1859-62 almost matched the rate of increase in average weekly wages of farm labourers, and therefore outpaced the estimated 21 per cent advance in the unit cost of land improvements, as may be seen from Table 1. Further, like drainage and related land improvements, harvest mechanization *per se* was becoming more economically advantageous during the 1850s: the purchase price of a manual sheaf-delivery reaping machine remained essentially unaltered while agricultural money wages rose. Thus we find that *c*. 1861 mechanization-cum-improvement on a farm with 21 acres under wheat and oats held out the prospect of a 3.5 per cent annual net rate of return on the land improvement expenditures – the same rate that, ten years earlier, had only been attainable on farms where over twice the acreage of those crops were involved. Putting the position at the beginning of the 1860s another way, if new improvement outlays could be repaid over a twenty-two year period in annual instalments of 6.5 per cent of the principal, the threshold wheat and oats acreage for mechanization-cum-improvement had become roughly coincident with the 19.6 acre threshold relevant in the case of farms whose terrain already was well suited to the use of the reaping machine.

But when the price of grain stopped moving upward, which is what happened for all intents and purposes during the 1860s, the precariousness of a high farming approach relying on rural labour-intensive capital formation to save land became more readily discernible. For money wage rates in agriculture continued rising during the 1860s, and real farm wages reckoned in terms of grain increased about twice as rapidly as they had in the preceding decade. This was enough to drive up the threshold farm size required for barely profitable new investment in mechanization-cum-land improvement – even though the concurrent 35 per cent reduction of the reaping machine's price in relation to harvest wage rates served to further encourage substitution of mechanical for hand methods of cutting grain. By the opening of the 1870s, according to the evidence of Table 2, purchase of a manual sheaf-delivery machine and preparation of the land for its effective use had ceased to make economic sense if the improvements were to be financed at the 3.5 per cent rate of interest implicit in the terms of the government subsidized drainage loans.

For us to recognize the existence of a more complex set of connections linking mechanization and the adoption of high farm practices, beyond the primitive interrelationship between land improvement and the effective use of the early reaping machines, can scarcely weaken the line of argument advanced here. In general it may be said that although the illustrative case examined in Tables 1 and 2 is rather generous in its evaluation of the direct, grain-yield-raising effects of land improvement outlays, it does omit consideration of many potential secondary benefits — especially those connected with the mechanization of other field operations, such as sowing, and the cultivation of row crops. Quite obviously, removal of obstacles to the movement of mechanical reapers would permit more effective use of grass mowers and hay-tedders, as well as of wheeled cultivators and grain drills, thereby generating labour cost savings that might be applied against the original capital charge for the improvements. It need not automatically follow, however, that the result was to reduce the size of the farm on which fuller mechanization became just profitable — bringing it below the threshold farm size defined for partial mechanization of the sort treated here.

There is even some reason to think that the opposite might have been closer to the truth of the matter, and that the replacement of sickles and scythes in the harvesting of wheat and oats comprised one of the more notably profitable among the various possibilities for mechanizing field operations which were available to British farmers during the 1850s and 1860s. Steam ploughing, however impressive a technical achievement, does not appear to have been a close contender [84]. Coming nearer to the specific activity examined here, we might briefly consider the possibility of a tenant of an improved farm pressing on beyond mechanization of the wheat and oats harvest, to replace hand mowing of his barley as well. A swath-delivery machine — such as Crosskill's version of the Bell reaper, or the adaptations of McCormick's machine developed by the firm of Burgress and Key — would serve this purpose in a way in which, for reasons already mentioned, the rear-delivery hand-rake models could not [85]. Evidence available for the early 1860s, however, makes it apparent that swath-delivery reaping machines were not only somewhat more costly to purchase than the hand-rake models, but that they saved considerably less labour expense per acre harvested when set to work in wheat, or in wheat and oats. Indeed, it turns out that the unit labour saving per representative acre of wheat, oats and barley — in the respective acreage proportions 42 : 31 : 27 observed nationally in the late 1860s and early 1870s — was greater for the manual sheaf-delivery machine than for the swath-delivery reaper, despite the latter's saving of labour in cutting barley where the former might be supposed to save nothing [86].

These being the basic facts of the case, it follows that on an

improved farm *of a given size* and representative mix of the major
cereal crops, there was no way to proceed to mechanize the harvesting
of all three grain crops using a 'swather' — either alone or in conjunction with a manual sheaf-delivery reaping machine — which would not
reduce the farmer's rate of return on his total investment in reaping
machinery, driving the latter below the rate he could obtain by remaining content to have partially mechanized the corn harvest. This is
tantamount to concluding that only the larger grain farmers could
employ swath-delivery reapers to cut their barley and still expect to
earn a rate of return on their machinery outlay identical to the rate
their lesser neighbours might obtain by investing in a device suited to
mechanization of the wheat and oats harvest alone.

Such findings can be no more than suggestive. Were one to insist that
harvest mechanization be evaluated in the context of the full array of
new methods employed on improved farms, it should be remembered
that the domain of profitable high farming remained quite rigidly
circumscribed throughout the period under consideration. As Chambers
and Mingay recently have pointed out, high farming was found to be
economically advantageous only on large holdings, namely those about
300 acres [87]. Yet medium and small units continued to predominate
in the structure of British agriculture: the Census of 1851 had reported
16,840 farms in the size class above 299 acres in England and Wales,
comprising about 7.5 per cent of the total number of holdings, and
occupying approximately one third of the agricultural land covered by
the returns [88]. Over the next three decades, farm consolidation failed
to augment this large scale segment of the industry. Such concentration
as did take place at the national level was slight, and appears to have
resulted mainly from consolidations of unviable smallholdings — of less
than 50 acres — into farms of under 100 acres [89]. Either in terms of
absolute numbers, or absolute extent of acreage controlled, or relative
share of the nation's agricultural acreage, the picture revealed by the
available statistics for 1851 and 1885 — riddled as these are with
elements of incomparability — is one of stability, and in some respects
contraction of the potential segment within British agriculture that
might profitably have taken up mechanical reaping as a part of a
thoroughgoing shift to high farming after 1850.

But the same conditions that were ultimately to spell the doom of
high farming in Britain lay at the root of the problem exposed by the
more restricted analysis pursued here. The price of grain prevailing in
international markets simply was not high enough to warrant con-

tinuing British land improvement expenditures on the basis of the direct benefits conveyed in the form of higher cereal yields. Hence such investments could be recouped only when the indirect effects of the improvements, such as those obtained by reducing unit costs of field operations like the corn harvest, were exploited to the fullest. And still, the expected rates of return to landlord and tenant were scarcely high enough to assuage the doubts that would beset even the mildly risk averse rational investor. That so much in the way of drainage and land improvement was accomplished in the face of such odds is remarkable. One is obliged to acknowledge that if the diffusion of mechanical reaping was at all held back by farmers' irrational resistance to innovation, surely it had been no less advanced by the monumental investment miscalculation on the part of British landowners.

To drive home the point that the heart of the problem lay in the long-run unprofitability of a post Corn Law repeal system of husbandry built around cereal production, it is worth stressing that the reason farm terrain and farm layouts in mid-Victorian Britain remained an obstacle to the further diffusion of the reaping machine is not properly traceable to the alleged 'abundance' of rural labour. At least not if that were meant to describe a situation in which farm labourers' wage rates remained so low in relation to prevailing grain prices that little effective inducement was afforded the substitution of other inputs in their place. As has been seen, rising real wage rates in agricultural districts, instead of promoting the replacement of Britain's old farms with modern ones *á la* Salter, acted as an inhibitor of the preparatory investments that Jacob Wilson had urged upon all those who sought to mechanize their corn harvest. By the close of the 1860s a substantial part of the arable farming sector was being forced to struggle on in awkward accommodation to the outmoded tangible legacies of its past, because within the then existing state of technology the transition to higher rural wage levels rendered it less and less economically worthwhile to erase the durable impress of history from the agricultural landscape and begin afresh.

EPILOGUE

In this tale the penalties of having had an early start in the accumulation of farm capital began to weigh heavily only when the advantages conveyed by taking the lead were already largely lost, when capital-intensive cereal production in Britain had ceased to be competitive with extensive grain farming in the regions of recent settlement across the Atlantic. But it is not also plausible to think that the tug-of-war between 'Ricardo effects' and 'Wicksell effects', whose outcome restricted the introduction of new labour-saving methods in agriculture, may have been still more directly responsible for the industrial dilemma of the late nineteenth-century British economy to which Veblen directed notice?

Certainly it now seems relevant to again look more closely at the difficulties created by the presence of strong elements of *technical* interrelatedness between equipment and long-lived physical plant. For, by analogy with the case examined, we can see that limping productivity advance in the building trades would have made the costs of modifying structures, or actually tearing down and replacing plants inherited from earlier phases of the First Industrial Revolution, particularly sensitive to the upward movement of the urban-industrial wage structure in Britain during the second half of the nineteenth century. In the absence of strong product market incentives for rapid expansion of industrial capacity – which would have occasioned the building of new, 'best practice' plants suited to the most advanced machinery designs – an important segment of the domestic demand for capital equipment would thus be comprised of calls for replacements of old-style machinery compatible with the existing factories, mills and mines. Equipment producers looking at the home market would thereby have been given a strong inducement to concentrate upon the perfection of older vintage machine designs, rather than upon applications of the latest in technical knowledge. As real wage rates continued to rise, some of the more up-to-date equipment could perhaps be profitably installed even in sub-optimal operating conditions; but the fact that it was not being efficiently utilized – in the technical sense, at least – might well have had the perverse result of misinforming potential purchasers as to the true advantages of the equipment when installed in new facilities.

As a consequence of the direction in which machinery producers were encouraged to channel their energies, we might anticipate a tendency for the purchase costs of older styles of equipment to fall in relation to the prices of technically more advanced machinery – which would only serve to reinforce the rational decision of industrial firms to carry on with their outmoded physical plant instead of investing in thoroughly modernized facilities. And so on, in a vicious circle broken only by the eventually rising costs of maintaining increasingly decrepit structures, or the appearance of dramatically superior innovations in equipment designs — quite likely from abroad. We have here the core of an explanation of how, even in an era of rising real wages, an industry or sector that initially operated with the most up-to-date capital-intensive production processes could be guided by strict adherence to cost considerations into a position of protracted technological back-wardness.

In the agricultural sector of the economy, with the route to more complete diffusion of mechanical reaping via renovation of the landscape being gradually sealed off, the immediate avenue of advance remaining open lay through the introduction of machinery on less-than-optimal terrain. Movement in this direction was, of course, fostered by the mounting real costs of labour in the harvest season — quite possibly receiving significant added impetus from the threat posed by Joseph Arch's organizing activities among the agricul-tural labourers in the 1870s. But after 1873 other forces were set in motion, which also worked to reduce the proportion of the British grain harvest that was left for the sickle and the scythe. The collapse of the level of grain prices under the onslaught of American wheat exports finally blocked further significant investment in land improvements, but by the same token it compelled a contraction of arable farming. And in the course of that painful readjustment it was the unimproved holdings, on which ridge-and-furrow remained pronounced, that were among the first to be left to 'tumble down to grass'; the nature of the terrain surface that had persisted on these sub-marginal arable farms is evident to this day in the undulating pastures of the East Midlands. The proportion of the British grain harvest that was machine-reaped thus tended to go on rising, in part because the segment of the now declining industry's capacity least well suited to mechanization was the first to be withdrawn from cereal production.

Then, too, technological progress continued in the development of farm machinery. The reaper-binder began to come into use in America in the mid-1870s, opening a new phase in the mechanization of harvest tasks, and it was not long in appearing on the British scene. Increased technical possibilities for saving labour promoted the use of new machinery under less than optimal conditions; and, in the longer run, the mounting potential benefits of farm mechanization — heightened by the exigencies of the nation's needs in wartime — became potent enough to once again initiate significant renovations of the landscape to make way for the tractor and the combine harvester. But in 1875 all that lay in the future, and would form part of a far more complicated story than the one I have sought to illuminate here.

NOTES

[1] C. S. Orwin and E. H. Whetham, *History of British Agriculture 1846-1914* (London, Archon Books, 1964), p. 10.
[2] F. Dovring, 'The transformation of European agriculture', in M. M. Postan and J. H. Habakkuk (eds.), *Cambridge Economic History of Europe*, vol. 6, pt 2, p. 645 (Cambridge, Cambridge University Press, 1965). Dovring's statement is not unrepresentative in its lack of precision regarding 'scarcity'; since all economic goods are scarce, something more must be meant. But if increased scarcity relative to other goods, or a rise in relative price compared with the relative price of the commodity in another country or region, is what we have in mind in speaking of farm labour 'becoming scarce', then the required conditions cited by Dovring are palpably not necessary. For parallel statements relating specifically to Britain, among recent contributions to the literature cf., e.g., John Saville, *Rural Depopulation in England and Wales 1851-1951* (London, Routledge & Kegan Paul, 1957), pp. 140–1; E. L. Jones, 'The agricultural labour market in England 1793-1872', *Economic History Review*, 2nd ser., vol. 17, 1964, pp. 322–38; W. Harwood Long, 'The development of mechanization in English farming', *Agricultural History Review*, vol. 11, 1963, p. 22; J. D. Chambers and G. E. Mingay, *The Agricultural Revolution 1750-1880* (London, Batsford, 1966), pp. 186–90.
[3] Although the choice of techniques in both industry and agriculture received attention in H. J. Habakkuk's stimulating book, *American and British Technology in the Nineteenth Century* (Cambridge, Cambridge University Press, 1962), the discussion provoked subsequently in the journals has dealt almost exclusively with industrial technology and the influence exerted upon it by national factor endowment. Cf., e.g., Peter Temin, 'Labor scarcity and the problem of American industrial efficiency in the 1850s', *Journal of Economic History*, XXVI, September 1966, pp. 277–98; R. W. Fogel, 'The specification problem in economic history', *Journal of Economic History*, XXVII, September 1967, pp. 298–308.
[4] The present paper forms part of a comparative, monograph-length work now in preparation: *American Reapers and British Fields, The Mechanization of Grain Harvesting in Britain and America Before 1875*. I have made use here of some findings contained in this larger study, without presenting explicit documentation on points that are ancillary to the central argument of the present paper.
In the course of my research on harvest mechanization in Britain I have had the benefit of comment and criticism from many friends and scholars on both sides of the Atlantic. Proper acknowledgement of these debts must wait until the study as a whole is published. Meanwhile, for having extended their financial support at one time or another to this undertaking (as part of an on-going project on the Trans-Atlantic Diffusion on Technology in the Nineteenth Century), the Ford Foundation, the Warden and Fellows of All Souls College, Oxford, and the Stanford University

Committee on Research in International Studies, all have my expressed gratitude.

[5] The basis and full import of this assertion cannot be adequately discussed here. Sceptics may, however, consult the data presented below (in Table 2), which pertains to the threshold wheat, rye and oats acreage for 'simple mechanization' in 1851. Note, then, that the average amount of arable devoted to wheat, rye and oats on *all* farms in England and Wales at the time was probably close to 23 acres. On what James Caird called 'the corn side of the island', the average would have stood well above the 25 acre break-even point indicated by Table 2.

[6] The details of the estimates of the overall extent of diffusion of mechanical reaping are too lengthy to be reproduced here, but a preliminary draft of the chapter of the larger study in which they are developed can be made privately available to the impatient. It should be noted that the figures cited in the text for the U.S.A. relate to the proportion of national acreage under wheat, oats, rye *and barley*, and supersede the diffusion measures offered in P. A. David, 'The mechanization of reaping in the ante-bellum Midwest', ch. 1 in H. Rosovsky (ed.), *Industrialization in Two Systems* (New York, Wiley, 1966), p. 10, n. 16. Keen-eyed readers will also note that the figures given here for Great Britain differ from those attributed to me by E. J. T. Collins, 'Labour supply and demand in European agriculture 1800-1880', ch. 3 in E. L. Jones and S. J. Woolf (eds.), *Agrarian Change and Economic Development, The Historical Problems* (London, Methuen, 1969), p. 75. The preliminary estimates cited by Collins, though in error, are nevertheless sufficiently accurate for the comparative use that Collins makes of them. As for the extent of harvest mechanization in the Lothians, cf. the data for the East Lothian harvest of 1860 from the *North British Agriculturalist*, cited by Jacob Wilson, 'Reaping machines', *Transactions of the Highland and Agricultural Society of Scotland*, 3rd series, XI, January 1864, p. 144; R. Scot Skirving, 'Ten years of East Lothian farming', *Journal of the Royal Agricultural Society of England*, 2nd series, I, 1865, p. 108.

[7] Cf. David, 'The mechanization of reaping', esp. pp. 26–8, for discussion of the relationship between the effects of the Midwestern economic environment and the effects of the physical environment on mechanization in the U.S.A.

[8] P. Pusey, 'On Mr McCormick's reaping-machine', *Journal R.A.S.E.*, XII, 1851, p. 160.

[9] *Farmer's Magazine* (London), September 1856, p. 189.

[10] Cf. Orwin and Whetham, *British Agriculture*, p. 112, on the problems caused by inefficient gearing, especially noticeable on Bell machines, where the cutter was placed far forward of the driving wheels. The use of additional horses would not, however, significantly increase speed in the case of 'pusher'-type machines on the Bell pattern. Cf. Wilson, 'Reaping machines', p. 131.

[11] *Farmer's Magazine*, September 1856, p. 189.

[12] John Wilson, *British Farming* (Edinburgh, 1862), pp. 147–8.

[13] Cf. William Wright, 'On the improvements in the farming of Yorkshire since the date of the last Reports in the Journal', *Journal R.A.S.E.*, XXII, 1861, p. 127, on the contrast between the type of reaping machine that could be used in the North Riding and on farms in the Yorkshire wolds. For parallel evidence primarily relating to Scotland, cf. Wilson, 'Reaping machines', pp. 131, 135–9. On the progress of 'agricultural mechanics', as applied to building mechanically more efficient reapers, cf., e.g., John Coleman and F.

A. Paget, 'General report on the exhibition of implements at the Plymouth meeting', *Journal R.A.S.E.*, 2nd series, I, 1865, pp. 373–405.

[14] Cf. W. J. Moscrop, 'A report on the farming of Leicestershire', *Journal R.A.S.E.*, 2nd series, II, 1866, p. 321, on irrigation trenches preventing the use of grass mowing machines, although hay-makers and horse-rakes could be used.

[15] James Caird, *English Agriculture in 1850-51* (London, 1852); G. E. Evans, *The Horse in the Furrow* (London, Faber, 1960), pp. 30–1.

[16] Evans, *The Horse in the Furrow*, p. 31.

[17] C. Lawrence, 'Letter on the use of the reaping machine, and the rootcrops in 1860', *Journal R.A.S.E.*, XXI, 1860, p. 551.

[18] J. H. Clapham, *An Economic History of Modern Britain* (Cambridge, Cambridge University Press, 1952), II, p. 269, citing the *Journal R.A.S.E.* prize essay for 1868.

[19] Cf. John Algernon Clarke, 'Farming of Lincolnshire', *Journal R.A.S.E.*, XII, 1851, p. 346.

[20] Caird, *English Agriculture*, p. 153.

[21] Cf. Evans, *The Horse in the Furrow*, pp. 30–1; Caird, *English Agriculture*, p. 153. Where 8.5 foot stetches called for uncommonly wide sowing and cultivating instruments, the gateways into the fields also had to correspondingly enlarged.

[22] Wilson, 'Reaping machines', p. 149.

[23] Reported in the *Farmer's Magazine*, XXII, July 1850, pp. 20–1, and quoted by Clark C. Spence, *God Speed the Plow, the Coming of Steam Cultivation to Great Britain* (Urbana, Ill., University of Illinois Press, 1960), p. 121. Mechi's theme on this occasion was the physical requirements for the successful application of steam power to cultivation, but with the exception of the special importance of field *shape* for efficient steam ploughing, many of the same considerations are relevant to the case of mechanical reaping. Cf. Spence, *God Speed the Plow*, pp. 120, 143–4.

[24] On Devonshire enclosures, cf. Caird, *English Agriculture*, p. 52, who regarded the presence of hedgerows as terribly injurious even before the appearance of mechanical reapers and mowers: 'Every operation of husbandry is impeded, a constant shifting of implements from field to field occasions waste of time, and does positive damage to the implements and the fields through which they passed . . . .' Cf. also Thomas George Bell, 'A report upon the agriculture of the country of Durham', *Journal R.A.S.E.*, XVII, 1856, p. 111.

[25] Wright, 'Improvements in the farming of Yorkshire', p. 127. This criticism was lodged particularly against the versions of the McCormick reaper built and marketed in Britain by Burgess and Key.

[26] James Slight, 'Report on reaping machines', *Trans. H.A.S.*, 3rd series, V, January 1852, pp. 193–4.

[27] This is based upon a set of calculations of the 'threshold' acreage, at which it would begin to be profitable to adopt Bell's machine, given the factor prices prevailing in Scotland during the period from *c.* 1828 to *c.* 1851, and assuming optimal terrain conditions such as those available to Patrick Bell's brother George, who continued to operate the machine on his farm in the Carse of Gowrie, Forfar, until some time in the early 1840s. Slight's 'Report on reaping machines', pp. 193–4, gives some of the details of George Bell's practice. The nature of the 'threshold calculation' for the case of simple mechanization is reviewed by Paragraphs 1–3 of the Technical Notes in Appendix A below.

[28] Wilson, *British Farming*, p. 148. Cf. also *The Encyclopaedia Britannica*, 9th ed. (Edinburgh, 1875), vol. I (A-ANA), p. 322, for a reiteration of this argument in the article on 'Agricultural implements and machinery', contributed by John Wilson.
[29] Cf. Clapham, *An Economic History*, II, pp. 270–1, for contemporary estimates of the cost and volume of drainage improvement work. The reference to James Caird appears in Orwin and Whetham, *British Agriculture*, p. 101. On the operation of the government loan programme, including estimates of expenditures during 1847-72 under the various Drainage and Improvement of Land Acts, cf. Orwin and Whetham, *British Agriculture*, pp. 194-200.
[30] Orwin and Whetham, *British Agriculture*, p. 101.
[31] Cf. Clapham, *An Economic History*, I, pp. 458–61, on the introduction of pipe-making machinery in the 1840s. See Appendix B below for the cost of drainage pipes and their installation.
[32] Cf., e.g., W. E. G. Salter, *Productivity and Technical Change,* 2nd ed. (Cambridge, Cambridge University Press, 1966), p. 52: '... the industrial plants in existence at any one time are, in effect, a fossilized history ....'
[33] It is possible that when the advantages offered for application of new techniques in some sub-set of complementary activities are terribly strong, the attempt to introduce a process innovation will issue in the fragmentation and ultimate transformation of a previously interlocking set of operations, or system of husbandry. In Britain during the 1890s the efforts of a few enterprising arable farmers to use tractors to mechanize their field work led to the demonstration that specialized grain farming was feasible. Since the early tractors could not deal with row crops, these were dropped from the rotation; and since the tractors were inefficient at haulage and often could not get into the cattle yards through the narrow entrances, as did the horses, stall-feeding of livestock and the carting of their dung was also dispensed with. The stockless grain farm in Britain was thus the logical consequence of the dogged effort to accommodate the early, non-versatile tractor as a satisfactory replacement for the horse. Cf. Whetham, 'Mechanization of British farming 1910-1945', *Journal of Agricultural Economics*, XXI, 2, May 1970, pp. 6–7.
[34] Cf. M. Frankel, 'Obsolescence and technological change', *American Economic Review*, vol. 45, June 1955, p. 296. The term 'interrelatedness' is Frankel's, but the modifier ('technical') has been added here to distinguish the class of relationships discussed by Frankel from the problems of institutional and market interdependence, which are treated under the same heading in C. P. Kindleberger. *Economic Growth in France and Britain 1851-1950* (Cambridge, Mass., Harvard University Press, 1964), pp. 193–47.
[35] Cf. *Report of the Cotton Textile Mission to the U.S.A.* (London, H.M.S.O., 1944), and *The Jute Working Party Report* (London, H.M.S.O., 1948), both of which are discussed by Salter, *Productivity and Technical Change*, p. 85.
[36] Cf. Thorstein Veblen, *Imperial Germany and the Industrial Revolution* (New York, Macmillan, 1915), pp. 126–7. Veblen actually referred to the necessity of changing 'terminal, facilities, tracks and shunting facilities', but cf. Kindleberger, *Economic Growth in France and Britain*, p. 142, n. 27.
[37] David, 'Mechanization of reaping'. For convenience, the variables and parameters entering the determination of the choice between mechanical and hand methods of harvesting grain are defined in Appendix A of the present paper – see Paragraphs 1, 2 and 3.

[38] If a reaping machine employed on a farm of a size equal to the threshold (defining 'size' here in terms of grain acreage) must earn – by definition – the annual imputed rental rate, which covers interest and amortization charges, on a farm with twice as much grain acreage the same machine would earn a gross rate of return equal to twice the rental rate. It seems equally obvious that for a farm of a *given* size, the gross rental rate earned on a single machine must vary *inversely* with the level of the threshold acreage. Nevertheless, since the point apparently eluded at least one reader of my earlier analysis (cf. George G. S. Murphy, 'Review of *Industrialization in Two Systems*', *Journal of Economic History*, XXVII, September 1967, p. 421, on the irrelevance of the concept of the threshold to any wealth-maximizing decision), a formal proof that the threshold acreage is the 'dual' of the gross rate of return is supplied by Paragraph 4 of the Technical Notes in Appendix A below.

[39] Note the important theoretical implication of this definition: over time it would be possible for the proportion of farms in the 'unimproved' category to decline, without any change in the total number of farms, or any physical improvements having been made. Progress in the design of machinery could increase its versatility in coping with a variety of terrain conditions. In such circumstances we would be justified in saying that outmoded farms had been directly 'improved' by subsequent technical progress in the farm machinery industry; and – so long as the manufacturers of machinery were unable to act as a discriminating monopolist would in setting different prices for their different farm customers – we might expect to find the 'improvement' reflected in a relative rise of the rental value of such *formerly* outmoded farms. The analogous point may be made in regard to the case of existing industrial buildings. Within the period with which the present analysis deals, however, there were no radical design advances of this sort in reaping equipment.

[40] *Productivity and Technical Change*, 2nd ed. (Cambridge, Cambridge University Press, 1966).

[41] Elements of indivisibility in the expenditures required to make the indicated improvements, leading to high fixed 'installation' costs, could give rise to this. Such indivisibilities need not have resulted from strict engineering considerations, and it should be noted that it was not *technically* impossible to drain and level, say, a single field, or even some portion of a field. Without indivisibilities, it is still possible that the fixed cost of preparing the land to permit effective mechanical reaping of a single acre of grain would largely offset the saving in labour costs per acre, thereby making it possible to cover the fixed annual rental charges for the machine only on big farms.

[42] *Farmer's Magazine*, XXII, July 1850, p. 20 (reporting a speech by Alderman Mechi to the Coggleshall Institute), quoted in Spence, *God Speed the Plow*, p. 120.

[43] Cf. Caird, *The Landed Interest and the Supply of Food* (London, 1878), pp. 46–7, 58, 60; G. C. Brodrick, *English Land and English Landlords* (London, 1881), pt II, ch. IV.

[44] Cf. J. D. Chambers and G. E. Mingay, *The Agricultural Revolution 1750-1880* (London, Batsford, 1966), pp. 160–1, 164–6; F. M. L. Thompson, *English Landed Society in the Nineteenth Century* (London, Routledge & Kegan Paul, 1963), p. 203–4, 227–31, on the question of leases in the period under consideration. For an example of restrictions

imposed in short, three to seven year leases, cf. Bell, 'Agriculture of the country of Durham', pp. 99–100.
[45] Cf. Caird, *English Agriculture*, pp. 503–10, and *The Landed Interest*; Alderman Mechi's address to the London Farmers' Club, *Farmer's Magazine*, XX, July 1849, p. 20; Léonce de Lavergne, *The Rural Economy of England, Scotland and Ireland* (Edinburgh, 1855), p. 294; Skirving, 'East Lothian farming', p. 111.
[46] Cf. Clapham, *An Economic History*, II, pp. 256–6, on the permissive legislation of 1875 and the Agricultural Holdings Act of 1883. Even when resort to the Act of 1883 became possible, it is questionable how much security tenants actually derived on durable improvement investments. Claims under the Act required documentation, and exposed tenants to counterclaims for violations of restrictions and to substantial penalties. Cf. Kindleberger, *Economic Growth in Britain and France*, p. 246, n. 147.
[47] Cf, Caird, *English Agriculture*, p. 328; Thompson, *Landed Society*, p. 250; Bell, 'Agriculture of Durham', pp. 99, 144. The typical charge in Durham seems to have been 5 per cent in the mid-1850s, but this was low by the standards that generally came to prevail. See further discussion below.
[48] Caird (*English Agriculture*, p. 328) rather confusedly castigates the landlord who would do this, for 'putting into his pocket 1 per cent, besides [sic] securing a permanently higher value for his land by an outlay to which he does not contribute a single farthing.' Note that Caird also got the landlord's profit rate wrong: twenty-two annual instalments of 6.5 per cent on the principal yielded the 3.5 per cent per annum interest rate charged under the government subsidized drainage loan programme initiated by Peel in 1846 and renewed in 1849. Analogously, annual instalments of 7.5 per cent would have yielded a 5 per cent per annum rate of return – a 1.5 per cent pure profit rate. On the government drainage loan schemes, cf. Orwin and Whetham, *British Agriculture*, pp. 195–6; Clapham, *An Economic History*, II, p. 271. Variants of these arrangements were set up by land improvement companies in the 1850s and 1860s (cf. Clapham, *An Economic History*, II, p. 272).
[49] Cf., e.g., Thompson, *Landed Society*, pp. 240–1.
[50] C. I. C. Bosanquet, *Farm Structures, Farm Mechanization (1946-47)*, p. 51, quoted in Whetham, 'The Mechanization of British Farming 1910-1945', p. 3.
[51] Where realignment of field boundaries of neighbouring tenant holdings was contemplated, such as was often the case in the conversion of farms to steam ploughing, for example, the number of interested parties would exceed the landlord and a single tenant. Cf. Spence, *God Speed the Plow*, p. 121. And where technical 'externalities' in maintaining an efficient system of field drains made it necessary to consider other people's ditches, streams and outfalls, several neighbouring landlords might have to combine. They were encouraged to do so by the Land Drainage Act of 1861 – which provided machinery for setting up Drainage Boards to deal with the improvement of a large area comprehensively. Cf. *Parliamentary Papers*, 1873, IX, House of Lords S.C. on Improvement of Land, pp. 344–52. This early legislative recognition of a classic 'non-pecuniary externalities problem' is noticed by Orwin and Whetham, *British Agriculture*, pp. 102, 198.
[52] Kindleberger, *Economic Growth in Britain and France*, p. 247.
[53] This is an objection that must be levelled at Kindleberger's more clearly elaborated analysis (*Economic Growth in Britain and France*, pp. 141–4) of

the failure of British railways to adopt larger coal cars. If the railway companies would have saved enough on operating costs to justify the change under a system in which coal cars and all related facilities would be owned by the railways, why could they not have arranged to compensate the mining companies (which owned the coal cars) for the investment in making the switch? Kindleberger does not examine whether sufficient compensation could have been paid to make collaboration attractive to the colliery-owners, or even whether the return on the total investment would have justified the investment under conditions of complete integration of activities, i.e. internalization of all benefits.

[54] Alternatively, the land rent savings could be added to the difference in operating costs in determining whether or not the conversion would be profitable for a farm of the size initially stipulated. Either procedure would amount to treating the capitalized value of the land rents saved on a par with the resale value of any other assets that could be disposed of in 'modernizing' the farm without reducing its output level. Cf. Salter, *Productivity and Technical Change*, pp. 55–8, for discussion of scrapping and replacement criteria in the case of industrial plant and equipment.

[55] Cf. Chambers and Mingay, *Agricultural Revolution*, p. 176.

[56] On the changing balance of grain and livestock profitability within mixed farming enterprise, cf. E. L. Jones, 'The changing basis of agricultural prosperity, 1853–73', *Agricultural History Review*, X, 1962, pp. 102–19.

[57] Cf. Thompson, *Landed Society*, pp. 250–3.

[58] Cf. H. S. Thompson, 'Account of a subsequent trial of the American reapers' (appendix to Implement Report), *Journal R.A.S.E.*, XII, 1851, p. 648.

[59] The use of swath-delivery reaping machines – of native British design – in this connection is referred to below. With manual delivery reapers fitted up with tipping platforms rigged for side-discharge, it was possible either to rake off the cut grain continuously, effectively laying it in swath, or to form sheaves. Such contrivances were developed during the 1860s as modifications of the original Hussey and McCormick devices, but unfortunately there is little information about their purchase costs and the per acre labour requirements associated with their use.
  Self-acting sheaf-delivery reapers, which also began to be marketed in Britain in the early 1860s, would only make work in the barley harvest – though they might afford side-delivery; barley delivered automatically in sheaf would have then to be spread out by hand to dry. The limited appeal of the 'self-rake' reaping machines in Scotland appears to have been due in large measure to essentially the same problem: they gave farmers no flexibility in handling grain that was too wet when cut to be safely bound into sheaves. Cf. the letter of 20 September 1865 from E. Alexander, of Stirling, to C. H. McCormick, cited by William T. Hutchinson, *Cyrus Hall McCormick*, vol. II (New York, Century, 130), p. 414, n. 19.

[60] See Appendix B, Table B.1.

[61] For the use of the standard annuity formula in making the calculation, see Paragraph 3 of the Technical Notes in Appendix A.

[62] Once the landowner had committed himself to a general policy of improvements – and announced the yearly improvement rental charge – his tenants would commonly have to apply to have specific changes made on the farms they occupied. Cf. Thompson, *Landed Society*, p. 255: 'It was very usual, as on the Northumberland estate, for the owner to fix the total annual appropriation for expenditure on his estate, but for its detailed farm

by farm application to be determined by the requests made by individual farmers for the draining of a field, the erection of a barn or the removal of a hedge.' The argument being advanced here, of course, holds that the rational landowner would not fix an estate improvement budget without reference to the charges he could anticipate extracting from those of his tenants who would apply to have specific projects carried out. The alternative interpretation of Table 2 is thus to treat it as depicting the marginal efficiency of (landlord's) investment as a function of the size of his tenants' grain acreages.

[63]   It is the maximum net rate of return on improvement net capital that would be compatible with minimally profitable mechanization by the tenant.

[64]   It certainly belongs in a category with the scale economies in the management of sheep flocks and the utilization of horses and carts, described for eighteenth-century English farms by John Arbuthnot of Mitcham, *An Inquiry into the Connection between the Present Price of Provisions and the Size of Farms. By a Farmer* (London, 1773), p. 8, to which reference is made in T. S. Ashton, *An Economic History of England: The 18th Century* (London, Methuen, 1955) pp. 43–4.

[65]   The situation just described is denoted by the zero entries for the mechanization-cum-improvement threshold in Table 2.

[66]   Cf., e.g., the use made of this rate by R. J. Thompson, 'An enquiry into the rent of agricultural land in England and Wales during the nineteenth century', *Journal of the Royal Statistical Society*, LXX, 1907, p. 619.

[67]   *Parliamentary Papers*, 1873, IX, House of Lords, S.C. on Improvement of Land, 'Report' para 9, subsec. 3, cited in Brodrick, *English Land,* pp. 69–70.

[68]   See Appendix B for further discussion. One may arrive at this inference directly, from the information presented by Table 2: at $r_I = .035$ the mechanization-cum-improvement threshold (S_T^{**}) exceeds the threshold applicable in the case of 'simple mechanization' – S_T^*, shown by the last line of the table. This indicates that some of the pure gains from mechanization must be applied to cover the improvement rental charges.

[69]   As the last row of Table 2 reveals, *c.* 1851 a manual sheaf-delivery reaper (in lieu of scythe-mowing of wheat and oats) would cover its own annual rental costs on the first 25.5 acres harvested, yielding pure profits – or quasi-rents – on the remaining 17.5 (= 43.0 – 25.5) acres up to the mechanization-cum-improvement threshold.

[70]   For $r_I = .0375$, $R_I = .0667$, from which the data in Table 1 enable us to calculate the $S_T^{**} = 80.0$ acres. Referring to the required improvement outlay per acre harvested *c.* 1851, we then find that $S_T^{**}(C_I A') = £2052$.

[71]   The following statements draw upon an examination of the characteristics of the size distribution of British farms, farm acreage and grain acreage, based on the complete census of agricultural holding in 1851 and data for a sample of seventeen counties from the census of 1871. The full details and documentation are too lengthy to give here, but will be provided in the larger monograph now in preparation.

[72]   Cf. Thompson, *Landed Society*, ch. IX, esp. pp. 248–55. 'Disappointingly' is used here with conscious intent, despite the view advanced by Thompson (*Landed Society*, p. 254) that landowners regarded their estates as assets whose very ownership constituted a luxury, and which *could not be expected* to yield financial returns of more than 2 or 2.5 per cent per annum on the purchase cost. There is a relevant distinction to be made between finding consolation for low monetary returns in the social

advantages conferred by landownership, and proceeding to sink more
money into the improving of estates whose ownership already conferred
prestige. Before arguing that mid-Victorian landowners looked forward with
equanimity to low rates of return on improvement expenditures it is
necessary to posit that in this era – and not only in eighteenth-century
England – the improvement of estates, not simply their ownership, was
considered socially prestigious.

[73] Cf. Thompson, *Landed Society*, pp. 250–1. Repairs of buildings are
excluded from the underlying expenditure figures in this calculation.

[74] Cf. Chambers and Mingay, *Agricultural Revolution*, p. 177.

[75] The average yield on 3 per cent Consols during 1850-9 was 3.16 per cent;
during 1860-9 it was 3.27 per cent; and during 1870-9 it was 3.19 per cent.
Cf. Sidney Homer, *A History of Interest Rates* (New Brunswick, N.J.,
Rutgers University Press, 1963), Table 19, pp. 195–7.

[76] *Parliamentary Papers*, 1873, IX, House of Lords S.C. on Improvement of
Land, 'Report', pp. iii–iv, quoted in Thompson, *Landed Society*, p. 251.

[77] The reader may find it easier to grasp the essence of the following argument
and counter-argument by turning at this point to a short mathematical
treatment of the effects of price and wage changes upon S_T^{**}. Such a
treatment is supplied by Paragraphs 5 and 6 of the Technical Notes in
Appendix A below. The verbal statement of the argument given in the text
is, nonetheless, complete and self-contained.

[78] Cf. Salter, *Productivity and Technical Change*, pp. 50–4 and ch. V.

[79] Evidence of the relatively slow rate of productivity growth in the British
construction industry is, admittedly, rather shaky – a rather firmer case can
be made in regard to the U.S. construction trades during the latter half of
the nineteenth century. But cf., e.g., G. T. Jones, *Increasing Returns*
(Cambridge, Cambridge University Press, 1933), pp. 58–100, on cost and
price movements in the London building trades, 1845-1913.

[80] See Appendix B for discussion of the estimated wage share in improvement
costs.

[81] This theoretical proposition is demonstrated in Paragraph 6 of the
Technical Notes in Appendix A.

Imposing the condition

$$\tilde{C}_m = \left[\frac{dC_m}{C_m} - \frac{dp}{p} \right] = 0,$$

equation (8) in Paragraph 5 of the Technical Notes may be rewritten as
follows:

$$dS_T^{**} = \left(\frac{pS_T^{**}}{g_m + g_I} \right) [\tilde{C}_I(I/p) - \tilde{w}(g_m/p)]. \qquad (8a)$$

This expression mirrors the statement in the text above, showing that the
threshold acreage will be raised if the term in the square brackets on the
R.H.S. of the equation is positive –,which it may well be even though real
wages are rising in accord with the conditions

$$\tilde{w} = [(dw/w) - (dp/p)] > 0, \text{ and } [\tilde{w} - \tilde{C}_m] > 0.$$

By imitating the proof given in Paragraph 4 of the Technical Notes in
Appendix A, the reader may readily satisfy himself that the pure profit rate
and the gross rate of return on a total investment for harvest mechanization

and complementary improvement of a farm with G acres under small grains – an investment of $(C_m + IG)$ – must vary inversely with the mechanization-cum-improvement threshold S_T^{**}.

[83] The connection between high farming's profitability and the adoption of new machinery is usually asserted in much looser fashion. It is suggested that 'prosperity' resulting from the level of grain prices in the 1853-73 era – in contrast with the plight of grain farmers in the last quarter of the century – encouraged (or, in some accounts, permitted) investment in farm equipment. Cf., e.g., Chambers and Mingay, *Agricultural Revolution*, pp. 177 ff.

[84] Cf. Spence, *God Speed the Plow*, pp. 103 ff. An exact analysis of the economics of steam-ploughing remains to be carried out, but Spence's interesting study makes it clear that 'the simple matter of expense' was a problem that continued to plague steam plough enthusiasts. During the 1860s and 1870s the question whether steam cultivation was or was not economically advantageous remained a subject of controversy. The Royal Agricultural Society concluded that, because of the initial expense entailed, for the equipment alone – leaving aside complementary land improvements – a steam plough would be an asset 'only on farms of more than 250 acres of heavy arable land' (Spence, *God Speed the Plow*, p. 118).

[85] Cf. Orwin and Whetham, *British Agriculture*, p. 112, for a convenient, brief account of these machines. Further details are to be found in James Slight and R. Scott Burn, *The Book of Farm Implements and Machines*, ed. Henry Stephens (Edinburgh, 1858), esp. pp. 357–9.

[86] A comparison of average savings in mower-equivalent man-days for manual sheaf-delivery and automatic swath-delivery machines working in the several grain crops, and for representative mixes of wheat, oats and barley suggested by the acreage figures for Great Britain in the late 1860s and early 1870s, is to be found in Table B.1 of Appendix B. Corresponding purchase prices for various designs and makes of reaping machinery in the early 1860s have been drawn from Wilson, 'Reaping machines', pp. 131–9. The details of the threshold calculation are omitted here in the interest of brevity.

[87] Cf. Chambers and Mingay, *Agricultural Revolution*, pp. 172–6. Farms of 300 acres, if they followed the pattern of land allocation characteristic of the agricultural sector in England and Wales as a whole, would have had approximately 60 acres under wheat and oats (and rye) – a figure quite consistent with the findings reported by Table 2.

[88] Cf. *Parliamentary Accounts and Papers, 1852-3*, XXXII, 1851 census, 'Report', p. lxxx. The totals cited by Clapham, *An Economic History*, II, p. 264, differ slightly from these, for reasons not altogether clear.

[89] Cf. P. G. Craigie, 'Agricultural holdings in England and abroad', *Journal R.S.S.*, L, 1887, pp. 86 ff.; Clapham, *An Economic History*, II, pp. 264-5, thought it most likely that the throwing together of little hill farms in Wales had figured significantly in these developments reflected by the farm size distribution statistics for 1885.

TECHNICAL NOTES

Paragraph 1: Definition of the threshold acreage for simple mechanization, S_T^*.

Let the imputed annual money rental cost of a single reaping machine be (M), and the money gain through the reduction of harvest labour costs by mechanization be $(g_m)_k$ for the kth acre of grain harvested. The threshold acreage for adoption of mechanical harvesting is then defined by the equality,

$$(1) \qquad M = \sum_{k=1}^{S_T^*} (g_m)_k .$$

As it is legitimate to treat the difference between the variable cost functions for the hand and machine methods of harvesting as linear over the relevant operating range, S_T^* in eq. (1) may be estimated from

$$(2) \qquad S_T^* = M/(g_m).$$

Paragraph 2: The saving in harvest costs per acre, g_m.

For the choice between harvesting with a manual delivery reaping machine and harvesting with scythes ('harvesting' including all operations from cutting to stooking), the following notation is relevant:

Hand method labour coefficients, in man-days per crop acre,

ℓ_1 = mowers;
ℓ_2 = gatherers; $\qquad \ell_3$ = binders and stookers.

Machine method labour coefficients, in man-days per crop acre,

m_1 = machine drivers and rakers;
m_2 = binders and stookers.

Note that $m_1 = N_1/a$, where N_1 is the number of drivers and rakers per machine, and (a) is the normal daily cutting rate of the machine, in acres.

Relative wage rates exclusive of food, and food costs,

$v_1 = w_1/w_1 = 1$,   mower's wage rates being the numeraire;
$v_i = w_i/w_1$,   for hand method wage rates in general;
$v_j = w_j/w_1$,   for machine method wage rates in general;
f,   daily food cost per worker;
$f' =$ $(f)/(w_1 + f)$.

Total labour costs per acre harvested, inclusive of food are therefore:

$$w_1 \Sigma_i v_i \ell_i + f \Sigma_i \ell_i, \quad \text{for the hand method,}$$

and

$$w_1 \Sigma_j v_j m_j + f \Sigma_i m_j, \quad \text{for the machine method.}$$

The difference in operating costs per acre harvested may then be represented as

$$(3) \qquad g_m = w(L_s^*),$$

where

$w = (w_1 + f)$, is the mower's daily wage rate including food,

and

L_s^*, the labour savings in mower-equivalent man-days per acre, is given by

$$L_s^* = (1 - f')(Q_h \Sigma \ell_i - Q_m \Sigma m_j) + f'(\Sigma \ell_i + \Sigma m_j),$$

defining

$$Q_h = (\Sigma v_1 \ell_i)/(\Sigma \ell_i) \quad \text{and} \quad Q_m = (\Sigma v_j m_j)/(\Sigma m_j).$$

Paragraph 3: Determination of the imputed annual rental cost of a reaping machine.

Let C be the money purchase cost of a reaping machine, and R be its annual imputed rental cost to the farmer, such that

$$(4) \qquad M = R(C).$$

Given the rate of interest (r) and the service life of the machine, in years, (D), the standard annuity formula may be employed to determine

$$(5) \qquad R = r(1 - e^{-rD})^{-1}.$$

Note that this involves setting

$$C = \int_0^D M(t)e^{-rt}dt,$$

taking $M(t) = M$ for all $t = (0, \ldots, D)$, whence, upon evaluation of the definite integral we obtain equation (5).

Paragraph 4: To prove: The gross rate of return on a reaping machine is, for any given farm, inversely proportional to the threshold acreage.

Consider a farm with small grain acreage G. After covering interest and depreciation charges on a reaping machine in the given year, the pure (or super-normal) profit rate on the original investment in the machine is

$$\pi = [(G - S_T^*)g_m]/C,$$

since, by definition, S_T^* is the break-even point in the farmer's harvesting operations. However, from equations (1) and (4) we have

$$S_T^* = RC/g_m,$$

which, upon substitution in the expression immediately above, yields,

$$\pi = R[(G/S_T^*) - 1].$$

The *gross* rate of return on the original investment in the machine is $(R + \pi) = \rho$, from which it follows directly that

$$(6) \qquad \rho = R(G)/(S_T^*). \qquad\qquad\qquad\qquad \text{Q.E.D.}$$

Paragraph 5: Effects of price and wage rate changes on the mechanization-cum-improvement threshold acreage.

In the case of technical interrelatedness considered, we arrive at an augmented expression for the threshold acreage at which it would just begin to be profitable to mechanize the harvest by first making the required farm 'improvements':

$$(7) \qquad R_m C_m - (p\dot{y}G' + wL_s^* - C_I R_I A')S_T^{**} = 0.$$

Note the following:

(i) The direct gain from improvements, per acre of small grain harvested, is a function of (p) the price of grain and two parameters.

(ii) Subscripts m and I distinguish between the capital outlays for the reaping machine and those for 'improvements', respectively.

(iii) The capital outlay on improvements, per acre of small grain harvested, is

$$I = A'C_I,$$

where A' is a parameter of proportionality, between acreage required to be improved for every acre harvested annually by the machine method. Furthermore,

$$C_I = C_I(w, z),$$

indicating that capital outlays on improvement are a function of agricultural wage rates and prices of materials (z).

Paul A. David 195

Taking the total derivative of (7), under the following conditions,

$$\left.\begin{array}{l} \partial G'/\partial p = dG' = 0 \\[6pt] \partial A'/\partial p = dA' = 0 \end{array}\right\}$$ there is no adjustment in crop mix within the arable;

$$d\dot{y} = 0$$ physical yield effects of improvements are constant;

$$\partial L_s^*/\partial w = dL_s^* = 0$$ there is no autonomous or induced innovation in reaping machinery, or in hand methods of harvesting small grain;

$$0 = dR_m = dR_I = dz$$ rental rates, and the price of materials used for improvements are fixed parameters;

we therefore obtain the following expression;

$$(8) \qquad \frac{dS_T^{**}}{S_T^{**}} = \frac{I}{(g_m + g_I)}\,\tilde{C}_I + \tilde{C}_m - \frac{g_m}{(g_m + g_I)}\,\tilde{w},$$

in which the notation and definitions given below are employed.

$$\tilde{w} = \frac{dw}{w} - \frac{dp}{p},$$ the percentage change in the real wage rate.

$$\tilde{C}_m \equiv \frac{dC_m}{C_m} - \frac{dp}{p},$$ the percentage change in the real (grain) price of a reaping machine.

$$\tilde{C}_I \equiv \epsilon\frac{dw}{w} - \frac{dp}{p},$$ the percentage change in the real (grain) cost of the improvement of an acre, due to the change in the wage rates of agricultural labour, $\epsilon \equiv (\partial C_I/C_I)/(\partial w/w)$.

$$(g_m + g_I) = R_m C_m/S_T^{**}$$ the initial monetary gain, per acre of small grains harvested, arising from mechanization-cum-improvement.

Paragraph 6: To prove: In the absence of other changes the perverse effect of a rise in real wage rates upon the mechanization-cum-improvement threshold is not restricted to the class of technically complementary improvements whose production is a labour-intensive process.

From equation (8) we can write the general condition for a perverse change in the threshold acreage:

(9) $\dfrac{dS_T^{**}}{S_T^{**}} > 0$ when $\tilde{w} > 0$, if $[(g_m + g_I)\,\tilde{C}_m + I\tilde{C}_I] > g_m\tilde{w}$.

For simplicity let us impose the further restrictions, and consider the situation in which

$$\tilde{C}_m = 0 \text{ and } \qquad \frac{dp}{p} = 0,$$

noting that $dw/w > 0$ still implies a rise in the price of labour relative to the price of the reaping machine and relative to the price of grain.
The condition for a perverse movement in S_T^{**} then simplifies to:

$$(\tilde{C}_I/\tilde{w}) > (g_m/I).$$

But since under the assumed restrictions we now have $\tilde{w} = dw/w$, and $\tilde{C}_I = \epsilon\,dw/w$, ϵ being the elasticity of C_I with respect to w, the condition for the perverse wage-effect is fulfilled for $(\epsilon < 1/2)$ relatively capital-intensive 'improvements' whenever $(g_m/I) < \epsilon$.

                                                                    Q.E.D.

SOURCES OF THE ESTIMATES OF PARAMETERS
AND VARIABLES EMPLOYED IN TABLE 1

*1   Costs of improvements per acre of wheat and oats harvested, C_{IA}
c. 1851.*

(*a*) C_I, the cost of improvements per acre, represents the sum of
unit costs $(C_{I,i})$ in each of three improvement activities: draining,
spreading the subsoil, and levelling.

The costs of drainage: At any given date the cost of installing
subsurface drains depended upon how widely apart the pipes were
placed. The maximum spacing that seems to have been thought still
worthwhile was 30–36 ft. Installation of pipes on this basis cost £5 per
acre drained at the beginning of the 1850s, exclusive of the cost of
carting the pipes – as carting was normally provided by the farmer
rather than the landlord (cf. Lord Wharncliffe, 'On draining, under
certain conditions of soil and climate', *Journal R.A.S.E.*, XII, 1851,
pp. 56–7, for estimates of costs of £5.7.9. per acre drained with 30 ft
spacing, and £4.9.10½. with 36 ft spacing. On soggy land, however, this
would prove inadequate and 24 ft between drains most likely would be
required, which would run about £6 per acre – according to the
information showing the variation of unit installation costs as a
function of spacing, in *The Encyclopaedia Britannica*, I, 1875, p. 334.
Moscrop, 'The Farming of Leicestershire', pp. 306–7, refers to £6 as the
usual, historical cost of draining an acre of clay land. Further
contemporary testimony to this figure's appropriateness, drawn from
the *Transactions of the Surveyors Institution*, 1871-2, pp. 66, 102, is
cited by R. J. Thompson, 'The rent of agricultural land'. As one
seeks contemporary evidence at later points in the century, e.g., in
Albert Pell, 'The making of the land in England', *Journal R.A.S.E.*,
series 2, XXIII, pp. 335 ff., the representative historical drainage
cost figures tend to drift upwards – which is precisely what is to be
anticipated.

Spreading subsoil: Spreading the subsoil raised by digging trenches
for the drains was thought to be very beneficial in its effects upon grain
yields, particularly when the subsoil was mixed with chalk. Hamilton
Fulton, 'Drainage of Hethel Wood Farm', *Journal R.A.S.E.*, XII, 1851,
pp. 150–1, mentions 19*s.* per acre as the cost of spreading the subsoil on
a Norfolk farm on which the spacing between the trenches was closer to
30 ft than to the 24 ft assumed here. Adding 20*s.* to the drainage costs

estimated above will bring the combined figure up to £7 per acre, without running a serious risk of overstatement.

Levelling: The cost of levelling the tillage once drained is more difficult to estimate. On the basis of statements as to the costs of ploughing up the topsoil and levelling the field by casting the soil into adjacent furrows, the unit price of the completed work may be put at £2 per acre. This makes use of Chandos Wren Hoskins, 'On "ridge-and-furrow" pasture land, and a method of levelling it', *Journal R.A.S.E.*, XVII, 1856, pp. 327–31, omitting the costs attributable to the operation of paring and rolling the turf back before ploughing on the crown of the ridge, and then rolling the turf back into place. On tillage land, obviously, the extra expense for the preservation of the turf during levelling would not arise. Note, however, that the cost estimate may well be on the low side, as the levelling of pasture land was undertaken to prevent burning of crown grass on drained land still lying in ridge and furrow, and would not have been carried out as thoroughly as improvement work undertaken to prepare a field for reaping machines.

Together, the cost of these operations c. 1851 comes to £9 per acre of land drained (C_I), a figure that is not out of line with the improvement expenditures per acre of *all* land – arable and pasture – reported for large landowners by Thompson, *Landed Society*, p. 250.

(*b*) A', the ratio of arable acreage to the acreage under wheat and oats is treated as a parameter in this analysis. From the *Agricultural Statistics* for the years 1867-72 it appears that approximately 35 per cent of arable was devoted to the two crops here assumed to be machine cut (cf. B. R. Mitchell and Phyllis Deane, *Abstract of British Historical Statistics* (Cambridge, Cambridge University Press, 1962), p. 78); the representative British farmer, whose arable was distributed like that of the country at large, would thus have to drain $(1/0.35) = 2.85$ acres per acre of wheat and oats.

(*c*) ϵ, the share of C_I attributable to labour costs is a parameter that is relevant in estimating the influence exerted by changes in the level of agricultural wage rates upon unit improvement costs after 1851. It is found that labour costs comprised 57 per cent of the expense of installing pipe drainage, exclusive of haulage, and that this share was essentially invariant with respect to the spacing of the pipes. *The Encyclopaedia Britannica*, I, 1875, p. 334, provides data from which we can compute that the labour share moved from 57 per cent to 58.4 per cent as the width of the spacing increased from 24 to 30 ft, and declined to 56.6 per cent when pipes were densely laid at 18 ft intervals. (Because it is argued that we can reasonably expect reductions in the relative price of drainage pipe *vis-à-vis* labour to have led to a higher pipe-labour input mix, and thus closer spacing of drains, which permitted adequate draining of heavier soils, it is important that the labour share appears to have been an elasticity parameter that would remain unchanged in the face of the rise of wage rateś relative to the price of drainage materials.) The other two operations – spreading the subsoil and levelling – particularly the latter, would involve the use of horses; but, as this work would be done at times during the year when the farmer's horses were not otherwise engaged, the two activities can justifiably be treated as having been purely labour-using.

Thus, for all three parts of the improvement work combined, the labour bill would amount to approximately 70 per cent of the estimated outlay – i.e. weighting the shares, we find $\epsilon = [.57(6/9) + 1.0(3/9)] = .713$.

2 Value of the direct benefit from land improvements per acre of wheat and oats harvested, $(p\dot{y}G')$, c. 1851.

(*a*) $\dot{y}$, the incremental wheat yield, in bushels per acre sown, is estimated on the assumption that the farmer would enjoy a 15 per cent improvement in the level of his cereal yields as a consequence of drainage and spreading the subsoil – without any other changes in farm practice, such as manuring with solid or liquid fertilizers. The proportional improvement in yields is suggested by the few and scattered contemporary reports of what seem to have been noteworthy increases in yield following drainage: Caird (*English Agriculture*, p. 374) cites the case of a Northumberland strong-land farmer who was extremely pleased to find his farm 'had been increased 20 per cent in its produce of wheat by pipe drainage'. There were other, still more optimistic figures mentioned, but they all are hedged with qualifications that lead one to rather discount them. For example, a civil engineer, writing in 1851, thought there was 'little doubt' that spreading the subsoil 'in conjunction with *perfect* drainage' would raise yields 30 per cent (emphasis mine) (cf. Fulton, 'Drainage of Hethel Wood Farm', p. 151).

Starting from an average wheat yield of 26.67 bushels per acre, as estimated for England as a whole in 1850-1 (cf. Caird, *English Agriculture*, p. 480), a 15 per cent gain in yield would provide $\dot{y} = 4.0$, bringing the average above 30 bushels per acre. It can be argued that, historically, the reductions in the relative price of drainage pipe encouraged closer spacing of drains (requiring more pipes per acre) and thus permitted cheaper attainment of *adequate* draining on heavier land, rather than better and better drainage – with consequently greater yield increases – on moderate and light soils. These calculations therefore make no allowance for a rise in *average* cereal yields per acre in response to alterations in the price of drainage materials relative to rural labour wage rates.

   (*b*)   ($p\dot{y}$), the value of the additional grain yield per acre drained *c.* 1851, is determined by referring to the prevailing price of wheat per bushel (*p*). The average *London Gazette* price of wheat for 1849-52 stood at 41*s.* per imperial quarter, according to the data reproduced in Mitchell and Deane, *British Historical Statistics*, p. 488. Taking 40*s.* per quarter as a notional price, and reckoning 8 bushels of 63 lb to the quarter, we find *p* = 5*s.*, and (*py*) = 20*s.* at this date.

   While ($p\dot{y}$) is estimated on the basis of the value of the yield increment when the drained land was sown with wheat, this does not imply that all the cereal acreage of the farm need have been devoted to that crop. Bushel yields of oats and barley per acre were higher than the average wheat yield, so that an appreciation of 15 per cent would imply larger absolute incremental bushel yields of those grains as a result of drainage. But the bushel price of oats and barley was correspondingly lower than that for wheat. Indeed, if the farmer had achieved an efficient allocation of his cereal acreage, the marginal value product of his land (and of land improvements) would be identical for all the cereals – relative quantity yields varying inversely with relative prices – and it would make no difference which of the grains was considered for the purpose of estimating ($p\dot{y}$) at the margin. Note that this holds true among the cereals, as there were, to all intents and purposes, pure substitutes in the rotation; it would not be correct to assert that in equilibrium the market value of an additional acre of root crops would equal the market value of giving that acre over to cereals. The shift away from the root crops, or rotation grasses under a regime of convertible husbandry, could be expected to lower the steady-state yield on the intra-marginal cereal acreage.

   (*c*)   A generous estimate of the value of the additional cereal yield per acre of wheat and oats harvested ($p\dot{y}G'$), *c.* 1851, is obtained by putting $G' = 1.6$. The *Agricultural Statistics* for the late 1860s and early 1870s suggest that for Britain as a whole approximately 66 per cent of cereal acreage was devoted to wheat and oats, which would imply

$G' = (1/0.66) = 1.5$. The stability of the relative position of wheat and oats, taken together, among all cereal crops in England and Wales throughout the last quarter of the nineteenth century is strikingly evident in the analysis of the acreage statistics presented by R. H. Best and J. T. Coppock, *The Changing Use of Land in Britain* (London, Faber, 1962), pp. 88–9.

(*d*) A check on the plausibility of the present set of estimates is provided by considering their implications regarding the anticipated rate of return to investment in land improvements *c.* 1851, in the absence of mechanization.

The government's programme aimed at encouraging drainage investment was established during 1846-9, and, as noted in the text (pp. 153, 170), offered financing at 3.5 per cent per annum over a twenty-two year amortization period – with annual repayments running at 6.5 per cent of the principal. If Robert Peel and the other sponsors of the Drainage Act had in mind the draining and spreading of the subsoil of the entire arable (omitting levelling) at a cost of £7 per acre, and the value of the incremental yield with wheat at 40*s.* per quarter, they were contemplating a subsidy to landowners of 2.0 or 2.5 per cent per annum. This would follow from consideration of the value of the annual incremental yield as a fraction of the total capital expense: $(20s.)(1.6)/(140s.)(2.85) = (32s.)/(399s.) = .0802$, which would be sufficient to amortize the principal in twenty-two years and yield a compound rate of return between 5.5 and 6.0 per cent per annum.

It is not inconceivable that in the late 1840s Peel and his friends had in mind an even more generous compensation to the landowning class for the injury so recently done them by the repeal of the Corn Laws. The average price of wheat during the 1840s had stood above 50*s.* per quarter, so that were the latter taken as the notional price in valuing the incremental yield of grain – instead of the 40*s.* price that actually prevailed *c.* 1851 – the implied anticipated rate of return on the expenditures just considered would have been upwards of 8.0 per cent per annum. Were the levelling of the drained fields to be undertaken, however, the initial outlay would have been larger, so that even with wheat at 50*s.* per quarter the annual proportional return $[(4 \text{ bush})(6.25s. \text{ per bush})(1.6)/(180s.)(2.85)] = (40s./513s.) = .078$, would generate an average annual compound rate of return of only 5.5 per cent over the twenty-two year amortization period. As it was, *c.* 1851, with wheat fetching 5*s.* per bushel the annual value of the yield enhancement as a proportion of the corresponding total improvement outlay was (0.0624) insufficient to generate the 3.5 per cent per annum rate of interest made available to landlords by the Drainage Loan Acts.

3   The per acre savings in harvest labour due to mechanization, (L_S^{**}).

The saving in labour realized through the use of mechanical reapers has been estimated on the basis of a comparison with the labour required when standing grain was mown by scythesmen, rather than cut by small hand tools such as sickles or reaping hooks. E. J. T. Collins, 'Harvest technology and labour supply in Britain, 1790-1870', *Economic History Review*, 2nd series, XXII, 3, December 1969, pp. 453–73, provides a convenient description of the different hand techniques and some of the available evidence indicating that per acre labour requirements were lower for mowing than for the other methods. On harvest cost differences between standing grain and laid grain, cf. P. A. David, 'Labour productivity in English Agriculture, 1850-1914: some quantitative evidence of regional differences', *Economic History Review*, December 1970, and available in mimeograph as Research Memorandum No. 68, Stanford University Research Center in Economic Growth (July 1969). The comparison between hand method and machine method labour requirements per acre of wheat and oats is made for the entire harvest operation – cutting, binding and stooking, as described in Paragraph 2 of the Technical Notes in Appendix A.

Full details of the estimates made, with appropriate comments and corroborative evidence cannot be presented in the space available here. The L_{iS}^{*}-coefficient for the manual sheaf-delivery reaper, which has been employed in Tables 1 and 2, is drawn from Table B.1: it is the weighted average of separate coefficients of labour-saving estimated for wheat and for oats, on the basis of A. Hammond's Practice. Note, from Table B.1 that the L_{iS}^{*}-coefficient used is on the generous side of the estimate derived on the basis of P. Love's practice with manual sheaf-delivery machines. Love, however, managed his harvest labour on a piece-work system known as 'thraving', and appears to have been uncommonly economical in the use of ancillary workers in gathering, binding and stooking behind the mowers: the overall labour savings he reported having realized through instituting machine-cutting were rather smaller than might otherwise be anticipated. Cf. Peter Love, 'On harvesting corn', *Journal R.A.S.E.*, XXIII, 1862, pp. 217–26, for the data underlying estimated labour-savings in harvesting wheat with the hand rake, and the swath-delivery machines, which are shown in Table B.1.

TABLE B.1
*Savings of mower-equivalent man-days of labour per acre
for different grain crops*

	L_S^*-coefficient with a single machine		
Per acre of harvested:	Manual sheaf-delivery reaper,		Swath-delivery reaper,
	Hammond's practice	*Love's practice*	*Love's practice*
WHEAT, cut (gathered), bound and stooked:	1.416	1.100	0.712
OATS, cut (gathered), bound and stooked:	0.667	0.413	0.440
WHEAT and OATS [a]	1.096	0.804	0.594
BARLEY, cut:	0	0	0.361
WHEAT, OATS and BARLEY [b]	0.800	0.587	0.532

(a) Wheat and oats coefficients weighted in proportions of 57 : 43.
(b) Wheat, oats and barley coefficients weighted in proportions of 42 : 31 : 27, respectively.

The sources of the estimates based on A. Hammond's practice may be briefly indicated, following the approach outlined in Paragraph 2 of the Technical Notes. The latter, of course, refers to the computation of L_S^* for a single homogenous grain crop; thus,

Harvesting wheat: the ℓ_i- and m_j-coefficients are derived from Anthony Hammond, 'Use of reaping-machines', *Journal R.A.S.E.*, XVII, 1856, pp. 339–40; the relative wage structures v_i and v_j are based on information in the same source, and the representative wage quotations for England, *c.* 1851, in Henry Stephens, *The Book of the Farm*, 2nd ed. (Edinburgh, 1955), II, pp. 345–6; daily food costs per worker, as a fraction of mowers' daily wages inclusive of food (*f*) are based on Stephens, *The Book of the Farm*, II, p. 346, and ibid., 3rd ed. (Edinburgh, 1871), II, p. 313.

Harvesting Oats: The ℓ_i-coefficients derived for wheat from Hammond 'Use of reaping-machines', were adjusted downward using a factor of 0.667 derived from John Taylor, 'On the comparative merits of different modes of reaping grain', *Trans. H.A.S.*, July 1844, pp. 262–3. According to the latter source, a force of 7 workers – 2 mowers, 2 gatherers, 2 binders and 1 boy, raking – in 10 hours cut 2.75 acres of wheat (2*A*.3*R*.0*P*.); working in oats and barley the same force cut 4.125 acres (4*A*.0*R*.20*P*) in the same time. Consequently, the same downward adjustment of the ℓ_i-coefficients provided by Love ('On harvesting corn') for wheat were made in order to estimate the L_S^*-coefficients for barley harvested with the swath-delivery machine. Otherwise, all the data employed in estimating the L_S^*-coefficient for oats harvesting with the hand-rake reaping machine following Hammond's practice were drawn from the sources described above.

4   *Wages and prices – w, p, C_m, and C_I – from c. 1851 to c. 1871.*

(*a*)   Mowers' daily wage inclusive of the cost of food, (*w*), is estimated as having been 3*s*. for England in general *c*. 1851, on the basis of Stephens, *Book of the Farm*, pp. 345–46. This initial observation was extrapolated to later dates on the basis of an index of harvest labour wage rates in England's corn counties in 1850, 1860 and 1870. The index was formed by first computing an average of the daily farm money wage indexes for a representative group of twelve counties in England drawn from A. L. Bowley, 'Statistics of wages in the United Kingdom during the past hundred years', *Journal R.S.S.*, LXI, December 1898, pp. 704–6.

The resulting average index numbers resemble the daily wage series for Northumberland quite closely, permitting the use of the relationship between the wage rates of 'ordinary' and 'harvest' workers observed in Northumberland on these three dates to convert the index based on Bowley's data into a harvest wage rate index. Cf. A. Wilson Fox, 'Agricultural wages in England and Wales during the last fifty years', *Journal R.S.S.,* LXVI, June 1903, p. 320, for the harvest differential in Northumberland. The resulting index, based on 1850 = 100, is: 131.3 in 1860, and 154.5 in 1870. The decadal movements have been put at 30 per cent and 50 per cent, respectively, for the 1850s and 1860s in Table I.

(*b*)   The price of wheat per bushel, (*p*), *c*. 1851 was roughly extrapolated on the basis of the *Gazette* quotations of the price of wheat per imperial quarter averaged for 1849-52, 1859-62 and 1869-72; 41*s*., 51*s*. 8*d*., 52*s*. 2*d*., as computed from Mitchell and Deane, *British Historical Statistics*, p. 488. The decade averages show a slightly different course: for 1841-50, 53*s*. 3*d*., for 1851-60, 54*s*. 7*d*.; for 1861-70, 51*s*. 1*d*.

(*c*)   Estimated delivered cost of McCormick Hussey type, manual sheaf-delivery, reaping machines (C_m); based on quotations of £30 *c*. 1851 and *c*. 1861, and £21 *c*. 1871, with 10 per cent delivery charge added. Cf. Slight, 'Report on reaping machines', p. 197; Hammond,

'Use of reaping machines', p. 49; Wilson, 'Reaping machines', p. 135; Coleman and Paget, 'Exhibition of implements', p. 389; Orwin and Whetham, *British Agriculture,* p. 110 (for price of two-horse machine quoted at the Manchester Exhibition of 1869).

(*d*)   The unit cost of improvements (C_I) after *c.* 1851 has, for simplicity, been estimated in Table 1 on the assumption that the elements of the farm wage structure moved together. This allows the use of the percentage rate of rise in (*w*) to serve as a proxy for the percentage increase in wages paid workers engaged on land improvement projects. Table 1 further assumes that the money price of agricultural pipe and other materials used in drainage remained essentially unchanged. Thus the decadal changes in C_I are estimated from the percentage change in (*w*) and the estimate of the elasticity parameter (ϵ).

Chairman: P. Temin

Prepared Comments: E. H. Hunt, Barbara Solow

Hunt: David's paper was an interesting and formidable one. Like many other papers at the conference, it is a study of Victorian entrepreneurship: British farmers and landlords emerge from the analysis with their reputations enhanced. To the extent that general themes and impressions can arise from a series of conference papers, the most evident here is that, taken together, the papers constitute a formidable rebuttal to charges of entrepreneurial shortcomings over considerable sectors of the British economy. The central thesis in David's paper is that the relatively slow adoption of harvesting machinery was far more a consequence of Britain's uncongenial farming landscape than of either entrepreneurial deficiencies or relative labour abundance. This is entirely convincing. A half or more of total man-hour requirements on arable farms was concentrated in the harvest period: at this time labour was not abundant, nor was it cheap, because harvest work was relatively well paid. These points tend to be overlooked in explanations of slow harvest mechanization that stress labour abundance.

There are some points that require clarification, especially in that part of the paper devoted to statistical exercises. The exactitude suggested in this part is less convincing than the general impressions that emerge from the literary evidence, although this impression may well be modified when David publishes his evidence in full. Three points in particular stand out. First, a problem acknowledged in the paper as likely to introduce uncertainty into the 'threshold' calculation, but not satisfactorily resolved, is that the land improvements that were usually a prerequisite of harvest mechanization were also necessary before mowing, drilling and other non-harvest machines could be used; their costs, therefore, should be distributed over these various operations and not considered as part of the cost of introducing reapers alone. A second difficulty concerns the cost of operating reapers. Doubtless one reason why farmers hesitated to purchase reapers in the early 1850s was that professional repair facilities were inadequate and because they doubted the ability of their own men to cope with minor breakdowns. It is reasonable to suppose that over time repair facilities improved and farm labourers acquired some degree of mechanical competence. As this occurred, the 'threshold' size (that is, the acreage at which it became worthwhile for a farm to buy a reaper) would fall.

The third point, on which the paper is curiously silent, concerns cooperation. To what extent were farmers able to reduce the cost of mechanization and so lower their 'threshold' by cooperating, either formally or informally, in the purchase and use of reapers, or by hiring reapers from contractors?

While the general conclusion on the relative unimportance of labour abundance and the importance of the 'farming landscape' is convincing, it would be wrong to ignore labour entirely. In some areas, particularly in East Anglia, farmers had less control over harvest operations than the paper implies. At harvest time part of the managerial function was transferred to the labour force; they selected two of their members, the lord and lady of the harvest, to negotiate with the farmer for a lump sum to cover the entire cost of harvest labour. In such cases labour may have resisted attempts to introduce machinery because they depended on high harvest earnings to pay their rent, the shoemaker, and similar accounts settled annually and too onerous to be met from their normally low earnings. Another variable that should find a place somewhere in the paper is climate. There are contemporary references to Scottish farmers buying reapers, not because harvest labour was scarce or dear but because reapers allowed maximum exploitation of limited periods of fine weather. In those areas where harvesting was hampered by a fickle climate the mechanizing 'threshold' was likely to be lower than in more favoured regions.

Some of the digressions in the paper, and the implications that David suggests might follow from his findings, are less convincing than his central theme. Conditions at harvest time were exceptional. During most of the year, across large areas of Britain, labour was abundant and badly paid and this was, as in the case of the threshing machine, almost certainly a barrier to mechanization in general. For these reasons the paper's conclusions are probably more specific to reapers than David suggests. His comments on the cost of introducing reapers after 1873 also require clarification. He considers that, although labour costs increased in these years, mechanization still lagged because the saving that might have been expected to follow harvest mechanization was offset by the increased cost of land improvement necessary before reapers could be used. The suggestion is ingenious but entirely unsubstantiated. Did farmers and landlords think in these terms? Are there figures of improvement costs that show an increase at this time? Is it possible that high wages were not accompanied by higher costs (because at this time farm workers' productivity was closely related to diet, which, in turn, was a function of income)? The cost of improvement varied also according to season. In the winter, when underemployment was widespread, the real cost of labour used for land improvement may have been very low indeed. Appendix B discounts the cost of horsepower used in the winter on the grounds that the horses would not be otherwise occupied at this time: surely it would be reasonable to discount part of the cost of manpower for very similar reasons. As they stand, the comments on mechanization after 1873, in short, are highly speculative. It would be no less plausible to argue that rising real wages encouraged farmers to use their labour more efficiently in the winter by engaging in *more* land improvement, thus facilitating an acceleration in harvest mechanization. An index of reaper sales would show which of these speculations is nearer the truth.

The part of the paper with which even more people might take issue concerns the system of land tenure and its effects on investment between 1850 and 1873. David asserts that the division of the managerial function between landlord and farmer reduced the incentive and ability to invest, a curious assertion considering that others working in this field have discovered the very opposite of a reluctance to invest. Michael Thompson describes landlords 'pouring money into their estates' and 'lavishing money on improvement' to an extent that returns were below those obtainable on government securities. David's assertion is the more remarkable because towards the end of the paper he appears to accept the established interpretation: he argues then that overinvestment may have resulted in harvest mechanization proceeding faster than a rational consideration of profit opportunities would have dictated.

Solow: It appeared plain that David's paper was proof in itself of the powerful illumination that modern analytical techniques can throw on important historical questions. David has set a splendid example in the optimal allocation of intellectual resources. Out of the huge question of choice of production techniques, he has chosen a manageable topic, has pushed beyond its narrowly economic limits, and has not asked us to consider his results as more conclusive than he ought to.

The first proposition, that one aspect of the cost of the introduction of reapers was the undoing of the old ridge-and-furrow landscape, would have gladdened the heart of her teacher, A. P. Usher, and it would not be surprising to find some of David's observations on the interrelatedness of landscape and drainage and the profitability of reapers in her old lecture notes − or at least something about the relation of soil type, shape of field, and technical aspects of medieval ploughs – though there would be nothing about Ricardo and Wicksell effects.

About the second proposition, that 'the form of land tenure greatly diminished not only the incentive but also the financial ability of Britain's farmers to undertake substantial improvements of any sort', there are grounds for more scepticism. David tells us that 'the serious problems of investment coordination to which the system of tenancy gave rise have tended to go insufficiently noticed and analysed.' Now the notion that the tenure system diminished investment incentives was in fact the dominant explanation of Ireland's agricultural backwardness in the nineteenth century after the Famine, and in connection with Ireland the proposition certainly has a very ancient history. The theoretical skeleton of the tenure question is well understood: where compensation for unexhausted improvements is not provided for, investment disincentives exist; where externalities can be internalized to the firm there need be no problem of misallocation of resources; yet the setting is one in which risks and uncertainties can easily be imagined that will prevent the smooth cooperation of landlord and tenants.

These words are chosen carefully – as David chose his – disincentives *exist*, there *need be* no misallocation, risks and uncertainties *can be imagined*. For nothing but a close examination of the agricultural history of the period can tell whether in fact these tenure factors seriously affected investment decisions. In the case of Ireland, after looking at the historical record, at the customs that prevailed, and at the empirical record of rents and evictions and tenant and landlord investment, she had concluded that the importance of tenure arrangements as an explanatory variable in Irish economic development was not great.

It would be hazardous to guess about its importance in England without an equally close examination. The argument has a strong flavour of the nineteenth century about it: if the legal (and other institutional) barriers to factor mobility are removed, the presumption is that economic growth will take place. Where economic growth apparently did not take place, the classical economists tended to look at the legal barriers as culprits. Yet nowhere is the assumption that legal arrangements correspond to actual historical fact more treacherous than in agriculture. For example, while nothing sounds more precarious than yearly tenancies, in fact in Ireland they were generally preferred to long leases on account of their security, and yearly tenancies commonly descended from father to son. Such is the stuff of which agricultural history is made.

A critical feature of David's analysis, however, is his choice of corn farming as the industry. If wages and wheat prices stay constant and the price of reapers falls, then mechanization is profitable in the way we learned at our mothers' knees. It is only if wages rise *relative to the final product* that the cost in landscape improvements in terms of wheat output foregone can outweigh the benefits of mechanization. This is all to be found in the paper, though perhaps the statement of it could be put more clearly. But if we have advanced beyond Lord Ernle at all, it is that we no longer equate the history of English agriculture with the history of arable. The old tradition left a sort of anthropomorphic view of English agriculture, rising in the course of the eighteenth century, basking in the glow of the mid-Victorian sun, sinking sadly in the 1880s. From a different viewpoint the history of English agriculture is not such a sad one. The responsiveness of factors to changes in their rewards has meant that whatever its *absolute size* agriculture never became the sick man of the British economy. Productivity in English agriculture has maintained itself admirably compared with manufacturing. How many other countries could make that claim? Once we begin to look at the factors that lie behind this achievement, we shall be asking different questions than about mechanization in arable farming. And we shall need someone with David's combination of economic technique and historical judgement to find the answer.

David: The objection that Mrs Solow raised to the argument about tenancy arrangements may reflect an expositional weakness in the paper. One has to read it closely, but the paper does admit that compensations could have been arranged between tenant and landlord. The question becomes, then, whether the improvements were worthwhile *even if* all benefits and costs were internalized. The answer, given in the succeeding parts of the paper, is that it was not. That is, even under conditions of owner-occupancy the 'reaper-cum-improvement' project would have been unprofitable. We cannot say very much about the importance of what Kindleberger called the 'disarticulated structure of agriculture', then, because we do not observe an otherwise profitable undertaking being ignored. Only in that case could we attribute the failure to mechanize to the lack of owner-occupancy.

Hunt asserts that labour was not abundant and cheap in Britain. The question is, compared with what? Surely by comparison with the United States labour was indeed cheap relative to capital. The reason that mechanization of the harvest was profitable on *improved* land in Britain was that the yield per acre was higher than in the United States. Consequently, the great saving of labour on this densely planted land from displacing labourers with machines offset the relatively low British wage. In other words, one can grant Habakkuk the supposition that labour was relatively abundant in Britain, yet still maintain that the price of labour relatively to capital is not the whole story: there is a third factor of production, namely, land.

Another point is that the cost of the improvement of land should have been spread over all field implements, not just the reaper. Towards the end of the paper, however, it is argued that the proportion of the size distribution of farms that could have profitably undertaken mechanization of other tasks in the field, aside from reaping, was quite small.

McCloskey: The new drainpipes are the key, because they permitted levelling of the ground to accommodate the reaper. But better drainage than the old ridge-and-furrow system surely had advantages independent of making the land suitable for mechanical reapers. Moreover, the additional cost of making the land flat need not have been incurred: if drainage by pipe was independently profitable, the land could have been ploughed flat at no additional cost by simply installing the drainpipes and gradually ploughing the earth off the ridges and into the furrows in the normal course of preparing the land for seed.

David: The problem was that the varying depth of drainpipes under the option of gradual flattening of the land significantly reduced the advantages of drainage.

Harley: What temporal pattern of land-flattening can actually be observed?

David: It was generally done all at once rather than gradually. There was a good deal of regional variation. Laxton was never enclosed because the ridge-and-furrow system worked well, while in other places the excessive height of the ridges made the installation of pipes and flattening of the land 'in one go' profitable.

Trace: Flattening the ridges required a plough whose mould-board could be adjusted to plough to either the right or the left. Were such ploughs available?

David: Yes. And steam ploughs, which were available at this time, were always adjustable.

Floud: Had there been attempts to design reapers to fit British conditions? The early versions were essentially American machines. How much effort went into circumventing their drawbacks in British terrain?

David: A good deal of effort went into redesign, but most of it can be traced to the special problems of the barley harvest. The cut barley was left in the fields to dry, and, in order to avoid it being trampled by the horses, farmers adopted one of two alternatives. The first was the pusher or Bell machine, with the horses behind the reaper. This arrangement, which hobbled the horses, involved a sacrifice of speed. To compensate, the number of horses was increased and the cutter bar was extended, allowing the cutting of a broader swath, but this made the machine still more cumbersome than it already was. The alternative was to keep the horses at the front but to redesign the machines so that the barley was delivered to the side, into the swath cut on the last run down the field, rather than to the rear, as in the American machines.

Although harrows and seed drills, which are easier from the engineering standpoint to modify, were adapted, there were no attempts to adapt the reaper to the local conditions of the land in wheat harvesting. The sheer variability of British conditions, making standardized designs impossible, made machinery more expensive in Britain than on the American plains.

Mathias: How would the possibility of joint use of machinery and horses change the analysis? Would the size of the farms matter in that case?

David: There was no difficulty introduced by the sharing of horses, at least, because they were in fact not shared. Farmers generally had a plough team of four horses in any case, and only on the Bell machines for cutting barley was additional horsepower needed. Indeed, the Bell machines were used only on very large farms, probably precisely because of the additional horsepower. The other question is that of the sharing of the machine itself. If a machine could be shared among several farms, the threshold acreage at which they could be introduced profitably would presumably fall. There were some scattered cases of landlords buying reapers for the use of all their tenants together. The infrequency of this arrangement is perhaps attributable to the inevitable disputes to which it would give rise over who was responsible for maintaining the machine, who could use it first in the harvesting season, and so on. Again, there were a few scattered cases of farmers renting out their machines to neighbours when their harvesting was completed.

But the question is, could they depend on this additional work and did they take it into consideration when contemplating the purchase of a machine?

Supple: Independent entrepreneurs could also set up as harvesting contractors.

David: He had not come across any cases of contract reaping – although there was, to be sure, contract steam ploughing. The limitations on contract harvesting were that the season was short, the capacity of the machines was fairly small, it was difficult to move them around from farm to farm, and their set-up and knock-down costs were high. Even in steam ploughing, as Spence's book shows, the contract rental price observed in the market was higher than the imputed rent on the machines because the farmers gave the contractors the more difficult bits of field. The steam ploughing companies made a great number of moves each day, from one 3 acre piece of field to another, and went out of business at a great rate. There were, then, economies of scale even in the provision of rented ploughing services. And the same holds for reapers: access to the market does not imply unlimited divisibility. Consequently, the threshold point may have to be restated as a range, but the range was still narrow and the main point is not disturbed.

McCloskey: The problem of scattered fields applies to one farm as much as to several farms. The fields in one British farm are often scattered and therefore there is no high differential between the cost of moving from one farm to another as a contractor and the cost of moving from one field to another as the operator of one's own machine.

Mathias: The issue was that two farms of 50 acres, if they lay close to each other, would be able to afford a reaper as well as one farm of 100 acres.

David: It was much more costly in terms of transaction costs to assemble a job for a reaper consisting of several different farms than one consisting of one large farm.

Engerman: Could not the high transaction costs to some extent have been offset by designing machines to fit the smaller jobs: making them more mobile, for example?

David: The scale of production of each type of machine adapted to local conditions was just not large enough to make feasible still more adaption to the smaller jobs. The broader question of why there were not reaping contractors is an intriguing one. In the United States there was contract ploughing and even contract fencebuilding and in Britain contract steam ploughing, but there are no cases before the invention of the combine of contract reaping in either country. Combines had larger fixed costs, so that even large farms formed part of the extensive market for their rental.

McCloskey: The size of farms is treated as being as exogenous in David's model. Would not farm size change?

Harley: In response to McCloskey's question, even on the large farms David had shown that the reaper was not very profitable. If it had in fact been very profitable for a generation or so, one probably would have observed a move to either rental of machines or consolidation of farms. But it was not.

David: He agreed with Harley. The mechanization-cum-improvement project yielded less than 4 per cent on investment, even on the optimal size farm. But the question still remains why reapers were not introduced on farms *without* improving the land. At acreages higher than the threshold the return to investing in a machine by itself, accepting the inconveniences of ridge-and-furrow land, could be quite large. It is because of this that the argument requires some factor limiting the rentability of machines, by adding the cost of negotiations and of forming a market.

Temin: The issue becomes, then, one of how high precisely these costs were.

David: The difficulty was that there were no reaping contracting firms in existence and therefore no firms whose books can be examined to establish how high they were. In steam ploughing, as was noted before, the market rental was considerably above the imputed rental, the difference being accounted for by the costs of negotiation and other transaction costs.

6

The shift from sailing ships to steamships, 1850–1890: a study in technological change and its diffusion

CHARLES K. HARLEY

Radical improvements in transportation were one of the hallmarks of the late nineteenth century. Alfred Marshall believed that 'probably more than three quarters of the whole benefit [Britain] has derived from progress of manufactures during the nineteenth century has been through its indirect influences in lowering the cost of transport' [1]. The technological changes involved were primarily the railroads and the improvements in ocean shipping; surprisingly there has been little recent research on the improvements in late nineteenth-century shipping. A casual debate exists in the literature about the relative importance of improvements in sailing ship technology and in steamship technology, but the analysis is either very loose or seriously misleading [2]. This paper attempts to analyse systematically one aspect of the technological change in shipping between 1850 and 1890; the process by which steam gradually displaced sail as the source of power for ocean transportation.

The shift from sail to steam during the late nineteenth century was a process of technological change and its diffusion and should be analysed as such. Both historians and economists have tended to view technological change and its diffusion as separate events. Joseph Schumpeter's vision of economic growth as consisting of spurts of innovation followed by periods of diffusion has influenced much economic thinking in this field. Edwin Mansfield's recent econometric work on technological change is in this same vein. His basic model of diffusion is explicitly a learning model and implicitly assumes that innovations appear and that during the period of diffusion production is in disequilibrium — that is to say, producers are not minimizing costs in light of the best available technology. In the case of nineteenth-century shipping, at least, an alternative model of the process of technological change appears more appropriate. Technological change and its diffusion in shipping is more fruitfully regarded as a process than as an event. The displacement of sail by steam occurred gradually between about 1850 and the beginning of the twentieth century as technological change proceeded.

The model underlying this investigation is based on the assumption that shipping and shipbuilding markets were generally in long-run competitive equilibrium (or perhaps better, fluctuating around that equilibrium). This implies that both sailing ship freights and steamship freights were governed by the technology of production and input prices. The proportions of any given trade carried by steam and sail were determined by the relative costs of shipping by steam and sail. For the bulk of the cargo the lower cost method was preferred. The shift from sail to steam occurred as technological change, occurring faster in steam than in sail, and changing relative prices lowered the costs of steamships relative to those of sailing ships.

The most important technological change specific to steamships was the more or less continuous improvement that occurred in the fuel consumption of the marine engines throughout the latter part of the century. In general, with the possible exception of the introduction of the compound engine, the improvements in the machinery were marginal and were introduced continuously by the marine engineers. The sailing ship competed with steam for some fifty years after 1850, not, as Schumpeter suggests, because of 'extra rational preference or habit' [3], but rather because of the nature of the costs of steam transportation. Steam could provide lower cost transportation than sail on short routes while coal consumption of marine engines was still quite high, but could not successfully compete with sailing ships for bulk cargoes on long routes, even though, in some cases, steamships quickly captured the passenger trade even on these routes. The displacement of sail on short routes in the 1850s and 1860s, while sail remained dominant in very long voyages until the turn of the century, resulted not from chance but from the nature of the technology of production of shipping services. As marine engines improved the steamships gradually took over longer trades.

Fortunately there exist sufficiently extensive technological data, primarily in the nineteenth-century engineering journals and company records [4], to approximate the production functions for ocean transportation services at various times during the late nineteenth century. In addition, quite extensive price data also exist [5]. In this paper these data have been used to investigate the changing relative cost of shipping bulk cargo by steamship and sailing ship on various voyages at various times.

The analysis in this paper is strictly applicable only to the ocean transportation of bulk cargoes. For these cargoes the transportation services provided by sailing ships and steamships can, for purposes of analysis, be considered perfect substitutes. Speed of shipment, the most important qualitative difference between sailing ship services and steamship services, was of little, if any, significance to the shippers of these bulk cargoes. Although the study of non-bulk trades and specific trade routes will require information beyond what is available in this paper, the basic technological and price relationships involved in the switch from sail to steam for bulk cargoes discussed here must form an important part of any such analysis.

In order to understand the process by which steam displaced sail it is necessary to specify the nature of the production functions and substitutions involved. The basic input substitution involved in the comparison of the production of sailing ship services with the production of steamship services is one of coal for capital and labour (and other factors). The greater speed and regularity of steamships reduced capital and labour costs per ton mile; the increase in speed more than compensated for the increase in capital embodied in the steamship and the larger crew carried by steamships. Greater speed was obtained primarily through greater coal consumption (larger engines, etc., were, of course, also involved). At low speeds (up to about 12 knots) resistance and thus power consumed increase with the cube of speed. Distance, of course, increases proportionately with speed, thus coal consumption per mile increases with the square of speed. At higher speeds resistance increases with speed at an even higher rate.

The single most important reason for the long period of transition from sail to steam resulted from the necessity of a steamship's transporting its fuel. As a result, the factor inputs and costs of steamship transportation varied inversely with the length of the voyage from the source of coal. The longer the voyage, the greater was the proportion of the ship's capacity that had to be devoted to coal bunkers rather than to cargo. Throughout the late nineteenth century Britain was the world's primary coal source, so steamship costs increased as the distance from Britain. Since the source of coal was Britain, the possibility of a steamship recoaling at coaling stations along its route did not remove the increased cost associated with increased distance. By carrying less coal a steamer could carry more cargo and earn freight on that cargo. There would be no net gain, however, since that freight earned on cargo would have to be immediately paid out in the higher cost of coal freighted to overseas bunker stations.

Consider, for example, a steamship in 1855 burning 5 lb of coal per indicated horsepower per hour designed to carry 1000 tons of deadweight cargo. On a 500 mile coasting voyage at 5.5 knots (the most economical speed for that length voyage), this required a ship of 1446 tons displacement with an engine of 85 indicated horsepower. The coal burned on the voyage would be about 17 tons. On a 3000 mile voyage at 5 knots, the ship would have to be 1550 tons displacement, the engine 67 indicated horsepower, and 90 tons of coal would be burned on the voyage. A 10,000 mile voyage at 5 knots would have required a vessel of 1940 tons displacement and 78 horsepower and burned 350 tons of coal on the voyage. The cost of transportation per million ton miles would increase from £138 on a 500 mile voyage to £150 at 3000 miles and £183 at 10,000 miles or one third above the cost on a 500 mile voyage.

TABLE 1
1872: Cost per million cargo ton miles
various length voyages
ship 2000 tons cargo capacity

Voyage length (miles)	Optimal speed (knots)	Cost (£)
1 000	7.0	100
3 000	7.0	103
5 000	6.5	111
7 500	6.5	111
10 000	6.0	115

The nature of the trade-offs and the influence of length of voyage on inputs per million ton miles for a steamship carrying 2000 tons deadweight cargo in 1872 can be seen from Figure 1 and Table 1. The curved lines in Figure 1 refer to steamships. On the axis labelled capital and labour (a necessity forced by the two-dimensional nature of the diagram), capital and labour services have been combined on the basis of price and measured in pounds sterling. The production function for shipping services produced by sailing ships contains no coal and thus is represented by the appropriate point on the *x* axis, £106 per million ton miles. Sailing ship costs are not influenced by the length of the voyage as sailing ships carried no fuel for propulsion. A price line showing relative prices of capital and labour and coal has been drawn through the point for sail. Steam is cheaper than sail if the steam isoquant is to the left of this price line and more expensive if it is to the right. These figures imply sail was clearly preferable for bulk cargoes on voyages over 5000 miles in length [6].

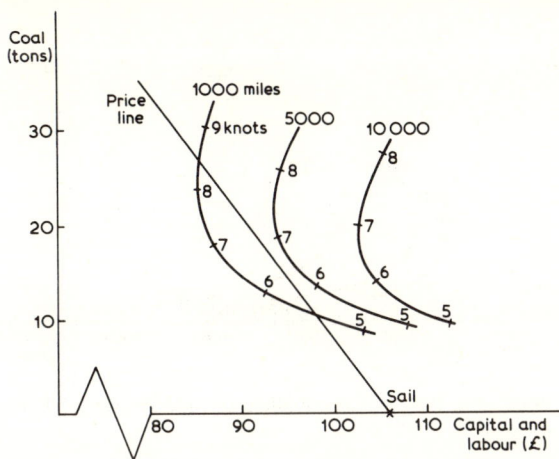

Figure 1   1872: Production function per million ton-miles of shipping services, steam and sail voyages: 1000, 5000, and 10 000 miles length.

During the last half of the nineteenth century the production functions for ocean steam transportation moved relative to that for sailing ship transportation. Figure 2 presents isoquants representing the inputs required to produce a million cargo ton miles in 1855, 1865, 1872, 1881 and 1891. Along the horizontal axis capital and labour services have been aggregated on the basis of 1872 prices. The inputs required for sailing ship transportation are plotted as appropriate points on the *x* axis. The effects of technological change are dramatically evident over the half century. Although there was considerable techno- logical progress resulting in lower labour requirements in both steam- ships and sailing ships, the principal technological improvements caus- ing a shift from sail to steam occurred in marine engines. The most important aspect of this improvement was the dramatic reduction of the coal consumption of the marine engine. This reduction, of course, had a twofold impact on the production function for steam transporta- tion. First, the coal input itself was reduced; second, the amount of ship, crew, and coal devoted to the transportation of bunker coal was reduced. The second impact was greater on long voyages where a considerable portion of the deadweight capacity of the ship was devoted to coal for bunkers in contrast to short voyages where bunkerage was a small portion of capacity.

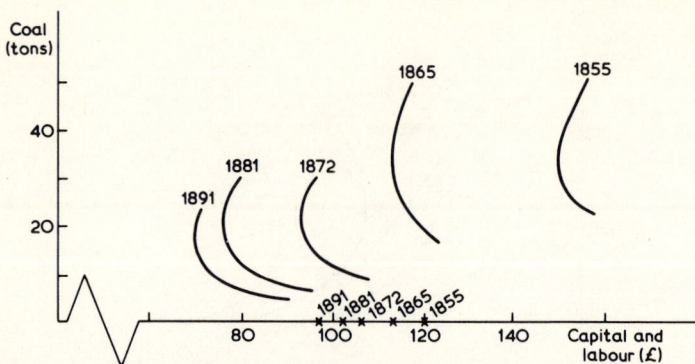

Figure 2   Production functions per million ton-miles, voyage 5000 miles length:
1855, 1865, 1872, 1881 and 1891.

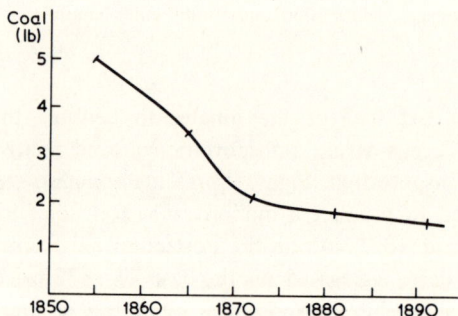

Figure 3   Coal consumption per indicated horsepower per hour: 1855-1891.
Source: 1855: based primarily on the Reports of the British Association
Committee on Steamship Performance, *Reports of the British Association,* 1859,
1860, 1861, 1862, 1863; 1865: various engineering articles; 1872: F. J. Bramwell,
'On the progress effected in economy of fuel in steam navigation', *Proc. Inst.
Mechanical Engineers,* 1872, pp. 125–85; 1881: F. C. Marshall, 'On the progress
and development of the marine engine', *Proc. Inst. Mechanical Engineers,* 1881,
pp. 449–509; 1891: A. Blechynden, 'A review of marine engineering during the
past decade', *Proc Inst. Mechanical Engineers,* 1891, pp. 306–71.

The specific form of this model of the shift from sail to steam
occurring as a result of faster technological change in steam than sail
clearly implies that steam would displace sail on short routes close to
coal sources (in the late nineteenth century Britain was the major coal
source) first and spread to longer routes. A first step in investigating

the model is to observe the actual shifting pattern of sail and steam trades in the late nineteenth century. Clearly, sailing ship services and steamship services were not identical products. Steamships offered more rapid delivery and thus a saving of inventory costs on expensive non-seasonal goods. Speed was not, however, any advantage for seasonal agricultural products, which had to be stored between harvest and consumption. In fact, speed of delivery of cargo was sometimes a positive disadvantage; as contemporaries remarked, 'A ship's hold is admitted to be the cheapest warehouse in the world.' [7] Speed was not the only difference in service between steam and sail. Since the cost of waiting idle in port was approximately 50 per cent higher for steamships than sailing ships, steamship contracts required more rapid loading and unloading than did sailing ship contracts. This imposed higher loading costs on the shipper and frequently also forced the shipper to pay warehousing costs he could have avoided by shipping by sail. Consequently, for example, coal freights in the 1870s were consistently about 10 per cent lower for steamers than for sailing ships [8]. This difference in services obviously complicates analysis. However, the shift from sail to steam can still be seen in various trades. It is perhaps useful to assume a third of the freight was willing to pay a premium for speed and a third to pay a premium to warehousing. When steam takes a third of the trade it can conveniently be considered as fully competitive with sail, and when it takes two-thirds as having a clear cost advantage.

Steam first displaced sail on short routes over which passenger traffic was important and the bulk of the cargo was valuable and speed and regularity were of value. The passenger trade in the Irish Sea and across the Channel was primarily steam before the mid-century. By 1855 almost all the cargo entering Britain in the 'home-trade' (i.e. from Brest to the mouth of the Elbe) was carried in steamships, although the large export trade in coal from the north-east coast was still carried out under sail in wooden colliers, which returned in ballast [9].

Nearly a third of the trade with the Mediterranean was also carried by steam by 1855. Both the light, variable winds of the Mediterranean and the fact that perishable fruit was a significant portion of the homeward cargo speeded this takeover. By the mid-1860s the trade circulars were stating that both the fruit trade and the Alexandria cotton trade were exclusively steam [10]. At the same time steam was extending into the grain trades of the Baltic and the Black Sea, although the Baltic timber trade remained largely the preserve of sailing ships [11] . Glover Brothers Annual Circular for 1863 [12] sums up the situation in the mid-1860s:

> In the shorter trades all valuable goods are now carried by steam. The saving in insurance, and in interest of money, and the facility of being able to depend on a given number of days passage, secure for steamships a preference that sailing ships will never recover. Moreover, the great improvements in the construction of steamers, and the various arrangements by which it has become possible to move goods in larger bulks than formerly, enables the steamer to compete at nearly equal rates with sailing vessels. These observations, however, apply only to short voyages and valuable cargoes. In the long voyage trades steamers cannot compete with sailing vessels.

As the quotation implies, most of the uses of steamships prior to 1865 involved premium freights for speed and regularity. The entry of steam colliers into the coal trade from the north-east to London in the 1850s is, thus, of particular significance. It was the first bulk trade in which steam captured the trade, the cargo paid no premium for speed and where there was no passenger revenue. The steam collier of the 1850s can be regarded as the prototype for the steam tramps of the later nineteenth century. The first steam colliers were introduced in 1852 and 1853. These ships proved very successful as government transports during the Crimean War. Immediately after the war the steamers were carrying nearly 20 per cent of the coal brought coastwise to London; by 1865 over half this coal was carried by steam [13] . Clearly the old wooden sailing colliers were being replaced with steam as they wore out.

Thus, by the early and mid-1860s, steamships were firmly established in the short trade from Britain to the Continent and were extending into trades up to about 3000 miles in length (Alexandria is about 3000 miles by sea from British ports) particularly in the Mediterranean where variable winds seriously hamper sailing ship operation [14]. The North Atlantic trades with distances of about 3000 miles of open ocean were the next areas of expansion of steamship services. Steam was well established in the Atlantic passenger trade by mid-century. The Cunard Line began its transatlantic service in 1840 with an annual subsidy of £81,000. In 1850 the American Collins Line started in competition with the Cunard Line and with an annual subsidy of $385,000. The Collins Line failed in 1858 as a result, primarily, of poor management but also as a result of the misfortune of losing at sea two of the five magnificent (and extravagant) ships that made up their fleet. More important to the gradual development of steam ocean transport than the ill-fated Collins Line was the entry of the Inman Line into the transatlantic trade, also in 1850. Inman was able to develop a successful steamship line without the aid of government subsidy. Passenger revenue remained, however, the necessary base of the earning capacity of the Inman Liners. In 1856, 96 per cent of the passengers arriving in New York from foreign ports arrived in sailing ships. By 1862 the steamers carried 32 per cent of the westbound passengers to and almost all the eastbound from New York, although not from Boston or other ports [15]. In 1860 less than 15 per cent of the tonnage of ships entering Britain from the U.S. were steam; the liners of the steamship companies seem to have accounted for almost all of that.

During the second half of the 1860s steamships appear to have gained in the transatlantic cargo trades, particularly the grain trade. There is evidence of significant steam traffic from Montreal in the late 1860s [16]. The total Canadian trade, however, remained overwhelmingly sail because of the dominance of the timber trade. In 1870 nearly 60 per cent of the clearances from New York were steamships. This figure, however, is inflated by the importance of passengers in the trade of New York, only 6 per cent of the clearances from Boston and Philadelphia were steam, and 27 per cent from Baltimore [17].

By the early 1870s steam was well established on the North Atlantic on trade routes of about 3000 miles. In the cotton trade to New Orleans, a voyage of just under 5000 miles, the switch to steam came around the mid-1870s. In 1870 only 10 per cent of the ships clearing New Orleans for Britain were steam, in 1875 nearly half were steam, and in 1880 over 70 per cent.

In the European and Atlantic trade the diffusion by steam was a gradual process of steam displacing sail on increasing longer trade routes. The process was generally smooth, governed by the continuous improvements in marine engines. The long trades to India and the Far East would, presumably, have become steam trades gradually in the 1880s or 1890s, except for the discontinuity introduced into the process by the opening of the Suez Canal in 1869. The Canal radically shortened distances from Europe to the East. The sea distance from Britain to Bombay was reduced from about 11,500 miles to just over 6200 miles and the distance to Calcutta was reduced from 11,500 to

8200 miles. The fact that the Canal was unsuitable for sailing ships, primarily because of unsatisfactory wind conditions in the Red Sea, had even a greater influence on the relative position of sail and steam in the Eastern trades. Had the Canal been equally suitable for sailing and steamships, the Eastern trades involving distances in excess of 6000 miles would have remained sail well into the 1870s. However, the actual effect of the Canal was to shorten the steamship route but not the sailing ship route.

One immediate result of the opening of the Canal was a tremendous boom in the building of steamships at the expense of sailing ships. Only about 15 per cent of the tonnage of ships built in 1871 and 1872 was sail; in the late 1860s two-thirds of the tonnage was sail. These new steamers quickly entered the Bombay trade where their distance advantage over sailing ships was greatest. Prior to the opening of the Canal almost no steamships entered Britain from Bombay and Scinde. In 1870, 28 per cent of the tonnage was steam; by 1873, 65 per cent of the tonnage was steam and this percentage persisted through the 1870s. By the early 1890s all the cargo from Bombay was carried by steam. Even with the advantage of the Canal steam could only compete with sail at Calcutta in the early 1870s on the basis of a premium freight. In 1873, a quarter of the tonnage entering from Bengal and Burma were steamships; by the end of the decade nearly 40 per cent was steam. As late as the early 1890s about a quarter of the tonnage was still sail.

Surprisingly, the most dramatic shift from sail to steam after the opening of the Suez Canal occurred in the China trade, even though the distance was longer and the relative saving in distance considerably less than in the Indian trade. The distance from Britain to Shanghai is nearly 14,000 miles by the Cape and nearly 11,000 by the Canal. In 1869, 14 per cent of the tonnage entering the U.K. from China was steam. By 1873, 70 per cent of the trade was carried by steamships and by the end of the decade over 90 per cent. The nature of the China trade explains this dramatic change. Chinese exports were almost exclusively goods of high value, of which tea was the overwhelming proportion. These goods had paid premium freights in the days of sail for fast passages on clipper ships and quickly adopted the even faster delivery available with steam and the Suez Canal. The steamship quickly displaced the clippers since the steamships halved the time home at approximately the same freight as the clippers charged during the late 1860s. The advantage of steam was further enhanced by lower insurance premiums for tea shipped by steam.

In summary, steamships gradually displaced sail first on the short trades and then on the long. In the 1850s and 1860s steamships took the short trades to the Continent. In the late 1860s and 1870s they took the North Atlantic. In the 1870s and 1880s, with the aid of the Suez Canal, the steamship took over the trade to India and the Far East. But sail still held on in the round-the-world trades, the Australian trade and trades to the west coast of the Americas, into the twentieth century.

The preceeding discussion of the actual diffusion of steamship transport corresponds gratifyingly with the predictions of the theoretical model based on the production function discussed at the beginning of the paper. The model explicitly assumes competitive equilibrium at various points in time: steamship freights equal the minimum average cost of providing ocean steam transportation, and similarly sailing ship freights equal the minimum average cost of sailing transportation. There can be little doubt that the shipping industry in the late nineteenth century closely approximated the economist's model of perfect competition. There were very large numbers of participants in the market, and entry was open to anyone with £15,000 to £20,000 to invest in a ship. Lloyd's Register of 1893 lists 32,010 ships totalling 24 million gross tons. In addition, it lists 218 five-column pages of shipowners and managers with their ships. The largest fleets (British India Steam Navigation Co. and Navigazione Generale Italiana) consisted of just over 100 ships each and occupied a column of type. The majority of owners owned only one or two ships. Under these conditions, although liner conferences might have had some control over some line freights, it seems impossible that tramp freights could have been anything but competitively determined. The existence of an auction market for shipping service – the Baltic Exchange – and of professional brokers, both characteristic of a competitive market, reinforces this belief.

The mere existence of a competitive market does not, of course, imply that price must always equal minimum average cost. Both negative and positive quasi-rents are possible, at least until the market has adjusted fully. The specific issue in this case is whether, during the transition from steam to sail, sailing ships were earning negative quasi-rents or steamships earning positive. Sailing ships earning negative quasi-rents implies that the present value of expected net earnings were below the market price for new sailing ships. This in turn implies that profit maximizing entrepreneurs would not purchase sailing ships. The continued production of sailing ships during the 1870s and 1880s, and in the early 1890s (the largest tonnage of sailing ships launched in Britain in a single year was launched in 1892), strongly suggests that sailing ships continued to earn enough to cover their capital costs throughout the period to at least 1895. It also seems unlikely that steamships earned persistent positive quasi-rents over the period of transition. In a competitive industry with free access, entrepreneurs will react to positive quasi-rents by continued purchase of ships. British shipbuilding, particularly steamship building, however, experienced sharp cyclical fluctuations throughout the late nineteenth century. There was considerable excess capacity in the British shipbuilding industry during cyclical troughs in the late 1870s, the mid-1880s and in the early 1890s. This implies a lack of demand for steamships, which in turn implies an absence of positive quasi-rents in steamship operation.

Comments of contemporary observers support the contention that sailing ships were not earning persistent negative quasi-rents, nor steamships earning persistent positive quasi-rents. The following statement from the annual report of Messrs Rucker, Offer and Co. (London) for 1871 [18] is typical of the comments of shipbrokers from 1872 to about 1875.

> The business of shipowning was more profitable in 1871 than in 1868, 1869, or 1870 – the improvement being especially marked in the East India trade, in which, notwithstanding the opposition of steamers via the Suez Canal, sailing vessels realized remunerable freights. Whether the working of steamers has realized as favorable results is another matter, the heavy expense attending even the most modest constructions, and the keen competition – particularly for outward freights – having already provoked an outcry against the overbuilding of this description of shipping property.

The relative position of steam in the Indian trade worsened further in 1873 with a 30 per cent increase in Canal dues and very high coal prices. In 1884, John Hughes and Co. made the following statement in their annual circular [19].

> In the present state of affairs, and being guided by past experience, we think investors may reasonably consider new iron sailing vessels the best permanent investment they can find, as when business is good they make very large profits, and when freights are low they possess the best staying power, being capable of management on most economical principles, and requiring almost no outlay

for repairs during the first 12 years of their existence, so that handsome average dividends are obtained over a course of years without deduction for repairs, and only a very trifling rate of depreciation.

Although all the preceeding discussion suggests strongly that during the period of transition from sail to steam, long-run equilibrium tended to exist in both the sailing ship and the steamship markets, it remains useful to attempt to test this proposition directly. It is possible to estimate sailing ship costs and steamship costs on various routes at various dates from engineering and price data. The engineering data is, in fact, the same as was used in the production functions presented earlier [20]. The results of several calculations for representative trades at various dates are presented below.

TABLE 2
Cost of round trip voyage per 1000 tons of cargo capacity
by steam and sail, various dates and various trades

Trade (distance)	Date	Cost of sail	Cost of steam
U.K. to			
1 (*a*) New Orleans (5000			
miles)	1872	1230	1400
(*b*)	1876	1100	1180
(*c*)	1881	1310	1280
2 (*a*) Bombay (Cape:11 500)	1865	2839	3901
(*b*) (Suez:6200)	1872	2610	2165[1]
3 (*a*) Calcutta (Cape:11 500)	1872	2610	2640[1]
(*b*) (Suez:8000)	1873	2950	3040[1]
(*c*)	1881	2470	2389[1]
4 (*a*) San Francisco (13 500)	1881	2840	3140
(*b*)	1891	2000	2100

[1]Contain downward bias; assumes coaling at Port Said but charged no port charges.

The calculations presented above must be regarded with judicious scepticism. Despite the various possible sources of imprecision in the calculations, they do tend to confirm that the timing of the switch from sail to steam was governed by technical considerations. Further, the calculations confirm that sail was superior to steam in some trades until at least 1890.

The accumulated evidence all tends to support the contention that the switch from sailing ships to steamships during the late nineteenth century was accomplished in a shipping market that adjusted quite rapidly to equilibrium. Steam displaced sail as the cost of transportation by steam fell relative to the cost of transportation by sail. Most of the fall in the cost of steam relative to the cost of sail occurred as a result of improvements in marine steam engines. The contribution of various factors in the fall of sail and steam freights between the 1870s and the 1890s can be illustrated in Table 3, which presents calculations for the California grain trade and the Bombay trade [21].

TABLE 3
*Annual rates of charge in freights and the contribution
of various factors to the decline*

	Sail: California 1875-1890	Steam: Bombay 1873-1890
Freight	− 3.8	− 5.7
Contribution of:		
Ship prices	− 1.1	− 1.9
Ship size	− 0.9	− 0.7
Coal consumption	−	− 1.1
Weight of ship	− 0.4	− 0.4
Crew size	− 0.4	− 0.4
Other input prices	− 0.5	− 0.7
'Residual'	− 0.5	− 0.5

Table 3 presents a perspective on the importance of the shift from sail to steam. The importance of the shift to the world as a whole must be judged by its effect on freight rates. The table clearly illustrates the effect of decreased coal consumption on the relative costs of sail and steam. It is equally clear that the impact of technological improvements in the marine engine was not the overwhelming factor in the decline of ocean freight rates. Declining ship prices, resulting from technological change in shipbuilding and lower iron prices [22], and technological changes in ships resulting in lower ship weight and smaller crews for both sailing ships and steamships made major contributions to the decline in freight rates. Since the Bombay trade was the longest trade in which steam was dominant by the early 1870s, it was also the trade where the decline in coal consumption had its greatest impact on freights. The calculations in Table 3 thus represent an upper bound on the importance of the improvements specific to steam.

On shorter routes there was less saving from the reduction in bunker coal and thus less savings in cost. On longer voyages the earliest savings in steamship costs did not influence freights. The initial savings were necessary to make steam competitive with sail; bulk freights were influenced by improvements in steam technology only after steam became dominant in the trade. Thus, while faster technological change in steam than sail·explains the shift from sail to steam, it is by no means the whole story of late nineteenth-century shipping.

The shift from sailing ships to steamships during the late nineteenth century occurred as shipowners made adjustments in their fleets primarily in response to improving steam technology. The nature of the factor substitutions involved in the shift offers an explanation for the long coexistence of sailing ship construction and steamship construction that does not require any assumption of market imperfection. The factor inputs per ton mile for steam transportation increased with the length of the voyage, but the inputs per ton mile for sailing ship transportation were largely unaffected by voyage length. Thus sail remained the lower cost alternative on long voyages while steam captured shorter voyages. Eventually by the early twentieth century the improvements in marine engineering make steam competitive on the largest voyages. Finally although improvements specific to steam were responsible for the changing composition of the world's merchant fleets, they were by no means the whole explanation for the decline in freight rates during the late nineteenth century.

NOTES

[1] *Principles of Economics*, 8th ed., p. 675.
[2] Gerald S. Graham, 'The ascendancy of the sailing ship 1855-1885', *Economic History Review*, IX, August 1956, pp. 74–88, remains the best work in the debate. He points out the persistence of sailing ships in long trades where freights fell dramatically. Douglass North, on the basis of his own study of freight rates and the timing of their decline, also argues that sailing ships were important in the decline of freights after the mid-nineteenth century (see 'Ocean freight rates and economic development 1750-1913', *Journal of Economic History*, XVII, 1958, pp. 542–3. In a recent article, Ramon Knauerhase ('The compound steam engine and productivity changes in the German merchant marine fleet 1871-1887', *Journal of Economic History*, XXVIII, 1968, pp. 390–403) has maintained that the shift to steam was of primary importance, at least for the German merchant marine. These results, however, are based on a productivity measure of clearance per man employed and must be regarded very suspiciously. Labour was a relatively minor input (about 20 per cent of costs in sail and 10 per cent in steam). The use of steamships involved a substitution of coal for capital and labour.

Finally, the analysis does not consider the effect of different voyage
lengths.

[3] *Business Cycles*, p. 369.

[4] Primarily the records of William Denny and Brothers of Dumbarton. The
technological data are at the National Maritime Museum in Greenwich and
the commercial records are in the Adam Smith Building the University of
Glasgow.

[5] Such contemporary journals as the *Economist, Engineering*, and the
Engineer, plus the Denny records and the records of Alexander Stephen and
Sons of Glasgow, also held at the University of Glasgow, are the main
sources of price data.

[6] For more detailed discussion of the construction of Figure 1 and Table 1,
see Appendix 1.

[7] Charles Wigram in discussion of J. D. A. Samuda, 'The influence of the Suez
Canal on ocean navigation', *Transactions of the Institute of Naval
Architects*, XI, 1870.

[8] See, for example, the Annual Report of Rucker, Offer and Co. of London;
'Economic history of 1871', *Economist*, 16 March 1872, p. 30; and appendix
table 13 to Giffen's Testimony to the *Royal Commission on Depression*,
PP. 1886, XXI, p. 169, for a table of steam and sail freight rates for coal
from 1872 to 1885.

[9] *Trade and Navigation Accounts 1855.* In 1855, 285,564 tons of shipping
entered the U.K. with cargo from the German Hanse cities; of this, 229,592
tons was steam. 83,413 tons of sail entered Newcastle in ballast; the total
entries from the Hanse into the U.K. were 627,127 tons. The Dutch trade
was similar. 309,385 tons of 385,245 tons entering with cargo were
steamships and 126,849 tons of sail entered Newcastle in ballast. The total
Dutch entries into the U.K. were 717,955 tons. Unfortunately, data for
Sunderland, the other great coal port, are unavailable (all U.K. trade and
navigation data in this paper are from the *Trade and Navigation Accounts*
and are not noted separately).

[10] Glover Brothers Circular in *Mitchell's Maritime Register*, 7 January 1865, p.
19, and C. Moller's Circular in *Mitchell's Maritime Register*, 6 January
1866.

[11] Throughout most of our period wooden sailing ships remained important in
the timber trade of the Baltic and North America. Wooden ships no longer
fit for the carriage of dry and perishable cargo would find employment in
the timber trades. The same is true to a lesser extent in the coal exports
from the north-east of England.

[12] *Mitchell's Maritime Register*, 2 January 1864, p. 19.

[13] The cargo carried by steam colliers annually from 1852 to 1869 are given
by C. M. Palmer, 'On iron as a material for shipbuilding and its influence on
the commerce and armaments of nations', *Journal of the Iron and Steel
Institute*, II, 1870, p. 59. The total sea coal shipped coastwise to London is
given in B. R. Mitchell, *Abstract of British Historical Statistics* (Cambridge,
1962), p. 113.

[14] See Evidence of C. Richards before the *Select Committee on The Transport
Service*, PP. 1860, XVIII, QQ 370–3.

[15] John G. B. Hutchins, *The American Maritime Industries and Public Policy,
1789-1914* (Cambridge, Mass., Harvard University Press, 1941), p. 319.

[16] Unfortunately, there is no direct breakdown of clearances from Montreal
by sail and steam. However, by the late 1860s there are regular quotations
of steamer freight rates (see *Canada Year Book 1915*, p. 201). Also in

1865-6, 141 ships of 119,553 tons cleared seaward from Montreal with
cargo. These ships carried 5351 men (*Dominion of Canada*, S.P. 1867-8, I,
p. 22). This is 4.46 men per 100 tons. The average number of men on
British ships in 1855 was 2.9 per 100 tons on sailing ships and 5.1 on
steamships (*Trade and Navigation Accounts*, 1865). If these crew figures
were also true in the Montreal trade, it would imply that 70 per cent of the
tonnage was steam. This figure appears high but may be accounted for by
the advantage steamships must have had over sail in the navigation of the St
Lawrence to Montreal.

[17] *U.S. Report of Commerce and Navigation*, 1870, p. 739.
[18] 'Commercial history and review of 1871', *Economist*, 18 March 1872, pp.
      29, 30.
[19] *The Shipping Gazette and Lloyd's List Weekly Summary*, 4 January 1884,
      p. 7.
[20] The various assumptions involved in the cost estimates are discussed in
      Appendix 1.
[21] For the basis of the calculation, see Appendix 2.
[22] See C. K. Harley, *Changing International Competitive Positions in Ship-
      building 1850-1885*, Discussion Paper, Dept of Economics, University of
      British Columbia, 1971.

A. *Calculation of the 'Production Function' for Steamships*

1. The basic technological information required is that power of a ship increases as the cube of the speed and with the two-thirds power of the displacement. During the late nineteenth century this information was embodied in a so-called Admiralty Constant:

Admiralty Constant = speed^3 x displacement$^{2/3}$/indicated horsepower of the engine

This concept is no longer generally used, since the Admiralty Constant embodies both the resistance of the hull and the efficiency of the engine and transmission. However, the general validity of the calculation for quick, approximate results is still reorganized. For the purpose of this paper, the concept has thus been used.

2. Given this technological relationship and various other physical relationships, it is possible to calculate input quantities for various speeds and voyage length for various capacities. Cargo capacity has been increased through time to approximate new ship sizes.

(*a*) The hull size is the most complicated calculation:

Hull displacement (H) = cargo capacity + engine weight + hull weight + coal bunkerage

(i) engine weight is proportional to IHP $\left(= \dfrac{\text{speed}^3 \text{disp.}^{2/3}}{\text{Ad. Con}} \right)$

(ii) hull weight is proportional to displacement
(iii) coal bunkerage is proportional to engine size and the time occupied on the voyage.

This results in a complicated equation involving odd powers of H, which has been solved on a computer using an interative procedure.

(*b*) Engine size: IHP = speed^2 x disp.$^{2\,3}$/Admiralty Constant
(*c*) Coal: per IHP per hour x hours on the voyage x IHP
(*d*) Crew: deck crew is assumed proportional to displacement and engine crew proportional to IHP.

3. Physical relationships and prices used at various dates

		1855	1865	1872	1881	1891
(*a*)	Admiralty Constant	250	250	250	250	250
(*b*)	Coal consumption *IHP*					
	hour	5lb	3.5	2.1	1.8	1.6

		1855	*1865*	*1872*	*1881*	*1891*
(c)	Hull weight/ton displacement	.26 tons	.26	.25	.25	.25
(d)	Engine weight/service IHP	.5	.33	.27	.21	.18
(e)	Crew/100 tons displacement	1.6	1.4	1.4	1.2	1.0
(f)	Crew/100 *IHP*	2.6	2.2	1.9	1.5	1.1

4.   Prices

		1855	*1865*	*1872*	*1881*	*1891*
(a)	Hull/ton displacement	£8.10/−	£8.14/−	£8	£6.8/−	£4.16/−
(b)	Engine/service IHP	£20	£12	£14	£9	£6
(c)	Coal/ton	10/−	9/−	15/−	8/6	11/−
(d)	Wages/month	52/−	56/−	65/−	56/−	78/−

B.   Cost of various voyages

The physical quantities calculated as described above have been multiplied by relevant prices. Steamships are assumed to coal in Britain for the entire outward voyage. Homeward, via the Suez Canal they are assumed to coal at Port Said. Other voyages assume all homeward coal was purchased at the destination. Overseas coal is priced at the U.K. price plus freight.

The 'production function' refers only to costs at sea. Port time has been assumed on the basis of loading and unloading rates of 400 tons per day. The cost of port time overseas includes capital cost plus wage cost. In Britain the cost of waiting is only the capital cost as crews were dismissed on arrival in Britain.

Sailing ship costs have been calculated from capital and wage costs. Sailing ships have been assumed to travel at 4 knots. Waiting costs calculated in the same manner as for steamships.

Port dues, loading costs, etc., were a considerable part of the freight costs. These have been ignored in the cost calculations. It has been assumed that these costs were similar for sail and steam.

Table 3 rests primarily on a simple total derivative. In competitive equilibrium price per unit equals the sum of the quantities of imputs per unit of output times their respective prices:

$$(1) \qquad P_q = \frac{A}{Q} P_a + \frac{B}{Q} P_b + \ldots$$

where Q is quantity of output and A and B are inputs. The total derivative of (1) for a given Q is:

$$(2) \qquad dP_q = dA \frac{P_a}{Q} + dP_a \frac{A}{Q} + dB \frac{P_b}{Q} + dP_b \frac{B}{Q} + \ldots$$

Simple arithmetic operations and minor rearrangement yields the following expression. P_q^* equals dP_q/P_q and S_a equals $P_a A/P_q Q$, the share of A in total cost.

$$(3) \qquad P_q^* = A^* S_a + P_A^* S_a + B^* S_b + P_b^* S_b + \ldots$$

The contribution of changing quantities of factor A, for example, is then $A^* S_a$.

In this specific case a few additional comments are necessary. The influence of increasing ship size over time has been treated separately. Larger ships required smaller crews and larger steamships required less than proportional increases in power (resistance increases with the two-thirds power of displacement). The weight of the vessel (including engines in the case of steamships) and the influence of reduced weight of bunker coal as a result of lower fuel consumption of steam engines through time have also been treated separately. A reduction in these weights allowed greater cargo with given factor inputs.

More detailed information on the calculations embodied in the conclusions of this paper are available from the author on request.

DISCUSSION 6

Chairman: S. B. Saul

Prepared comments: S. Pollard

Pollard: He had no criticism of the conclusions of the paper, which were uncontroversial but very well supported, nor of the mathematical methods used. But the paper does, as it were, only half the job.

The argument has four steps. First, the central proposition is stated. Second, the proposition is refined and simplified, leaving out a great number of unsettling and complicating facts. Third, calculations are performed on the simplified set of variables. Finally, broad conclusions about the behaviour of the industry are adduced. Now it would be unfair to previous literature to say that the paper was revolutionary, and Harley is suitably modest on this score. His characterization of the process of technological diffusion as gradual, keeping the industry close to equilibrium at any moment of time, for example, is not new. What is new is the precision of the demonstration. But the precision, achieved in the refining stage of argument, is partly illusory. For example, in the first few pages of the paper the variations in the demand characteristics of steam and sail are eliminated. The array of services that could be provided by each, however, was in fact vast: rapid steamships and slow sailing ships serviced different sorts of demands in the market. And their safety as well as their speed differed markedly. Again, many of the early steamships were subsidized, another complicating fact that is refined away in order to yield a simple model for the purpose of the paper. There is even the complication that steamers and sailing ships were not distinct pieces of equipment. For many years all steamers carried sail and later all sailing ships had donkey engines. In short, although the paper is a very neat piece of work, the neatness in the refining stage of the argument is obtained at the cost of simplifying, perhaps oversimplifying, a very complex situation.

Harley: Clarity requires simplification. There are, of course, many factors left out, but, if we are to advance beyond playing hunches, we have to take the initial step of reducing the factors to the few that seem to be the most important.

McCloskey: He agreed with Harley on Pollard's methodological point. A complete explanation of any historical event no doubt requires the inclusion of an unlimited number of variables. But if two or three explain 90 per cent of the event, then the ball, as it were, is in the court of those who stress the complexity of the issue. They must offer evidence that the many other variables bearing on the event significantly alter the explanation given by the few variables.

David: It was not clear what the paper is trying to show. The process described is *not* a gradual diffusion of a discrete innovation taking place early in the period as is claimed in the paper, but a series of small innovations adopted as soon as they were discovered throughout the period. The shift from sail to steam depends on the interaction between these gradual improvements and the price of coal, ships and men in the United Kingdom. But are the prices of new British ships and the wages of British seamen relevant? After all, there was a secondhand market in ships, the ships could be registered abroad, and they could be staffed with foreign crews. This international feature of the market deserves more emphasis.

Harley: Virtually all of the sailing ships and steamships made in Britain were registered and owned by British firms and their crews were picked up and discharged in British ports. Apparently, then, the international character of the industry was unimportant.

McClelland: Would the data on cost shares give some insight into David's point that the factors of production in shipping were internationally mobile?

Harley: They do: the operating costs of production – especially manpower – were a small share of the total.

Landes: Were there data on the proportion of British-built ships that were in fact British owned?

Harley: He did not have the exact data at hand, but in the 1880s and 1890s a substantial share of the *sailing* ships were built for Norway. The data are readily available in Lloyd's Universal Register.

Von Tunzelmann: Could the equilibrium model of diffusion that Harley used to explain the shift from sail to steam really be used to explain the diffusion of the marine steam engine itself? His own work with land engines in early nineteenth-century Britain had uncovered no short term relationship between engine productivity and coal prices; the main determinant of productivity in the short run was rather the state of demand. Only in the long run, outside the time-horizon of a diffusion model, did coal prices have a significant impact.

Harley: There was a significant short-run impact on the adoption of the marine engine in the period of most rapidly rising coal prices, represented by the kink in the productivity curve of Figure 3. Over the whole period, though, von Tunzelmann was correct in supposing that there was no large impact in the short run.

Vamplew: Were difficulties in raising capital important in delaying the move to the steamship, as they definitely were in Norway?

Harley: No. The owners and builders were well connected with the capital market.

David: Responding to Pollard's earlier point on the composition of demand, the paper offers convincing evidence that fof the main bulk trades, which are its concern, the elasticity of substitution between sail and steam was infinite. This undermines Pollard's point, for there was therefore no apparent difference in these trades between the service provided by the steam ship and that provided by a sailing ship.

Pollard: It was only by ignoring the non-bulk trades that Harley got this result. And the other problem is that mere freight mileage is not the only important characteristic of a voyage.

Imlah: By the 1890s there was excess capacity in sail and much idle port time.

Harley: It is plausible that there was excess capacity. Sail by that time was confined to the long Pacific bulk routes.

7

*Yardsticks for Victorian Entrepreneurs**

PETER H. LINDERT AND KEITH TRACE

I

While no major question in economic history can be said to have been 'fully' researched, coverage of the quality of Victorian industrial management has been relatively heavy. Authors seeking to generalize about the role of entrepreneurial failure in Britain's relative decline after 1870 have been able to draw on numerous contemporary and retrospective industry studies. Perhaps as a consequence allegations concerning the quality of management have abounded. Writers stressing the shortcomings of businessmen [1] have linked them to amateurism, the family ownership of firms, complacency based on past achievements, an underemphasis of technical education and a range of other factors. Others, sceptical of explanations of retardation reliant on entrepreneurial failure, have provided alternative explanations focusing on (amongst others) international factor price differentials and the size of available markets [2]. Yet we find ourselves disturbingly short of conclusions when summarizing this literature in the classroom. The extensive commitment of scarce research time to this issue seems to have yielded little more than a long listing of alleged examples and counterexamples, the trivial rejection of monocausal explanations, and the reminder that entrepreneurship is a hard thing to measure and weigh.

More is at stake in the question of entrepreneurial deficiency than may be evident at first glance. Seemingly independent arguments about growth rates in fact depend on the demonstration that managers did or did not pass up profitable opportunities. In particular, the 'early start' hypothesis is plausible almost solely when it stresses the entrepreneur himself as the transmitter of the retardative influence of past success. One variant of the 'early start' theme — the theory of 'momentum' or 'over-commitment' — explicitly emphasizes conservative and counterproductive attachment of managers to established patterns of production and marketing [3]. Even the argument that the existence of outdated capital equipment can bring loss of leadership is usually an

* Earlier versions of this paper were read at seminars at the universities of Essex, Kent and Manchester. The authors wish to thank the participants in those seminars and Mr D. W. F. Hardie for their comments and suggestions.

assertion that the managers of the established firms were failing to maximize profits. Old equipment is a gift from the past that a rational manager will accept only so long as it offers him an alternative superior to buying the latest. Except for the costs of razing structures and retraining or relocating permanent employees [4], past investments do not place the leader at a competitive disadvantage relative to newcomers, since it can choose to change techniques. Any claim that the legacy of sunken costs caused an older company or nation to lose markets thus rests on the proposition that either managers or suppliers of capital acted irrationally so far as the economist is concerned. Similarly, the technical 'interelatedness' of new and installed plant and structures [5] can impose a competitive handicap on the early starter in the wake of innovations only through lack of entrepreneurial vigour or through the inability of firms owning the complementary units of capital to reach a mutually beneficial agreement.

The debate over the causes of Britain's relative industrial decline is essentially between explanations like these, stressing the shortcomings of her entrepreneurs, and those absolving them from blame by pointing to such external constraints as market size, consumer tastes and the supply of inputs. Our objective is to show how more careful measurement of entrepreneurial deficiency and its impact promises to place the debate on a firmer footing. Two types of measures will be developed: direct detailed comparisons of the profitability of actual and alternative techniques of production, and a set of related indicators that economize on primary research inputs. Both yardsticks are used to judge investment decisions taken in selected branches of the U.K. chemical industry in the last quarter of the nineteenth century. In the cases in which deficiency is demonstrated, its impact on national product will be quantified. Finally, some suggestions are offered to aid further research in this area. We are not at present disposed to prejudge the importance of entrepreneurial failings for British industry as a whole. We do not insist that entrepreneurship is an appropriate focal point for interdisciplinary explanations of prewar growth rates, nor are we so wedded to models of *homo economicus* as to deny that entrepreneurial irrationality and miscalculation could have been a prime source of British retardation.

II

The calibre of entrepreneurship has yet to be quantified satisfactorily, and there is little reason to expect consensus on a single summary index of entrepreneurial talent in the near future. It is frequently asserted that country X or industry Y is better endowed with 'enterprise' than other countries or industries. Unfortunately, we cannot in the social sciences undertake controlled experiments as one would in a laboratory and we would be fortunate indeed to observe, say, two countries in which industrialists faced sufficiently similar social and economic conditions to enable us to formulate a test to discriminate between degrees of 'enterprise'. We can, however, identify the *economic consequences* of this quality. If earnings are sacrificed because of 'leads lost, opportunities missed, [and] markets relinquished that need not have been' [6], their amount can be estimated by comparing actual returns with those that would have been reaped had some better choice been made. The scope for such comparisons is unlimited. One can compare choices of machinery, research efforts, work rules, recipes, marketing strategies, corporate structures, asset portfolios, or plant locations. A nation's entrepreneurs can be criticized (or credited) for not adopting a particular practice whether the product in question exists in other countries or only on paper. Even the definition of an 'entrepreneur' could cover anyone making a decision with economic consequences, though the present paper will perpetuate the usual focus on the technical and marketing decisions of business managers [7]. The one cardinal rule is that the comparison must reflect the conditions faced by the individuals or firms whose performance is being judged. It will not do, for example, to fault Victorian manufacturers for not having adopted techniques that were preferable under American or German, but not British, price relationships.

We do not believe that past studies have conformed to this standard. Authors seeking to substantiate the charge of entrepreneurial failure have drawn upon two unsatisfactory forms of evidence: the opinions of others and general economic indicators that reveal competitive decline but not its causes. The opinions are primarily those of official boards of inquiry, consular attachés and financial engineering journalists, and tend on balance to be critical of management. One suspects, however, that indictments of entrepreneurs by such sources were coloured by a desire to blame somebody (business leaders) for the nation's commercial slippage, and an attraction to things new and mechanized. As Professor Landes has acknowledged,

> . . . the evidence is biased, to a degree that is hard to assess. Contemporary observers emphasized the failures of British entrepreneurship and the imminent dangers of German competition . . . That was the way one sold articles or attracted the notice of

officials in London. Besides, there is such a thing as fashion in opinions, and this was clearly one of the popular dirges of the day. [8]

Contemporary journalists and officials were not, however, unanimous in their criticism [9], nor is it easy – without a detailed examination of costs and prices – to decide what weight to assign to contemporary accounts that were critical of management as against the implied convictions of the industrialists that they were doing the best they could.

Passages purporting to illustrate entrepreneurial backwardness too often and too casually display data on declining market shares, scale of operation, capital intensity, capital vintage and average labour productivity, as if these pinpointed such backwardness. To refer without qualification to Britain's failure to conform to a world wide 'best practice' or to her 'failure to mechanize' and 'failure . . . to modernize her plant or to adopt new processes' is to confuse modernity and machinery with profitability [10]. As for data on the level and growth of output-labour and capital-labour ratios, it would not be necessary to mention them in this context were it not for the fact that they continue to be cited as telling evidence on entrepreneurial quality [11].

It is clear from recent industry studies that such evidence can be misleading. Against previous authors' condemnation of the long lag in switching from mule spinning to ring spinning in cotton textiles [12], Professor Sandberg has shown that the lag was rational in view of Britain's cost and market conditions [13]. And against figures showing lower labour productivity for British than for American pig iron production, Professor McCloskey offers indirect evidence that the British industry maintained a higher level of total factor productivity than the American firms until at least 1900 [14]. It is not beyond the bounds of belief that the whole array of testimonial evidence of flagging entrepreneurship will prove on closer examination to be a mirage created by differences in price ratios and factor proportions.

On the other hand, authors questioning the importance of entrepreneurial shortcomings have at times leaned too heavily on the argument that if other major sources of retardation can be identified, entrepreneurial explanations carry less weight. But indirect arguments seldom suffice. Thus, for example, even if the entire drop in Britain's growth rates after 1870 could have been attributed to exogenous shifts in export demand and their input-output effects on related industries [15], a separate inquiry might nonetheless be able to attach equal weight to a decline in entrepreneurial vigour. A similar qualification should be attached to Professor Temin's demonstration that tariff and transport barriers could have deprived even the most efficient British steel industry of sufficient export markets to prevent its matching German and American growth rates [16]. It might seem that this finding places a ceiling on the contribution of weak entrepreneurship to the relative decline of British steel. But to show that tariff and transport barriers suffice to explain 100 per cent of the differences in steel growth rates does not demonstrate the unimportance of incorrect production techniques either for steel or for the whole economy [17]. As long as both positive and negative contributions can be included in the balance, a 100 per cent explanation (of steel growth rate differentials) can be an incomplete one. The importance of entrepreneurship can be appraised directly, but not by showing the importance of other factors.

III

A straightforward cost-benefit calculation can be used to measure the private profits foregone by a non-optimal choice of techniques. The actual or foreseeable earnings associated with such a choice can be compared with data on an optimal practice suggested by theory or actual performance elsewhere. The value *(PV)* of the incremental profits viewed from the time of entrepreneurial decision is obtained by discounting all increments occurring over the time span in which earnings are likely to have been affected. The expected value of the profit difference *(D)* for any time span is related to the average prices and physical amounts of all inputs and outputs by the identity

$$D \equiv \pi^* - \pi \equiv \sum_{j=1}^{n} P_j Y_j^* - \sum_{i=1}^{m} w_i N_i^* - \sum P_j Y_j + \sum w_i N_i$$

The asterisks here refer to the hypothetical alternative technique of production (e.g. American practice in a particular industry), while the symbols without asterisks refer to the practices being judged (e.g. British). P_j and Y_j are the price and volume of the *j*th output, and w_i and N_i are the average unit price and level of employment of the *i*th input. If an input is an asset that the decision-maker could invest elsewhere (financial assets, land, personal effort and talent), an opportunity cost must be added into its w_i [18]. If the input is a fixed asset already installed, the cost of acquiring this gift from the past must, of course, be excluded from the estimated cost of continuing production with the same technique. For the present, assume that the average prices of outputs and inputs are independent of the decision. Should this assumption be invalid, the task of measuring the D's and PV is rather more complicated [19], although their signs are unlikely to be reversed. Adjustments for price changes will be made in one of the cases below.

Entrepreneurs have forgone profits whenever

$$PV = \sum_{t=0}^{\infty} D_t/(1 + r)^t > 0, \text{ or in,}$$

the continuous-time case,

$$PV = \int_0^{\infty} D_t e^{-rt}\, dt > 0,$$

where the null subscript refers to the time of decision and r is the rate of return on the asset sacrificed (or the liability incurred) in order to change techniques.

The proposed measure can be employed either with or without hindsight. In order to determine the *ex post* impact of a decision on subsequent incomes, the actual subsequent movement of prices and volumes should be examined. If, however, one wishes to ask what levels of profitability could reasonably have been foreseen at the time of decision, judgements can be made about the movements in markets and technology that might have been (or were) predicted by informed contemporary observers. The 'predictable' and observed profit performances may differ sharply. Both will be discussed in connection with chemicals.

We anticipate that some readers may object to our calculation on the grounds that the entrepreneurs being judged may not have set out to maximize the estimated or expected value of profits. Risk avoidance, continuity in policy and practice, and relaxed enjoyment of the fruits of attained wealth are among the many non-profit goals that may have been pursued. The profit yardstick is nonetheless employed, for one negative and one positive reason. To take the negative reason first, if an entrepreneur has a multiplicity of objectives with unspecified utility weights that can change over time, there is no way of saying whether he is acting rationally or correctly. For example, conservatism can always be excused as rational if the analyst rightly admits that risk aversion is justified to some unknown degree. Under such charitable criteria for optimality, non-optimality could never be revealed. The second, positive reason is that the profits measure can be objectively linked to the entrepreneur's contribution to the national product, another one-dimensional risk-neutral measure central to economic analysis. It is moreover clear that writers who have contributed to the debate believe that 'entrepreneurial failure' has implications for the rate of growth of national product. Dr Aldcroft, for example, advances 'the hypothesis that Britain's relatively poor economic performance can be attributed largely to the failure of the British entrepreneur to respond to the challenge of changed conditions' [20]. The legitimacy and durability of this interest in the growth of national income thus leads us to judge entrepreneurs by a standard they may not have fully shared. In this paper, such terms as 'deficiency' and 'failure' apply only to this narrow income-maximization criterion.

The rule that the price structure must be that faced by those being judged has implications that deserve emphasis here. For one, the proposed measure does not possess *transitivity* or *symmetry*. If British steel producers are deficient relative to American techniques, and their American competitors would be better off switching to German techniques, it does not follow that German entrepreneurs are correct in not using British and American techniques. Or again, American and British firms could be simultaneously irrational in not adopting each other's methods. Of course, the reverse case, that of mutual rationality of technical choice, is more likely: if all production is optimal, every firm's decisions are superior to all others — given the conditions facing that firm. The *PV*'s, in other words, would all be negative if entrepreneurship were flawless.

A further implication of the measure chosen is that because simple aggregation is likely to yield negative sums of *D*'s and *PV*'s, it would be unduly biased against the hypothesis that entrepreneurial deficiency had serious retardative effects. As we intrepret it, the deficiency hypothesis simply states that the gross effect of all of those instances where wrong decisions were made (or right ones not made) can explain 'much' of Britain's retardation. Therefore, the finding that a particular set of producers used techniques better (for them) than known alternatives means that deficiency fails to appear, but it does not mean that the impact of other mistakes is lessened. To allow satisfactory performances to offset errors is to pursue once again the will-o'-the-wisp called the 'overall quality' of British entrepreneurship.

Finally, accurate portrayal of the price structure that would have been produced by hypothetically superior decisions becomes an increasingly formidable task as the inquiry becomes more aggregative. Cost-benefit studies tend to have their comparative advantage in the analysis of marginal changes, as Prest and Turvey have reminded us:

> If investment decisions are so large relative to a given economy (e.g., a major dam project in a small country), that they are likely to alter the constellation of relative outputs and prices over the whole economy, the standard technique . . . is likely to fail us, for nothing less than some sort of general equilibrium approach would suffice in such cases. [21]

Some suggestions for the partial solution of this problem are given in the final section of this paper.

In the interests of economizing on the cost of primary data collection, further inquiries may benefit by a restatement of the above formula for D into expressions using more commonly available data. The expressions for D shown in Table 1 allow the researcher to avoid multiplying every physical volume of inputs and outputs in the alternative context by a price facing the firms under scrutiny. Instead, the same result can be reached using, say, a single representative detailed set of cost accounts, price ratios (more readily available than physical volumes), total revenues, and one profit margin. The choice among these and equivalent formulae is a matter of convenience. If the group or country being 'judged' does not produce the range of commodities at all, the first and third expressions will prove especially convenient. If the data permit a calculation of the total factor productivity (*TFP*) of the alternative (American) production pattern using British weights, such a measure can be incorporated into Formula

---

Symbols:

* = Data from the 'alternative context' (e.g. America) with which existing (British) practice is being compared.

α_i = Share of cost of ith input in total revenue = $w_i / N_i / \Sigma^i P_j Y_j$.

β_j = Share of revenue from jth output in total revenue = $P_j Y_j / \Sigma^i P_j Y_j$.

π = Profits above opportunity costs earned by the producers being judged.

π^{**} = Profits above opportunity costs earned by producers in the alternative context.

TFP* = Index of total factor productivity of producers in the alternative context, using British data as a weight base and a comparison base.

For other symbols, see text.

TABLE 1

Selected formulae for D, the profit increment resulting from a change in technique

Formula No. and name	Expression for D	Data required (a) to quantify D	Data required (b) to determine its sign
(1) Price ratios minus actual profits	$\Sigma P_j^* Y_j^* [\Sigma \beta_i^* P_j/P_j^* - \Sigma \alpha_i^* w_i/w_i^*] - \pi$	(1) * revenues (2) actual profits (π) (3) * cost shares (α_i^*) (4) price ratios	same
(2) Price and revenue ratios	$\Sigma P_j^* Y_j^* [\Sigma \beta_i^* P_j/P_j^* - \Sigma \alpha_i^* w_i/w_i^*$ $- \dfrac{\Sigma P_j Y_j}{\Sigma P_j^* Y_j^*}(1 - \Sigma \alpha_j)]$	(1) all revenues (2) profit margin $(1 - \Sigma \alpha_i)$ (3) * cost shares (4) price ratios	same, but with estimates of revenue ratios sufficient if data are lacking on levels
(3) Profits and price differences	$\left[\Sigma \beta_i^* \dfrac{P_j - P_j^*}{P_j^*} - \Sigma \alpha_i^* \dfrac{w_i - w_i^*}{w_i^*} \right.$ $\left. + \dfrac{\pi^{**} - \pi}{\Sigma P_j^* Y_j^*} \right] \Sigma P_j^* Y_j^*$	(1) % price differentials (2) * cost shares (3) profits and * revenues	same
(4) Total factor productivity	$\Sigma P_j^* Y_j^* \left(1 - \dfrac{\Sigma \alpha_i}{TFP^*}\right) - \Sigma P_j Y_j (1 - \Sigma \alpha_i)$ $\text{or } \Sigma P_j Y_j^* \left(1 - \dfrac{\Sigma \alpha_i}{TFP^*}\right) - \pi$	(1) outputs and one set of prices (2) profit margin (3) TFP^* index	In some cases the ratio of total revenues and the value of TFP alone suffice to determine sign

(4). Again, if the data on physical volumes used in the definition of total factor productivity,

$$TFP^* = \frac{\Sigma P_j Y_j^*}{\Sigma w_i N_i^*} \cdot \frac{\Sigma w_i N_i}{\Sigma P_j Y_j} = \frac{\Sigma P_j Y_j^*}{(\Sigma \alpha_i) \Sigma w_i N_i^*} \, ,$$

are scarce, the price dual of this measure may prove more useful [22] :

$$TFP^* = \frac{(\Sigma \alpha_i) \Sigma \beta_j^* (P_j/P_j^*)}{\Sigma \alpha_i^* (w_i/w_i^*)}$$

In this way conclusions about entrepreneurship could be reached as byproducts of international productivity comparisons.

The savings in research cost made possible by Table 1's formulae are not likely to be dramatic. If the inferiority of one method of production to another could be demonstrated quickly and simply, the mode of demonstration would have been common business knowledge years ago. But the scholar can equip himself with useful clues and rough impressions by sacrificing rigour for speed when applying Table 1's formulae. He can, for example aggregate over inputs or ignore minor input items in order to concentrate on a small number of items whose volumes and prices are likely to be crucial in the comparison of techniques. If there is approximate equality between the scales of production being compared (each $Y_j^* \simeq Y_j$), the formulae can be simplified further. In some cases, observed profits can be used in place of the π and π^{**} measures, which reflect imputations for opportunity cost. Such short cuts can of course mislead, and should be used only in developing preliminary clues.

For the present we shall revert to the more pedestrian original profit-difference formula, in order to make the basis for our calculations as explicit as possible.

IV

The chemicals sector, though employing only about 2 per cent of Britain's labour force toward the end of the nineteenth century, was conspicuous as a rising research-based industry in which advances in knowledge and efficiency held out the promise of substantial economies for a cross section of British industry. Yet these opportunities were not fully exploited, according to practically every author dealing with chemical entrepreneurship. Britain appears to have held a strong lead in chemical production in 1870, but was far behind

Germany and America by 1913 [23]. Even the history of alkali production, the most important line in which Britain's lead was retained until the war, has been seen as a dreary tale of defensive and overcautious entrepreneurs clinging to the obsolete Leblanc system long after the superiority of Solvay soda production was recognized by their Continental and American counterparts [24]. Germany's conquest of synthetic dyestuffs is also cited as a classic case of British sluggishness, amateurism, and neglect of science [25]. Britain (and France) 'watched other countries take the lead' [26] in the electrolytic production of chlorine and caustic soda from the 1890s on. At the same time, Britain lost her lead in the production of sulphuric acid,

> ... due to falling demands from the Leblanc makers and Britain's laggardliness in superphosphates production and retention of out-of-date technical methods, particularly the lead-chamber process rather than the new contact acid process widely used in Germany by the early 1900s. [27]

In this paper we will concentrate on the allegations regarding alkali, sulphuric acid, and dyestuffs. We wish to stress, however, that this choice of subject matter is not random and probably not representative. The chemicals sector is one in which we initially suspected a high probability of detecting entrepreneurial errors, if only because the opinion of outside observers has been so unanimously critical in this case. How the frequency and importance of profit-sacrificing decisions in chemicals compares to overall British performance can be determined only after a broader and more systematic investigation.

The Leblanc soda producers certainly looked like men being punished for backwardness. They had been warned in the mid-1880s [28] that they would have to scrap their plant and start all over with the ammonia process patented by Solvay if they were to continue producing soda at a profit. Yet Britain continued to lag behind in the conversion to ammonia soda. In 1894 over 65 per cent of British soda production still came from Leblanc plants, while no other country produced as much as 22 per cent by this process [29]. From the mid-1870s on, Brunner Mond and Company, Britain's leading Solvay firm, consistently announced annual dividends above 25 per cent. Leblanc production and profits began to slump across the 1880s despite numerous minor technical advances. Merger into the giant United Alkali Company in 1890 failed to produce a better profit record, despite the closing of less efficient units and the opening of one ammonia soda plant. Dividends on ordinary shares were small and infrequent, and the share reached with Brunner Mond, with other domestic caustic makers, and with German bleach producers on increasingly concessionary terms. United Alkali apparently ceased production of Leblanc soda ash altogether around 1902 and abandoned the remaining Leblanc alkali lines sometime during World War I.

Such outward signs of morbidity do not prove that significant amounts of profits and value added were sacrificed by retention of the Leblanc system. Comparison with Continental profit margins and choice of technique, for example, may be misleading because cost conditions differed. Three of the four largest items in the extra cost of Leblanc soda over Solvay – coal, pyrites and capital – were cheaper in Britain than on the Continent. Labour alone was more expensive in Britain. Such differences in costs help to explain why an allegedly inefficient industry felt so little competition from imports despite free trade; it is conceivable that these differences might also have sufficed to erase the cost margin in favour of ammonia soda. Nor do references to the unit costs of Leblanc and Solvay soda ash deal directly with the profitability of Leblanc by-products (bleach via the Weldon or Deacon process, sulphur via the Claus-Chance process, and pyrites cinders) or the shift from soda ash to caustic soda, on which Leblanc producers placed so much hope in the 1880s and 1890s. Although the dramatic contrast between the profits of Brunner Mond and those of the Leblanc producers suggests that the latter missed an opportunity worth millions in the early 1870s, the name of the company seizing this opportunity was of no consequence for the economy as a whole. Furthermore, the rapid growth of Brunner Mond, and the attacks launched after 1895 by electrolytic producers on the final Leblanc citadels, bleach and caustic soda, may have made the obsolescence of the Leblanc system so rapid that it dragged down total British efficiency only for a few years. Even if the Leblanc system had proved unprofitable, in other words, Britain may have succeeded in burying this mistake before it could 'significantly' retard the growth of the industry.

The consequences of shifting over to ammonia soda production thus seem sufficiently uncertain to require a detailed calculation. The outcome hinges critically on the answers given to four questions:

(1)   What product mixes are to be compared?
(2)   Who are the hypothesized investors in the new Solvay plant?

(3)   What effect would their investment have had on input and output prices and volumes?

(4)   At what date is the critical decision hypothesized to have been taken?

The set of products called 'soda' or 'alkali' consists of four main types of soda ash (sodium carbonate), five types of caustic soda (sodium hydroxide), soda crystals (carbonate), and sodium bicarbonate. Demand and cost conditions were such as to split this product range into two distinct groupings: soda ash (now including crystals and bicarbonate) and caustic soda. The basic product in the Leblanc trade was carbonated soda ash having 48 per cent Na_2O content, or about 82 per cent pure sodium carbonate [30]. Soda crystals, refined soda ash, and 'caustic soda ash' could be sold in place of carbonated soda ash at prices that seem to have reflected the latter's Na_2O content plus a mark-up covering the net cost of product alteration (refining, crystallization, etc.), so that all of the products in this group tended to yield similar profit margins per ton of Na_2O content. The ammonia process, on the other hand, initially yields soda ash of 58 per cent Na_2O (or about 98 per cent pure Na_2CO_3), a degree of purity that the Leblanc process could not have achieved without prohibitive outlays for fuel and labour. As long as the two processes competed openly (up to about 1894), the price ratio of carbonated Leblanc ash to Solvay ash tended toward the ratio of the purities of carbonate (.84) [31]. That is, consumers implicitly demanded the two in proportion to their carbonate (or sodium monoxide) contents. We can therefore view the ton-equivalent of pure sodium carbonate as a homogeneous product, whether it was sold as 1.22 tons of '48 per cent' ash or as 1.008 tons of '58 per cent' ash.

With caustic soda, as with soda ash, each type of final product was apparently priced so as to yield about the same profit margin per ton-equivalent of the basic product, in this case white caustic of 60 per cent Na_2O. It was also the case that the price ratio of Leblanc caustic to Leblanc ash was usually near the ratio of their Na_2O contents. It is important, however, to treat ash and caustic separately. Producing caustic from soda ash was considerably cheaper with the old Leblanc process, which could causticize from an intermediate product (black ash), than the causticization of ammonia soda. As a result, the Leblanc firms retained a large share of the caustic market despite steady retreat from soda ash, bicarbonate and crystals. Consequently, the ash-to-caustic price relationship became more and more a reflection of the cost of causticization by the ammonia process [32].

To complete the comparison between the profits on one ton-equivalent of 98 per cent sodium carbonate and its equivalent in '60 per cent' caustic soda, it is necessary to allow for the profits on Leblanc byproducts. For each ton of 98 per cent carbonate ash, or for each 0.967 tons of caustic soda, produced by Solvay plant instead of Leblanc, proportionate values of profits on 35 per cent bleaching powder, recovered sulphur (after 1888) and pyrites cinders would also be forgone. If this abandonment of the final (soda and sulphur recovery) phases of the Leblanc process were complete, the Leblanc trade would have consisted of the production of sulphuric acid, pyrites cinders and small amounts of bleaching powder [33] and saltcake (sodium sulphate) for direct sale only. As it was, this change was not complete until World War I.

The hypothetical investors in new Solvay plant either could have come from the ranks of the major existing alkali producers or could have been new entrants seeking to wrest markets from these established suppliers, perhaps with the direct backing of soda-using firms (e.g. in soap, paper, dyestuffs or textiles) or a foreign bleach competitor [34]. If the investor had been one of the hitherto Leblanc-based firms it is possible that despite the change in method of production no change would have been made in soda prices or sales volume. Our first set of calculations will estimate the gains from this sort of fixed-output, fixed-price cost reduction. If, on the other hand, the new investment was accompanied by fresh competition, prices would have fallen and output would have risen, making the computation of incremental earnings more difficult. To analyse such cases, we utilize two generalizations about the prewar soda industry: it was characterized by flat long-run cost curves, and it was governed (after 1894 if not earlier) by price and market-share agreements.

Leblanc and Solvay cost accounts, mostly pertaining to the years between 1860 and 1894 [35], appear frequently in the technical press and in industry studies. While these reveal considerable improvements in efficiency up to the mid-1880s, the economies achieved seem to have been independent of the scale of operation. For each of the major processes, including causticization and the Leblanc byproduct processes, the ratios of inputs to output are similar for several quite different scales of production, all of which were well below the level of replaceable Leblanc production [36]. Serious inaccuracies are thus unlikely to arise from the assumption that the shift from Leblanc to Solvay soda would not have altered the ratios of each input to output in the production of ammonia soda or the leftover production of Leblanc products.

The unit prices of inputs, like the physical input-output ratios for each separate process, would not have been significantly altered by the change in technique. The discussions given to the issue of input price changes in the 1880s found little basis for expecting the prices of coal, limestone, lime, salt, saltpetre, labour or capital to r *Caustic soda* level or technique of soda production. Only two of the relevant inputs showed any signs of possible inelasticity. A rise in the price of the ammonia compounds purchased in rapidly increasing amounts by Brunner Mond was hopefully awaited by the Leblanc producers [37]. By the mid-1880s, however, it was clear that ammonia compounds collected from coke ovens and blast furnaces were being exported in large amounts, and that their production could be increased tenfold with the slightest extra incentive and effort [38]. Similarly, by 1890 it was clear that a major cutback in Leblanc manufacture would not significantly reduce the price of Sicilian sulphur (thus adding to the gains for large Leblanc firms switching to ammonia soda production while continuing to produce sulphuric acid), since any slight drop in the f.o.b. price of sulphur would have forced a large number of Sicilian mines to close [39]. A combination of circumstances thus made the prices of all inputs and long-run average costs unresponsive to the levels of Leblanc and Solvay soda output.

Other circumstances restricted competition in soda throughout the period to be examined. In 1872 Solvay granted the first British ammonia soda licence to Brunner Mond and Company for a royalty of eight shillings per ton. This agreement also stipulated that no other British licence was to be granted for less than £1 a ton. On these terms a new ammonia soda firm would have required high efficiency and generous financing to survive the competition of Brunner Mond until the Solvay patent legally expired in Britain in 1886 [40]. From 1886 to the early 1890s the prospects for individual firms were unstable and uncertain, with the breakdown of price collusion in bleach and caustic soda, the formation of United Alkali in 1890, and a continued rise in Brunner Mond's market share. By about 1894, however, Brunner Mond and United Alkali had clearly reached an agreement on price levels and market shares for each soda product [41], and other

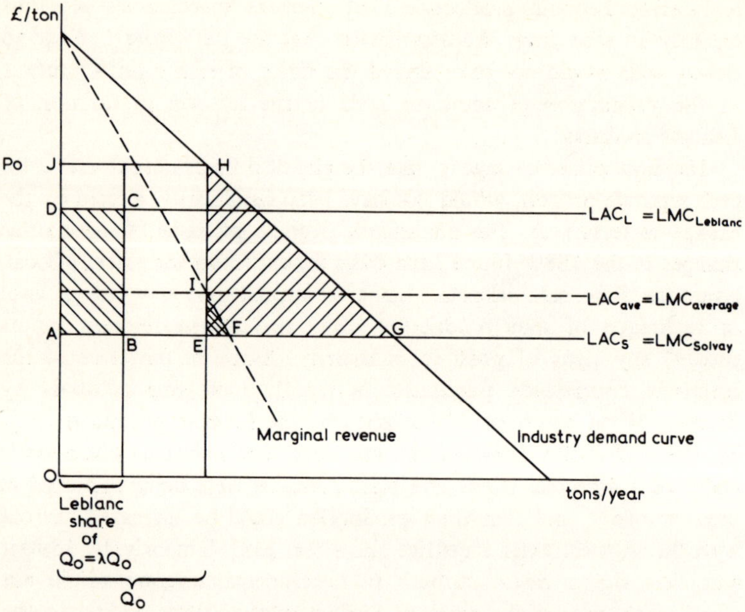

Figure 1   Collusive monopoly in British soda products, *c.* 1894-1914.

companies soon joined the alliance. The agreement was maintained until the war, with a major renegotiation of prices occurring in 1900 and 1901.

The truce seems to have resembled a collusive monopoly solution like that portrayed in Figure 1, in which a high-cost (Leblanc) and a low-cost (Solvay) set of firms first agree on market shares and then set prices so as to maximize joint profits. The marginal revenue curve will intersect (at Point I) a long-run [42] marginal and average cost curve (LAC_{ave}), the level of which depends on the provisions of the agreement regarding marginal buyers. If, for example, market shares are rigidly fixed, the relative distances of LAC_{ave} from the Leblanc and Solvay lines will correspond to the Leblanc and Solvay shares of the market. Alternatively, but with little change in the estimates that follow, the colluders might have acted as a single firm and produced output *AF*. In any case, the level of LAC_{ave} is bounded by LAC_L and LAC_S.

Under such collusion, there are two useful formulae for capturing the gains from replacing Leblanc with Solvay soda (assuming for the

moment that Leblanc production was in fact more costly). If the
changes in technique were effected by the existing firms, they would
gain the area of rectangle *ABCD* plus, if the present theoretical
assumptions are accurate, the area of the triangle *EFI*. With a linear
demand curve it can be shown that

Area of $ABCD = \lambda Q_0 (LAC_L - LAC_S)$, where λ is the Leblanc share
of total production, and

$$\text{Area of } EFI \simeq \frac{(LAC_{\text{ave}} - LAC_S)^2 P_0 Q_0}{2(P_0 - LAC_{\text{ave}})(LAC_{\text{ave}})}$$

If, however, the Leblanc producers had been driven from the field by
new entrants using the ammonia process, the total cost saving to
soda-using firms minus the loss of profits to soda producers could have
been as high as the sum of the area of *ABCD* plus

$$\text{area of } EGH \simeq \frac{(P_0 - LAC_S)^2 \cdot Q_0}{2(P_0 - LAC_{\text{ave}})}$$

This extreme result would have obtained if the new entrants had
completely destroyed the monopoly powers of soda producers. Thus, if
the old processes were in fact more costly on balance, the national gain
in profits could have been considerably greater if the builders of the
new plant had also chosen to undercut any attempts at monopoly
pricing. A rough measurement of these extra gains for 1894-1914 will
be attempted below.

The choice of decision date is the final issue to be resolved before
estimates can be made of the profitabilities of the two processes. Three
plausible alternatives present themselves. We shall first examine the
incremental profits that would probably have accrued to British
chemical firms if one of them, instead of Ernest Solvay, had perfected
and wholly adopted ammonia soda production in the late 1860s and
early 1870s. A second calculation determines the returns from
converting to the Solvay process between 1872 and 1886, given that
Solvay had already established his patent and had sold a licence to
Brunner Mond. Finally, we shall appraise the results of a decision to
switch techniques in the late 1880s and early 1890s. The three
alternatives yield quite different results. The fact that the dicovery and
rapid development of the Solvay process was not led by British firms
around 1870 was to cost the nation considerable sums *ex post*, but they
could not reasonably be 'blamed' for this outcome. Given the necessity
to pay out royalties to Solvay, there were in fact no net incremental
soda profits to be had for the period 1872-86, and again entrepreneurs

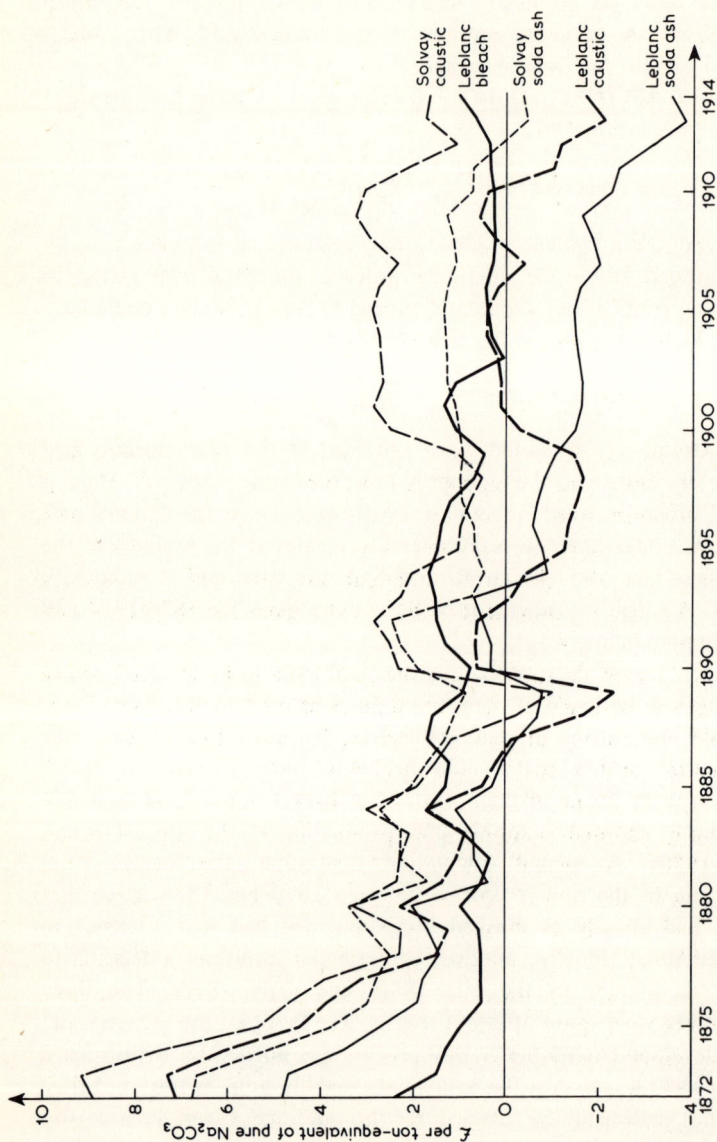

Figure 2 Profit margins on Leblanc and Solvay products, 1888-1914. *Note:* The Leblanc ash and caustic figures are calculated as though the HCl used in bleach manufacture were wasted. Correspondingly, the bleach data treat HCl as a free input. The pre-1886 Solvay royalties have been ignored in computing the Solvay ash and caustic profit margins.

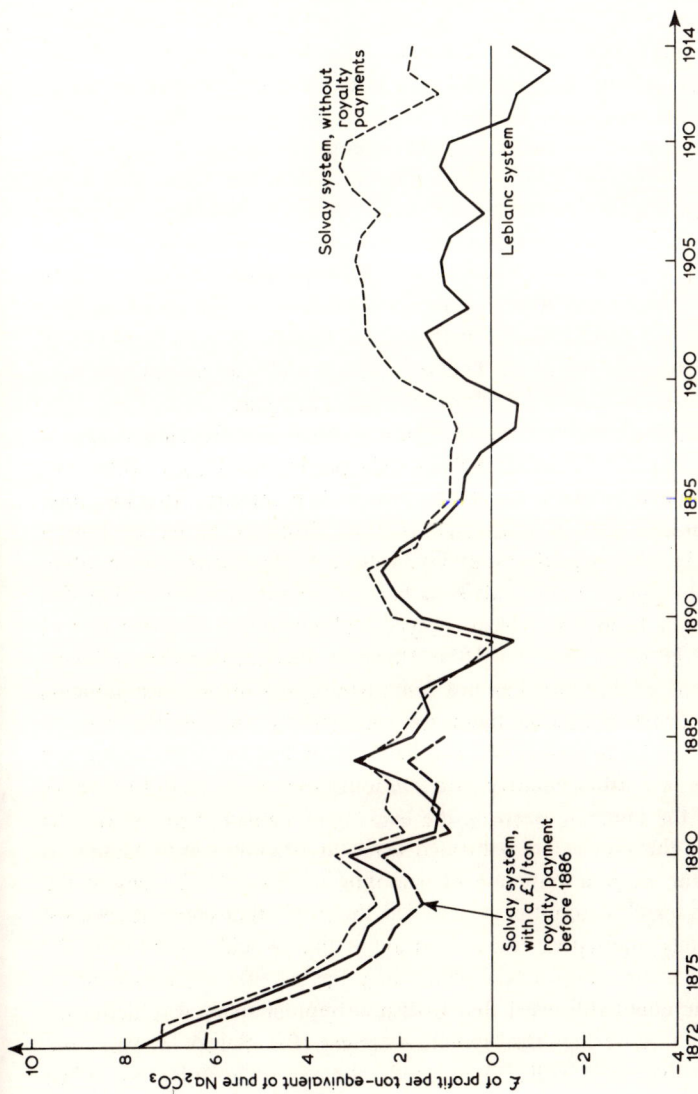

Figure 3 Overall profit margins on the Leblanc and Solvay systems, 1872-1914.
Note: The data refer to the total Leblanc and Solvay profits per unit of alkali output attainable on the combination of soda products actually made by Leblanc plants in these years. The returns from bleach production, sulphur recovery and resale of pyrites cinder have been included in the Leblanc calculation.

are to be excused. But for the years after 1888, significant amounts of forgone profit are evident whether one uses hindsight or not, and the charge of entrepreneurial 'deficiency' is sustained.

The profitability of the two soda processes is displayed in Figures 2–4. The profit margins on each product in Figure 2 have been derived by combining benchmark estimates of the volumes and costs of each input per unit of output [43] with price data for the final products. The results [44] are broadly consistent with the observed profit performances of the two major soda companies. After the turn of the century, however, the profitability of ammonia soda ash seems somewhat underestimated by our figures, which do not allow for any of the savings on raw materials reportedly achieved by Solvay firms after 1894 [45]. Figure 3 combines the profit margins of Figure 2 into average Leblanc and Solvay margins obtainable on the set of outputs actually produced by the Leblanc process. Figure 4 applies these overall margins to the estimated Leblanc caustic and ash output, yielding best-guess estimates of the values of forgone earnings.

The hindsight calculation in Figure 4 shows that Britain's failure to develop, patent and adopt Solvay soda production in, say, 1866 cost her income throughout most of the next half century. This loss took the form of royalty outpayments from Brunner Mond to Solvay (1874-85), the royalties that could have been received from other nations by granting ammonia soda licences, and the incremental profits that British firms could have enjoyed had ammonia soda been free of royalties between 1872 and 1886. However, the fact that Ernest Solvay was not an Englishman does not demonstrate that British entrepreneurs made a decision costing them the opportunity to lead the way to ammonia soda. Britain appears to have put at least as much money and effort as any other country into ammonia soda research before 1870, some of the research receiving the backing of Leblanc firms [46]. The fact that the crucial breakthrough came in Belgium can be viewed as merely the *ex post* outcome of gambling in research. As long as the British research commitment matched those of other countries, we see no obvious alternative research strategy that would have raised the expected value of profits – even when the payoffs are measured *ex post*. One could still insist that British entrepreneurship was 'deficient' for not discovering the specific designs for Solvay towers and ammonia-recovery stills, but this choice transcends our own (admittedly arbitrary) threshold of tolerance for hindsight.

Once Solvay had secured the crucial patents and set his price for an

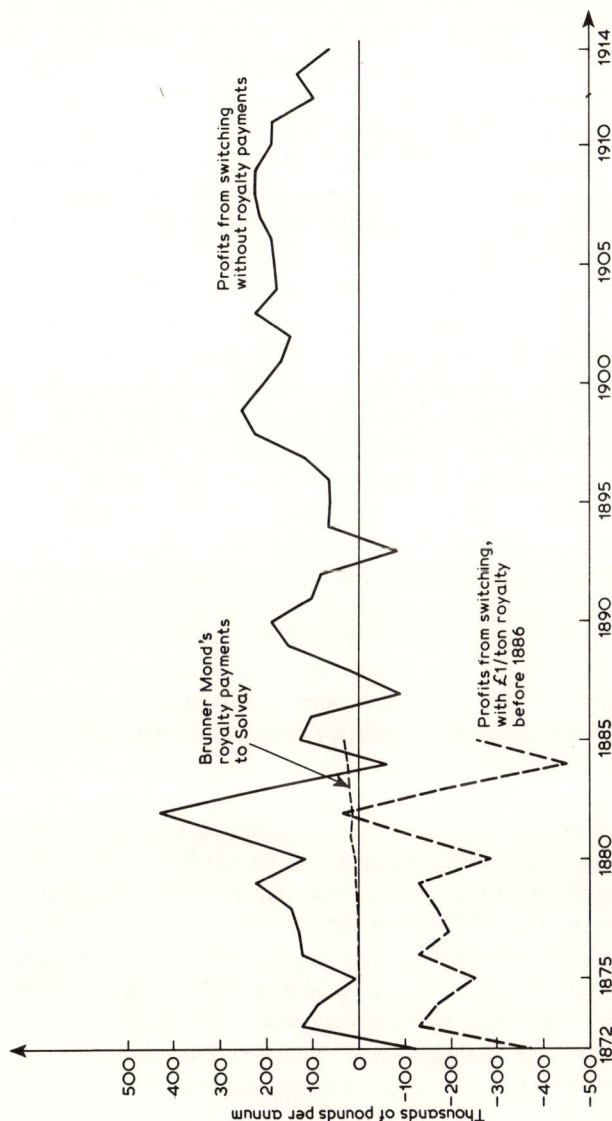

Figure 4 Profits gained by switching from Leblanc to Solvay production, 1872-1914.
Note: The series on profits from switching have been calculated under the assumption that the output prices and volumes would not have been affected by the change in techniques. For calculations that do not make this assumption, see Table 2. Allowances for previously sunken Leblanc costs have not been made in these series. For estimates reflecting the pre-existence of Leblanc fixed capital, see the Discussion of this paper, pp. 280–2.

English licence, replacement of Leblanc with Solvay plant would not have brought any clear net gains until the patent legally expired in Britain in 1886. Figures 3 and 4 reveal that the pound-per-ton royalty stipulated for new entrants by the 1872 contract between Solvay and Brunner Mond was sufficient to make conversion truly unprofitable for the following fourteen years. Brunner Mond, entitled to pay only eight shillings a ton, might have profitably expanded and competed even more vigorously than they did, especially in markets for soda ash and crystals, but the range of error in our estimates is too wide for rejecting the null hypothesis that the true increments forgone by Brunner Mond were zero before 1886 [47].

The expiration of the patent in 1886 combined with a number of other issues to make the late 1880s an especially plausible time for a major review of the Leblanc-Solvay cost comparison by Leblanc firms. By this time, several issues had resolved themselves. The Solvay process was well known, so that the costs of acquiring and perfecting the technique were negligible. By 1888, the hopes for Leblanc sulphur recovery had been fulfilled by the Claus-Chance process, which offered a small profit on this byproduct. As noted above, it was clear by this time that ammonia prices would not rise and choke off the growth of ammonia soda output. Many of the previously anticipated economies in coal and salt consumption had already been achieved. Capital markets were also receptive to new issues around 1888. Finally, rationalization was reportedly an agreed goal of the merger negotiations under way among Leblanc firms by 1888, and large-scale conversion to Solvay production could have accompanied the formation of the United Alkali Company.

Our hindsight calculations show that a wholesale conversion to Solvay plant, if ordered in 1888 and fully installed by the start of 1890, would probably have brought the new United Alkali Company extra profits in every remaining prewar year except 1893. The annual increments averaged £147,600 over the entire period, and maintained an average of £201,600 per annum for the 1898-1911 subperiod. Discounting these returns back to the middle of 1890 at the prevailing consol rate of 3 per cent yields a capitalized value of £2,536,500. Deducting from the Leblanc cost estimates an allowance for pre-existing fixed capital reduces, but does not eliminate, this margin of forgone profits.

These estimates, however, are subject to considerable errors. It is entirely possible that our estimates of Leblanc and Solvay unit costs are each wrong by as much as 10 per cent. The important series on unit coal costs has, say, a 5 per cent chance of being off by 20 per cent, a margin that must be weighed against the convenient constraints imposed on other input costs by the laws of chemistry. Another weak link is the set of output estimates used to convert the unit profit margins of Figures 2 and 3 into the total profits of Figure 4. The reluctance of United Alkali to disclose output figures has left us only a handful of benchmark estimates after 1893. These estimates nonetheless give a broadly consistent and plausible portrayal of the rate of decline of Leblanc output [48]. All things considered, it seems conservative to say that the 95 per cent confidence interval for any quinquennial average of our unit profit and total profit estimates from the period 1889-1914 excludes errors as great as 100 per cent. In other words, we are quite confident that the true value of the forgone profits is neither zero nor twice our estimates for these years.

Once the United Alkali Company was formed and price agreements concluded with other alkali producers, purchasers of alkali had a clear collective incentive to break up this collusion and drive prices down to costs. Doing so would have brought them extra profits equal to the area *AGHI* in Figure 1, while the nation as a whole would have gained an amount represented by triangle *EGH* plus rectangle *ABCD*. Even if the price agreement were left unchallenged, the Leblanc producers could profitably have renegotiated a slightly lower price if they had converted over to ammonia soda production, the amount of the extra gain being their share of triangle *EFI*. Subdividing the period 1894-1914 at years in which prices were apparently renegotiated yields Table 2's rough estimates of the relevant income increments. Perhaps the most interesting hypothetical outcome is the extreme one represented by Rows (5) and (6): by installing their own ammonia soda plants and triggering a complete breakdown of soda monopoly, the soda users might have gained over a million pounds a year after the turn of the century and raised the approximate social gains to a figure (£630,000) three times as great as the cost savings plotted for these years in Figure 4.

Further adjustments could be made to the social-saving calculations. One could add in the small public savings that could have been gained by conversion to the cleaner Solvay process: the country could have spent less money on paying the Alkali Inspector to sniff the chimneys and drainpipes of pollution-prone Leblanc plants. Nor should one conclude directly from Figure 4 that the effects of the technical change

TABLE 2

Approximate private and social gains from switching
To Solvay soda production with lower prices and higher
outputs, 1894-1914
(thousands of pounds per annum)

	Soda ash, crystals and bicarbonate			
	1894-1901	1902-1914	1894-1899	1900-1914
(1) Area *EFI* (Figure 1)	10	0	50	40
(2) Area *EGH*	180	40	220	420
(3) Gains from cost reduction alone (Area *ABCD*)	60	0	110	170
(4) Area *AEHJ*	290	80	180	610
(5) Gains to purchasers from new ammonia-plant competition (Area *AGHJ = AEHJ + EGH*)	470	120	400	1030
(6) Social gains from new ammonia-soda competition (*ABCD + EGH*)	240	40	330	590
(7) Gains to colluding firms from scrapping Leblanc plant and renegotiating prices (*ABCD + EFI*)	70	0	160	210

on national income had become small once again by 1914. To equate the social savings generated in a particular year with the increments to consumption or national product experienced in that year alone is to assume that social savings are consumed at once. Making allowances for profit recipients' propensities to save and the average rate of return on their savings would shift much of the benefits of social savings forward in time [49]. The increments to consumption and national product in 1914 would thus be larger, and earlier increments smaller, than is indicated in Figure 4. We shall omit such adjustments, however, and simply offer Table 2 and Figure 4 as our portrayal of the time path of social gains from new ammonia soda plant with and without changes in price and output.

Are these gains 'large' or 'small'? The cost savings alone matched or exceeded the actual profits recorded by the United Alkali Company on all of its operations. Capturing these extra profits would have brought handsome capital gains to the company's shareholders. The much larger returns to be had by breaking up the soda price conspiracy would also have cheered investors in soap, paper and textiles, relatively competitive industries for which alkali took up a significant share of total costs. It is more difficult to render an impression of the importance of these magnitudes for aggregate conclusions relating entrepreneurial decisions and economic growth. Since national product is a sum either of industries' final output values or their values added, it is perhaps natural to extrapolate on the basis of the ratios of the measured gains to industry output or industry value added. In 1907 the cost savings (from Figure 4) and the gains from breaking the soda monopoly with new Solvay production (from Table 2) would have been about 4.6 per cent and 13.4 per cent of the value of the soda, sulphuric acid and bleach output. Their shares of value added in the same sector would have been about twice as great [50]. Repetition of such gains in all industries for a decade or more might have sufficed to bring Britain's 1870-1914 growth rate up to American or German rates. But the logic of projecting the gains to an industry value base is hardly compelling, and the present result may well be atypical: the Leblanc-Solvay case has been viewed by many as a prime example of entrepreneurial failure. We are thus forced to await the appearance of similar calculations for a few other key sectors before incorporating the present result into an overall conclusion.

Should the gains revealed by hindsight have been foreseen in the late 1880s and early 1890s? We know of no development that would have made Leblanc producers think their system was actually superior to Solvay's in the late 1880s. In fact, between 1887 and 1889 the breakup of the 1883 price agreements for bleach and caustic soda threatened to cheapen these crucial Leblanc outputs. Only if the 1890 merger were expected to peg bleach and caustic prices well above ash prices should Leblanc producers have been optimistic about the old system. They may have had such an expectation in the late 1880s, but it had to rest on the assumption that United Alkali need not fear new entrants in either bleach or caustic. By about 1897, the appearance of electrolytic bleach and caustic should have dispelled such illusions.

Explaining the costly conservatism of the Leblanc producers requires a certain amount of conjecture. Our principal sources of information are the tragicomic minutes of United Alkali's shareholders' meetings and a couple of retrospective volumes published by the company itself [51]. Both sources reveal only the flimsiest combinations of *ad hoc* excuses for company policy, without any direct explanation for their reluctance to expand the Fleetwood ammonia soda plant at the expense of others. Our tentative inference is that the Leblanc management exhibited the early-start mentality, with its profit-losing attachment to continuity and its reluctance to admit a major mistake. United Alkali avoided for years the systematic independent audit of its properties that would have given only scrap value to much of its plant [52]. The president, the director of research, and several members of the board, were responsible, or related to men responsible, for many of the technical advances that prolonged the life of the Leblanc system. One can imagine their reluctance to recognize that their contributions to knowledge merely furthered an ultimately lost cause. This attachment to improvements along Leblanc lines would partly account for the tendency of executives like E. K. Muspratt to hold out continued hope for new Leblanc economies (though Muspratt in 1886 underrated the imminent gains from sulphur recovery) while dismissing electrolysis as a passing fad.

The other group whose foresight needs to be judged is the set of soda purchasers. They were surely aware of the importance of the soda price agreements, and at issue is whether they could have been confident of surviving the counterattacks from Brunner Mond and United Alkali that would have followed their installing their own ammonia soda plant. Because they would sell alkali to themselves, they would, unlike Brunner Mond or other interlopers, look with equanimity on a protracted alkali price war. They could not, however, be indifferent to a retaliatory entry into their own industry, and precisely this tactic for expanding the theatre of war was used by Brunner Mond against Lever between 1911 and 1913 [53]. Had the paper makers, the soap makers or the textile firms acted collectively, they need not have feared such a wider war. But in the absence of such cooperation among habitual competitors, few were willing to step forward alone to play the role of giant killer. Lever's finally did so, but the soda price concessions they won on the eve of the war applied only to their own purchases. The threat of all-out war thus may have sufficed to justify the timidity of the soda purchasers. Table 2's hindsight nonetheless displays the consequences of their inaction.

V

What prospect is there that an examination of decisions taken in other sectors will yield conclusions like those just reached for the classic case of Leblanc versus Solvay soda? Extrapolation beyond the chemical sector is clearly out of place in this paper, but brief references to other technical choices within the chemical industry will serve to indicate the variety of results to be expected in future investigations.

Britain's lag in the adoption of the contact process of sulphuric acid production from the late 1890s on apparently cost her nothing before 1914. The lag itself was less dramatic than the Solvay soda lag: Germany, the leader in developing the contact process, apparently produced only 25 per cent of its sulphuric acid by this process by 1914, while the American and British proportions were 14 per cent and something under 11 per cent respectively [54]. The new process was found to be economical only for the very highest strengths of acid. The relative advantages of the two processes for different strengths of acid are shown by the following cost comparisons for 1902 [55]. Under either country's price structure, the region of equal profitability for the two processes lay around 93 per cent H_2SO_4. One drawback of adopting the contact process, according to American experience, was the heavy cost of highly trained chemists to supervise production [56], a cost that may have been understated in the available sample accounts.

Unit costs in £ per ton of pure H_2SO_4, 1902:

	At German input prices	At British input prices
Regular 'chamber' acid (60%–80% H_2SO_4)		
Contact process	1·233 to 1·461	1·088 to 1·193
Lead chamber process	1·138	0·931
Concentrated acid (97–98% H_2SO_4)		
Contact process	1·25 to 1·43	1·01 to 1·16
Chamber process plus Heraeus		
condensing stills	1·572	1·317

The prewar demand for highly concentrated acid was quite limited. The war created a temporary brisk demand for high-strength acid for use in making TNT, but in the 1920s the share of concentrated acid and the contact process in total acid production dropped off again [57]. The principal prewar user of concentrated acid was the synthetic dyestuffs sector, and this fact may help to explain why Badische Anilin- und Soda-Fabrik, a leading German dyestuffs firm, was the developer and largest user of the contact process [58]. With a much smaller dyestuffs sector, Britain had much less use for concentrated acid [59], and appears to have met this from its three prewar contact-process plants.

The choice between the chamber and contact processes, however, is not the only possible source of relative entrepreneurial deficiency in sulphuric acid. A host of unnamed minor technical improvements might have been adopted elsewhere and overlooked in Britain without this gap being detected in the literature. This possibility can be tested by using cost accounts anonymously given to Georg Lunge by an 'old established German works' and a 'first-class English works' in 1889. While the figures are rough and exclude amortization and interest, they show that a ton of ordinary chamber acid would have cost the British firm about 8 per cent more if it had achieved the input-output pattern of the German firm (the German firm, on the other hand, would have fared no better or worse had it achieved the British physical results instead of its own [60]. Thus no net deficiency of British practice is revealed in this case.

The well known case of synthetic dyestuffs can either yield complete absolution of Victorian entrepreneurship from all indictments for passing up profits or it can make those forgone profits seem enormous in relation to actual output, the outcome depending on what one considers to be within the entrepreneur's control. If scientific discoveries are viewed as beyond their control, British entrepreneurs cannot be blamed for leaving the lion's share of British and world dyestuff markets to German and Swiss firms. Once a key discovery was made and production successfully launched elsewhere, two external circumstances prevented British competition. The first was the threat of vigorous retaliation by the prosperous German firms, a threat made credible by their predatory dumping of alizarin in Britain when domestic production was starting up in 1883 [61]. The other was the defective British patent law of 1883, which effectively allowed patentees to leave their patents unworked in Britain without forcing them to grant licences. The German firms took out hundreds of British patents, many of them vaguely worded for maximum coverage, in order to prevent British manufacture [62]. Legal action by potential domestic producers must have seemed unrewarding when cases like Levenstein *v.* Hoechst (1889) found the plaintiff bearing considerable expense and the onus of proof [63]. The defect was not remedied until the Patent Reform of 1907, which took effect the following year.

It would, however, seem valid to blame British entrepreneurship for not making the original discoveries. Research in dyestuffs, unlike that in ammonia soda, was not undertaken with nearly so much energy and expense as in Germany. Greater research outlays in the 1870s and

1880s could have made the defect in the patent law irrelevant for dyestuffs. Armed with such patents, British firms might have been able to capture the profits that actually accrued to German and Swiss firms on their exports to unsheltered markets. If we assume that German, Austrian and Russian markets would in any case have been sheltered from British dyestuffs, there would remain, for 1904, £6,354,210 as a world demand for British dyestuffs [64]. The cost at which this demand could be met is highly uncertain, as we have few cost data for this highly diversified and secretive industry. Levinstein once argued that the sum of labour and capital costs would come out about the same for England as for Germany, leaving England with cheaper benzene, toluene, ammonia, coal, salt, pyrites, sodium nitrate and iron inputs. They should, he argued, be able to produce alizarin and perhaps other dyes 10 per cent more cheaply than Germany [65]. Against these advantages must be reckoned the higher cost of industrial alcohol in Britain [66]. On balance British patent holders might have enjoyed the same handsome profit margins that allowed the German firms to pay dividends equalling 22 per cent of share capital or about 10 per cent of output. Such a margin they might have applied to a world market about twenty times the actual value of British output of coal-tar dyes. It appears unlikely, in other words, that a closer study would revise the standard view of the dyestuffs example as a classic lost opportunity for Britain.

The soda, sulphuric acid and dyestuffs cases have thus illustrated almost the full range of possible outcomes for economic judgements for entrepreneurs [67]. Some of the missed chances for extra profits could not have been foreseen or more soundly pursued than they were (ammonia soda research before 1870), some should not have been missed (ammonia soda after 1886, dyestuffs research before about 1890), and some proved to be in fact unprofitable (ammonia soda for 1873-86, the contact process case, and dyestuffs production in German-patented lines). Each of the missed chances documented here seems to have been of major consequence to the industry itself. We presume that other studies could easily turn up the kind of outcome missing here: clear mistakes that were of negligible consequence for the firms and industry involved.

The aggregate issue remains unresolved, but the present paper is intended as an exercise of a sort that should hasten resolution when applied to a few other key sectors. Although we have here focused on choices between technical processes already known by name to

---

economic historians, we look forward to a more systematic method of search in the future. Instead of following the literature to individual technical choices, future studies should use variations on the measures in Table 1, especially the price duals of total factor productivity indices, to uncover inefficiencies and monopolistic distortions. Wherever a single set of reliable and detailed cost accounts can be combined with price data from two contexts, this procedure yields valuable results. The choice of industries should depend on their relative shares of total British output as well as data availability; on this criterion Bessemer steel and coal mining should continue to be prime targets for inquiries interested in the aggregate importance of entrepreneurial shortcomings.

There remains the basic problem of combining partial-equilibrium estimates for individual industries into a plausible portrayal of the aggregate consequences of hypothetical improvements. Basic as this difficulty is, we suspect that it will prove tractable even without major additions to our set of tools. Where the interrelatedness of supra-marginal changes seems to invalidate simple addition of the income increments from individual sectors, sensible adjustments and iterations should prove possible. If, for example, a significant opportunity for cutting coal costs and prices and raising tonnage is documented and these changes quantified, an inquiry into Bessemer steel could suggest how any forgone gains from technical changes in this sector would be affected by the improvements in coal supply. The procedure is rough and ready, but we are optimistic about the possibility of using such methods in a few major sectors to appraise the consequences of Victorian entrepreneurial decisions.

NOTES

[1] Some examples are David Landes, 'Technological change and development in western Europe, 1750-1914', in *The Cambridge Economic History of Europe* (Cambridge, Cambridge University Press, 1965), Vol. VI, part I; his 'Factor costs and demand: determinants of economic growth', *Business History*, VII, No. 1, 1965, pp. 15–33; A. L. Levine, *Industrial Retardation in Britain, 1870-1914* (Basic Books, 1967); T. S. Orsagh, 'Progress in iron and steel, 1870-1913', *Comparative Studies in Society and History*, III, 1960-61, pp. 216–30; and three articles by Derek H. Aldcroft reprinted in D. H. Aldcroft and H. W. Richardson. *The British Economy, 1870-1939* (London, Macmillan, 1969), pp. 126–89. In each case qualifications are acknowledged.

[2] See Peter Temin, 'The relative decline of the British steel industry, 1880-1913', in Henry Rosovsky (ed.) *Industrialization in Two Systems:*

Essays in Honor of Alexander Gerschenkron (New York, 1966); Donald N. McCloskey, 'Productivity change in British pig iron, 1870-1939', *Quarterly Journal of Economics*, LXXXII, May 1968, pp. 281–96; his 'Did Victorian Britain fail?', *Economic History Review, New Series*, XXIII, December 1970; *American and British Technology in the Nineteenth Century* (Cambridge, Cambridge University Press, 1962), ch. VI.

[3] Ingvar Svennilson, *Growth and Stagnation in the European Economy* (Geneva, United Nations, 1954), chs. I and II; W. Arthur Lewis, 'International competition in manufactures', *American Economic Association Papers and Proceedings*, May 1957; and H. W. Richardson, 'Overcommitment in Britain before 1930', *Oxford Economic Papers*, XVII, 1965, pp. 237–62, reprinted in Aldcroft and Richardson, op. cit.

[4] It might be thought that the leading firm or nation bears a cost for all labour transfers, and not just for those to whom it is committed to provide uninterrupted employment. But training and relocation expenses must also be borne by firms and nations beginning production in any product line and there is no clear net disadvantage to the early starter (for a contrary argument, see Richardson, 'Overcommitment', p. 261).

[5] On 'Interrelatedness' see Marvin Frankel, 'Obsolescence and technical change in a maturing economy', *American Economic Review*, 45, No. 3, June 1965, pp. 296–319; C. P. Kindleberger, 'Obsolescence and technical change', *Bulletin of the Oxford University Institute of Statistics*, 23, No. 3, August 1961, pp. 284–9; and E. Ames and N. Rosenberg, 'Changing technological leadership and industrial growth', *Economic Journal*, LXXII, 1963, pp. 13–31.

[6] Landes, 'Technological change', p. 558.

[7] We would include as examples of entrepreneurial error instances in which managers had to forgo investment projects because the capital market underestimated their returns. The 'blame' in such cases would rest with those whose scepticism kept them from lending or holding shares on terms that would have proved profitable. Others may prefer a narrower definition of entrepreneurship.

[8] Landes, 'Technological change', p. 565. Landes fails to give this remark its due weight as a rebuttal to his own citations of such opinion. Similarly, he cites lags in British adoption of new techniques as demonstrations of managerial backwardness, despite the brief observation that 'modernity is often meretricious, and ... even in technologically oriented industries, the law of relative factor costs was operative' (p. 590).

[9] See, for example, the American praise for British practices cited in S. B. Saul, 'The American impact on British industry, 1895-1914', *Business History*, 3, No. 1, December 1960, pp. 25–8, and his 'The market and the development of the mechanical engineering industries in Britain, 1860-1914', *Economic History Review*, XX, April 1967, p. 118.

[10] See Levine, op. cit., ch. 2, especially pp. 32–4, 40; Landes, op. cit., especially pp. 490–2; and Aldcroft, in Aldcroft and Richardson, op cit., especially p. 145.

[11] Levine, op. cit. p. 32; Aldcroft, op. cit., p. 146; and T. H. Burnham and G. O. Hoskins, *Iron and Steel in Britain, 1870-1930* (London, Allen and Unwin, 1943), p. 138.

[12] Levine, op. cit., p. 34; Aldcroft, op. cit., p. 138; and the book by Chin cited by Sandberg (following footnote).

[13] Lars G. Sandberg, 'American rings and English Mules: the role of economic rationality', *Quarterly Journal of Economics*, February 1969, pp. 25–43.

The rationality of avoiding the latest machinery has also been argued in connection with the automatic loom as well as ring spinning by R. E. Tyson, 'The cotton industry', in D. E. Aldcroft (ed.), *The Development of British Industry and Foreign Competition, 1875-1914,* (London, Allen and Unwin, 1969), p. 122.

[14] Donald N. McCloskey, 'Productivity change in British pig iron, 1870-1939', pp. 290–6.

[15] See J. R. Meyer, 'An input-output approach to evaluating the influence of exports on British industrial production in the late nineteenth century', *Explorations in Entrepreneurial History,* VIII, 1955.

[16] Temin, op. cit.

[17] Temin acknowledges that steel entrepreneurship has not been assessed with any accuracy (op. cit., pp. 151, 155). His attempt to argue that obsolescence was forced onto the British industry by its slow growth rate rests on a crude accelerator model with a constant capital-output ratio plus the assumption that investment grows steadily. Missing are the necessary demonstrations (1) that actual behaviour confirmed to this model, (2) that such behaviour would have been rational at the time, and (3) that *any* profit-maximizing producer conforms to a simple accelerator except under very restrictive assumptions. Lacking these, we infer that Professor Temin has advanced a model in which old equipment is retained irrationally. Thus here again an entrepreneurial-deficiency hypothesis is being offered without being identified as such.

[18] In the case of plant and equipment an implicit rental price of plant and equipment is appropriate, with account being taken of the rates of repair and replacement, a rate of interest, and movements in the price of new plant and equipment.

[19] Adjustments must be made, for example, in outputs and productivity ratios when the scale of operation observed in the alternative context (America) is larger than output-demand and input-supply curves will permit for the (British) entrepreneurs being judged.

[20] Aldcroft, 'The entrepreneur and the British economy, 1870-1914', in Aldcroft and Richardson, op. cit., pp. 141–42.

[21] A. R. Prest, and R. Turvey, 'Cost-benefit analysis: a survey', in American Economic Association and Royal Economic Society, *Surveys of Economic Theory,* Vol III, 1967, p. 157; cited in Paul A. David, 'Transport innovation and economic growth: Professor Fogel on and off the rails', *Economic History Review,* December 1969, p. 513.

[22] Here, as in Table 1, α^*_i and β^*_j are the shares of the ith input and the jth output in total revenue. Other authors have employed price duals, but have assumed that management is only paid its marginal product and receives no costless rents, so that $\Sigma\alpha_i = 1$. See Dale W. Jorgenson and Zvi Griliches, 'The explanation of productivity change', *Review of Economic Studies,* Vol. XXXIV (3), No. 99, July 1967, pp. 249–62; and Douglass C. North, 'Sources of productivity change in ocean shipping. 1600-1850', *Journal of Political Economy,* vol. 76, December 1968, pp. 953–70. In the present paper, however, $\Sigma\alpha_i \leqslant 1$.

[23] Output and value-added data for chemicals have yet to be gathered together in any systematic way. The principal figures available have been discussed in H. W. Richardson, 'Chemicals', in Aldcroft (ed.) *The Development of British Industry and Foreign Competition, 1875-1914,* pp. 278–9; L. E. Haber, *The Chemical Industry during the Nineteenth Century* (Oxford, Clarendon, 1958); and, especially for 1913, Ingvar Svennilson, *Growth and*

Stagnation in the European Economy (Geneva, United Nations, 1954), pp. 160–7, 286–92. The detailed output breakdown in the 1907 census of production (*Parliamentary Papers*, 1910, Vol. CIX, pp. 192–5, 200–1, 229–31, 239–40) should be used with caution.

[24] The tale is told by Haber, op. cit., chs. 6, 7, 9 and 10; Landes, op. cit., pp. 497–501; and Richardson, 'Chemicals', pp. 281–6; and thus need not be repeated here.

[25] Landes, op. cit., pp. 501–4; Haber, op. cit., chs. 6, 8–11; Richardson, 'Chemicals'. pp. 286–8; Richardson, 'The development of the British dyestuffs industry before 1939', *Scottish Journal of Political Economy*, IX, No. 2, June 1962, pp. 110–14; and the contemporary sources cited by these authors. French producers of alkali and (especially) dyestuffs have come in for similar criticisms. C. P. Kindleberger, *Economic Growth in France and Britain, 1851-1950* (London, Oxford University Press, 1964), pp. 299–300; and Haber, op. cit., pp. 109–14.

[26] Landes, op. cit., p. 500.

[27] Richardson, 'Chemicals', p. 280.

[28] By, among others, Ivan Levinstein, 'Observations and suggestions on the present state of the British chemical industries, with special reference to coal-tar derivatives', *Journal of the Society of Chemical Industry (JSCI)*, 29 June 1886, p. 356. The same warnings were sounded, but given a curiously hopeful final twist, by one of the most respected scientists in the Leblanc trade: Walter Weldon, 'On the present condition of the soda industry', *JSCI*, 29 January 1883, pp. 2–12.

[29] 'Report on chemical instruction in Germany and the growth and present condition of the German chemical industry', *Parliamentary Papers*, 1901, LXXX, No. 561, p. 192 (46).

[30] For a description of soda technology and products, the reader is again referred to Haber's *Chemical Industry during the Nineteenth Century* and also to the 11th edition of *The Encyclopaedia Britannica* (1911).

[31] This, at least, was the pattern shown by monthly price data in the later 1880s and early 1890s. In the 1870s Brunner Mond apparently had temporary difficulty convincing customers to accept the new, purer soda at a price reflecting its carbonate content (Haber, op. cit., p. 158).

[32] The statements in this paragraph imply that the reported price of Leblanc 48 per cent soda ash became increasingly irrelevant over time. This was apparently the case. From 1901 on the price of 48 per cent ash was fixed by agreement at a level that far exceeded that of 58 per cent ash. As we shall note again in discussing output estimates, this strongly suggests that Leblanc ash was no longer sold at all after about 1902.

[33] The drop in bleach production might have raised its price for the years before the appearance of electrolytic bleach in the late 1890s. The possibility of such price improvement for the hypothetically shrunken Leblanc sector would make the conversion to Solvay soda seem slightly *more* attractive to a large diversified Leblanc firm than it will appear in the calculations below, which ignore this price effect.

[34] Such outside support for new entrants was a possibility. During the negotiations forming the United Alkali Company, the Paper Makers' Association threatened to build their own alkali plant or finance a Brunner Mond expansion if the merger led to higher prices (Haber, op. cit., p. 181, citing *The Times*, 19 August 1890). Around the turn of the century one major soap manufacturer undertook to produce caustic soda from Brunner Mond ash, in amounts exceeding its own input needs (A. E. Musson,

Enterprise in Soap and Chemicals: Crosfields of Warrington, 1815-1965 (Manchester University Press, 1965), pp. 203–40). Another soap firm prepared to enter alkali production in 1903 and again in 1911 and ultimately won, after hard fighting, partial concessions on alkali supply from Brunner Mond (Charles H. Wilson, *The History of Unilever* (London, 1954), vol. I, ch. IX). Whoever the owners might have been, the new facilities could have been erected either in southern Lancashire or in Cheshire without any difference in unit costs.

[35] More recent prewar cost accounts are available for sulphuric acid and saltcake, but not for the final Leblanc phases of soda production or for ammonia soda production. Most of the accounts referred to were diligently cited and reproduced by Georg Lunge in his multi-volume work, *A Theoretical and Practical Treatise on the Manufacture of Sulfuric Acid and Alkali,* of which five English editions appeared between 1886 and 1923 (the last posthumously).

[36] While each of the Solvay ash cost studies refers to a plant much smaller than the large complex operated by Brunner Mond alongside its original plant in Winnington after 1881, they led us to cost estimates that are broadly consistent with the profit record of Brunner Mond and Co. in the 1880s and 1890s. We infer that the economies of scale are very slight above a very small scale of operation.

[37] D. W. F. Hardie, *A History of the Chemical Industry in Widnes* (Widnes, Imperial Chemical Industries Limited, 1950), pp. 137–8.

[38] See Weldon, in *JSCI*, 29 January 1883, pp. 5–6, and Local Government Board, *26th Annual Report of the Alkali Inspector* for 1889 (H.M.S.O., 1890), p. 12.

[39] *26th Annual Report of the Alkali Inspector,* p. 14. It was also argued (by A. M. Chance in 1888), after a major reduction in Spanish pyrites prices had been won in 1883, that the mines would not be able to cut prices much further if demand fell. Thus both pyrites and sulphur, the alternative sulphur-compound Leblanc inputs, were in elastic supply.

[40] The only firm to try it before 1886 sold out to Brunner Mond in 1878, within four years of its formation (Haber, op. cit., p. 158).

[41] The agreement was acknowledged at a Brunner Mond shareholders' meeting early in 1896 (*Chemical Trade Journal*, 29 February 1896, p. 145). Establishing such 'friendly arrangements' with Brunner Mond was in fact a major reason for forming the United Alkali Company (United Alkali Company, *The Struggle for Supremacy* (Liverpool, 1907), p. 40).

[42] The 'long run' here is the length of time sufficient to adjust the number of units (boilers, vats, stills, etc.) to shifts in demand, thus returning to the original level of average costs. As noted above, this basic constancy of average costs in the absence of input price changes seems to be characteristic of this industry.

[43] Unit capital costs were estimated by the implicit-rental-rate formula

$$(C/Y) = P_K(K + L) \ (i + \delta)/Y,$$

where C is the implicit unit rent; Y is the level of output in tons of pure carbonate; P_K is a benchmark-based price series for capital and land (using Feinstein's index); $(K + L)$ is a benchmark cost of plant, equipment and land; i is the yield on consols and δ is the rate of replacement (excluding repairs, which are estimated separately). The interest-cost calculation slightly underestimates the rate at which chemical firms would have floated debentures, but slightly overestimates the principal being borrowed when current capital-good prices are above historical ones (as they were in the last twenty prewar years).

A separate constant capital-output ratio was used for each major process being costed, so that the overall ratios would have varied with the product mix.

[44] The derivation of the numbers plotted in Figures 2 through 4 is laid out in detail in a data appendix obtainable from the authors on request.

[45] For an estimate of these later economies, see Geoffrey Martin *et al., The Salt and Alkali Industry* (London, Lockby Crosswood, 1916), p. 77.

[46] Haber, op. cit., pp. 87, 88.

[47] It should also be repeated that the calculations behind Figures 2–4 have been designed to determine cost savings and profits *in the absence of changes in soda output and prices.* By competing more vigorously Brunner Mond would have experienced lower marginal profits than the present figures suggest.

[48] The output estimates are discussed further in the data appendix available from the authors.

[49] For example, if c is the marginal propensity to consume out of current income and r the rate of return on savings, the incremental national income and consumption in Year t would be

$$Y_t = D_t + r(1 - c) \sum_{i=0}^{t-1} D_i,$$
and
$$C_t = cY_t,$$

respectively, where the D's are the amounts of social saving. As the years progress, first Y_t and later C_t will exceed D_t.

[50] The value of output and value added were reportedly £23,447,000 and £9,464,000 respectively for the entire chemicals sector. The value of soda, sulphuric acid and bleach output alone was £4,715,000. *The 1907 Census of Production, Parliamentary Papers,* 1910, vol. CIX, pp. 21, 58. These are probably slight overestimates.

[51] E. K. Muspratt's *My Life and Work* (London, John Lane, 1917) hardly mentions the challenges posed by ammonia soda and electrolysis. This omission is perhaps information of a sort.

[52] *Chemical Trade Journal,* 25 March 1899, p. 204. The company apparently did not formalize its capital losses until a wholesale reduction of its equity value in 1913.

[53] C. H. Wilson, op. cit., vol. I, IX.

[54] T. Kreps, *The Economics of the Sulfuric Acid Industry* (Stanford, 1938), pp. 65, 66.

[55] The data refer to German experience reported by Niedenführ and Lüty and have been converted into sterling, first at German then at British input prices. The original data are cited in Lunge, op. cit., 3rd ed. (London, 1911), vol. I, part II, ch. 10.

[56] Kreps, op. cit., pp. 63–64.

[57] *The Times of Trade and Engineering Supplement* 26 November 1927, p. 6.

[58] Haber, op. cit., pp. 108, 121, 122; and Herman Schultze, *Die Entwicklung der chemischen Industrie in Deutschland seit dem Jahre 1875* (Halle, 1908), pp. 68–70.

[59] The shares of oleum, the highest strength category, were about 10 per cent for Germany and 2 per cent for Britain (Schultze, op. cit., p. 69; H. A. Auden, *Sulphur and Sulphur Derivatives* (London, 1921), p. 87).

[60] Lunge also presents some American cost accounts for 1888 and 1893, which seem to make the American performance look no better. A number of difficulties make the comparison unreliable, however. (Lunge, op. cit., 3rd ed., vol. I, part II, ch. 10).

[61] I. Levinstein, 'Observations and Suggestions . . .', *Journal of the Society of Chemical Industry*, 29 June 1886, p. 354.

[62] This distortion has already been noted by Haber, op. cit., pp. 199–200; Habakkuk, op. cit., p. 216; H. W. Richardson, 'The development of the British dyestuffs industry before 1939', *Scottish Journal of Political Economy*, IX, No. 2, June 1962, p. 111; and R. J. S. Hoffman, *Great Britain and the German Trade Rivalry, 1875-1914* (Philadelphia, University of Pennsylvania Press, 1933), pp. 98–100.

[63] Levinstein, 'Section 22 of the Patents Act, 1883, and its bearing on British Industry', *Journal of the Society of Chemical Industry*, 30 April 1898, p. 321.

[64] Schultze, op. cit., pp. 193, 194; and Haber, op. cit., p. 223.

[65] Levinstein, 'The development and present state of the alizarin industry', *Journal of the Society of Chemical Industry*, 29 May 1883, p. 215; and his 'Observations and Suggestions', pp. 352–3.

[66] Richardson, 'Dyestuffs', p. 112.

[67] It has not been possible to include a judgement on Britain's relative lag in adopting the electrolytic production of bleach and caustic soda because the key data on the British costs of generating electric power were not available at the time of writing. The success of the Castner-Kellner Company suggests that other British firms passed up a valuable opportunity by not following this lead. On the other hand, prewar power costs were quite location-specific, and others may not have had the opportunity to obtain cheap gas- or hydro-generated power. Our impression about international differences in power costs and the profitability of Leblanc bleach and caustic production is that the optimal share of electrolytic in total bleach and caustic production would have been lower for Britain than for the U.S. or Germany. Further cost studies of electrolysis can profitably begin by consulting Victor Englehardt, 'Cost of alkali chloride electrolysis', *Metallurgical and Chemical Engineering*, Vol. 9, 1911 (also in *Chemiker Zeitung*, 1911, pp. 573, 582); J. B. C. Kershaw, 'The present position and future prospects of the electrolytic alkali and bleach industry', *Transactions of the Faraday Society*, Vol. III, Part I, 1907, pp. 38–49; and P. Ferchland, *Die elektrochemische Industrie Deutschlands* (Halle, 1905), chs. II and III.

Chairman: S. B. Saul
Prepared Comments: D. H. Aldcroft, L. Sandberg

Aldcroft: He welcomed the attempt in this paper to put the entrepreneurial debate on a firm footing. Though fairly narrow in focus, the paper is interesting because it shows quite clearly the variations in the strength of enterprise between different branches of the same industry – a fact noted for some other industries, e.g. engineering by S. B. Saul. The authors attempt to quantify the calibre of entrepreneurship in certain branches of the British chemical industry by measuring private profits forgone as a result of the non-optimal choice of techniques. The method used is not above criticism but it does have the advantage that it produces some identifiable quantity, which can be related to other economic variables. The authors effectively reach three conclusions which can be summarized briefly. First, some missed chances for extra profits could not have been foreseen or more vigorously pursued than they were – for example, ammonia soda before 1870. Second, some should not have been missed – ammonia soda after the mid-1880s, dyestuffs research before 1890. Third, some proved unprofitable – ammonia soda between 1873-86, the contact process for sulphuric acid, and dyestuffs production in the German line. Each of the missed chances was of major consequence to the industry itself.

The findings of this research do not provide us with a definitive assessment of the performance of the chemical industry in the later nineteenth century. For one thing, only part of the chemical industry has been analysed. Second, there is the awkward question as to what profits forgone should be related to in making the final judgement. Third, the choice of the technique for measuring efficiency needs to be examined more closely. It would also be interesting to discover whether in those sectors in which no opportunities were missed this was accidental or planned, or alternatively, if new techniques of a more profitable type had appeared, whether they would have been missed.

This paper, along with a number of others presented at this conference, raises an issue that has been the subject of much debate in recent years – namely, whether or not British enterprise was inefficient in the later nineteenth century. Unfortunately, we are still a long way from a final solution to this vexed question. Clearly we require many more rigorous studies of the type under discussion before we have a large enough sample from which to make generalizations. But before embarking on such studies we need to address ourselves to two important issues, which arise indirectly out of the work carried out so far.

It is important, first, to decide in advance the industries or branches to be studied. We need to choose a representative sample of the whole population if we are to derive some worthwhile results with general applicability. Data limitations will, of course, circumscribe the choice to some extent. Having made the selection, it is essential that the analysis of the sample be carried out on a uniform basis. Uniform questions must be posed and the method of analysis must be the same or very similar for each branch. If these conditions are not fulfilled we shall end up with a selection of projects examining different aspects of the situation, or similar aspects examined in different ways, from which it will be impossible to make useful generalization. Here a good case can be made for a team project financed by external funds.

The second major problem is that concerning the yardsticks. There are at least three ways in which the performance of enterprise may be assessed, all of which are defective in some respect. They are profit maximization, the use of best practice techniques, and productivity. As Lindert and Trace point out, the first of these, profit maximization, ignores rewards that are largely non-pecuniary, e.g. avoidance of risk, the satisfactions of a quiet life, and so on. The danger is, of course, that by introducing these factors a non-optimal position is never exposed. A profit maximization criterion also suffers from other defects. Profits may be maximized in imperfect markets by appropriate (monopolistic) pricing policies. Conversely, profits may not be maximized because of subsidy elements or social cost considerations. In other words, profits may well be maximized in the absence of best-practice techniques or under sub-optimal productivity situations, or they may not be maximized even when techniques and productivity are optimal.

Similarly, best-practice techniques may be employed without profits being maximized because of defective pricing policy or inefficient commercial policy. There is also the difficult question of defining best-practice techniques. We should be wary, too, about the obstacles to transferability of best-practice techniques. Techniques that constitute best practice in one country cannot necessarily be transferred to another country since much depends on relative factor endowments and their price relatives.

There are also snags in using productivity as a yardstick. Productivity may be maximized under best-practice techniques but need not necessarily be. Here, of course, much depends on how best-practice techniques are defined. If narrowly defined to cover only new machinery, better tools, and so on, a situation can be envisaged where the returns from using such best-practice techniques as are available are not optimized because of defective infrastructure. For example, cases could be imagined in which new machinery is introduced to produce a given product, but then yields sub-optimal productivity returns because of bad plant layout or inefficient labour organization. And even if best-practice techniques are employed and productivity yields are optimized it does not follow that profits will also be maximized.

We also need to resolve the question of measuring productivity itself. Clearly the productivity of labour, which is a commonly used measure, is only partial in scope. Both McCloskey and Vamplew recognize the need for a more comprehensive unit of measurement, that is, at least a two-factor measure using capital and labour as the main inputs. We certainly need a more satisfactory index of productivity for the British economy for the period 1870 to 1914. Before we go further with the micro studies it is essential to establish the productivity record of the British economy more firmly. Otherwise we may be trying to find answers to questions that do not really need to be posed in the first place.

The most efficient firm will be near the optimum in all three respects but this is an ideal case, which in practice is rarely attained. Most firms and industries will lie at sub-optimal positions in each case, though of course that position will not be the same for all three criteria. Ideally we should try to use all three measures, but there are practical difficulties with such an inclusive approach. Consequently, we first need to select the most useful criterion and then decide upon a feasible sub-optimal position, which might be attained by all industries or firms and which can be used as the yardstick or ultimate goal.

Sandberg: This paper contains two notable contributions. The first is the useful discussion of the problems of quantifying and aggregating the costs of managerial failure. It should be noted that even if we succeed in the difficult task set us by Lindert and Trace of obtaining an aggregate measure of the costs of managerial mistakes in Britain between 1870 and 1914, this alone would not finish the job. Surely there can hardly have been any period anywhere in which some amount of managerial failure did not occur. A measure for late Victorian Britain could only be interpreted properly in relation to similar measures for other countries at the time and for Britain at other times.

The second contribution is the careful quantitative analysis of managerial behaviour in the British chemical industry. There is one bothersome point about the calculations involved. Lindert and Trace claim that substantial losses were experienced by the United Alkali Company as a result of the company's failure to carry out 'a wholesale conversion to Solvay plant' (p. 260) between 1888 and 1890. In constructing an estimate of the losses they have compared the total cost of the Solvay and the Leblanc methods. This is clearly the appropriate calculation to make if the question is which type of equipment should be installed once a decision has been made to *increase* capacity. It is not appropriate, however, if the question is (as it seems to be in this case) whether or not to junk technically well functioning Leblanc equipment and replace it with new Solvay equipment. In such a situation the relevant comparison is between the *total* costs of the Solvay method with the *variable* costs of the Leblanc method. Keeping the Leblanc method requires no capital outlays. Installing the Solvay equipment, on the other hand, requires outlays for the new equipment, for alterations in the buildings, and for changes in the workforce as well as the costs of closing down the plant while the conversion is in progress. Even if the question is which method to install when old equipment has worn out there are still probably some additional expenses in changing over to the new method. This would be the case, for example, if it was necessary to make alterations in the factory buildings. The problem, then, is the interrelatedness of different parts of the capital stock.

The asymmetry in the relevant costs also implies that when junking is being considered the alternative of adopting new equipment is much more capital-intensive than the alternative of retaining the old. This, in turn, greatly increases the importance of the rate of interest used in the calculations. There is in any case always some interest rate high enough to make the more capital-intensive alternative unattractive. Lindert and Trace use the 3 per cent rate on consols, but this rate is surely much too low. As they themselves state in note 43, even debentures could not be issued at this low rate. And the interest rate on debentures is held down by the fact that there is some equity capital available to reduce the risk of loss. The true cost of capital to a firm is some combination of the cost of issuing debentures and common shares. The earnings needed to finance such a combination were certainly well above 3 per cent. Phelps-Brown and Weber estimated that the average rate of return on all industrial investment in Great Britain at approximately this time was around 15 per cent per annum. Although this figure, together with the logic of the borrowing alternatives open to the firm, casts serious doubt on the 3 per cent figure used by Lindert and Trace, it does not, unfortunately, reveal what the corresponding marginal rate of return was. An alternative approach might be to compare the two opportunities by comparing their implicit rates of return on invested capital. The rates of return, in any case, should allow for less than 100 per cent capacity utilization: this is especially important when comparing alternatives with radically different capital intensities.

There are, too, some more general questions suggested by the paper. For one thing, why did British industry tend, as it apparently did in the chemical industry, to underinvest in research? For another, what was the relation between market structure and managerial failure? That is, was a cartelistic arrangement such as that in the chemical industry an important support of large scale mismanagement?

Lindert: He agreed with Sandberg that the point about the relevance of comparing full costs in the new Solvay process with variable costs in the old Leblanc process was not covered in the paper, but this would be unlikely to change the results substantially. Capital costs were not zero in the older process: investment in replacement, if not in expansion, was still required to operate it. The relevant fixed costs in the Solvay process, in any case, were not large. And the move from the Leblanc to the Solvay process was not itself expensive. No shutdown of the plant or laying-off of skilled personnel (who were in fact unskilled from the 1880s on) was required, nor was the cost of learning about the new process high.

David: The objection by Sandberg has some force. There are two separate questions. First, what sort of plant do you build if you are going to build a *new* one? For this question, the full average costs of both processes, as calculated in the Lindert and Trace paper, are relevant. The second question is, what do you do with Leblanc plants given that they are in place? That is, do you scrap them just because a Solvay plant would offer lower total costs, including the capital costs of setting up new plants? Obviously you do not: if the Leblanc plants earned any positive quasi-rents they should have been kept in operation. The distinction between average variable costs and average fixed costs then becomes critical.

Lindert and Trace: A fixed-cost legacy can be a powerful inertial force, particularly where such costs are a high proportion of total cost, and it would not be surprising to find cases in which otherwise advantageous changes would be rationally passed up on this account.

It would be useful to make explicit the bearing of the fixed-cost legacy on one of the findings, namely, that Leblanc soda producers were among those who could have gained by installing Solvay plants at any time from the late 1880s on.* The best illustration of the role of fixed costs is the case in which all Leblanc producers decided in 1888 on a wholesale conversion to Solvay production to begin 31 December 1889, in new plants on the same company sites, employing basically the same labour force. The profitability comparison in this case should subtract from the Leblanc costs in Figures 2–4 in the paper those fixed costs that were incurred on plant and equipment installed by the end of 1889. Take the extreme assumption that none of the £1,875,000 of Leblanc plant and equipment could have been resold or re-used in Solvay production. At an interest rate of 3 per cent and a (linear) depreciation rate of 8.13 per cent, this equipment was implicitly reflected in the Leblanc cost calculations in amounts that declined in linear fashion from £200,000 in 1890 to zero in 1902. Removing these amounts from the cost of continuing Leblanc production changes the Solvay-minus-Leblanc profit increments for these years to the figures displayed in the left-hand column in the table opposite.

In this case the beginning of sustained forgone profits is pushed back from 1890 (with 1893 as an exception year) to 1897. The capitalized mid-1890 value of the 1890-1914 gains and losses from conversion to Solvay is still significantly positive, though reduced from £2,536,500 to £1,905,600 by the fixed-cost removal.

With or without fixed costs, the choice of an interest rate for costing capital and discounting future returns is crucial to the profitability of switching. A higher interest rate would raise the total cost of Leblanc production more than it would raise the total cost of Solvay, thereby raising the gains from conversion. On the other hand, the gains from scrapping Leblanc and installing Solvay will appear smaller the greater is the fixed interest cost removed from total Leblanc costs. The overall effect of higher interest rates when pre-1890 capital is left out of Leblanc costs is to lower the 1890-6 profit increments and to raise

* The following estimates by Lindert and Trace were presented after the conference.

Solvay Minus Leblanc profit increments,
1890-1914, with fixed costs removed from
Leblanc estimates (£1000s)

	With the interest rate equal to	
	3%	6%
1890	−10.3	−27.8
1891	−82.4	−98.6
1892	−82.2	−97.6
1893	−212.2	−243.6
1894	−65.7	−76.5
1895	−52.5	−61.5
1896	−33.9	−38.8
1897	26.1	33.4
1898	162.3	202.9
1899	208.0	247.5
1900	177.6	218.3
1901	156.0	191.5
1902	146.9	177.0
1903	225.7	250.9
1904	179.0	204.2
1905	184.4	209.5
1906	188.7	214.0
1907	218.9	246.1
1908	224.9	251.1
1909	214.4	240.9
1910	188.6	212.2
1911	184.1	203.9
1912	98.4	115.9
1913	130.7	144.6
1914	61.6	70.6
Value discounted back to mid-1890	1896.7	917.7

those for 1897-1914. As shown in the table, using a 6 per cent instead of a 3 per cent rate cuts the discounted gains in half (from £1,905,600 to £917,700 on an 1890 discount base). An 8 per cent rate would make the net gains over variable Leblanc costs roughly zero.

What interest rate is appropriate to the alternatives facing the founders of the United Alkali Company at the end of the 1880s? They were earning under 3 per cent on their holdings of consols and other financial assets, which were worth roughly a third of the hypothetical value of new Solvay plants. Their credit rating was probably such that they could have borrowed at about 4 per cent. The marginal rate of return on *all* of their operations was some undetermined fraction of their average rate of return on all capital, which — to judge from their published account — varied from 3 to 7 per cent after 1890. It would seem that none of the plausible alternatives facing Leblanc management offered a high enough rate of return (8 per cent) to make scrapping plus installation of Solvay plants look unprofitable. The overall interest rate that was appropriate in reckoning the cost of capital to these particular entrepreneurs, in short, cannot have been far from the consol rate used in the paper.

In short, reasonable allowances for the pre-existence of fixed capital and alternative discount rates do not alter the conclusion that conversion to Solvay production would have been profitable for the Leblanc producers in the late 1880s.

David: One can quarrel a little with Aldcroft's comment on the paper. Aldcroft implies that the burden of proof lies with those who reject the hypothesis of entrepreneurial failure, and suggests that the entire economy must be studied, industry by industry, before a conclusive judgement can be rendered against the hypothesis. But why should the burden of proof lie with the revisionists?

Temin: Along the same lines, the observed differences between America and Britain may have been the consequence of differing opportunities facing the two. American opportunities may have been many times as great, yielding rapid growth even if American entrepreneurs had failed to exploit them to the fullest extent. British entrepreneurs may have been better at exploiting the opportunities they had, but, because they had fewer of them, they may have been unable to expand their industries as rapidly as could American entrepreneurs.

Engerman: Another question brought up by Sandberg, that of the appropriate discount rate to use, was important. But on another matter, how was the pricing of patents treated? This is a critical issue in determining the rate of adoption of the Solvay process.

Lindert: The price of licences was determined in direct negotiations between the patent holder and the prospective buyer. There were opportunities, therefore, for price discrimination in classic form.

Hunt: What did the records of United Alkali and Brunner Mond show about the costs of the *new* process?

Trace: Unfortunately, the records of these companies for 1890-1914 seem to have been destroyed.

McClelland: What was 'failure' in entrepreneurship taken to mean? The issue of the divergence between social and private returns, which has been mentioned here several times, is not what proponents of the hypothesis of failure seem to have in mind. They believe that entrepreneurs neglected to some extent even *private* returns. But to assess the significance of this neglect in, say, the chemical industry, do not we have to look at the performance of entrepreneurs in other countries, other industries, and other times?

Hughes: He agreed with McClelland. We need an answer to the question posed earlier by David of what would constitute proof of British entrepreneurial failure or success.

David: The issue was a critical one. There had to be a reference standard of performance and the question is, what threshold of performance would push one who adheres to the thesis of 'failure' into the other camp? Better yet, what exactly is meant by 'failure'? One comprehensive measure of performance might be the dispersion among various industries of the rates of return to capital. If there was a low dispersion in Britain compared with the United States it would be apparent that British entrepreneurs had been in fact quick to move from bad to good opportunities.

Temin: The agreement on this question of standards seemed to be general. Some opportunities in all industries and countries were missed and some were not. Is that 'good' or 'bad' performance?

Lindert: There had to be a standard. The usual one, as in McCloskey's paper, is American (or German) performance. That is, the question usually posed is whether the earnings forgone on alternatives adopted elsewhere, but not in Britain, could have raised British income sufficiently to bring her growth rate up to the American (or German) rate.

8

International differences in productivity?
Coal and steel in America and Britain
*before World War 1**

DONALD N. McCLOSKEY

The assumption that the New World has yielded unusually high returns
to the factors of production has been a part of our thinking from the
time of Adam Smith and before. It is a congenial assumption, suggesting as one might wish that the right to life, liberty and the pursuit of
happiness had material as well as moral advantages. The evidence for it,
however, has been collected somewhat casually. In the nineteenth
century Anglo-American comparisons were made with scattered data on
real wages, that is, data on labour's marginal product. After the first
British census of production in 1907 they were made with data on
labour's average product. In either case the comparisons reflected the
productivity of one factor of production alone, although, to be sure,
the excess of American over British labour productivity was so large
that it appeared that no reasonable allowance for larger inputs of other
factors could account for it. The findings for the 1920s of A. W. Flux,
the director of the British census, that real value-added per worker in
British manufacturing was half the American average was confirmed in
later studies by L. Rostas for the late 1930s, by M. Frankel for the late
1940s and, most thoroughly, by a series of studies by the Organization
for European Economic Co-operation and the Cambridge Department
of Applied Economics on real national income in Europe and America
for the early 1950s [1]. The OEEC-Cambridge studies, which were
based on careful international comparisons of price levels rather than
on the par exchange rate and included all sectors of the economy rather
than manufacturing alone, found that British gross national product per
worker was about half the American level and value-added per worker
in manufacturing alone was still lower [2].

In his study of *Why Growth Rates Differ* Edward Denison attempted
to explain this gap in the levels of income per worker for 1960 [3]. The

* I should like to thank Michael Edelstein of Columbia University, Stanley L.
Engerman of the University of Rochester, Peter Temin of M.I.T., and the
members of the Columbia University Seminar on Economic History, for their
helpful comments on earlier drafts of this essay.

gap between the United States and the United Kingdom was then 41 per cent of the American level. He found that only 11 percentage points of it could be explained by total factor input corrected for quality and a mere 0.7 percentage points by misallocation and economies of scale; the rest, or about three-quarters of the total gap in 1960, had to be attributed as a residual to 'lags in the application of knowledge, general efficiency and errors and omissions' [4]. This result is both disappointing and remarkable. It is disappointing because it implies that even an imaginative use of conventional economic theory leaves the greater part of productivity differences unexplained [5]. It is remarkable because it implies that the productivity of the British economy was very far behind: as Denison put it, the level of total productivity, after allowing for economies of scale, the quality of the labour force, misallocation and conventionally measured inputs of capital, was about 20 per cent lower in the United Kingdom in 1960 than it had been in the United States in 1925. The gap was apparently a large, persistent fact.

Explanations of the fact have consumed many hours of after-dinner conversation, and their origin in the mental haze of brandy and cigars is sometimes apparent in their printed expression. After a nod towards the evidence, the writer loosens his tie and his standards of logic, and launches on one of several speculations. In reading the literature of Anglo-American comparison, one is struck by the attraction that certain of these speculations appear to have, irrespective of their empirical merit: repeatedly the story is told of cheap land causing mechanization, a large free-trade area encouraging economies of scale, rapid growth of industrial plant permitting the use of the most modern equipment in the New World, and the inevitable 'clogs to clogs in three generations' crushing the spirit of enterprise in the Old.

The persistence of the gap through many generations creates difficulties for some of these. For example, it is plausible perhaps that the vigour of an immigrant population yielded higher productivities, but the mass immigrations were confined to the second half of the nineteenth century, too late to explain any American superiority before 1850 and too early to explain it after 1920. Allyn Young, among others, doubted that there was evidence of greater vigour in the United States and supposed instead that economies of national scale were the dominant factor [6]. On the other hand, as E. Rothbarth pointed out, the scale of the American economy was not always larger than the

British [7]. He suggested that the higher ratio of land to labour was the true cause of American superiority. Yet land was not always an important factor of production: indeed, by the time estimates of factor shares are available, in the late nineteenth century, the share of land in national income was well below 10 per cent in the United States and below 15 per cent in the United Kingdom [8]. Though for particular industries, as will be shown later, the amount and quality of land in the United States may explain high labour productivities, for the economy as a whole it is doubtful that it can. If the arguments had been framed in quantitative terms, such difficulties as these would have been immediately apparent and would have inspired more critical examination of the explanations of American superiority, but they have generally been left in the pre-quantitative form in which the after-dinner speakers first expressed them. And many of them, of course, do not seem to fit easily into quantitative categories. This is especially true of the assertion, which has done good service as a residual explanation when others have proved wanting, that American businessmen were able to seize and retain a technological lead over Europe.

It is not generally recognized how puzzling would be the existence of a persistent and large American technological lead. If the difference between American and British production functions were as little as 10 per cent, say, and the share of entrepreneurial returns in total costs as much as 30 per cent, the adoption of American methods would increase returns to entrepreneurship by at least a third: a British firm could reduce its costs by 10 per cent and take the reduction in additional profit [9]. With the easy transport and communication that developed during the nineteenth century between the United States and the United Kingdom, with the frequent migrations of managers and the absence of a language barrier between the two, and with the competitive markets of both, it is hardly credible that such a large reward for imitation would go unclaimed. Recently D. W. Jorgenson and Z. Griliches have expressed scepticism about the significance of technological change, or costless increases in output for a given input, over time, asserting that 'the accumulation of knowledge is governed by the same economic laws as any other process of capital accumulation. Costs must be incurred if benefits are to be achieved' [10]. If this view has some plausibility for technical change between two years it has still more for technical differences between two countries. Investment in imitation is surely a less risky undertaking than investment in research, especially when the imitation can take the form of the mere purchase of improved machinery or the hiring of better managers from the leader. It would be strange if large technical differences persisted.

But this line of reasoning seems to be contradicted by the large, persistent gap in residual productivity [11]. The national comparisons of Denison register a gap of 35 per cent between the average levels of total productivity in the two countries and the earlier studies of labour productivity suggest that the same order of magnitude of difference has existed for a century and a half. One necessary downward revision should be mentioned. National comparisons give an exaggerated impression of the typical degree of American superiority. To get a true impression the comparisons must be made at the level of industrial detail corresponding to individual firms, because the national comparisons ignore intermediate inputs. If the United States had typically a 20 per cent advantage in efficiency, the advantage would be amplified by the cheapness of intermediate inputs, yielding a national productivity difference larger than 20 per cent [12]. If the United States, for example, produced iron ore and coal, as well as finished iron and steel, with 20 per cent less inputs than the United Kingdom did, the total direct and indirect resource costs of American iron and steel would be more than 20 per cent less than British resource costs. Put the other way, the national difference of 35 per cent in productivity corresponds to a smaller difference at the level of industrial detail where comparisons of costs and decisions to innovate take place. This is the level of the firm. The higher the typical share in total costs of purchases from other firms, the lower will be the productivity difference. In the United States the share was around 44 per cent of costs, implying a typical difference in productivity of about 20 per cent [13].

A gap of 20 per cent is still large. In view of it, one strategy of research would be to examine in detail the channels of technological flow in an attempt to find where they were blocked. Another, which will be pursued here, is to subject the difference in productivity to creative disbelief. The working hypothesis for this task is that British and American industries operated on substantially the same production functions. The appropriate production functions are those for the products of individual industries including materials in costs as well as value-added. For practical reasons the industries must have easily measured inputs and outputs and must be few in number. To offset their fewness they must be large. In order to put the working hypothesis in the most jeopardy, finally, they should be industries whose technological performance in late nineteenth-century Britain by the conventional measures was bad. Two industries that satisfy these requirements are coal and steel.

COAL

Historical opinion on the performance of the British coal industry before 1913 is not uniformly unfavourable. The industry grew much more slowly than the American or German industries, but there are adequate explanations from the side of demand for this, as there is for the worldwide shrinkage in the market for coal after the early 1920s, an event that casts a shadow back on the prewar history of the industry. Clapham, for example, concluded that in the quarter century before 1913:

> The whole industry, though full of conflict, was active and expanding both commercially and geographically. Its best units were admirably equipped. . . . [14]

Still, he noted that most British mines ignored equipment that had become common abroad. The mechanical coal-cutter is the best known, but the list includes as well steel pit props, electric haulage of coal and concrete and cement liners for shafts and tunnels. A. J. Taylor, the leading student of the industry, has emphasized these deficiencies, and his views are more representative of historical opinion on the matter than Clapham's. He mentions diminishing returns to land and other extenuating circumstances, yet concludes that

> It is still valid to speak of a hard core of recognizable inefficiency existing in the pre-1914 coal industry . . . in terms of diminished labour effort, unwillingness to accept innovation and the failure to provide a structure for the industry suited to the opportunities and needs of the twentieth century. . . . In all this the experience of coal was no doubt symptomatic of trends which were widely operative in British industry, more particularly in its older and deeper rooted sectors. [15]

This assertion does not bear up under close examination.

The chief evidence that an unwillingness to accept innovation altered the industry's history is that after the 1880s output per man-year in British coal mining declined, which, were this by itself an acceptable measure of productivity, would certainly suggest that there was an important failure of spirit in industry. The evidence of productivity is certainly more relevant to the issue than selected cases of the slow adoption of new equipment: indeed, the only way to determine whether the equipment was an important and profitable novelty is to perform a productivity calculation before and after its adoption. The average product of British labour, however, is a poor indicator of the course of British productivity. Average product fell, to be sure, but it fell or stagnated everywhere in Europe before World War I and does not suggest therefore any peculiarly British failure [16]. On the contrary it suggests that the natural conditions of coal mining dominated the determination of the average product of labour, driving it down as the coal beds were depleted. The rise in the average product in the United States during the period does not contradict this interpretation, since American coal reserves were so enormous that their depletion, except in the anthracite region, was negligible [17]. And comparisons of the level of the average product in various countries confirm it, suggesting that American product per man was high because the margin of cultivation of coal reserves had not been pushed far and that Belgian product, for example, was low because the margin had been pushed very far indeed. In comparing American and British productivity, however, most observers have resisted attributing all the difference in labour's average product to differences in the input of land. A resolution of the issue requires an estimate of how large the impact of the quantity and quality of cooperating factors was on the average product of labour.

The estimation of the average product of British and American labour is not as straightforward as the mass of statistics on the industry, the result of thorough and sustained official scrutiny in both countries, might lead one to hope. The data requirements of productivity measurement are great and in making comparisons between countries the sources of error are great as well. The output of coal, for example, seems to be a simple concept, but is not. Differences in the quality of coal mined may bias the measurement of output in one country in terms of another, because coal with good qualities and therefore high value per ton warrants more intensive mining at higher cost — that is, lower productivity. A similar problem afflicts the measurement of labour input. Ideally each quality of coal and labour should be weighted by its economic value in one country to form an index for one country in terms of the other, but the data are not good enough to do this [18]. Even the comparison of the crude aggregates, presented in

Table 1, which is based on the British Census of Production 1907 and
the American Census of Mines and Quarries of 1909, is difficult.
Through the statistical haze, nonetheless, comes the impression that
output per man in Britain was half or perhaps a little more than half
that in America before World War I.

The input of capital cannot explain any of this difference, since
capital per man was about the same in the two countries. Horsepower

TABLE 1
Yearly output per man employed, U.K. 1907 and U.S.A. 1909

	Output (millions of long tons)	Wage earners employed (millions)	Tons of output per wage earner year
U.K.	267	.812	325
U.S.A.	408	.667	613

Sources:
U.S.A.: U.S. Bureau of the Census, Thirteenth Census, vol. XI, *Mines and Quarries
1909* (Washington, D.C., Govt. Printing Office, 1913), pp. 186 ff. The employment figure given on p. 186 excludes coke workers, as it should to be comparable
with the British figure. It relates to 15 December. December, however, was the
month of peak employment in the industry (100 compared to 93.4 for the entire
year; ibid., p. 30). The figure given here is corrected for this overstatement.
    U.K.: Board of Trade, *Final Report on the First Census of Production of the
United Kingdom (1907)* (London, H.M.S.O., 1912), pp. 42 ff. The employment
figure has been reduced by an allowance for iron miners working in mines under
the Coal Mines Regulation Act (which are included in the definition of the coal
industry in the British census). It relates to four Wednesdays during the year and
reflects the normal absenteeism of 10 per cent: the census figure is roughly 10 per
cent below the Home Office figures, which relate apparently to people employed
whether actually working or not. The hours worked per year by each of these
wage earners was probably somewhat higher in the U.K. than in the U.S.A.; the
eight-hour day was introduced in unionized mines in the U.S.A. in 1898 and by
1909 the day was 8.6 hours (U.S. Geological Survey, *Mineral Resources of the
United States 1922* (Washington, D.C., Govt. Printing Office, 1925), p. 503). In
the U.K. the eight-hour day was introduced in 1908, after the census.

per man, for example, according to the census data was virtually
identical in the two: 2.82 per man in Britain and 2.85 in America.
Horsepower statistics are very crude measures of capital, since they
reflect only the stock of a certain kind of equipment rather than all
equipment, structures and inventories together, yet there is reason to
accept their surprising testimony that high American wages did not lead

to higher capital per man. The reason is that capital was a substitute for land as well as labour: bad and expensive coal land, such as Britain had relative to America, could be worked profitably only by investing in deep shafts and long tunnels to ferret out the coal. This heavier capital investment meant, for example, that British mines were much larger than American mines. It is plausible, then, that the substitution of capital for labour in the United States was matched by a substitution of capital for land in the United Kingdom. In any case, only if the measure is very much in error would capital have any great effect on output per man because capital's share in total costs was small. In the United Kingdom its share was around 12 per cent and in the United States only 4 per cent [19].

Land's share was small, too, but its small weight in the calculation of productivity was offset by the enormous differences in its quantity and quality in the two countries. The ideal measure of land input, like the ideal measures of coal output and labour input, would add up different units weighted by their value in producing coal [20]. This value – the coal land's price – is determined by characteristics such as its closeness to consumers, the ease of mining it, and the quantity of coal it contains. If the separate effects on price could be measured with acceptable accuracy, the production function, as it were, for land in terms of these characteristics of quality could be written down and the land input in the two countries compared precisely. The price of coal land classified by quality, however, is not available. Fortunately, the case to be made here, that differences in resource endowments explain most of the difference in output per man, can rest on a very rough approximation to the ideal programme.

The sheer quantity of coal land per worker was clearly larger in America than in Britain. The exact meaning of the 'sheer quantity' of land is somewhat elusive. Is it coal land in existence or coal land in use, tons of reserves under the ground or acres of land on the surface? The unit of measurement chosen should satisfy the specification of the production function that doubling it and all other inputs results in a doubling of output. Moreover, the unit represents a property right that is bought and sold and should therefore correspond to the unit employed in these transactions. The situation is obscured by the differences in mineral property rights in America and Britain: in America the surface land and everything under it was sold as one, while in Britain the surface and mineral rights were sold separately, often to the extent of selling different seams under one surface to different mining companies [21] . A reasonable compromise is to take the right to mine a certain quantity of tons of coal reserves as the unit of land. In any case, it should be the number of the units, however defined, that mining companies actually own or lease. Land that contains coal but is not considered worth holding by the coal companies should not be included in the coal industry's inputs. The American census gives acres of coal land owned or leased by the industry, but the British census does not and there is no corresponding statistic available in other sources. There are no statistics on the land 'in use', however, that might be defined. The only alternative is to use the tons of reserves in actively mined regions as an estimate of the land employed in the industry [22] . This is a crude procedure and it is prudent therefore to bias it in the direction of lowering the American measure of land employed. Accomplishing this by using in the measure only the reserves of the six most intensively mined states (Pennsylvania, West Virginia, Ohio, Indiana, Maryland and Arkansas), American land input in 1910 in terms of reserves was about 400,000 million metric tons [23] . Total reserves were eight times this: many of them lay fallow in the Rocky Mountains, to be sure, but the reserves of such large coal producing states as Illinois and Kentucky are also excluded from this figure. In comparable units, the entire reserves of the United Kingdom, whether intensively mined or not, were about 100,000 million metric tons [24]. British land input, then, was a quarter of the American and land input per worker was in the ratio of 0.205 to 1.000. The difference is about 80 per cent of the American level of land per worker. The difference in output per worker was 47 per cent of the American level. Since the share of land was about 0.08 in costs, the difference in the quantity of land per worker explains about 6.4 percentage points of the total difference of 47 points.

Not only was the quantity of coal land large in America compared with Britain, but, more important, its quality was high. American seams were generally thicker, closer to the surface, freer from faults, flatter and drier than British seams [25] . American coal land in 1910 had been blessed with a fortunate geological history and a brief industrial history. In using the meagre data to count these blessings, it is important to keep in mind that the quality of land to be worked was to some extent a matter of choice. If unusually thin seams were to be worked profitably in competitive circumstances they must have been unusually close to the surface, have been unusually free from faulting, or have had some other compensating virtue. Thick seams, on the other hand, would have been worked at great depths and with very faulted contours [26]. The result is that a simple plot of output per man against one of these qualities (such as thickness, shallowness, faultlessness) will give an impression of the impact of the quality biased towards no impact at all: as the thickness of seams rise, for example, their average depth will increase, reducing on that account output per man and resulting in an understatement of the true impact of changing thickness alone. It is important, therefore, to hold the other variables constant [27].

There is widespread evidence that in the range usually observed the thickness of seams had a large effect on output per man. One of the few opportunities to control for depth as well as thickness for a good sized sample is the data collected for forty-eight American shaft mines by Carroll Wright as Commissioner of Labor in his *Sixth Annual Report 1890, Cost of Production: Iron, Steel, Coal, etc.* [28]. A regression of output per man on thickness, depth, and the size of the screen separating coal into 'screenings' and more valuable large sizes, yielded an R^2 of 0.39, which is hardly impressive, and a coefficient on depth insignificantly different from zero. It is not too surprising that in the shallow American mines depth was unimportant (the average in Wright's sample was only 178 ft compared with a British average of around 1000 feet) [29]. The effect of seam thickness, however, is clear and strong: the coefficient is five times its standard error and the elasticity of output per man with respect to seam thickness is over 0.5. The weight of evidence, indeed, is that the effect of thickness was even greater, with an elasticity of around 1. In an unusual sample of outputs per tonnage worker and seam thicknesses collected for 1921 in Illinois, for example, the implied elasticity in the range of 5.5 ft is about 1.2 [30]. The consequences are important. The average seam worked in Britain in 1924, when the matter was first investigated systematically, was 50 in; the average in America in 1920-2 was about 65 in [31]. With an elasticity of about 1, this difference would explain about 25 percentage points of the total difference of 47 per cent in the average product of labour.

The 15.6 per cent difference remaining after the effects of land and thickness are extracted is more than explained by the great depth of British mines. The effect of depth can be approached through its close correlation with thickness. In contrast with the United States, in which the distances between coal markets created wide divergences in price, the United Kingdom was one market for coal. The market as well as technology worked to limit the dispersion of behaviour in the industry.

All combinations of thickness and depth could be observed in the United States because a poor combination was protected by the distance to a competitor. British mines, however, were all forced to lie close to the same curve of equal average product relating thickness and depth [32]. The slope of this curve expresses, then, the change in thickness required to compensate for a given change in depth. The elasticity of thickness with respect to depth appears to have been in 1924 about 1.2 [33]. Since the average depth of mines in the early 1920s was about 1000 ft in Britain and only 280 ft in the United States, the equivalent change in thickness is very high. Any reasonable elasticity of output per man with respect to thickness, then, will permit the depth of the coal to explain the remaining difference in average product. Indeed, the quantity and quality of land available to the American industry explains much more than is necessary to absolve the British industry of the charge of failure, especially in view of the biases introduced against this hypothesis in the course of the argument. A weaker argument, weighted still more against the hypothesis of British competence, would suffice.

The exercise is crude, to be sure, but its very crudeness suggests that it requires no delicate and uncertain inquiry to explain the difference between labour productivity in the American and British industries in terms of the large differences between the resources with which the two worked. The case for a failure of masters and men in British coal mining before 1913, in short, is vulnerable to a most damaging criticism: there was clearly no failure of productivity.

STEEL

It is commonly believed, with even more conviction than for the coal industry, that the steel industry in late nineteenth-century Britain performed poorly. The managers in coal could be excused on the grounds that the quality of the natural resource with which they worked was deteriorating, but the steelmakers could not: indeed, the chief history of the industry, D. Burn's *The Economic History of Steelmaking 1867-1939* [34], faults them for ignoring, in the phosphoric ores of Lincolnshire, the natural resources they did have. Burn emphasizes repeatedly the 'personal deficiencies', 'attachment to routine', and 'inadequate education' of British managers, and T. H. Burnham and G. O. Hoskins in their history of the industry sum up a similar indictment as follows: 'There is, in fact, good evidence to believe that the British iron and steel industry would not have declined so fast or so far during the period reviewed had the men at the head possessed greater vision and a bolder and more energetic capacity for organization, direction and administration' [35]. This view of the industry is widely accepted. The steel industry, in fact, almost invariably plays a large role in discussions of American technological superiority. If most observers believe that British coal mining was inferior, virtually all believe that British steelmaking was.

The evidence for a large technological difference in steel, as in coal, is dubious and it is fairly easy to show that the difference did not exist. In coal it was convenient to begin with the average product of labour in measuring productivity, since labour costs were 60 to 70 per cent of the total. In steel the direct costs of labour were much smaller. Most of the costs were materials, especially pig iron, but because the materials were used in relatively fixed proportion to output during the period the measure cannot use their average product. In any case the data on quantities of labour and pig iron used in steel production are poor. The way around this obstacle is to use the inputs' prices relative to the price of output rather than their quantities – that is, their marginal rather than their average products [36].

The best sources for comparing prices of inputs and outputs in steel, as for comparing their quantities in coal, are the prewar censuses of production in the United States (1909) and the United Kingdom (1907). Market prices reported regularly in the trade journals are useful checks, but the census data has the critical advantage of wide coverage. Wide coverage has drawbacks, too, often concealing rather than curing the heterogeneity in such categories as 'American pig iron' or 'British wage earners'. Market prices, in contrast, refer to a specific commodity at a specific location sold under specific terms, although it is often difficult to determine exactly what these specifications were. The average values in the censuses, then, must be handled with care. For example, the British census gives values and quantities for 'thick plates', which include ship plates and boiler plates, while the American census gives data for 'plates and sheets', which include sheets as well. Since sheets required much more rolling than plates, they were more expensive per ton and their effect of raising average values must be removed if the American industry is not to appear spuriously inefficient [37]. A similar problem of heterogeneity occurs in the measure of pig iron input. Low phosphorous (or 'acid', 'Haematite', or 'Bessemer') pig iron was more expensive because it was cheaper to use and more costly to make than other varieties. Because the British industry used more of it than the American industry the categories given in the censuses must again be broken down into more detail to avoid spurious productivity differences [38].

The results of the various corrections are exhibited in Table 2, which gives the names and average values of comparable American and British products. The values that it was necessary to estimate are bracketed. The marginal product of pig iron implied by this table — that is, the ratio of the price of pig iron to the price of a steel product is invariably

TABLE 2
Rolled iron and steel:
census values of labour and pig iron inputs and major products

U.S.A. 1909		U.K. 1907	
American name	*American value*	*British name*	*British value*
(dollars/ton or man-year)		(shillings/ton or man-year)	
Bessemer pig iron	[$15.70]	Haematite pig iron	72.5s.
Other pig iron	[$14.68]	Other pig iron	55.4
Average, all pig used	$15.10	Average, all pig used	[63.3]
Yearly earnings, wages	$679	Yearly earnings, wages	[1690s]
Plates ≤ gauge 16	[$36.10]	Plates ≤ 1/8″ thick	138.7s.
Rails	$28.38	Rails (including train	
Bars and rods	$31.97	rails	120.0s.
Structural shapes	$30.90	Steel bars, angles	133.8
Black plates and sheets	49.00	Girders, beams	128.0
		Black plates and sheets	188.0

Source: The source for the U.S.A. is the 1909 Census, pp. 238–40, and for the U.K. the 1907 Census, pp. 101–3 (see sources for Table 1). The coverage is roughly half of the value of rolled products and steel (i.e. excluding cast iron) in both the U.K. and the U.S.A. The bracketed figures were estimated as described in previous footnotes. The U.K. average value of pig used was estimated from the average values given in the Census (for forge and foundry, haematite, and basic) weighted by estimates of the haematite and non-haematite pig iron used to make steel and wrought iron (i.e. excluding cast iron and exported pig iron). These estimates, in turn, were based on the acid/basic proportions of steel output and an assumption that all puddling was done with non-haematite pig.

higher in Britain. This is not surprising, since labour was, of course, much cheaper relative to pig iron in Britain than in America, causing labour to be used intensively and raising the marginal product of pig iron. What is surprising, in view of the usual assumption of overwhelm-

TABLE 3
Productivity differences for major steel products

	Marginal products of pig iron U.S.A.	U.K.	% difference in marginal products of pig iron (U.S.A. higher = +)	% difference in total productivity (U.S.A. higher = +)
	1	2	3	4
Heavy plates	.418	.471	−11.92	−1.57
Rails	.533	.545	− 2.22	+8.13
Bars, rods, etc.	.473	.488	− 3.13	+7.22
Structural shapes	.488	.510	− 4.41	+5.94
Black plates and sheets	.308	.348	−12.20	−1.85

Source: Table above. Columns 1 and 2 are the average price of pig iron divided by the price of the product. Column 3 is $[(1) − (2)]/[1/2(1)+1/2(2)]$. Column 4 is column 3 minus the share of labour (assumed to be 0.192, which is the American value and is high for the U.K.) times the percentage difference in the price ratio of labour to pig iron (W/P). That is, column 4 is (denoting percentage differences in the variables with asterisks)

$$A^* = (P_I/P)^* + S_L(W/P_I)^*$$

The result assumes that labour and pig iron are the only two factors of production. In the United States they accounted for about 0.68 per cent of the costs of production, excluding steel inputs into steel in the total cost.

ing American superiority, is that this higher marginal product of pig iron in Britain is not outweighed by a correspondingly lower marginal product of labour. That is, as shown in Table 3, the uniformly high price ratio of pig iron to steel in Britain was just barely offset by a uniformly low price ratio of labour to pig iron, leaving very small differences in the total productivity of the American and British industries.

On this reckoning, which agrees with the pattern of comparative advantage that might be expected, the American industry was slightly superior in the making of rails, bars and structural shapes, and the British industry in the making of plates and sheets. The assumption that the share of labour was the same for each product when it was not imparts a small bias to the results, as can be seen from the steady relative improvement of British performance as the degree of fabrication (and labour-intensity) increases from rails to sheets. If this bias were corrected, the productivity differences would be more uniform from product to product, with perhaps a 2 or 3 per cent average superiority for the American industry.

The negligible difference in output for a given input suggests that entrepreneurial failure had little to do with the relative positions of the British and American supply curves, especially in view of certain biases against the British industry in the measure. Two years of productivity growth between the years of the British and American censuses would account for some of the difference. Moreover, 1907 ánd 1909 in the two countries were at different stages of the business cycle. The productivity measurements assume that the industries were in long run equilibrium, that is, that their cost curves were horizontal. When a cyclical increase in demand has raised output to a new peak, straining capacity, this assumption is violated and productivity appears lower than it is. It is likely, in fact, that the British industry suffered more from this downward bias in the measure [39]. In any case, though the measure in steelmaking as in coal mining is crude, the result is plain: the total productivities of the American and British industries before the War, when the allegations of American skill and British ineptitude were already many decades old, were virtually indistinguishable.

The apparent lack of any failure of productivity in coal and steel suggests that the traditional contrast between managerial vigour in America and sloth in Britain may be in need of critical re-examination. The measures of productivity proposed here are far from perfect and apply to only two industries. Yet the alleged superiority of American over British technique does not register in either, even though the superiority in coal and steel has usually been thought to have been especially great. Apparently, technology in these two industries was international. This is not a very surprising conclusion, given the sample means of communicating knowledge and the strong incentives to use it. In this view, the differences between the Old World and the New were differences in the quantity and quality of inputs, not in vigour and technology.

NOTES

[1] A. W. Flux, 'Industrial productivity in Great Britain and the United States', *Quarterly Journal of Economics*, 48, November 1933, pp. 1–38; L. Rostas, *Comparative Productivity in British and American Industry* (Cambridge, Cambridge University Press, 1948); M. Frankel, *British and American Manufacturing Productivity* (Urbana, University of Illinois Press, 1957); M. Gilbert and I. B. Kravis, *An International Comparison of National Products and the Purchasing Powers of Currencies* (Paris, OEEC, 1954); M. Gilbert *et al.*, *Comparative National Products and Price Levels* (Paris, OEEC, 1958); D. Paige and G. Bombach, *A Comparison of National Output and Productivity of the United Kingdom and the United States* (Paris, OEEC, 1959).

[2] Gilbert and Kravis, op. cit., p. 22, recalculated from *per capita* to per worker; Paige and Bombach, op. cit., p. 21. Taking as 100 the geometric average of American manufacturing value-added per employee in British and American prices, the British level given in Paige and Bombach for 1950 was only 36.5.

[3] Washington, D.C., Brookings Institution, 1967.

[4] Denison, op. cit., p. 332. His findings for the other western European countries studied were much the same.

[5] Denison's theoretical framework is essentially the Cobb-Douglass production function under conditions of equilibrium and perfect competition. A slightly more general framework is that of K. J. Arrow, H. B. Chenery, B. S. Minhas and R. M. Solow in 'Capital-labor substitution and economic efficiency', *Review of Economics and Statistics,* 43, August 1961, pp. 225–50. They, too, find large unexplained differences in productivity between countries, in their case between the United States and Japan.

[6] 'Increasing returns and economic progress', *Economic Journal,* 38, December 1928, pp. 527–42.

[7] 'Causes of the superior efficiency of U.S.A. industry as compared with British Industry', *Economic Journal,* 56, September 1946, pp. 383–90. Recent work on early national income by R. Gallman for the United States and C. H. Feinstein for the United Kingdom suggests that at the par of exchange the income of the two was approximately equal in the 1850s. The argument has the further difficulty that Britain sold to a world market: the market for British cotton textiles, for example, was surely larger than the American market throughout the nineteenth century.

[8] Series 66, p. 141, in U.S. Bureau of the Census, *Historical Statistics of the United States* (Washington, D.C., Govt. Printing Office, 1960) estimates rent as around 8 per cent of American national income from 1870. P. Deane and W. A. Cole in *British Economic Growth 1688-1959* (Cambridge, Cambridge University Press, 1964), p. 247, estimate rent, including apparently some rents of buildings, at around 13 per cent from 1860 to World War I.

[9] The basis for the estimate of a 30 per cent share is the sum of entrepreneurial income and dividends in American national income in the late nineteenth century given in *Historical Statistics* at the place cited above. The reason the share in national income is an upper bound on the relevant share is that, as discussed below, the share relevant to a particular industry's production function would include intermediate goods as well as value-added.

[10] 'The Explanation of Productivity Change', *Review of Economic Studies,* 34, July 1967, 249–84, p. 274. E. Denison has subjected this article to searching criticism, pointing out, among other things, that they did not offer evidence for the assertion quoted here ('Some major issues in productivity analysis: an examination of estimates by Jorgenson and Griliches', *Survey of Current Business,* 49, No. 5, pt II, May 1969, pp. 1–27.

[11] Denison himself admits that he is puzzled by it and remarks that his 'inability to decompose residual productivity or analyze it satisfactorily is surely the greatest gap in the present study' (Denison, op. cit., p. 340).

[12] Cf. E. D. Domar, 'On the measurement of technological change', *Economic Journal,* 71, December 1961, pp. 709–29.

[13] It can be shown, as in Domar, op. cit., that the typical productivity measure is the national measure multiplied by the share of inputs not purchased

from other firms. In the 1947 input-output table for the American economy (given in H. B. Chenery and P. G. Clark, *Interindustry Economics* (New York, Wiley, 1959), p. 222) purchased inputs were 44 per cent of total domestic sales. In the first British Census of Production it was found that 58 per cent of the costs were purchased from other firms (*Final Report on the First Census of Production of the United Kingdom (1907)* (London, H.M.S.O., 1912), p. 19). For a similar group of industries in the American input-output table (excluding, that is, agriculture, fishing, transport, trade and services), 47 per cent were purchased from other firms.

[14] J. H. Clapham, *An Economic History of Modern Britain* (Cambridge, Cambridge University Press, 1938), Vol. III, p. 168.

[15] 'The Coal Industry', chapter 2 in D. Aldcroft (ed.), *The Development of British Industry and Foreign Competition 1875-1914* (London, Allen and Unwin, 1968). p. 69.

[16] Cf. Taylor, op. cit., p. 46.

[17] In anthracite mining output per man-day declined after 1899, while in bituminous it continued to rise (U.S. Geological Survey, *Mineral Resources of the United States 1917* (Washington, D.C., Govt. Printing Office, 1920), pt II, p. 932).

[18] Because the price of any particular ton of coal or man-hour of labour reflects many different quality components, the components would need to be separated by some such method as regressing coal prices on BTUs per ton and other qualities. The analysis should not include costless quality differences in the inputs such as the presence of more vigorous men in America than in Britain; it should include education, experience and other qualities of the inputs requiring investment.

[19] The share of capital and land, calculated as a residual from labour and materials, was 19 per cent in the U.K. in 1919 (*Report of the Coal Industry Commission* (Sankey Commission), SP 1919 XI, p. xii) and 12 per cent in the United States in 1909 (*Census of Mines and Quarries*, pp. 183–229). Assuming that land and capital earned roughly similar returns, these can be split into land and capital by using their shares in total asset values. C. H. Feinstein's data on the coal industry in his *Domestic Capital Formation in the United Kingdom 1920-1939* (Cambridge, Cambridge University Press, 1965, pp. 80 ff) imply that the depreciated value of fixed capital in historical prices plus the value of stocks in trade was £146 million in 1920, while the value of coal deposits and surface land was £96 million. According to D. B. Creamer, S. P. Dobrovolsky and I. Borenstein's *Capital in Manufacturing and Mining* (Princeton, Princeton University Press, 1960, pp. 274 ff.) in the United States in 1909 the value of capital ($486 million) was much smaller in relation to all land used in the industry ($1064 million) than in the United Kingdom. The upshot is that while the estimates of the shares of land in Britain and America are about the same (7.5 and 8.2 per cent), the British share of capital (11.5 per cent) is much higher than the American (3.8 per cent).

[20] Strictly speaking, a conversion of the stock of land into a flow of services from land is required. Jorgenson and Griliches (op. cit.) criticized J. W. Kendrick for aggregating stock of capital rather than service flows and the same point applies to land. The fullness of utilization of coal land may have been different in the two countries, yielding different flows from the same stock.

[21] Incidentally, the pattern of coal land tenure is a good example of the effect

of economic conditions on legal arrangements. In the United Kingdom, apparently, land was expensive enough to overcome the high transaction costs of selling mineral rights and surface rights separately and to warrant more specialization between ownership of the rights and exploitation of the rights (over two-thirds of American coal acreage was owned outright by the mining companies; in Britain, however, ownership of coal by the mines was exceptional).

[22] It might seem reasonable to weight the reserves by the share of the region—the state in America and the county in Britain—in total output. It is not: although this weighting scheme corresponds with what one does unconsciously in assessing the size of actively used coal reserves, it yields a statistic that varies with the degree of detail chosen, as an arithmetic example can make clear. Suppose there were three districts with outputs of 1, 1 and 1 and with reserves of 2, 3 and 4. If the statistic were calculated taking all three districts separately, it would be 9/3. Taking the first and second together, it would be 14/3.

[23] 12th International Geological Congress, *The Coal Resources of the World* (Toronto, Morang 1913), vol. II, article by M. R. Campbell, 'The coal reserves of the United States', pp. 525–39. The definition of the intensity of mining is the ratio of 1909 output to the states' total reserves. The definition and the truncation at six states is highly arbitrary. The implicit assumption is that in these states the exploitation of coal land was as intense per ton of reserves as in Britain. For Pennsylvania and Maryland this is no doubt true. For the others it is less plausible.

[24] To make the comparison with the United States (whose reserves were given for seams greater than 2 ft in thickness at a depth of less than 3000 ft), the British reserves of 171,000 million metric tons (International Geological Congress, op. cit., p. 628, with Scotland's probable reserves estimated on the basis of the ratio of 'probable' to 'actual' in England and Wales) had to be reduced by estimates of the British reserves between 3000 and 4000 ft deep and 1 to 2 ft in thickness (the estimates were 25 per cent of the total to correct for the different standards of depth and 20.7 per cent (given in Colliery Guardian, *Digest of Evidence Given Before the Royal Commission on Coal Supplies (1901-05)* (London, 1905-7), vol. I, p. xxxii) to correct for the different standards of thickness. This procedure entails the assumption that depth and thickness were not correlated. They would be at shallower depths and greater thicknesses because of selective mining of the shallower and thicker seams, but at these far limits of depth and thickness the assumption is reasonable.

[25] See, for example, F. G. Tryon and M. H. Schoenfield, 'Comparison of physical conditions in British and American coal mines', *Coal and Coal Trades Journal* 57, pp. 934, 956–7, 1087–9, 1202–6 (4 parts), autumn weeks of 1926. Tryon was the chief statistical adviser to the United States Coal Commission and was in charge of the U.S. Geological Survey coal statistics. Tryon and Schoenfield use the data on British mines collected for the Royal Commission on the Coal Industry (the Samuel Commission) of 1926. A table, also from the Samuel Commission, on the conditions of coal mining in the major coal-mining countries is reproduced in the League of Nations, International Economic Conference, *Memorandum on Coal* vol. I (Geneva, 1927), p. 39, as well as in Tryon and Schoenfield, op. cit., p. 1203.

[26] This point is made repeatedly in the testimony of the witnesses to the Royal Commission on Coal Supplies (1901-5). See Colliery Guardian, op.

cit., vol. 1, chapter 1, 'The working of thin seams'; chapter II, section 3, 'Evidence as to thickness of seams worked at great depths'.

[27] Errors in the independent variables will also bias the coefficient on thickness in a regression explaining output per man downward. Unfortunately, simultaneous equation bias, of which this is a classic case (because there exists another relation among the variables namely, the conditions of profit maximization), works in the other direction.

[28] Revised ed. (Washington, D.C., Govt. Printing Office, 1891), pp. 199 ff.

[29] Cf. Tryon and Schoenfield, op. cit., p. 1205, speaking of the 1920s: 'In the bituminous mines of the United States, no marked correlation between average thickness and average depth of working has yet developed simply because the readily accessible coals have not been exhausted.'

[30] *Report of the U.S. Coal Commission* (Washington, D.C., Govt. Printing Office, 1925), part II, p. 1079.

[31] Estimated from Tryon and Schoenfield, op. cit., p. 1088. American bituminous seams in 1920 averaged 63 inches and anthracite seams in 1922 80 inches. 1922 was a depressed year in anthracite mining and the figure of 80 inches may therefore be too high: in bad years thin seams were not mined. 1920 and 1924 were prosperous years for coal in the United States and Britain.

[32] Output per man was very uniform in the U.K. compared with the U.S.; cf. Tryon and Schoenfield, op. cit., p. 1204.

[33] Tryon and Schoenfield, op. cit., p. 1205, give the average depth of coal in seams under 2 ft in thickness as 517 ft, between 2 and 4 ft as 876 ft, between 4 and 6 ft as 1163 ft, and over 6 ft as 1351 ft.

[34] Cambridge, Cambridge University Press, 1940.

[35] Burn, op. cit., pp. 303, 213, 11; and Burnham and Hoskins, *Iron and Steel in Britain 1870-1930* (London, Allen and Unwin, 1943), p. 271.

[36] The equivalence of measures of productivity using prices and quantities has received attention recently. See, for example, D. W. Jorgenson, 'The embodiment hypothesis', *Journal of the Political Economy* 74, 1-17, February 1966, p. 3 n. An early use of the price measure, familiar to economic historians, is G. T. Jones, *Increasing Return* (Cambridge, Cambridge University Press, 1933), esp. p. 33 (Jones's index can be shown to be identical to the price measure given in Jorgenson). It should be emphasized that the price measure is not merely an approximation to the quantity measure: with consistent data it is identical to it and is therefore not more volatile or uncertain.

[37] The average value of plates and sheets is given in the American census as $40.00 per long ton (U.S. Bureau of the Census, Vol. X, *Manufactures 1909* (Washington, D.C., Govt. Printing Office, 1913), p. 240). The census gives tonnages, but not values, of plates and sheets by gauge (ibid., p. 238). Assuming that a gauge of 17 or lighter is comparable to the British category of 'sheets', and assuming further that sheets sold at the black plate and sheet price (a high estimate of the true price) of $50.00 per ton (given at p. 240), the heavy plate price can be estimated at $36.10 per ton.

[38] The object was to break the American census value of pig iron used in steelworks and rolling mills ($15.10 per ton; ibid., p. 252) into Bessemer and non-Bessemer prices, comparable to the values reported in the British census. The Census gives tonnages for five types of pig iron; the American Iron and Steel Institute's *Statistical Report for 1913* gives 1909 market prices for pig iron similar to each of the five types; from this information and the average census value it is possible to infer the appropriate census values for the Bessemer type and for the rest.

[39] 1907 was a peak year for British steel output and was not surpassed until 1912. In 1909, the American industry produced about 3 per cent more steel than in the previous peak, but the previous peak was three years before and was surpassed in 1910: the industry had ample time to adjust and was not pressed much beyond its previous peak output until 1910.

Chairman: S. B. Saul

Prepared comments: D. Landes

Landes: The coal and steel sections of the paper are not strictly comparable. The argument in the section on coal uses labour productivity, while that on steel uses total productivity. One question that comes to mind, then, is whether using labour productivity in steel might not give rather different results. In the section on coal McCloskey begins his argument by observing that 'average product fell, to be sure, in England, but it fell or stagnated everywhere in Europe before World War I, and therefore does not suggest any peculiar British failure.' This observation is based on Taylor's table of average labour productivity per man, and while McCloskey is, literally speaking, correct, his interpretation is a strange one in an otherwise carefully quantitative paper. The variations in behaviour brought out by the table are more striking than the particular uniformity he used. For example, in Germany labour productivity does level off after the 1880s, but over the whole period from the 1870s to the War there is a rise in productivity of one third. Over the same period, American productivity in bituminous coal doubles, while British productivity suffered a slight net decline.

In the subsequent calculations of the importance of the two geological factors in coal mining, thickness and depth of seam, a great deal depends on the particular elasticities chosen. In the argument on this point, McCloskey uses two small samples, which imply elasticities of output per man with respect to seam thickness ranging from 0.5 to 1.2. The calculation then proceeds on the assumption that the elasticity is 'around 1'. If the elasticity of 0.5 had been chosen instead, the significance of seam thicknesses in explaining output per man would be cut in half.

Having arrived at some estimates of the elasticities, the question becomes what the differences in the thickness and depth of seams actually were. Here McCloskey uses data from the 1920s, when they first became available. In applying these data to the Anglo-American comparison in 1907-9, however, the difficulty arises that British seams were becoming thinner and deeper as time went on, whereas American seams, it is argued in the paper, were not. The sharpness of the contrast in geological conditions, then, may not have been as great in 1907-9 as it was in the 1920s, and the power of the geological explanation is reduced, by an unknown amount.

The methodology underlying the calculations for coal raises some other questions. Taylor gives prominence to the increase in absenteeism in British mines. What one would like to see is some attempt to bring variables such as these, some of which are perhaps less quantifiable than absenteeism, into the analysis. The importance of other factors than the geological is suggested, too, by the great regional variations exhibited in one of Taylor's tables in the rate of growth of output per man in Britain in the late nineteenth century. By 1924, the paper notes, British output per man was uniform among districts, with mining concentrated on seams with similar geological characteristics. But the evidence from Taylor suggests that the correlation between geological conditions and output per man derived from the 1924 data might not hold at earlier times. That is, some factors other than geology were at work.

In the steel industry the argument is based on total productivity, measured, assuming that the industry was competitive, by the ratio of the prices of pig iron input and of steel output. The essential results are exhibited in Table 3. One problem with this procedure is that the ratio might fluctuate from year to year, leaving one in doubt as to which year to choose for the comparison. And, in fact, in McCloskey's Ph.D. thesis, from which the argument on the steel industry is taken, there appears a chart of the marginal product of pig iron in the production of steel, which does show substantial fluctuations from year to year. Another problem is that the measure focuses on steel alone: one might wonder, for example, whether similar results would emerge from a study of the industry as a whole, including pig iron.

There are a few larger issues suggested by the paper. Is it really relevant to compare British with American, rather than German, performance? The traditional story of the enormous superiority of American technology must certainly be revised in light of this and similar papers, but it remains to be seen whether the alleged German superiority was also illusory. Finally, McCloskey is troubled by the large residual gap in productivity between countries that Denison finds, and argues that such differences cannot be believed. If one starts from the other point of view, however, and believes in differences among people in different countries and the slowness of the transmission of technology that these differences imply, then the large residual gap in productivity is not troubling at all. This position, of course, is a matter of faith. But so, too, is McCloskey's position that the differences are unbelievable and must be explained.

McCloskey: On the issue of the view of the world or working hypothesis with which one starts, his has the advantage that it has observable implications. If you suppose to begin with that technology is international, you have a concrete standard against which to judge the truth of the supposition, by seeing whether you can or cannot explain international differences in total productivity. This may have something to do with the way the burden of proof is left with these who doubt rather than with those who support the hypothesis of entrepreneurial failure: the working hypothesis of the latter group gives them few ways of proving the truth or falsehood of their position.

The coal and steel sections of the paper do not really use different methodologies. The one uses average product and the other marginal product, but there is between these two what mathematicians call a relationship of 'duality'. The simplest way to see that this is true is to consider the simple case of one input, call it 'L', which is purchased at the wage 'w', and one output, call it 'Q' which is sold at a price 'p'. In competitive equilibrium there are no supernormal profits, so $PQ-wL = 0$. That is, $pQ = wL$, or $Q/L = w/p$. This last says that the average product of labour (Q/L) is the same as the marginal product (w/p). A change or difference in the average product would therefore equal a change or difference in the marginal product. In the general case, in other words, a measure of productivity based on quantities (a generalized average product) would give the same result as one based on prices (a generalized marginal product). The first part of the paper uses a quantity measure and the second part a price measure, but there is no difference in principle or in the results that they would give between the two.

It might be useful to mention the economic assumptions that lie behind productivity measures in this paper and in the others concerned with productivity at the conference. First, the industry is assumed to be perfectly competitive, so that no monopoly profits are being earned and, in the one-factor case, $pQ = wL$. Second, to make certain of this last result, long-run equilibrium is assumed. No Marshallian quasi-rents are being earned: entrepreneurs have had time to adjust their employment of each factor to the desirable level given the prices of the factors and the price of the output. Third, to facilitate the calculation given the difficulty of finding yearly data on the shares of the factors of production in costs, the shares are assumed to be constant. An equivalent assumption is that the production function of the industry is of the Cobb-Douglas form.

Feinstein: Returning to one of Landes's points, it was not helpful to make comparisons in the British coal industry with the United States. Conditions were so different there that one learns very little from the comparison. Germany would be a more sensible choice. Furthermore, the argument of the paper is that by 1907 the British industry could do no better. But in fact in later years it *did* do better. The question is, then, were there improvements that were achieved after the War that could have been achieved before it?

McCloskey: Feinstein's question was identical to the one he had asked in the paper. The question that is answered by a productivity calculation is precisely: was some other technique of production (in this case the American) superior to the one used in Britain? And the calculation involves the same logic, too, if the question is one of profitability, as in the paper by Lindert and Trace. The comparison with the United States is relevant (although, of course, it would be desirable to bring Germany, Belgium and France into the comparisons as well) because the United States had so much higher labour productivity in coal that contemporaries and historians have taken it for granted that technology there was superior, while conceding that geological conditions were better in the United States. The point of the paper is that the geological conditions can explain the entire large difference in labour productivity. Although some doubt is cast on the calculations for 1907-9 that used post-war data on geological conditions, the change in conditions in fifteen years are not enough to alter the results significantly.

Trace: There would have been pressure to open up new fields, as in Kent and the Midlands, which may indeed have altered the results.

McCloskey: These fields were known very early, and were in fact exploited when it became profitable to do so. As was argued in the paper, the British industry was geographically concentrated by comparison with the American industry and there was therefore strong pressure to open up new fields gradually as the balance of geological conditions warranted. This point answers one of Landes's questions as well. The paper did not say that geological conditions were uniform, but only that in all mines the increment to labour productivity from exploiting thickness was carefully balanced against that from exploiting shallowness. In the United States, by contrast, mining was widely scattered and many mines that worked seams that were both thin and deep could survive: there was more deviation possible from a single line of equal average product as a function of depth and thickness.

Thomas: It is not clear how the physical conditions could be separated from entrepreneurial performance in the explanation of average product per man.

McCloskey: The purpose of the paper is to estimate the magnitudes of the geological effects. The argument, then, is that once these have been properly measured there is no residual productivity difference to be explained by entrepreneurship.

Landes: He objected to precisely this residual procedure. If one started with the entrepreneurial explanation, one could exclude geological conditions just as well.

Lindert: Landes's point could be made in another way: even if 100 per cent of the difference was explained, it would still not follow that the one factor, entrepreneurship, was unimportant, so long as there were still other factors to be taken into account.

McCloskey: The point he began with was relevant here: if one does start with the entrepreneurial hypothesis, there are no guides as to how to put the argument in quantitative form.

IV Problems of Measuring Productivity:
The Capital Goods and Service Sectors

9

Changes in the productivity of labour in the British machine tool industry, 1856–1900

RODERICK FLOUD

Discussion of trends in the growth of labour productivity is central to an evaluation of the behaviour of the British economy during the second half of the nineteenth century. It has conventionally been argued that the growth rate of labour productivity fell during the period from 1.2 per cent per annum in the decade 1870-80 to a low point of 0.2 per cent per annum in the decades 1890-1900 and 1900-13, and that the overall growth rate for the period 1870-1913 was only 0.6 per cent per annum [1]. Other calculations have suggested that output per hour worked rose more slowly during this period in the United Kingdom than in any other industrialized or industrializing country, with the exception of Italy [2].

While there is now general agreement that this period saw a slackening in the rate of growth of labour productivity in the economy as a whole, there is much less agreement on the causes of this slackening, or on its implications for the position of the United Kingdom *vis-à-vis* the other industrial economies. In reopening the controversy in 1952 Phelps-Brown and Handfield-Jones argued that the cause was to be found in the diminishing effects of the major technological advances of steam and steel [3]. Coppock, in rejecting this explanation, saw the decline in the rate of growth of exports during this period as a cause of slowing investment, and hence of declining rates of growth of productivity [4]. D. H. Aldcroft, in a recent article, has argued that both these explanations are unsatisfactory, and that far more attention should be paid to the complex nature of technical change, and to the factors in the British economy that retarded the widespread acceptance of productivity-raising techniques. He argues that 'investment was not unduly low in British industry during this period but ... it was misallocated; that is, new investment was concentrated too heavily in the basic or old sectors of the economy, or, alternatively, replacement investment was either insufficient or of a traditional type.' Aldcroft places most emphasis on the second of these deficiencies, on those in replacement investment [5].

As Aldcroft recognizes, a hypothesis of declining rates of growth of

labour productivity explained by deficiencies in replacement investment requires a type of investigation that was not required of the
protagonists of the earlier explanations; their analysis was concerned
with the economy as a whole, and the variables whose behaviour they
examined were correspondingly measured at an aggregate level. Any
explanation involving differential rates of application of technical
innovations (and Aldcroft emphasizes that he is concerned with 'a delay
in the utilization of known productivity-raising or best-practice
techniques') requires to be explored not at the aggregate level but
rather at the level of the investment/replacement decisions of individual
industries or firms, since it is clearly at this level that any deficiency, if
it existed, must have appeared. Unfortunately, the statistical basis for
such an investigation at the micro-level is clearly inadequate; it is often
impossible, when investigating an individual industry, even to assume
that the rate of growth of labour productivity was declining. As has
been emphasized in a number of studies, some newer industries were
experiencing very considerable rates of growth, while others, notably
coal mining, were almost certainly suffering from a fall in labour
productivity [6].

In spite of these difficulties, analysis at the micro-level is clearly a
necessary condition of further progress in the examination of the
economy of the United Kingdom at this period. It is the purpose of this
paper to contribute to this analysis by the presentation of some results
from one firm, engaged in the production of machine tools. Since the
products of the machine tool industry were perhaps the major means of
enhancing the labour productivity of major sectors of British industry,
the examination of that industry has clear implications for the
discussion; furthermore, machine tools are made by machine tools, so
that the rate of growth of labour productivity achieved by the machine
tool makers is some guide to the rates of growth that could have been
achieved by the many industrial groups who bought and used the tools.

While the machine tool industry and its performance is therefore
important to the discussion, it is necessary to explain how the
behaviour of one firm within that industry can be a guide to the
performance of the industry as a whole. It is extremely difficult to
define a 'typical' firm or to establish whether a firm is 'representative'
of the industry of which it is a small part. Business historians are thus
often defensive when faced with the question of whether the firm
about whose activities they have so laboriously gathered evidence is
'typical' of the industry, or 'representative' of other firms in that

industry. In most circumstances, however, such defensiveness is not warranted, because it is normally not necessary to establish whether the firm is 'typical' or 'representative' in all respects; usually it is only necessary to know whether it is so in respect of the particular characteristics or facets of the industry that are to be explored. Thus if the subject of inquiry is, for instance, the trend of wages in the engineering industry, and it is known that, because of strong trade unions and employers' organizations, all engineering firms paid the same wages, then the experience of one firm would be a complete guide to the experience of the industry as a whole in that particular respect. That firm may be fifty times larger than any other firm in the industry, and totally atypical in all kinds of other ways, but in this particular case of wages it would be typical, and, for a study of wages, that is all that matters.

In most cases, however, this fortunate situation will not occur, and the main subject of inquiry will be into a characteristic of the firms which cannot be expected to be uniform over all firms. This is likely to be true of an inquiry into productivity change and its causes and results. It is likely that there are, in any industry, some firms whose labour productivity, for example, is very much higher than that of other firms; there will be, in the common terminology, a spectrum of firms ranging from best to worst practice, with respect to that particular characteristic. It would, of course, be possible to enquire exactly where a particular firm falls along the spectrum at each moment of time, but it is normally very difficult to answer such a question in a historical study, because of the likely scarcity of evidence on all but a few firms. Thus if one is attempting a static analysis of the state of the industry at one moment in its history, it is normally impossible to know whether the firm one is studying is in any sense representative of the industry as a whole.

The case is not, however, quite so hopeless when one is interested in long term trends in a characteristic of the industry – for instance, in the movement of labour productivity over time. In this case, it would not be necessary to know where one's particular firm lies on the best-worst practice spectrum, in any detail, but merely whether it seems to maintain whatever position it has over the period. If, for example, a firm begins as technically most advanced, but by the end of the period of study is generally known as backward and conservative, by comparison with other firms, then naturally its experience does not provide a good base for the drawing of general conclusions about the industry. If, however, the firm is known to stay, throughout the period, at roughly the same point on the spectrum, then it may be possible to extrapolate from its experience to that of the industry as a whole.

There still remains the problem of whether it is reasonable to assume that the length of the spectrum, the gap between best- and worst-practice firms, has remained constant throughout the period being studied. This problem is raised implicitly by Aldcroft in his explanation of retardation in the British economy in terms of a lag in technical innovation. Clearly, such a lag might have occurred either between the application of some new technique abroad and its introduction into England, or between its application by best-practice firms in England and its general use (or perhaps both of these). If retardation is to be explained by the second type of lag (and explanations using the first type run into many difficulties concerned with different factor costs in different countries) then it is necessary to show that the gap between best- and worst-practice firms, or the arrangement of firms along the spectrum, changed in such a way as to produce retardation. The experience of one firm (for example, a best-practice firm) would present an over-optimistic view of the progress of an industry in which such a lengthening lag, or rearrangement, was occurring. It is, however, still true that, unless the lag lengthens very rapidly, or the rearrangement is very drastic, the experience of one firm will still be a guide to the general trend of the industry, if only as an upper limit. Furthermore, if no evidence of such a rapid lengthening or rearrangement of the best-worst practice spectrum exists, this problem can be safely ignored.

This generalized discussion has suggested that it may be possible, under certain conditions, to generalize safely from the experience of one firm to that of the industry as a whole, when studying one particular facet of an industry. It will now therefore be argued that the relationship between the firm of Greenwood & Batley and the machine tool industry satisfied these conditions for a study of the changing productivity of labour.

GREENWOOD & BATLEY [7]

The partnership of Greenwood & Batley was founded in Leeds in 1856 by two employees of Sir Peter Fairbairn, Thomas Greenwood and John Batley. Thomas Greenwood had built up a connection with the managers of the Royal Arsenals, in particular with the small-arms factory at Enfield, and from the start the firm concentrated much of its effort, and Thomas Greenwood much of his inventive ability, on the manufacture of machine tools for making small arms. Throughout the period with which this paper is concerned, 1856 to 1900, they made not only such machinery, by its nature highly specialized, but also general purpose machine tools for a wide variety of engineering firms both in the United Kingdom and overseas. In addition, they were makers of many other types of engineering products, so many that in 1908 a writer in the 'Engineering Supplement' to *The Times* could report that they were:

> the most famous of all the Leeds firms. . . . They make such a bewildering variety of different things – torpedoes, turbines, electrical plant, cartridges, machinery for silk mills, oil mills, boot sewing, wood-working etc. – that the machine tool department is dwarfed; but it is large, extremely varied, and modern. [8]

In this involvement in the manufacture of many types of engineering products Greenwood & Batley were typical of almost all the machine tool and engineering firms of this period. The specialization said to be characteristic of the American engineering industry at this time did not spread across the Atlantic until the years around World War I.

It is, however, clear that the concern of Greenwood & Batley with many fields of engineering did not prevent them from being leaders in a number of different fields, both as inventors and as major suppliers. In particular, their interest in armaments machinery, both for heavy ordnance and for small arms, made them famous for their specialized machine tools. They were among the first makers of milling machines in Great Britain, and they pioneered the use of the capstan lathe in that country. They were exhibitors at many of the international exhibitions of the period, starting in London in 1862, when a machine with circular cutters for machining rifle muskets was described by the Jurors as showing the 'great ingenuity and originality of Greenwood and Batley' [9]. In 1867, although they did not show any machine tools at the Paris Exhibition, they were mentioned by the British Juror, John Anderson, as being one of the leading British machine tool firms [10] The tools made by the firm received prizes at the Philadelphia Exhibition of 1876, and at the Melbourne Exhibition of 1880, and in 1889 they demonstrated their strength in the field of heavy machine tools with an engine lathe made for Schneiders, which was described as the 'grandest machine in this class' (machine tools) by the United States

Commissioner to the Paris Exhibition of that year [11]. In 1900, with the general reduction in enthusiasm for international exhibitions, Greenwood & Batley were simply mentioned, with the other major machine tool firms, as 'conspicuous by their absence' [12].

Greenwood & Batley's importance as machine tool makers was shown not only by their success at international exhibitions, but also by the volume of their sales and the quality of their customers. They completed 4961 orders for machine tools (many of them for several individual tools) between 1856 and 1900, and these tools were sold to 653 customers. They received orders worth over £50,000 in both 1871 and 1886, and their normal yearly sales ranged between £15,000 and £30,000. While many of their tools were sold to British and foreign government arsenals, they also sold machinery to every British arms manufacturer, and to many of the most famous British engineering firms [13].

It is clear from this evidence that Greenwood & Batley were generally regarded as being one of the leading British machine tool firms, and as one of the most important makers of machinery for the production of armaments in the world. But for the purpose of considering trends in the productivity of the labour they employed, this evidence is not necessarily relevant. It is clear that high public regard for an engineering firm cannot necessarily be equated with best-practice production by that firm; the comments of Charles T. Porter on the production methods of the Whitworth company have often been quoted because they well illustrate the decline of a famous firm, but they also indicate how deceptive public regard could be [14].

There is however no evidence that Greenwood & Batley's production methods were as outdated as those of Whitworth; it is clear from the records of the firm that new machine tools were regularly brought into use in production, and although the financial administration of the firm was severely criticized after 1890, no similar criticisms were made of the quality of work. In an article in the *Financial Mail* in 1914, although the financial record of the firm was described as 'simply disastrous', the firm was also said to have 'a splendid name for quality. It is one of the best engineering works in Leeds' [15].

In other respects relevant to productivity measurement there is no evidence that Greenwood & Batley differed significantly from other firms in the industry. The engineering industry at this time was successfully unionized, and the rates of wages paid were common to all firms within each district, although there were minor regional differences [16]. Greenwood & Batley appear, from the evidence in the Minutes of the Board of Directors of the company, to have paid the rates of wages common in Leeds. The firm was also typical in adhering to the practice of neither giving nor receiving notice of leaving employment; a man could leave or be dismissed at any meal break, giving a highly flexible labour force. The labour force of the firm was certainly large by the standards of the engineering industry, but this reflected the range of products made rather than organizational differences.

In two respects the firm certainly was atypical. It made, firstly, many more types of engineering goods than was normal. In its internal organization, however, the production of each major type of product (for instance, machine tools) was segregated, so that it does not appear likely that the scale of the firm as a whole altered the conditions under which a particular product was manufactured; machine tool manufacture was carried out in separate shops in the works. The firm was secondly atypical in the closeness of its relationship with the government arms factories. The connection led to large profits for the firm, and it is possible that it also gave Greenwood & Batley access to new ideas and designs developed by the government engineers. It is possible that this gave the firm an advantage over other machine tool producers, but it does not seem likely that this advantage, if it existed, was very great, since any new ideas and designs were apparently quickly publicized in the trade press, and could be taken up at will by other firms.

Greenwood & Batley seem, therefore, to have ranked among the best-practice machine tool firms as far as technical advance and the quality of their products are concerned; in other respects, with the possible exception of their size and the number of products which they made, they do not seem to have been atypical in comparison with the leading firms in the industry. They are clearly unlike the smaller and less technically progressive firms in the industry who formed the tail behind the best-practice firms. Nor are they representative of the specialized firms making machine tools for such customers as the shipbuilding industry. Nevertheless, it is clear that Greenwood & Batley were consistently among the leaders of the machine tool industry in their working methods and in the quality of their products; in these circumstances, it is reasonable to regard the changes in labour productivity, which are observable in their records, as roughly representative of trends in best-practice machine tool production at this time. At the

least, the Greenwood & Batley data on labour productivity demonstrates what it was possible for one firm to achieve; at the most, if it
can be regarded as representative, it can provide some information on
the nature and causes of productivity change in British engineering as a
whole.

The records of Greenwood & Batley

The Greenwood & Batley records provide a great deal of information
that can be used to indicate trends in productivity in the manufacture
of machine tools. They consist of the order and cost books of the
partnership and the company, an unbroken series running from 1856 to
1900, and, in a different form, from 1900 to the present day. It is
possible to discover from these records, at the most detailed level, the
amount of work carried out on a particular order on a particular day,
and the records give details of the quantity and cost of labour and
material inputs on each order, total costs, weights, prices, and many
other data concerned with the customers of the firm.

The records have, however, one major deficiency from the point of
view of productivity analysis, in that it is impossible to estimate with
any accuracy the capital inputs. The aggregate financial records of the
firm, covering all aspects of their manufacturing, cannot be broken
down to reveal the capital inputs into machine tool production alone.
Secondly, while the number of machine tools made or bought for the
use of the firm is known with precision, it is impossible to allocate
these machine tools to any particular branch of the factory. Thirdly, the
method used by Greenwood & Batley itself to calculate the 'management' or overhead costs attributable to each order is unilluminating; the
method was to assume that these costs were equal to 100 per cent of
direct labour costs, although the firm itself was aware that, particularly
in times of full capacity working, overhead costs were very much less
than direct labour costs. It is unfortunately impossible to overcome this
difficulty by splitting the 'management cost' element into two parts,
overhead cost and a concealed profit, in accordance with an index of
the extent to which capacity was being utilized.

The records thus do not provide a useful indication of the capital
inputs into machine tool making by the firm. They provide information
on the cost and weight of each metal input, but the processing of this
data would have added approximately 25,000 items of data to a data
set consisting already of 135,000 items, and it was decided at an early
stage of the analysis that the metal inputs could be aggregated, and

total cost of materials and finished weight of the machine tool used as an adequate substitute.

A further difficulty is that some data were missing on a large number of orders. The exclusion of all orders for which any data were missing left a sample of over 2000 orders for the manufacture of 5551 machine tools, and it is on this reduced data set that the results given below are based. It is conceivable that this method of treating the missing data has introduced a bias into the results, but it is unlikely, given the large size of the data set that has been used, that any bias is serious enough to affect the results significantly.

The difficulties that have so far been described arose from the nature of the data and of the accounting methods of Greenwood & Batley. There are also, in the measurement of productivity change through these records, difficulties of greater theoretical complexity, stemming largely from the heterogeneity of the machine tool output of the firm. Greenwood & Batley made, in the period from 1856 to 1900, 793 differently named machine tools, of which 457 were ordered only once during the period. Many of the tools given different names were, of course, only slightly modified versions of general types, but it is clear that the lack of standardization revealed in these figures makes it necessary to proceed carefully in choosing a unit of output that is sufficiently invariant over time to use as a yardstick in the measurement of productivity change.

Two possible units of measurement of output are available, given the nature of the records; the number of machine tools made is known, and so is the net weight of each machine tool. Arithmetically either may be used as the numerator in a calculation of output per man-hour, but theoretically it is questionable whether either is sufficiently invariant; it may well be that quality change in machine tools between 1856 and 1900 was so great that implicitly to equate a machine tool built in 1856 with one built in 1900 makes productivity measurement based on such an assumption either ambiguous or meaningless.

Problems of aggregating output are, of course, common in economics, but the difficulties always encountered in dealing with such problems are compounded in the case of the machine tool industry by the fact that the output, a machine tool, is also an input into the productive process. Machine tools make machine tools. Thus an explanation or consideration of productivity change in the machine tool industry, embodied to some degree in the use of new machine tools in the productive process, may appear to run into the difficulty that by definition the output will be changing also, and that the rates of change of inputs and outputs will not necessarily be the same. It can be argued, however, that this difficulty is more apparent than real, in that the difficulty is caused by a verbal confusion. If one considers a machine tool that is being manufactured as a series of blocks of metal being machined and fitted together, and the machine tool that is being used in this process as a machine that is being used to machine metal, then it is possible to distinguish easily between machine tools as inputs and machine tools as outputs. If this can be admitted, then the difficulty of productivity measurement in the machine tool industry becomes one of discovering whether the machine tool (as a block of machined metal) was significantly changed over the period, even though its capabilities (as a machine for machining metal) obviously were.

There is considerable reason for arguing that such a distinction may usefully be made. It is clear from the treatises on machine tool development written by R. S. Woodbury, and from the recent history of machine tools by W. Steeds, that many of the innovations in machine tool design in the second half of the nineteenth century were of a very minor character in terms of changes in the physical appearance of the machine, although they gradually improved its efficiency and ease of operation [17]. In the absence of detailed engineering data, it is difficult to know how much difference was made to the process of manufacturing machine tools by such minor design changes (the introduction of totally new types of tools would clearly have made some such difference, but very few totally new tools were introduced by Greenwood & Batley, except at a very early stage in their operations, and this difficulty may safely be ignored). The probability is that minor design changes (for instance, the introduction of a new tool for a capstan lathe) did not make a great deal of difference to manufacture.

If a majority of the design changes were minor, and if they made little difference to the manufacturing process, then it is possible to utilize the distinction between machine tools as inputs and as outputs, and to measure productivity change through the records of Greenwood & Batley, using the weight of machine tools produced as the numerator in the calculation of production per man-hour. Further justification for such an attempt can be found in the certainty that any technical change in the period was positive, so that to assume that machine tools were the same in 1856 as in 1900 is to err on the side of caution, and to understate any improvement in the machine tool defined as a machine to machine metal. Furthermore, study of the Greenwood & Batley records demonstrates a close relationship, both in the long term and in individual years, between the weight and the price of machine tools, suggesting that the use of weight per man-hour as a measure incorporates the desired adjustment for quality change; this conclusion is supported by Professor Brady's findings for American machine tools [18]. It is clear that to use machines produced per man-hour as a productivity measure would, on the other hand, be misleading, because of the wide variety of machines produced, and this measure will therefore be used only for comparative purposes.

For all these reasons, it appears to be theoretically and practically justifiable to utilize the Greenwood and Batley data in the measurement of labour productivity; in the remainder of the paper the results of doing so are described and analysed.

Changes in labour productivity in the operations of
Greenwood & Batley.

As a first step in the use of the Greenwood & Batley data, yearly values were calculated for a number of variables relevant to the measurement of productivity change, principally measures of output relative to the factor inputs. In the absence of any adequate measure of capital inputs the 'margin cost' (total cost minus direct labour cost minus materials cost) was used as a substitute. Linear trends in these variables were then calculated over the forty-five year period (1856-1900), and these trends are presented in Table 1. Even with the large sample, some abnormal orders appear to have distorted some yearly results, but it can be seen from Graphs 1 to 4 that the linear trends calculated do not seriously misrepresent the underlying movements of the variables.

Calculation of compound growth rates on the basis of the linear trends shows that output per man-hour, expressed as cwts of metal produced per man-hour, rose by 2.4 per cent per annum over the whole period. If the hours worked are weighted by the wage rate of the worker, to standardize the labour input, the growth rate is 2.3 per cent. Over the whole period, this growth raised production per man-hour by approximately three times.

On the other hand, Table 1 also demonstrates that production of machines per man-hour fell during the period; the rate of change in machines produced per man-hour is −1.8 per cent per annum (or −1.5 per cent per annum if the labour input is weighted by wage rates). This is equivalent to a cut of one half in the productivity of labour,

TABLE 1
*Linear trends calculated in variables relevant to productivity changes,
Greenwood & Batley, 1856-1900*

Value added per cwt	$y_t = 3.57 + 0.001x_t$	S.E.E. = 1.24
Price per machine	$y_t = 47.49 + 3.27x_t$	S.E.E. = 49.68
Value added per machine	$y_t = 15.49 + 4.63x_t$	S.E.E. = 53.80
Weight per machine	$y_t = 5.23 + 1.47x_t$	S.E.E. = 26.86
Cwt per hour A	$y_t = 0.0097 + 0.0004x_t$	S.E.E. = 0.006
Cwt per hour B	$y_t = 0.0431 + 0.0017x_t$	S.E.E. = 0.271
Machines per hour A	$y_t = 0.00084 - 0.00001x_t$	S.E.E. = 0.00028
Machines per hour B	$y_t = 0.00369 - 0.00004x_t$	S.E.E. = 0.00118
Labour cost per machine	$y_t = 5.622 + 2.095x_t$	S.E.E. = 27.512
Labour cost per cwt	$y_t = 1.479 + 0.002x_t$	S.E.E. = 0.405
Metal cost per cwt	$y_t = 0.581 + 0.004x_t$	S.E.E. = 0.196
Metal cost per machine	$y_t = 2.256 + 1.064x_t$	S.E.E. = 19.27
Margin cost per machine	$y_t = 9.862 + 2.539x_t$	S.E.E. = 28.66
Margin cost per cwt	$y_t = 2.086 - 0.00075x_t$	S.E.E. = 0.897
Price per cwt	$y_t = 4.817 - 0.042x_t$	S.E.E. = 1.274

A. Denominator is the total number of hours.
B. Denominator is the number of hours weighted by the relative wage rates of each group of workers.
All prices and costs are in real terms.

measured in this way, over the forty-five year period. The explanation for this discrepancy in trends using different measures of output is that, as would be expected, the average weight of machine tools was rising, by 6.1 per cent per annum (or by 5 per cent per annum if the exceptional years 1856-8 and 1898-1900 are excluded). It is therefore clear that the average weight of machine tools was increasing over the period, but that each cwt of machinery was taking less labour, in terms of man-hours, to produce.

These two movements, the increase in the production of cwts per man-hour, and the fall in production of machines per man-hour, may be explained by the same factor, which stems from the nature of the machine tool as both the input and the output in the manufacturing process. It is likely that machine tools were, gradually, becoming more versatile and more efficient, but they were also becoming more complicated; they therefore took longer to make, although they themselves allowed the metal of which they were made to be machined more quickly and easily. The explanation for the changes in productivity that have just been observed may therefore be the effects of technical change, operating in this unique industry on inputs and outputs simultaneously. Labour productivity is thus both rising and falling, according to which measure of final output is used. But the

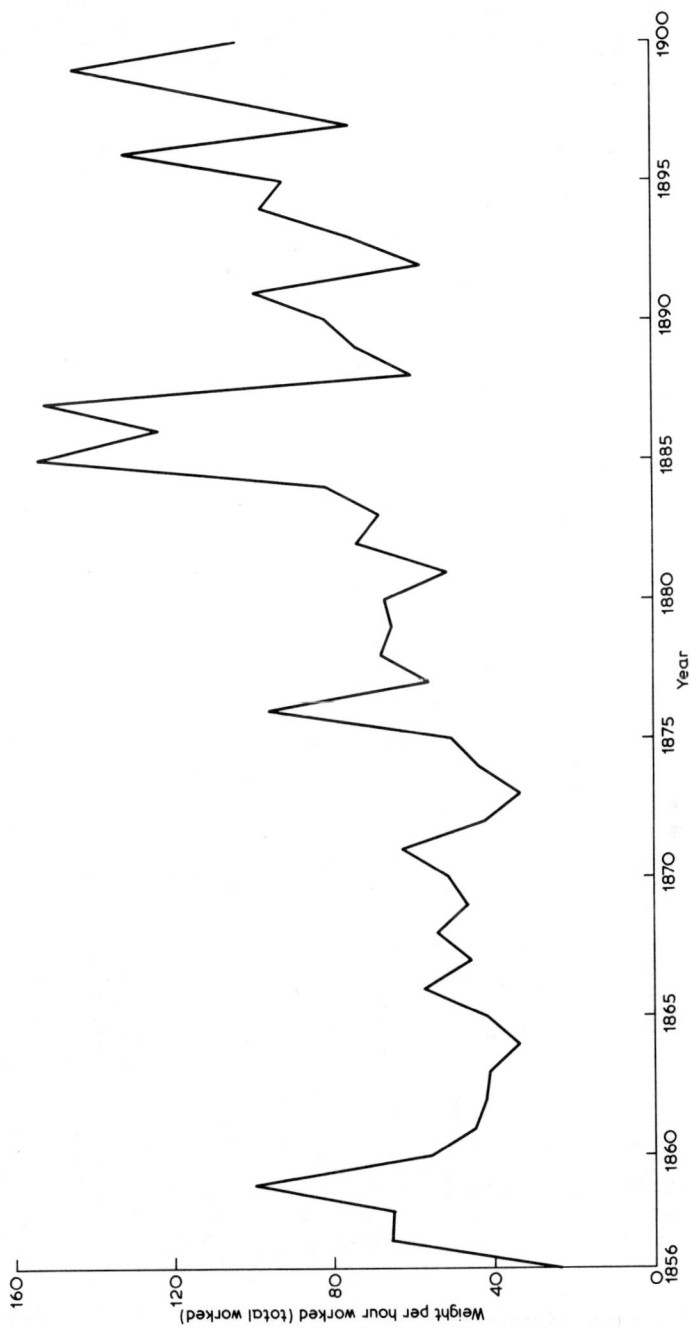

Graph 1 Weight per hour worked, in cwts, expressed as an index with base year 1859 (hours are total worked).

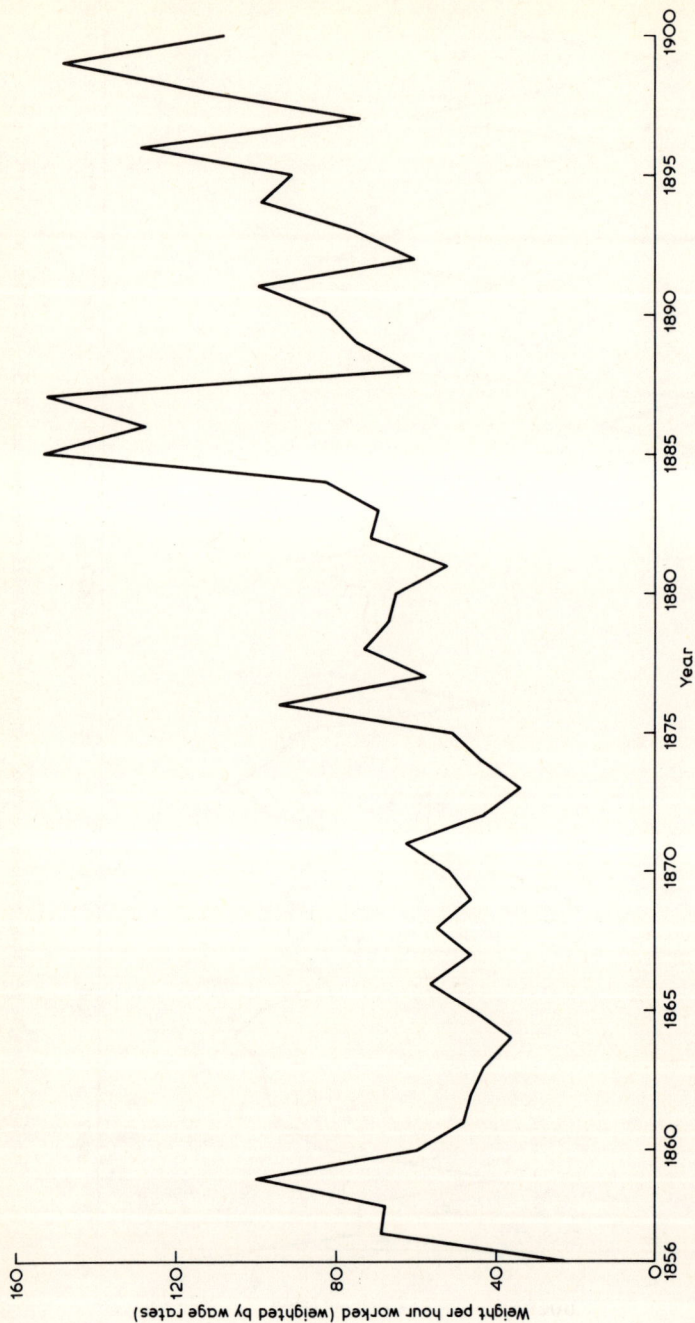

Graph 2 Weight per hour worked, in cwts, expressed as an index with base year 1859 (hours are weighted by wage rates of labour employed).

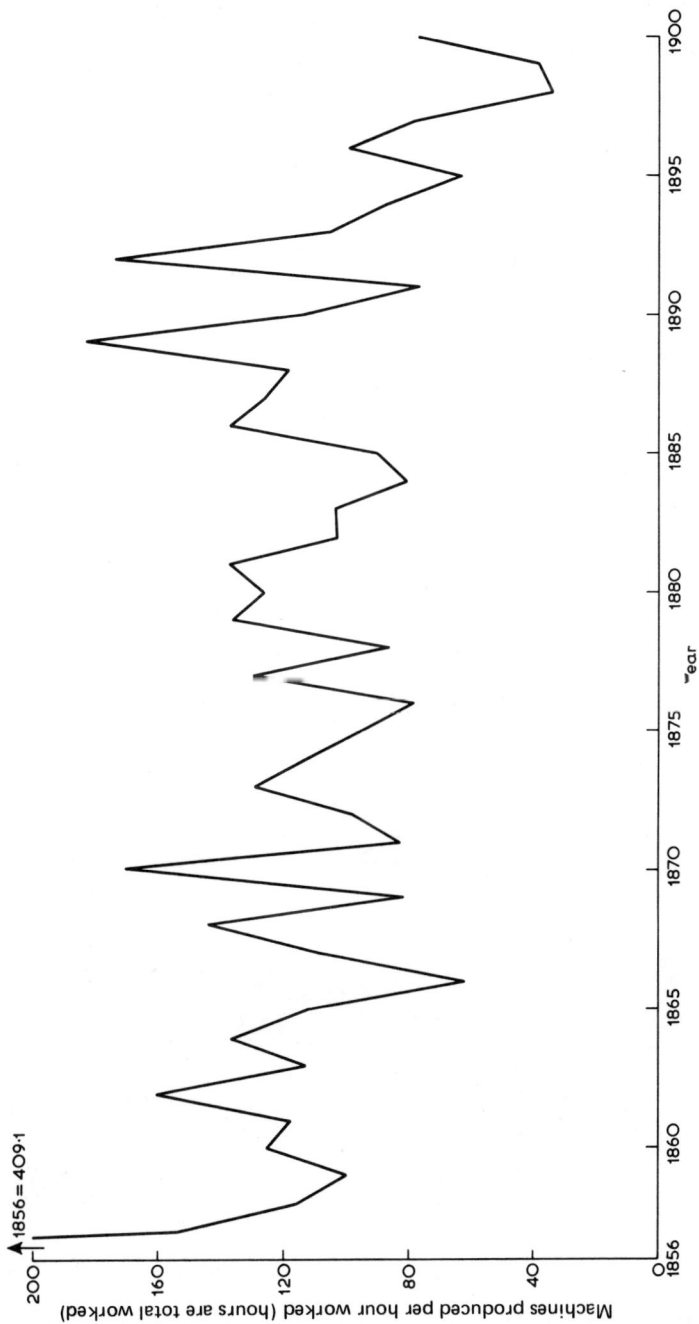

Graph 3 Number of machines produced per hour worked, expressed as an index with base year 1859 (hours are total worked).

327

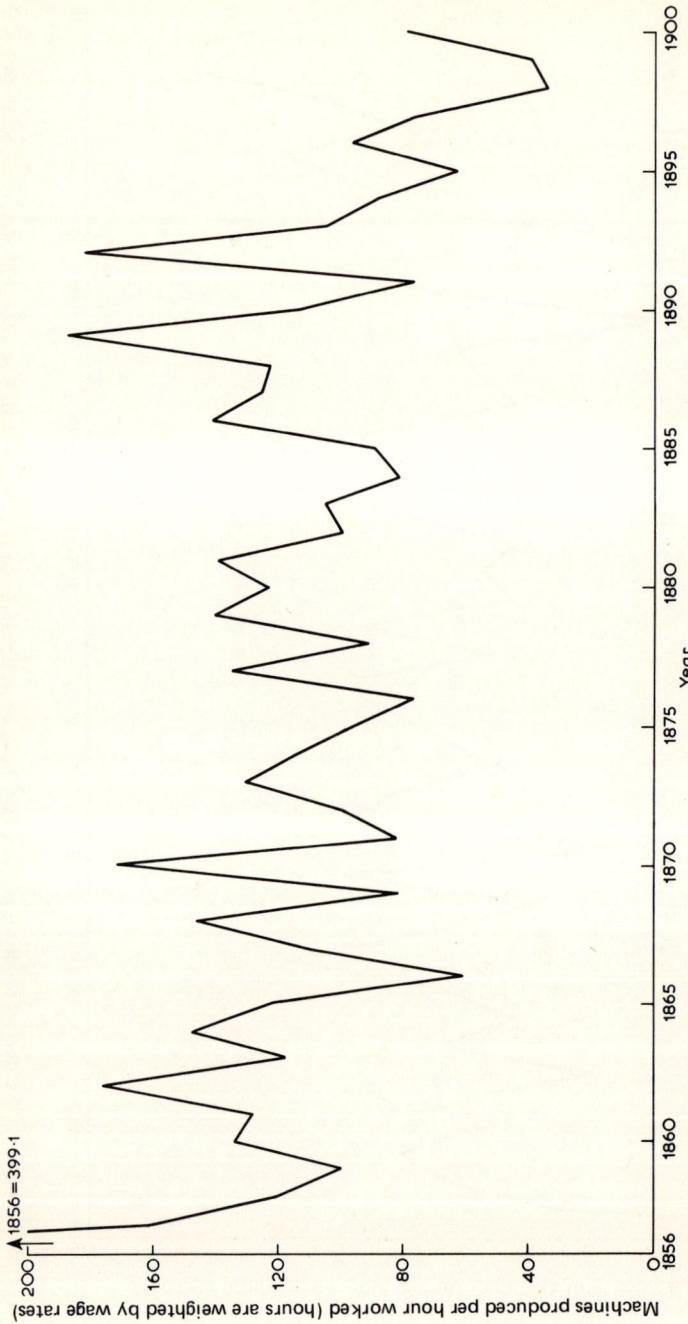

Graph 4 Number of machines produced per hour worked, expressed as an index with base year 1859 (hours are weighted by wage rates of labour employed).

efficiency of the firm in the machining of metal is rising, and it is this rising efficiency that could be passed on to the customers; they would be able to buy more efficient machine tools, produced more quickly than they would have been had the technical changes not taken place.

Before accepting this explanation, that technical change embodied in improved machine tools was the cause of increasing labour productivity, it is necessary to explore other possible causes of productivity change. In particular, since it is labour productivity rather than total productivity that has been measured, it is important to discover whether any substitution took place between the factors of production, increasing labour productivity at the expense of decreasing the productivity of capital, for example. Furthermore, there is the possibility that the increases in labour productivity were the result of economies of scale accruing to Greenwood & Batley as their machine tool business grew over the period.

Unfortunately, as has already been mentioned, the character of the accounting system of the firm makes it impossible to measure the capital inputs, and therefore the costs of such inputs, making it impossible to approach directly either the extent of, or the costs of, factor substitution in the form of the use of capital rather than labour. The accounting methods of the firm do allow the calculation of two measures, which throw some light on this question: the factor shares in final price and the remuneration and utilization of different types of labour.

The relevance of measurement of factor shares in final price is that, if factor substitution on a substantial scale took place in the operations of Greenwood & Batley, then such substitution should have been reflected in the remuneration of the different factors, in their shares in the final price of the products. In practice, the correspondence is unlikely to have been very exact, but there is no reason to think that there were any mechanisms at work that would, over the long run, seriously have distorted the predicted relationship. One possible source of stickiness in the shares, a failure of the share of labour to rise commensurately with improved personal productivity, seems unlikely to have occurred in this case, since the Amalgamated Society of Engineers was, at least until 1897, a strong and effective union.

Measurement of the factor shares is made difficult by the same deficiency in the accounts that makes it impossible to measure the capital inputs directly. The share accruing to capital has therefore to be calculated as a residual, and it includes expenditure on indirect labour and other overheads. This procedure is necessarily imprecise, but it is the only way out of the difficulty. The factor shares in final price, as mean shares over the period 1856-1900 were

Labour	36.4%	(coefficient of variability	14.8%)
Materials	16.1%	(„ „ „	39.1%)
Residual	47.4%	(„ „ „	14.8%)

and the shares are graphed in Graph 5.

It is clear that, over the forty-five year period, the factor shares were very steady, although there were some departures from the trend in particular years. It is possible that the residual category includes within it changes that, if they could be disaggregated, would alter this picture of stability. It is also possible that, if the firm was able to calculate its future prices on the basis of past experience of profits (as it probably could in some markets), an inherent stability in such prices and shares might result. A further difficulty is that expressed by W. G. Salter in the conclusions to his work on productivity and technical change, that 'relative shares are remarkably insensitive to factor substitution. . . . Large changes in the relative factor prices, or large differences in the strength of the opposing forces (as measured by the elasticity of substitution) are necessary to induce moderate changes in shares. Moreover . . . where there are more than two factors the change in relative shares is likely to be even less' (than those that Salter calculated for the two-factor case) [19].

In view of these difficulties, it would be unwise to conclude that the long term stability of the factor shares demonstrates the absence of factor substitution in Greenwood & Batley's works. At the same time, the stability of factor shares over such a long period suggests that any substitution of capital for labour, if it occurred, must have been slight in its effects, while the second set of evidence bearing on this point suggests strongly that factor substitution on a significant scale was not taking place. The firm had five different types of labour available for use in its operations, and it is likely that, if substitution of capital for labour had taken place, one of the motives for, and one of the consequences of, such substitution would have been changes in the utilization of these different types of labour. It is, of course, possible that organizational changes would produce reductions in the use of all types of labour, preserving the same relative usage but reducing the total labour input, but such changes are likely to have been of a once-for-all character, showing up as a sudden jump in labour

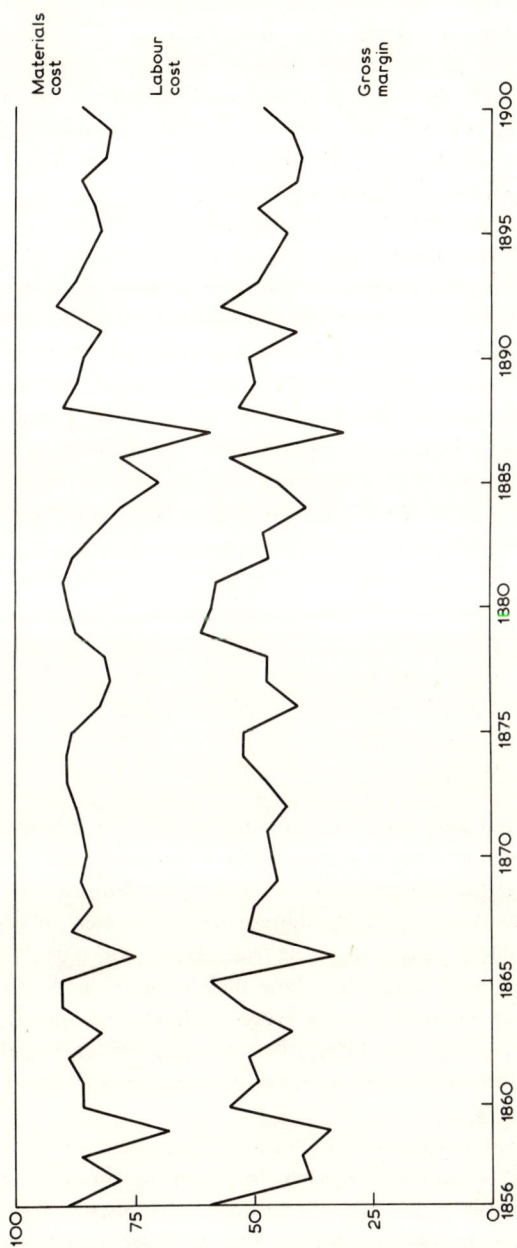

Graph 5 Factor shares as a proportion of final price, 1856-1900

productivity rather than as a long term trend. In all except unusual periods, therefore, one would have expected factor substitution to have affected the use made by the firm of different types of labour, particularly since the wage differentials would have constituted a considerable incentive to the firm to substitute less skilled for highly skilled labour; the desire of the employers to do this was the major cause of the nationwide engineering strike of 1897.

It is clear from Table 2, and by implication from Table 1, that very little if any substitution of one category of labour for another actually took place. The proportions of the total number of hours worked which are attributable to each category of labour remained remarkably constant over the whole period: Furthermore, the relative wages paid to the different groups also remained very constant; although wage increases were not granted simultaneously to each group, boys in particular lagging behind the adult groups, the differentials normally returned to their previous levels within a short time. As an illustration, relative wages paid to the five groups were, at the beginning and end of the period:

	1856	*1900*
Boys	10.1	9.5
Planers and borers	20.2	20.5
Turners and fitters	30.4	30.5
Boy joiners	10.1	9.5
Men joiners	29.1	30.5

It is possible that some form of concealed substitution was taking place; the titles given to different groups of labourers might, through inertia or tradition, remain the same while their tasks changed, but it is not easy to think of any form of substantial substitution of capital for labour that could, over the long run, affect all types of labour simultaneously, and could also allow such stability in the utilization and the relative wages of the five types of labour. The stability in the use of labour can therefore be regarded as further evidence against large scale factor substitution as a cause of the observed trends in the productivity of labour.

Another possible cause of the trends in labour productivity that have been observed is the possibility that the company was able to achieve economies of scale. It was argued by some contemporary observers that the achievement of such economies was one cause of the competitive

TABLE 2
Proportions of total number of hours worked
attributable to each section of the labour force,
Greenwood & Batley, 1856-1900

Year	Boys	Planers & borers	Turners & fitters	Boy joiners	Men joiners
1856	20	15	64	0	1
1857	27	20	51	0	2
1858	26	20	53	0	2
1859	20	21	52	1	6
1860	28	20	49	0	2
1861	30	20	45	0	4
1862	31	21	43	0	4
1863	26	20	50	0	4
1864	29	22	45	1	4
1865	31	20	46	1	2
1866	19	16	54	2	9
1867	22	22	53	0	3
1868	23	19	54	1	3
1869	22	16	58	1	3
1870	22	19	54	1	5
1871	22	15	59	1	3
1872	27	11	60	1	2
1873	27	9	62	1	1
1874	25	11	61	1	2
1875	25	10	60	2	4
1876	21	6	58	4	11
1877	29	8	56	2	4
1878	28	20	46	1	4
1879	19	33	44	1	4
1880	10	38	46	1	5
1881	17	34	45	0	3
1882	16	22	54	1	7
1883	24	18	55	0	4
1884	24	17	50	1	8
1885	21	17	52	1	8
1886	26	16	51	1	6
1887	21	19	53	1	6
1888	23	24	50	1	3
1889	24	19	54	0	2
1890	23	15	59	0	2
1891	22	16	58	1	3
1892	29	15	55	0	1
1893	23	14	59	1	3
1894	24	14	57	1	4
1895	19	19	57	1	4
1896	21	12	63	1	4
1897	21	12	63	1	3
1898	24	18	53	1	4
1899	23	18	54	1	3
1900	27	13	56	2	2

advantage held by the American over the British machine tool industry. Although this advantage is much more difficult to discern than those observers believed, and still more difficult to explain, the possibility that there were economies of scale in machine tool production cannot be dismissed.

Unfortunately, consideration of this possibility is hampered by the large amount of missing evidence in the Greenwood & Batley data. It will be recalled that the labour productivity calculations have been carried out using a data set from which observations with missing data have been excluded. Since the remaining sample size is still very large, it is unlikely that this has seriously affected the productivity calculations, but it clearly affects the measurement of economies of scale, since the scale (expressed either as numbers of machines or numbers of cwts produced) is affected by differential quality of the data in different years. Regressing cwts produced per man-hour on numbers of cwts produced gave an R^2 of 0.55, but little weight should be placed on this result.

It is also clear, however, that some necessary conditions for the achievement of economies of scale existed in the industry. For instance, Greenwood & Batley made some machine tools in considerable numbers, and there is evidence in the cost books of the beginnings of mass production of parts, at least towards the end of the period. A further reason for arguing that at least part of the increase in labour productivity may be attributed to economies of scale is that such an explanation would accord with the tendency for unit factor costs to move together over time, and for the use of different types of labour to remain relatively stable.

This discussion of the causes of changes in labour productivity revealed in the production of machine tools by Greenwood & Batley has been necessarily brief. Of the three major explanations of these changes – technical change, economies of scale and factor substitution – only the third can be fully examined, and only the third can be rejected as a major source of change. It seems likely, in fact, that this study must follow Salter in putting 'primary emphasis . . . on technical progress and economies of scale', and that Salter's conclusions, based on an analysis of twenty-eight industries in the twentieth century, are also applicable to a single firm in the nineteenth [20].

Discussion so far has been concerned with the causes of changing labour productivity. As to the results, it is clear that changes in the production of machine tools were passed on to those who bought the tools in two major ways. The engineering industry almost certainly received its tools at a slightly lower real price, although it is of course difficult to attribute this to productivity improvements rather than to other factors. But price per cwt of machine tools produced by Greenwood & Batley fell by 1.1 per cent per annum over this period, not so substantial a change as that in productivity, but, since it is a fall in real prices of machine tools, still giving a sizeable benefit to the engineering industry.

Secondly, since all the measurements of productivity and of price per unit have assumed, in the assumption that 'a machine tool' or 'a cwt of machine tool' is an invariant unit, that the quality of the machine tools produced by Greenwood & Batley remained the same between 1856 and 1900, the engineers who bought the machine tools were also receiving all the benefits of the increasing technical capabilities of the machine tools. They were getting not only machine tools at a lower real price, but the tools were being constantly improved at no cost to the consumer. Since Greenwood & Batley were only one among several best-practice machine tool makers at this period, and since it seems legitimate to assume that similar increases in labour productivity were being achieved by other firms in the industry, and similarly passed on to their customers, the British machine tool industry must have been making a substantial contribution to increasing productivity in the metalworking industries.

CONCLUSION

This paper has demonstrated many of the difficulties that are to be encountered in carrying the discussion of the British economy in the late nineteenth century down to the level of the individual industry or firm. In particular, the demonstration that one can discover both increasing and decreasing labour productivity, depending on one's choice of units of output, should reinforce doubts about the validity of some measurements of aggregate productivity that have been made for this period. On the other hand, it may be thought that the investment of time and effort in the measurement in detail of productivity of labour in one firm, while it may be more exact than aggregate discussion, does not necessarily take the argument much further.

Nevertheless, the evidence that has been presented in this paper, with its many admitted imperfections, suggests that one leading British machine tool firm was able to achieve, in its production of machine

tools and partly as a result of technical changes embodied in those
tools, an increase in labour productivity considerably higher than the
average for British industry as a whole. Furthermore, there are grounds
for believing, in the absence of evidence for substantial factor
substitution, that Greenwood & Batley were achieving considerable
increases in total productivity. Although it is still possible to argue that
British industry as a whole was unwilling to invest in new,
productivity-raising machinery, it is clear that one important, if not
vital, branch of industry was doing so. Furthermore, the tools made by
Greenwood & Batley, and by the other leading British machine tool
makers, were being sold in increasing numbers throughout the latter
part of the nineteenth century, as the work of Professor Saul has
demonstrated [21]. It is difficult, even with such precise data as that
afforded by the Greenwood & Batley records, to test Aldcroft's
suggestion that British industry was misallocating its investment and
concentrating on traditional lines, but in the machine tool field, and in
the engineering industry that bought the machine tools, it seems clear
that investment in technical change and in improved machinery was
achieving good returns.

NOTES

[1] Aldcroft, D. H., 'The Problem of productivity in British industry,
     1870-1914', in Aldcroft, D. H. and Richardson, H. W., *The British
     Economy 1870-1939*, pp. 126–9.
[2] Aldcroft and Richardson, op. cit., p. 7.
[3] Phelps-Brown, E. H. and Handfield-Jones, S. J., 'The climacteric of the
     1890s: a study of the expanding economy', *Oxford Economic Papers*, IV,
     1952.
[4] Coppock, D. J., 'British industrial growth during the "Great Depression"
     (1873-1896): a pessimist's view', *Economic History Review*, XVII, 1964-5.
[5] Aldcroft, op. cit., pp. 136–7.
[6] Aldcroft, op. cit., pp. 138–9.
[7] The bulk of the information in the succeeding parts of this paper is taken
     from my Oxford University D.Phil. thesis, *The Metal-Working Machine
     Tool Industry in England, 1850-1914, with special reference to Greenwood
     and Batley Ltd*. I am very grateful to Greenwood & Batley Ltd for their
     generous help and for permission to use their records, now deposited with
     the Leeds City Library. I am also grateful to Nuffield College, Oxford, for
     assistance in carrying out the analysis of these records. Above all, I am
     grateful to my supervisor, H. J. Habakkuk, for his advice and assistance at
     every stage in the preparation of my thesis.
[8] Shadwell, A., Engineering Supplement to *The Times*, 4 March 1908.
[9] London Exhibition, 1862, *Jury Reports* on Class VII, B, p. 5.
[10] *Report to Parliament on the Paris Exhibition of 1867* (P.P. 1867–8, XXX,
     pt II, 341), Report on Machine Tools by John Anderson, pp. 702, 722.

[11] *Report of the U.S. Commissioners to the Paris Exhibition of 1889*, vol. III, 'Machine Tools' by John H. Barr (Exec. Docs. House of Representatives, 1889-90, Washington, 1893), pp. 352–4.

[12] *Report of the Royal Commission to the Paris Exhibition of 1900* (P. P. 1901, XXXI, 1), Report by C. W. Burton, British Juror in Class 22, Machine Tools, p. 368.

[13] A complete breakdown of sales by Greenwood & Batley, by year, by country and by industrial group, may be found in my thesis referred to above, note 7.

[14] Porter, C. T., *Reminiscences of Life as an Engineer* (New York and London, 1908), pp. 115–134.

[15] *Financial Mail*, 4 July 1914.

[16] Ransome, J. S., 'Wages in the engineering trade' *Engineer*, vol. 81, 3 April, 8 May and 5 June 1896. Page, W., *Commerce and Industry* (London, 1919), p. 214.

[17] Woodbury, R. S., *History of the Gear-Cutting Machine* (Cambridge, Mass., 1958), *History of the Grinding Machine* (Cambridge, Mass., 1959) and *History of the Milling Machine* (Cambridge, Mass., 1960). Steeds, W., *History of Machine Tools, 1700-1910* (Oxford, 1970).

[18] Brady, D., 'Relative prices in the nineteenth century', *Journal of Economic History*, vol. 24, June 1964, pp. 164–166.

[19] Salter, W. E. G., *Productivity and Technical Change* (Cambridge, 1966), pp. 136–7.

[20] Salter, op. cit. p. 144.

[21] Saul, S. B., 'The machine tool industry in Britain to ¹914', *Business History*, X, 1, January 1968.

Chairman: P. Temin
Prepared Comments: M. Falkus

Falkus: Floud's argument involves four steps. First, there is an attempt to measure the growth of labour productivity in the firm from 1856 to 1900. Second, the growth is explained. Third, the question is raised of how representative this one firm is of the machine tool industry. Finally, the issue is raised of the performance of the British economy as a whole in the light of the experience of the machine tool industry.

Clearly, the key point is the appropriateness of the measures of productivity. A paradox in the paper is that the two measures presented yield opposite results: the number of machines per unit of labour fell over the period, whereas the weight of machines per unit rose. Floud rejects the first measure, and his reasons seem sufficient. What is worrisome is his acceptance of the second measure, which shows a 2.3 or 2.4 per cent growth per annum over the period. Consider, for example, the Graph 3 on page 327. It is quite clear that, if one breaks the trend into subperiods, productivity in terms of the weight of machines produced per man actually *fell* until about 1873 and stagnated until 1884. In 1885 apparently something quite spectacular happened, for productivity shot up. It is the high figures from this year onwards that give the impressive overall rates of productivity growth.

Several questions are suggested by these observations. Why was there a sudden improvement in productivity in 1885 and subsequent years? Was there some important technical improvement in the machine tools used in production? Presumably not, for we are told that few machines were developed by the firm after its early years and that design changes *gradually* improved efficiency and ease of operation thereafter. Was there, then, a relative increase in the demand for some especially heavy types of machines? It is relevant in this connection to point out the exceptionally low machine-per-man ratio in the critical year, 1885: in only six years previously had the ratio been lower. Some answer to this problem of the mysterious break in trend must be provided if we are to believe the index of weight of machines per man.

Furthermore, if we do believe it, there needs to be some explanation of why the trend in output per man ran precisely counter to that in other British industries; for it is well known that in these other industries there was a striking fall in the rate of growth of labour productivity after the 1870s or 1880s. Assuming that the measure is appropriate, the atypicality of the change in trend raises the question whether the experience of this one firm can in fact be generalized to the whole industry. Floud might perhaps have paid more attention to the subperiods, especially since the discussion of productivity in the British economy usually centre on changes in the the 1870s or 1890s, rather than on the trend, ignoring subperiods, over the whole of the second half of the nineteenth century. He might, too, have backed up the measure in terms of weight of machines per man with the available information on value-added and the prices of machines. This is especially important in view of the uncertain connection between the weight of machines per man and technical efficiency. As noted earlier, the demand for machine tools of different weights may well have changed without any change in efficiency.

The explanation of the productivity change needs further study as well. The basic proposition that improvements were due in part to technical change embodied in machine tools themselves is not proven convincingly. Economies of scale, for example, may well have contributed much more. And the quality of the labour input may have improved as the firm grew, drawing on the growing pool of skilled workers in Leeds.

Floud: It was to be expected that someone would raise the question of whether one should break the measure into various periods. The difficulty is choosing the periods and interpreting the results of a particular choice. The choice of the whole period is adequate for the task at hand — namely, measuring productivity over the long term.

Another point made by Falkus is that there may have been changes in the mix of machine tools, imparting a bias to the measure in terms of their weight. But the price per ton of machine tools, whatever their weights, was in fact constant over a wide range of weights of individual machine tools. This suggests that weight is a reasonable measure of machine tool output and does allow for changes in the mix of machine tools produced.

It is probably true, as Falkus argues, that the quality of the labour input improved, and the explanation of the productivity change given in the paper does not exclude this possibility. On the other hand, it is unlikely that it was a major influence on productivity, because the mix of skills used by the firm did not change very much over the period and it is unlikely that the quality of all types of labour improved uniformly, as would be necessary to accord with the lack of change in the mix. This proposition is difficult to test, but it does suggest that some other factor than the improvement in the quality of skilled labour was affecting productivity. The explanation of productivity change in the paper as due to technological improvements is, of course, a residual, as explanations of this sort must always be. It is, however, consistent with the qualitative evidence from the records of Greenwood & Batley and from the technical literature.

McCloskey: In his response Floud uses price as a touch-stone for the real value of machines. Why take this intermediate step? Why not construct an output measure by adding together the number of machines of a particular specification weighted by some base period prices? There are, to be sure, problems of changes in the quality of machines, but these can be handled, as they have been in recent studies of automobiles, by inferring from the prices of machines with slight differences what the economic value of the slight differences were.

Floud: The firm made 793 different machine tools. Several attempts to construct price indexes for various types failed because the firm usually made one, or at most five or six, tools of a given specification.

McCloskey: But is it really impossible to group the 793 into relatively homogeneous categories, to make some moves in the direction he had suggested? There is always a difficult aggregation problem, but there is apparently data for this firm to test whether it is a hopeless problem.

Temin: The question was whether most of the variance came within the broad categories – as seemed reasonable in this instance – or between them.

Edelstein: Dorothy Brady, in her study of the American machine tool industry, found that for a given price of a machine the power tended to increase over time and the weight tended to decrease.

Floud: She had, in fact, found virtually the same thing he had: in the one year for which there was evidence there was a constant price for each broad type of machine tool and after that price varies proportionally with weight.

Supple: It was true that machine tools were sold by weight. Falkus's point, though, is that what is being observed is an increase in productivity due to larger machine tools being demanded. The measure in terms of weight runs the danger of double counting because the output was the same as the input, namely bigger machines, which could have been made at any time, but were not demanded. Did one need bigger machine tools to produce bigger machine tools?

Floud: There was a difficult problem of the partial identity of input and output. The average weight of machine tools did rise over the period, because more tools were added to each machine, but it is not clear what happened to the weight of the machine tools used to make them. At the beginning of the period many machine tools were being made essentially with files: one started with a block of metal and made the tool by hand.

Supple: The key question is as follows. In the usual measurement of productivity one attempts to allow for changes in the quality of output. In Floud's paper the weight of machines is used as a measure of quality. It may be, however, that the machine tool industry had economies of scale to the weight of individual machines. What was measured through time, then, would not be an increase in technological knowledge, but spurious increases in productivity due to the change in the output mix.

David: The distinction Floud introduces between the output as a block of metal and the output as something useful to the consumer is not helpful. The issue is the other side of that raised by McCloskey. The block-of-metal approach taken by Floud probably arises out of a desire to measure productivity change in the productive process. But this neglects design changes that allow the firm to deliver a machine that is equally serviceable to the consumer as the old one, measured by price, yet requires less input. Why should one exclude product innovation from the measure? The paper uses a measure that assigns all the productivity growth to changes on the shop floor rather than to changes in the drafting room as well.

Harley: The problem raised by David was a quite general one in the study of engineering industries. In his own work on shipbuilding he had noticed, for example, that the use of the horsepower of marine engines as a measure of output misses the chief source of productivity change in the industry — namely, reduced coal consumption. There does not seem to be any way of collapsing the output characteristics into a single number. McCloskey's solution of using prices to isolate the value of certain characteristics is fraught with difficulties, especially when one is interested in change over time: there were 457 specifications of machines that occur only once in Greenwood & Batley's records.

Saul: There was another difficulty with the approach through prices. In modern studies of the armaments industry, for example, adding up the weights of airplanes would give, to be sure, misleading results. But adding up their values is liable to give misleading results as well, because the contracts will rarely be awarded on a truly competitive basis. The same difficulty may afflict measures in terms of value in Floud's case:

Greenwood & Batley were selling a good portion of their output to arsenals under non-competitive bidding.

Floud: He agreed with Saul. Another part of the Ph.D. thesis of which this paper is a part examines the firm's pricing policies and finds that it was involved heavily in price rings to set prices of machines sold to the government. The firm was selling the same tools at different prices to different customers. In the records of another firm there are exchanges of letters among the major government suppliers about agreements on the bids to be made for particular contracts. About 30 per cent of the value of Greenwood & Batley's output went to the British government and another 20 per cent to other governments buying specialized equipment from a handful of firms.

Engerman: The 50 per cent of output that was competitive might provide enough prices to run the regressions proposed by McCloskey on the characteristics of machines. On the larger issue of the performance of the industry, though, the criticisms of the measure of productivity make the argument Floud is putting forward stronger. Presumably he started with the number of machines as a measure of output, but decided this was inappropriate because weight captures the usefulness of the machines, as measured by price, better than the mere number of them. The alternative measure by weight, however, as David points out, omits part of the productivity change. Correctly measured, then, productivity growth would be even higher, and in terms of the larger issue of how the industry performed Floud's case is strengthened.

David: The bias may be in the other direction, for larger machines may have satisfied the uses to which consumers put them worse than small machines. In any case, the justification that Floud uses for the measure in terms of weight is that the weight of a machine reflects the difficulty of making it. The appropriate measure should reflect its usefulness to consumers. Detroit automobile manufacturers are now redesigning their product to make automatic welding possible, without changing its value to consumers. If output were measured by Floud's procedure, which adjusts for the difficulty of making the product, no productivity change would register, as it surely should.

Harley: David was misinterpreting Floud's purpose. He was not trying to allow for the difficulty of manufacture in his use of the weight of machines, but trying to capture the value to the consumer. He found that weight and prices were proportional at a given point in time and he did not have a homogeneous product whose price he could follow through time. Therefore he used weight to measure the output.

Mathias: Was there any evidence of increasing speed of machines? Speed, rather than horsepower or weight, might be a measure that could meet David's point.

Floud: Increases in speed waited on the development of harder steels. Such steels were introduced in the United States in the 1890s, but there was a delay in their introduction in Britain. When they came they forced the complete redesign of machine tools, but this was after the period under consideration.

Harley: There was a gradual increase in the speed at which marine engines were run throughout the period, related not so much to high speed steels as to steady improvements in ordinary steels. Was not the same sort of change occurring in machine tools? Marine engines, furthermore, were lighter, yet better, when made of steel rather than iron. Was this substitution occurring in machine tools as well? If it was, it would impart an upward bias to the measure of productivity change.

Floud: As far as could be ascertained from the engineering literature, the experiments in running machine tools at high speeds, largely American experiments, had little impact on average British practice before 1900. Machine tools used a great many different types of metal, but the Greenwood & Batley records do not distinguish the types. Admittedly, steel was probably used increasingly in preference to iron after 1880 or so.

Saul: The new materials, such as better steels, might have been easier to machine, giving an increase in productivity from the change in the material rather than from the factor emphasized in the paper, the change in machine tools used to make machine tools. This would give a downward bias to the measure, in the opposite direction to the one suggested by Harley.

Supple: He asked whether Falkus's earlier point that there was a spurt in measured productivity growth after 1885 would compel Floud to revise his argument that technological change was gradual in the industry.

Floud: The 2.4 per cent average annual increase in productivity cannot be interpreted to mean that in each year there was this increase without deviation. The spurts could reflect the variations in the price/weight ratio and in the rate of growth of productivity among machines, reinforced by variations in the composition of output. Over the long run, though, these variations even out.

Saul: Were some of the random movements in productivity the result of occasional long runs in orders of a particular machine tool, resulting in a temporary move down a learning curve for that tool? Greenwood &

Essays on a Mature Economy

Batley was a somewhat special firm in this respect. By the end of the century some other firms in the industry were concentrating on fairly long runs of fifty or sixty tools of a given type each year, whereas this firm continued to produce small orders. In other words, it was a jobbing firm, and changes in its productivity are not necessarily indicative of changes in the productivity of the industry as a whole.

Floud: The reasoning introduced by Engerman could be applied here: one would expect productivity change in the rest of the industry to be even higher than Greenwood & Batley's. Moreover, it is not entirely clear that the other firms were in fact producing in significantly longer runs. Alfred Herbert, the largest British machine tool firm nowadays, very rarely produces runs of more than five or six at a time. What is true now was truer still in the nineteenth century. The British machine tool industry was very largely based on small orders.

10

*Nihilistic impressions of British railway history**
WRAY VAMPLEW

I

Originally the intention of this paper was to investigate productivity on Scotland's railways between 1870 and 1900, in order to assess whether the railway sector shared the fate of the Scottish economy in general and slowed down in its rate of growth. Ample evidence exists to *suggest* that railway productivity growth was decelerating: increasingly adverse traffic patterns, high urban land costs for relocated termini, severe intercompany rivalry, the growing drag of interrelatedness, and unfortunate investment decisions in suburban railways and branch lines — 'more than half of the North British (the largest Scottish railway company) is made up of branches to mouldering old towns and cross lines over hills sacred to sheep and wandering botanists' [1]. Yet these facets of Scottish railway operations are not in themselves sufficient indication of declining or decelerating productivity; no definite statement can be made unless productivity is actually measured. Without quantification of inputs and outputs any remarks on productivity trends — no matter how substantial the data on which they are postulated — are mere hypotheses.

Essentially productivity is a measure of the efficiency with which inputs are converted into outputs. Often it is expressed in terms of output per man or per man-hour but the input is, of course, more than labour alone; and as the composition of the input most likely varies with time, partial productivity indices such as output per man are meaningless as measures of productivity change, except as indicators of the *direction* of the change and then only if the partial productivities for each input factor exhibit the same trend. Labour productivity could well rise through an expansion in the employment of capital equipment, though simultaneously the work force could utilize the equipment so inefficiently as to decrease overall productivity. As the late Dr Salter pointed out, 'we cannot divorce changes in the productivity of one factor from the productivity of other factors, or indeed, from all the elements in an interrelated economic system' [2].

---

* I am grateful to Dr Brian Mitchell of the University of Cambridge for valuable assistance in preparing this paper.

To obtain a meaningful productivity measurement it is necessary to relate output to all inputs. Still, since even modern transport economists, with all the statistical material at their disposal, find immense problems in considering all but labour and capital as inputs, it is surely reasonable for the economic historian similarly to limit himself and exclude purchases of coal and other intermediate products [3]. Not only the factor combinations changed with time; so did their prices and the price of the resulting output. As productivity is not the same concept as profitability, it is essential to allow for these price changes in the productivity index, so that the ratio between real output and real factor input can be established. This can be done only by constructing price indices for those aspects of the input-output factors measured in monetary terms. Obviously this raises many problems, not least the question of obtaining relevant data.

At first sight the chances of constructing a productivity index seem favourable for the Scottish railway historian is surprisingly well placed for source material. The voluminous records of the country's railway companies are retained in the Scottish Record Office, Edinburgh, along with a substantial compilation of family papers, happily indexed as regards references to railway enterprises. In addition, there are manuscript sources in the University of Glasgow, the Mitchell Library, Glasgow, and the National Library of Scotland, Edinburgh; this latter institution, being a copyright library, also contains a comprehensive collection of railway literature. Further surveillance, however, reveals this mine of information to possess seams of too low a quality to yield data adequate for constructing an acceptable productivity measure. Accordingly this paper's objective was changed from trying to measure productivity to explaining why this was not possible, and, leading from this specific failure, to commenting, with reference to recent work on British railways, on the statistical approach to economic history in general.

II

Turning first to the labour input, an immediate problem is the paucity of statistical information. Annual employment returns to the Board of Trade ceased after 1860 and quantified references in the company books after that date are few and far between. In any event, how valid would it be to assume that figures for any one company were illustrative of national trends? An alternative source lies in the occupational tables of the decennial population censuses but difficulty arises here from inconsistent occupational definitions, especially the tendency before 1901 to class an unspecified number of railwaymen in the ill defined group of 'labourers' and 'mechanics', and a failure to distinguish fully between construction and operating workers. Moreover, the figures apply only to single years that may not be typical; straight line interpolations could be made between the census years – as was done by Phelps-Brown and Handfield-Jones and accepted by Aldcroft [4] – but reference to an isolated employment return of 1884 suggests that this is liable to substantial (over 25 per cent) error [5].

Information on the hours worked – a more useful input concept than the numbers employed – by the railway servants is even more scarce. Theoretically the employees could be required to work twenty-four hours a day, though only rarely was anything near this level asked for. Still, systematic overtime was prevalent enough to render any assumptions of a standard working day invalid, and, unfortunately for the purposes of a productivity index, the extent of overtime was by no means uniform between occupations (affecting footplatemen, guards, shunters and signalmen more than platelayers or workshop employees) or geographically within the same occupation [6]. As information on the structure and geographical dispersal of the railway labour force in the years of this study is virtually non-existent, no realistic estimates can be made of the total hours worked. It is possible to calculate the wage bills of the various railway companies from their account books, but not knowing the number of men employed, their grades, or the rate at which overtime was paid, also renders this approach useless as an indicator of the hours actually worked.

In the absence of other information, however, the wage bill is the only feasible measure of labour input. Unfortunately, most of the reasons mentioned above operate against the creation of an index with which to deflate it so as to obtain figures for real labour input. How can weights be assigned without details of seniority or occupational and grade structures? How can allowances be made for fringe benefits, such as uniforms, houses and cheap travel, when there is no evidence of the number of workers to whom such benefits applied? The celebrated wages statistician, A. L. Bowley, believed that the construction of a wages index for railwaymen would be 'unlikely' [7]. How right he was, at least where Scotland was concerned; facts are hard to come by, usable information even more so. No staff records appear to exist for engine drivers, firemen or guards, and those for other grades are extremely fragmentary and thus perhaps atypical. Extensive research has yielded only two reasonably comprehensive sets of data on Scottish railway wages between 1870 and 1900, but unhappily they are for two consecutive years [8]. Otherwise all that has come to light are a few random references, which may or may not be typical. English wage data cannot be utilized in place of the missing Scottish information for it is generally accepted that 'throughout the entire period before the first world war, railwaymen in Scotland worked longer hours for less pay than their brethren south of the border' [9]. It is possible, of course, to construct a Scottish railway wage index, but this involves making several debatable assumptions: that the occupational structure changed uniformly between 1860 (the last year in which information is available from the Railway Returns) and 1891 (data from the *Abstract of Labour Statistics 1901*, LXXIII), continuing its trend thereafter at the same rate; that wage rates rose linearly between known points; that known wages were representative of the more numerous unknown ones; and that no allowances can be made for seniority. The validity of using such an index for deflationary purposes remains a question of conjecture and conscience.

TABLE 1

Labour input on Scottish railways 1870-1900 (1870-80 = 100)

	(A)	(B)	(C)	(D)
1870-80	100	100	100	100
1875-85	117	119	115	119
1880-90	141	135	130	138
1885-95	161	166	170	193
1890-1900	190	181	185	203

(A)   Men employed (straight line interpolation of census data).
(B)   Undeflated Wages Bill (calculated from company accounts).
(C)   Wages Bill deflated by Scottish Railway Wage Index.
(D)   Wages Bill deflated by U.K. average money wage (Mitchell and Deane, *Abstract of British Historical Statistics*).

Table 1 illustrates the variations in labour input obtained by varying the available evidence and the assumptions applied to it. There is some measure of agreement in the indices, especially in the early part of the period, but, given the unsatisfactory nature of their construction, this may be nothing more than coincidence or the influence engendered by the nearness of the starting date. The assumptions made probably render variant (*C*) extremely inaccurate and variant (*D*) is of dubious utility unless Scottish railwaymen kept pace in the wages race with other workers both north and south of the border. All that we can be reasonably sure of is that the labour input increased and it would have been most unexpected had it not.

III

The first step in estimating the input of capital is to calculate the annual capital expenditure of the companies, and from that obtain an estimate of their capital stock at any point of time. Of course, because of the longevity of most railway assets, to do this requires the tracing of capital spent long before 1870. Unfortunately, although the collection of accounts in the Scottish Record Office is fairly complete, the lack of standardization within the books makes for difficulties in their interpretation. As late as 1867 a Royal Commission could state that 'each company is at liberty to adopt the form it considers most convenient, and to vary that form from time to time' [10]. Happily, following this report, accounts became standardized by Act of Parliament and their interpretation becomes much easier. Until that time, however, personal judgement decided the format of the accounts, with the result that there was little uniformity between companies or even over time within the same company. Contemporary statements about the two leading companies in Scotland will illustrate the difficulties of using these early accounts. In 1850 *The Times* reckoned those of the Caledonian to be in 'just such a tangle as one might dream of after supping on lobster salad and champagne', and later in the century a lesser chronicle, with the benefit of hindsight, claimed that the 'North British accounts are intelligible only back to 1866. Before that it was the deluge pure and simple.' [11]

The strong element of personal discretion in the early accounts also allowed fraud occasionally to rear its head. In Scotland the prime example was on the North British where an inquiry subsequent to the discovery of malpractice yielded the following confession of company morality:

> *Question*: Have the annual accounts as laid before the share-
> holders been systematically cooked so as to mislead them
> as to the true position of the revenue and expenditure of

the company, and simply to exhibit an ability to pay the dividend desired by Mr Hodgson (the Chairman), regardless of the free revenue of the company being adequate for the purpose?

Answer: (from the company accountant): Yes, that has been the plan.

The unhealthy financial position of the company was consequently hidden from the shareholder by 'a careful and most ingenious fabrication of imaginary accounts' [12]. Fortunately, references to the auditors' reports in such instances of known fraud enable the accounts to be adjusted, though of course the extent of undetected malfeasance is open to conjecture.

Bearing these pitfalls in mind, the accounts can then be examined. From the capital accounts items that are not strictly of a capital nature must be eliminated: these include purchases of existing railway assets, expenditure placed in the account as a result of amalgamations, subscriptions to other companies for which separate accounts exist, capitalization of arrears of interest on dividends together with all nominal additions to capital made on the conversion or consolidation of stocks, capitalization of revenue account deficits and the repayment of loans. To the residue must be added entries in the revenue accounts that economists would normally class as capital spending; these include replacement and renewal of equipment and, more controversially, expenditure on repairs (deducting internal labour costs so as to avoid double counting), this being justified by there being no essential difference on the expenditure side, apart from altering the spending pattern, between replacing a worn out asset at a specific point of time and gradually replacing it over a period of time. Although the annual Railway Returns include data on repairs and renewals (for track and buildings from 1854 and for carriages and wagons from 1860) the more time-consuming method of searching the original accounts yields much better results. This is because assumptions have to be made as to what proportion of the amount recorded in the Returns can be taken as representing capital expenditure; reference to the actual accounts shows that this was not constant either over time or between companies.

Not all companies possessed comprehensive records in their early days and others appear to have died intestate. Much of the relatively small deficiency in information after 1845 can be made up from the summarized accounts published in the railway journals. These do not allow all the incorrect entries to be sorted out, but it is possible to exclude two major sources of potential trouble, namely subscriptions to other companies and the purchase of existing assets. However, this still leaves several gaps as regards pre-mania capital formation. Fortunately a Parliamentary return exists giving the amounts of money spent by individual railway companies in each triennial period ending 1 January 1841, 1844 and 1847 [13]. A few companies misinterpreted the instructions and gave all expenditure before 1841, but this can be allowed for by reference to the existing accounts and the appendices to the Select Committee Report on Railway Acts Enactments [14]. Figures for capital expenditure in the periods 1838-40, 1841-3 and 1844-6 can therefore be obtained. A total for the period 1831-7 can also be derived from the same sources, together with the appendix to the Report of the Select Committee on Railways of 1839 [15].

The problem then arises of how to produce annual estimates of capital expenditure from these statistics relating to periods of years. One way is to distribute the known expenditure in proportion to the capital authorized each year on the grounds that the money authorized would eventually be raised and spent, and that this would usually take place in the years immediately following the authorization. Allowance has to be made for abortive projects, but a more important problem is what lags to adopt between authorization and spending. Much depends on whether a new company was being set up or whether the authorization was for an established company determined on expansion. Surviving accounts, if typical, suggest that in the former case a pattern of expenditure of 12, 30, 35 and 23 per cent in successive years, and in the latter 20 and 80 per cent, would not lead to serious error, especially when over 70 per cent of the expenditure before 1843 and nearly 80 per cent before 1846 is directly traceable.

From 1843 the Railway Returns give statistics of paid-up capital, which can be used in conjunction with the surviving accounts to complete the estimate of capital expenditure. This was done by assuming that the companies for which accounts exist were representative, and then working on the basis that the ratio of their capital spending to their paid-up capital (after deductions for subscriptions to other companies, etc.) would hold for Scottish railways as a whole. As in all years the known capital expenditure group accounted for well over 90 per cent of the total paid-up capital, the degree of error emanating from these assumptions should be small.

So far so good: the estimate made is substantially accurate, especially after 1870; but at this stage two major problems emerge: those of price deflation and depreciation, both of which serve to shatter any illusions as to the feasibility of obtaining a reasonable capital input index. Brian Mitchell kindly supplied me with his indices of British railway construction costs 1831-1919, but they are, as he freely admits, rough and ready, especially in the case of rolling stock, where no account is taken of increasing technical sophistication. Moreover, he assumes constant weights throughout the period; this is unavoidable (because of data difficulties) but unlikely. The relevance of these British indices to the Celtic fringe of the United Kingdom is arguable, especially in the 1890s when the trend of Scottish railway investment was almost the inverse of the British experience. However, statistical information on the costs of railway building in Scotland is not good enough to allow the construction of a separate Scottish index. This is more feasible for rolling stock and differences were found, some of them significant. As to the question of capital erosion, it is essential that different depreciation rates be applied to different assets, otherwise serious error could arise from the concentration of invest-ment on one particular type of asset at a particular period of time. Estimates can be made of the longevity of the various assets; for rolling stock, statistics in a suitable form are conveniently available, but for permanent way material many assumptions are necessary, not all of them as convincing as the others [16].

TABLE 2

Capital input on Scottish railways 1870-1900 (1870-80 = 100)

	(A)	(B)	(C)	(D)	(E)
1870-80	100	100	100	100	100
1875-85	108	113	115	110	108
1880-90	115	120	121	126	123
1885-95	128	137	138	137	136
1890-1900	139	146	152	143	145

(*A*) Straight line depreciation over 25 years.
(*B*) Straight line depreciation over 50 years.
(*C*) Depreciation using normal distributions around assumed average lives; permanent way 15 years; locomotives 25 years; other rolling stock 30 years; stations and trackbed 100 years. Spending patterns of estimated expenditure assumed to follow the norm of known patterns (this is open to error where lines were worked by other companies).
(*D*) Deflated by Mitchell's railway construction cost index.
(*E*) As (*D*) but use of a separate Scottish rolling stock index.

As with the labour input, a table is provided to demonstrate the influence on the estimated capital input of varying assumptions as to depreciation and price adjustment. Again, little can be said. Given the inability to know how representative the data were on which the assumed average lives were calculated, who can tell whether or not straight line depreciations yield more accurate results than the more time-consuming method of variant (*C*)? As to the price deflation, which will produce the greater imprecision – an undeflated series that is known to be tolerably accurate, or one deflated by an index, perhaps adequate for England but certainly not so for Scotland? Given these unknowns, is it not a waste of time and effort to try to produce a capital input index both depreciated and price adjusted, since there would be no way of knowing if the results were anywhere near the actuality?

IV

The difficulties of measuring railway output are no less formidable than those involved in quantifying the input. Several aspects of railway product are quantifiable but all are subject to serious deficiencies. The Railway Returns give figures for both the total tonnage and the number of passengers carried, but, apart from passenger-miles in the 1850s, there is no indication of the distance travelled (occasional statistics exist for some companies, but how representative are either the figures or the companies?); both measures are thus open to gross inflation through the opening of one short but intensively used line, such as the Glasgow Underground in the 1890s. Anyway, how can the two be added? How many passengers equal a ton of freight? Train-miles run perhaps solves this problem but it, too, is subject to artificial distortion; if, for a given input, more miles are run but less carried, has productivity increased?

These physical measures at least avoid the deflation problem that the use of receipts as an output index would involve. In fact, it is impossible to construct a realistic railway price index: weighting as regards the class of passenger and type of good is feasible, but the critical question of what rates were charged is unanswerable. Few rate books have survived and those that have bear little relationship with reality, most companies by the 1890s agreeing with the Glasgow and South Western that 'the bulk of our traffic, passing both locally and through, is carried at exceptional rates' [17]. Unfortunately, most exceptional rate books appear to have. been destroyed when new arrangements superseded the existing ones. A final problem as regards rates is the allowances made to traders who supplied their own wagons; we do not know how many private wagons existed, or how far they ran, an important omission since the allowance varied with mileage. Lastly there is the perplexing problem of changes in the quality of railway output such as the size of wagons, the speed of trains, the frequency of services, the introduction of dining cars and sleeping compartments, and the provision of toilet facilities. All of these are amenable to some form of measurement but they are only aspects of railway output; how can we total them together? Consumer satisfaction is perhaps the only common factor but this is not fully measurable; saving time might save money, but what is a corridor train worth to a weak-bladdered passenger?

TABLE 3

Output on Scottish railways 1870-1900 (1870-80 = 100)

	(A)	(B)	(C)	(D)
1870-80	100	100	100	100
1875-85	112	117	122	118
1880-90	121	133	155	123
1885-95	136	156	192	140
1890-1900	160	181	246	164

(*A*)   Total gross receipts.
(*B*)   Tons of freight.
(*C*)   Number of passengers.
(*D*)   Train-miles run.

Again, a table is provided showing the indices obtained by making different assumptions as to what constitutes railway output. The wide disparity between the variants speaks for itself as to the impossibility of obtaining a realistic output measure.

V

What I hope that this paper has shown is not that Scottish railway productivity was immeasurable, but that it was not measurable with any degree of precision. I would now like to suggest that this inaccuracy renders the measurement *absolutely* useless as regards throwing light on productivity trends. It is possible to construct a range of productivities by permutating the input and output variants, but it is impossible to say which end of the spectrum lies nearer the truth, or if the true productivity is within the spectrum at all. Too often economic historians, not merely econometricians and their fellow travellers but any of us who utilize quantified information, seem to believe that any measurement is better than no measurement. Aldcroft's use of the labour productivity estimates of Phelps-Brown and Handfield-Jones to suggest that 'productivity on the railways remained practically stationary in the three or four decades before 1914' is a case in point [18]. Another is Hawke and Reed's analysis of the impact of regional railway development on the capital markets of Britain. They cheerfully present an argument based on the statistics of paid-up capital as given in the Railway Return, ignoring (because the figures are not presented in the Returns until 1890?) any nominal adjustments to capital before the last decade of the nineteenth century. When these do appear they reveal a startling disparity between the regions — nominal capital accounted for over 16 per cent of capital in Scotland's railways but less than 5 per cent of that of English and Welsh companies — which surely must affect their earlier discussion [19].

Many historical questions are unanswerable without reference to statistical data, but will we necessarily obtain the correct answers by using inaccurate information? Surprisingly, the answer to this question could be 'yes'. In this particular case of Scottish railway productivity, second best theory would suggest that it is feasible for the most inaccurate input and output series to yield a productivity index nearer the truth than if one measurement were perfect and the others inaccurate. This line of reasoning most likely applies to any historical study in which a mass of numbers is being reduced to a few. Should we therefore become utterly nihilistic in our approach and reject any arguments based on statistics that are not perfect? Surely this would be the end of economic history.

The way out of this dilemma, so long as we would be satisfied with establishing orders of magnitude rather than absolute rankings, could be to bias all our assumptions against the hypothesis that is being tested. Yet I would suggest that in many, if not most, cases this would prove impossible to do because we do not know how typical are the samples of data on which we base our estimates. Fogel, in his conceptually brilliant book on American railways, attempted to bias all his results in an upward direction, so as to increase the probability that his

calculations of the savings brought about by the railways was above
rather than below the true figure [20]. But did he really achieve his
aim? For example, one of his assumptions was that the average rates
(water and rail) for wheat and corn were equal to the Chicago-New
York rate on wheat. However, McClelland has since argued that this
rate, at least so far as water transportation is concerned, was by no
means representative and seriously understated the costs of U.S. water
transport and hence the savings of the railway alternative [21]. Most of
us are so glad to obtain any quantitative evidence at all that we use it;
perhaps with a qualitative comment on its chances of being representative, perhaps not. But unless it is a perfectly random sample, are we
not akin to the pollsters who predict a 100 per cent swing on the basis
of the first result? That information survives is no indication of its
typicality.

Recent railway history yields several examples of the use of isolated
data without any indication of how representative the information
might be. I may well be doing Dr Hawke an injustice in suggesting that
most of his examples of management attitudes toward pricing policy
are solitary ones — I appreciate that publishers insist on space limitation — but Brian Mitchell's method of estimating the output of the
engineering industry in the late 1840s is surely open to question [22].
How reasonable is it to hope that the proportion of wages to output in
1907 held good for the mid-nineteenth century? To be fair to Dr
Mitchell, he does allow for a potential error of 33 per cent in his results,
though he then discusses his results as though there was no error [23].
Mitchell also relies on a single piece of evidence in calculating the
demand for track renewal. This was an estimate of Lowthian Bell's that
the average life of iron rails was ten years. My own research on
Scotland's railways has shown that the picture is decidedly more
complex than Bell would have had us believe [24]. Still, to maintain
my line of argument, who knows how typical was Scotland's
experience? Should it be felt that I am merely taking an opportunity to
criticize others, may I point out that my own past record is no better
than those I have been taking to task? Perhaps I can illustrate this by
listing the assumptions necessary to my calculations of rolling stock and
permanent way demand for iron.

(1) Rolling stock of the minor companies bore some relation to
    train-miles run.
(2) Locomotives had a life of 25 years; carriages and wagons 30 years.

(3) Before 1861 all scrapped vehicles were replaced.
(4) Before 1850 there was some relationship between the numbers of locomotives and the numbers of other rolling stock.
(5) Locomotives and tenders consisted solely of iron and steel.
(6) All carriages were second class and all non-coaching stock were mineral wagons.
(7) Rolling stock built by R. & Y. Pickering was typical of that used on Scottish railways.
(8) Over time the ratio between tare weight and the amount of metal used remained constant.
(9) Companies did not stock materials substantially in advance of use.
(10) The ratio of sidings to track mileage was constant before 1867 and was typified by the ratio on the Caledonian. Between 1867 and 1904 the ratio rose linearly.
(11) The Caledonian was also representative in the age of its rails in 1866-7, in replacing all the components of the permanent way at the same time, and in introducing fishplates and longer rails.
(12) The average weight of rails and chairs increased linearly between known points.
(13) The ages of rails quoted by contemporary authorities were realistic.
(14) Renewals were normally distributed around an asssumed average age.
(15) The general pattern of the adoption of steel rails was illustrated by the Glasgow & South Western and North Eastern railways.
(16) Train-miles run reflect the intensity of use of a railway system and affected the general trend of the expected life of a rail.

One reviewer described my methodology as 'ingenious'; my dictionary defines this as meaning either 'skilful' or 'curious in design or contrivance', I have not yet had the courage to ask him which meaning he was applying to my study.

My final point is that, given the imperfect nature of our information, we have no idea whether sophisticated statistical techniques bring us any nearer the truth than simple arithmetic. Shortages of data may well exercise our ingenuity but is it merely an academic exercise?

NOTES

[1] *The Rialto*, 30 March 1889.
[2] W. E. G. Salter and W. B. Reddaway, *Productivity and Technical Change* (Cambridge, 1966), p. 3.

[3]   See, for example, B. M. Deakin and T. Seward, *Productivity in Transport* (Cambridge, 1969), Applied Economics Occasional Paper No. 17.

[4]   E. H. Phelps-Brown and S. J. Handfield-Jones, 'The climateric of the 1890s: a study in the expanding economy', *Oxford Economic Papers*, 1952, p. 294. D. H. Aldcroft, 'The efficiency and enterprise of British Railways, 1870-1914', *Explorations in Entrepreneurial History*, vol. 5, no. 2, 1968.

[5]   *Parliamentary Papers*, 1884, LXX.

[6]   *S.C. Railway Servants (Hours of Labour)*, 1890-1, XVI.

[7]   *Journal of the Royal Statistical Society*, vol. 69, 1906, p. 119.

[8]   *S.C. Railway Servants*, loc. cit.; *Abstract of Labour Statistics 1901*, LXXIII. p. 153.

[9]   P. S. Bagwell, *The Railwaymen* (London, 1963), p. 139.

[10] *R.C. Railways*, 1867, XXXVIII, xxiii.

[11] *The Times*, 30 September 1850; *The Rialto*, 30 March 1889.

[12] *Report of Committee of Investigation*, 14 November 1866.

[13] *Parliamentary Papers*, 1847, LXIII.

[14] *Parliamentary Papers*, 1846, XIV.

[15] *Parliamentary Papers*, 1839, X.

[16] See for example W. Vamplew, 'Railways and the iron industry: a study of their relationship in Scotland' in M. C. Reed (ed.), *Railways in the Victorian Economy* (Newton Abbot, 1969).

[17] *Herepath's Railway Journal*, 18 March 1893.

[18] Aldcroft, op. cit., p. 160.

[19] G. R. Hawke and M. C. Reed, 'Railway capital in the United Kingdom in the nineteenth century', *Economic History Review*, vol. XXII, no. 2, 1969.

[20] R. W. Fogel, *Railroads and Economic Growth* (Baltimore, 1964).

[21] P. D. McClelland, 'Railroads, American growth, and the new economic history: a critique,' *Journal of Economic History*, vol. XXIX, 1968, pp. 105–6.

[22] G. R. Hawke, 'Pricing policy of railways in England and Wales before 1881', in M. C. Reed, op. cit.

[23] B. R. Mitchell, 'The coming of the railway and United Kingdom economic growth', *Journal of Economic History*, vol. XXIV, 1964, p. 22.

[24] W. Vamplew, loc. cit.

Chairman: P. Mathias

Prepared comments: P. Deane

Deane: Vamplew's paper is a poignant document. He started out with the object of trying to produce a *definite* answer to the question whether the productivity of the Scottish railway sector slowed down over the period 1870-1900 – a modest enough question, one might think. He prudently adopted a limited definition of productivity by focusing on the labour and capital inputs and setting aside the land and raw material elements of input. He was confronted with a gratifyingly voluminous, well indexed and relatively comprehensive set of railway company accounts and other relevant sources. And he had the benefit of prior consultation with a research worker who had already mounted an assault on these materials. But in the end, after following a laborious trail, made increasingly uncertain by a multitude of unsignposted choices of method and sickening gaps in the data, he ends (or rather he gives up short of the end) by wondering whether his journey was more than an academic exercise.

Those of us who have stumbled through this kind of statistical morass, applied debatable assumptions to dubious data, leapt blindly over the gaps, and after much tedious calculation got back to a number we might have drawn out of a hat, will appreciate his agonies. Happily, the sensation of being completely adrift tends to fade when the results of the calculations achieve the sanctity of the printed word, but there is always a painful recurrence whenever an interested reader shows signs of either probing the methodology or trusting the conclusions, or indeed whenever one has occasion to retrace any part of the trail oneself.

However, what really piles on the agony is the delusion that historical quantification is ever likely to lead to a *definite* result, a precise or conclusive answer, to any of the really interesting questions that economists are likely to ask. What we may hope to do with it is to make conceptually consistent use of a great deal more quantitative or semi-quantitative information than could be taken account of by non-statistical techniques of analysis, and by this means to throw some light on the traditional hypotheses and possibly to suggest hypotheses that might never have emerged from the traditional analysis. True, a different set of assumptions applied to the same basis of information might lead the investigator to a totally different conclusion. But it is always true, whatever the methodology, that where the information is incomplete, different people will produce differing interpretations of the 'truth'. The advantage of the systematic quantitative approach is that the assumptions are more explicit and, to the extent that the researcher spells out his assumptions, those who differ can see exactly when and why they differ.

Vamplew is not really doubting the value of the statistical approach to history *per se*, but merely trying to probe the limits of its usefulness. It turns out that the question he chose to answer runs into extremely intractable conceptual and statistical problems. The economic concepts of input or output are not clearly reflected in the figures that appear in the railway company accounts. The supporting data that might make it possible to adjust these statistics so as to approximate the desired concepts are incomplete, unrepresentative, or simply non-existent. The more elaborate the method adopted to manipulate the data, the longer is the list of effectively arbitrary assumptions that has to be adopted. Where does one draw the line in following out the implications of these time-consuming fantasies?

There is, of course, no unequivocal answer to this question. In the end it is a matter for the judgement and the conscience of the investigator. There *is* a danger that a researcher who has invested time and effort in exploiting a mine of information that turns out to have seams of too low a quality to yield an acceptable productivity measure will go on to produce one. However, it is only at the last stage of the exercise that it becomes 'academic'. The sinking of the mineshaft may be justified as development expenditure even if it yields no product. A conscientious scholar will regretfully close up the shaft if the product is unacceptable. But even conscientious scholars differ on what is and is not acceptable.

On the other hand there is also a danger that investigators who have set their hearts on a 'correct' result will give too much weight to what are really rather minor variations in the results obtainable on different assumptions and despair too soon. The agreement between, say, column (*A*) and column (*C*) of Vamplew's Table 1 seems close enough to be encouraging for anyone ready to settle for order-of-magnitude answers, though before using the figures one would want to explore the reasons for the divergence that seems to relate to the second half of the 1880s. Similarly, the variations in Table 2, which stem largely from variations in methods of depreciation, are close enough (if we exclude column (*A*), which seems rather implausible) to be worth proceeding with. Nor do the indices in Table 3 look too wild, on the face of it, to operate with. As for the list of assumptions at the end of the paper – whether these are tolerable or not depends on Vamplew's judgement. It is reasonable to suppose that a research worker who has really immersed himself in the data, who has dug for himself in the mine and surveyed the accessible sources with some care, is more likely to be right than wrong in his choice of assumptions – even though he finds it difficult to regard many of them as more than 'hunches' and is genuinely indifferent about some of them.

Vamplew's final point concerns the choice between 'simple arithmetic' and 'sophisticated statistical techniques'. Here again, there can be no unequivocal answer. However, if more sophisticated techniques enable one to embody more information in the foundation, or to introduce a theoretical framework giving more consistency to the analysis, then there is an *a priori* case for the more sophisticated methodology. To evaluate the case, however, calls for something in the nature of a cost-benefit analysis that takes into account *inter alia* the costs (in research or computer time) and the significance of the question at issue as opposed to all the other questions that could be answered with these research resources.

Before one decides whether a question is worth investigating by relatively time-consuming statistical techniques, it is appropriate to explore rather fully the character of the non-quantitative evidence and one's theoretical expectations. The 'ample evidence' referred to by Vamplew in his first paragraph must be presented before deciding whether it was worth engaging in an intensive statistical study. And one would like to know what substantiation of the hypothesis that railway productivity growth was decelerating might contribute to a general theory of the sources of economic growth in Scotland over the period in question.

Engerman: What historical questions of any sort did Vamplew consider answerable? 'Old' economic historians have provided what they feel are answers to many historical questions without facing the statistical problems involved. For example, Hobsbawn, in his *Industry and Empire*, draws a number of conclusions from the fact, which is not subjected to criticism to ascertain its factualness, that British railways took 40 per cent of the output of iron in the 1840s.

Vamplew: His idea of an answerable historical question was a measure of productivity change for one company. The difficulties come when one tries to measure it for the entire industry.

Supple: Engerman's question could be put another way. The point is that the old economic history faces the same problems of the uncertainties of quantitative information as the new does, but chooses not to look at them. As Deane pointed out, the new economic history does look at the uncertainties and makes its more or less correct assumptions about them explicit. Is the paper, then, pointing out a difficulty that is really peculiar to the *new* economic history?

Vamplew: The question was: are we any better off with the new than with the old?

Supple: At least in the new economic history the implicit quantitative assumptions lying behind a historical argument are made explicit. Whether this approach has large payoff or not, of course, remains to be seen.

Hawke: The payoff seemed obvious to him. The assertion by Hobsbawn that Engerman refers to is based on one American visitor's impression quoted in one newspaper. There is no basis for it whatsoever. He, too, had experienced the sort of doubt that Vamplew expresses, but the difficulties often turn out to be less formidable than they look at first when one attempts to use the figures for a concrete purpose. For example, for 1847 to 1860 and for 1884 there are good figures for labour input on railways in England and Wales. In these years there is an extremely close correlation between labour input and the operating receipts of railways, partly because railways had recruiting programmes based on receipts. One can use the results of this correlation, then, to construct a reliable index of labour input, in years when the obstacles to measurement seem at first hopeless. It is possible to measure productivity in England and Wales, and only if there is something peculiar about the Scottish data would it be plausible that it is not possible in Scotland.

Feinstein: The absence in the paper of a discussion of the *magnitudes* of the errors was unfortunate. If the magnitudes are small enough to allow confirmation or rejection of the hypothesis being tested, the error in using the figures is not critically important. The statistician does not make only one estimate, but a number of them, staying within the margins of error he feels are reasonable: at the end of the day he has narrowed the range of uncertainty in the final result. Only if the margins of error are too large to draw conclusions from the final calculation does one have to be nihilistic.

Falkus: He agreed with Feinstein. The search for one, definite measure of productivity to many decimal places of accuracy is bound to be unsuccessful. The discussion of productivity at this conference has demonstrated that there are many different ways of measuring it.

McCloskey: He did not entirely agree with Falkus that the various ways of looking at productivity gave different results. On another issue, though, was Vamplew's working hypothesis that productivity growth had declined in the period?

Vamplew: His work had been inspired by Aldcroft's: he thought Aldcroft's estimates showed too much of a decline to be reasonable.

McCloskey: Vamplew was fortunate, for the figures, with all their faults, indicate a substantial increase in productivity on Scottish railways. In the light of Table 1, one could not be too far wrong to take the growth of labour input between the decades 1870-80 and 1890-1900 as 85 per cent (on a base of 1870-80 equal to 100). The capital estimate rises about 45 per cent. If the share of capital, just for illustrative purposes, is taken to be 50 per cent, then the growth of inputs as a whole lies half way between these figures — that is, at 65 per cent. Most of the difficulties are in the output estimates. But the numbers of passengers and the tons of freight carried are surely lower bounds on the growth of output: surely over this period each passenger and each ton of freight went further and got more associated services (such as speed). Taking freight and passengers together, then, the resulting productivity measure rises at 1.4 per cent per year, a quite respectable rate of growth.

Harley: The Glasgow underground was built in this period, which would in fact reduce distance travelled by each passenger.

Trace: Many branch lines were opened in this period, which may well worsen certain of the indices of quality.

Engerman: The point McCloskey was getting at was still valid. The choice of measures of input and output is not random: some of the measures presented by Vamplew, as also some of those presented by Floud in his paper, make more economic sense than others.

Feinstein: The issue was not whether there was productivity change in the period 1870 to 1900, but rather whether it had *decelerated* late in the period.

Engerman: The form of the calculation is the same. One simply has to pick a middle year and perform the calculation for two subperiods rather than the whole period. However that calculation turns out, the other point remains. In Table 3 there are four measures of output and the paper implies that these are all equally plausible measures. The issue is the same as that in the measurement of national income. A measure of national income that added tons of steel, tons of copper and tons of haircuts would not deserve the same attention as one that weighted these outputs by prices in the correct manner.

Harley: One can surely go further in narrowing the uncertainties in the measures of output in Table 3. It is argued in the paper that it is impossible to deflate the revenues by a rate index because there were a great variety of rates. But if the rates moved together this heterogeneity is not a serious problem. If they did not move together, it is still possible to use the information on how they did move to improve the measure. The resulting measure, taking account of the movement of freight rates, must certainly be closer to the truth than mere money revenues without deflation. Likewise, the information on the length of trains, such as it is, surely can be used to bring the estimates of ton-miles somewhat closer to the truth. By using all the information, in other words, one may be able to arrive at some measure to which all the alternative measures converge.

Vamplew: He was less optimistic than Harley. In passenger traffic, for example, tramways replaced railways in the early part of the period in some cities, but late in the period the Glasgow underground replaced some trams. And there are no data on how many passenger-miles were travelled on the underground.

Saul: It was not clear what the purpose of Table 3 was. Obviously, numbers of passengers, tons of freight, or receipts, are each by themselves inadequate measures of output.

Hawke: The statistics of numbers of passengers and tons of freight underlie the Phelps-Brown-Hopkins series used by Aldcroft. If Vamplew wishes to dispute with Aldcroft, he has to go beyond Aldcroft's statistical base. In the case of England and Wales it did prove possible to do this.

Feinstein: What was the conceptual basis of the measurement of capital in Table 2? In particular, was the length of life of capital used in building up the capital stock estimate the same as the one used in the estimate of depreciation? If the assumptions about the length of life were consistent, it is surprising to get such large variations between the different measures. Normally, the biases from taking the wrong length of life push the capital stock estimate in one direction and the depreciation estimate in another, with a strong tendency for the error in using the wrong length of life to cancel out, if it is taken to be the same for both calculations, as it should be. It may be, then, that inconsistent assumptions about the length of life are the explanation

for the wide variations in the estimates of Table 2. Another problem is
that Vamplew includes repairs in capital formation to arrive at a capital
stock. If repairs are included, however, the length of life of the capital
must be correspondingly reduced, because repairs, by definition, wear
out very quickly.

Floud: The earlier discussion, especially by Harley, of the criterion for
judging the truth of the measures is disturbing. The close correlation
between various measures of output is no evidence that their common
value is a true measure of output. If the measures do not make
economic sense, their correlation is irrelevant. He had faced the same
issue in his paper on machine tools. He confessed that if he had found
that the number of machines per man as well as the weight per man had
increased, he probably would have taken the increase in number per
man as an additional confirmation of the trend. But this measure is
economic nonsense and does not in fact add to the explanation.

Harley: The number of machines per man was not necessarily
irrelevant. If one had outside information that the sorts of machines
being built stayed roughly the same, the number would not be a
nonsense measure and would indeed confirm the other trend.

Pollard: It was a factual, not theoretical, issue. The series of numbers of
passengers given in Table 3 of Vamplew's paper is surely meaningless,
because of the increase in short journeys from new suburbs and so on.
Train-miles seem a more reasonable measure, giving a measure independent of the enormous changes in the travelling habits of each passenger.

Falkus: To return briefly to an earlier issue, was there any useful
information on capacity utilization?

Vamplew: There was virtually none. For one company there was some,
but nothing else.

Falkus: In view of that fact, there may be difficulties in the way of
McCloskey's programme of productivity measurement. The differences
in utilization may be large enough over the period to obscure the
pattern of productivity change.

McCloskey: There was a difficulty. The appropriate measure of capital
for productivity measurements is not the stock of capital in existence at
any time, but rather the yearly flow of services from the capital that is
in use, which is clearly affected by utilization.

McClelland: He wondered if Vamplew would accept the following
characterization of his position. McCloskey showed in a rough and
ready way that one can answer the question of whether productivity
change was positive or negative in the period 1870 to 1900. But if, as

Feinstein pointed out earlier, the question is the more delicate one concerning the rate of change of the rate of productivity growth, the statistics are too crude to use.

Vamplew: McClelland's characterization was reasonable. He felt now that the method of approach could be improved somewhat, but, given the problem of the atypicality of the statistics available as representing what was happening in the industry as a whole, it seemed reasonable that this further work would vindicate the position of nihilism.

11

Railway passenger traffic in 1865 *

GARY HAWKE

I

My invitation to participate in this seminar on the Application of
Mathematical Techniques to British Economic History was presumably
based on my recent work on the economic effects of the innovation of
railways in England and Wales between 1840 and 1870 [1]. That work
is too recent for me to engage in any comprehensive revision; too
recent, indeed, for me to review the reviewers if there are any reviewers.
But this invitation did provide an opportunity for me to pursue some
further thoughts, especially some thoughts of a mathematical kind,
with reference to the passenger traffic of the railways.

I suppose that to most readers my book appears 'mathematical'
because it contains many diagrams and tables, and because much of the
argument depends on arithmetical manipulation of statistical data.
Some readers might give more weight to the implicit and explicit
regressions or similar statistical tools contained among the wealth (or
plethora) of more everyday arithmetical operations. But even this
slightly more sophisticated attitude can be disputed. Mathematicians
have the same attitude towards arithmetic as many historians have
towards the memorization of chronology. Many mathematicians are
proud of being unable to do simple arithmetic, just as many historians
are proud of being unable to remember dates. Such trivia are beneath
them. Both professions are, I suspect, more unanimously agreed on
these attitudes than is the economics profession on the claim that an
economist's merit cannot be measured by his success on the stock
exchange. In this last case, those who do have the skill in question are
less likely to disclaim its importance.

To most mathematicians, especially pure mathematicians, mathematics is not so much the science of number as many dictionaries
define it, as the investigation of the properties of defined structures. Its
essence is the discovery of the implications of a given set of axioms. In
applied mathematics, and even more in statistical and numerical

---

* This paper has benefited from comments made on earlier work by Professors
R. W. Fogel and H. J. Habakkuk. It has benefited also from discussion with
Professor J. D. Gould.

mathematics, the manipulation of numbers, arithmetic, is more important but it is usually subordinate to the investigation of the more general properties of certain assumptions. Mathematics is more akin to logic than to the popular ideas of arithmetic.

Viewed in this light, *Railways and Economic Growth* is 'mathematical' in that it deals with a precisely defined problem. It deals with the interrelationships between specified variables and the implications of certain specified changes in those variables. It is mathematical in logic as well as having the 'mathematical appearance' of more popular ideas. The assumptions are, of course, somehow related to the reality of the English economy in the nineteenth century but this is irrelevant to the pure logic involved. The change that is central to the book occurs in the mind of the investigator rather than 'on the ground', but this, too, is irrelevant to the logic. Indeed, as has been shown many times, many arguments in economic history involve counterfactual arguments at least implicitly and any recent change in the treatment of such arguments has been only in making them more explicit. But a change in the questions asked by economic historians has made the role of the counterfactual more obvious. There has been some shift of emphasis from identifying čauses to measuring effects. In a complete analysis of '*A*' is a necessary and sufficient condition for '*B*' the study of causes and of effects would eventually be entirely integrated. But few studies are complete in this sense. When the economic historian is studying the causes of *B*, he is not inevitably led to consider counterfactual situations. If he starts with *B*, he may be able to identify

$$(A, x,y,z) \text{ implies } B$$

without ever considering any counterfactual conditions. Given some minor assumptions about the nature of the currency, changes in mint output can be traced to changes in mint price. The same question could be approached in a counterfactual way – suppose mint price had not behaved as it did, then . . . – but a historian is not naturally inclined to take this approach [2]. But when a historian is concerned with the effects of some event, he is concerned with a problem of the type; given

$$(A, x,y,z) \text{ implies } (B, u,v,w);$$

to assess the effect of *A*, we need to know what

$$(\text{not } A, x,y,z) \text{ would have implied.}$$

The problem is immediately seen to involve counterfactual analysis.

Whether or not explicit counterfactuals are involved in any particular study, recent changes should certainly have induced a greater awareness of the need for precision in arguments in economic history. The logical structure of any arguments and explanations are likely to be given more critical scrutiny. Economic history, like some other disciplines, has become more mathematical.

It is not intended here to denigrate the significance of statistical work. Economic history is very largely a quantitative subject and statistical techniques are methods of ensuring that the best possible use is made of available quantitative data. The techniques themselves often result from the mathematical investigation of the properties of variables given certain assumptions. More confident use can be made of statistical techniques if these mathematical properties are known. The usefulness of statistical techniques should be so ʌbvious as to require little discussion.

These reflections could lead us into a methodological discussion of such questions as the distinction, if any, between 'theory', 'model' and 'assumptions'; of the 'reality' of assumptions; of the role of 'literary' evidence, etc. Except for saying that I would not expect such a discussion to reveal any new methodological problems for an economic historian, and especially that the role of people is in no way necessarily forgotten in mathematical thinking, I prefer to turn to some more specific issues associated with railway passenger traffic on nineteenth-century English railways. Firstly, I want to review the question, 'At what cost could the economy have sustained the actual passenger traffic of 1865 had it been deprived of railways?'

II

In *Railways and Economic Growth* I have developed an estimate of the passenger-miles travelled on railways in England and Wales in 1865. This is shown in Table 1.

TABLE 1
Railway passenger output in England and Wales 1865
(million passenger-miles)

First class	368.5
Second class	659.3
Third class	1094.9
Season tickets, etc.	105.8
	2228.5

Source: Railways and Economic Growth, p. 43.

In the absence of railways, had the same transport services been required, the commodity of travel would have had to be supplied by coaches. The main routes for passenger travel were inland, especially from London to the north-west, and the alternative transport system would have had to be a land system. Sea transport did coexist with coaches before 1840 and it continued to exist beside railways later in the nineteenth century. But, in general, personal travel by ship did not directly or indirectly compete for most passenger traffic. Some capacity for carrying passengers exists on most ships that are intended primarily for the transport of goods and the charges made to such passengers bear little relation to the costs that would have been incurred had shipping attempted to carry all the passengers carried by rail. Similarly, although there was a little personal travel by canal, the inland waterways were not competing for the traffic carried by coaches. Nineteenth-century writers considered only coaches as an alternative to rail travel [3] and it is reasonable to follow their practice. Even though improvements to ships lowered the cost of travel by sea, the geographical location of rail travel meant that it could not be replaced to any significant extent, even indirectly, by sea travel.

The contemporary statistician, Porter, estimated the total passenger-miles travelled by coach in 1834 as 358 million [4]. We are therefore concerned with an approximately sixfold increase in the scale of personal travel. Coach rates fell in the years 1820-40, at least partly under the stimulus of potential rail competition, but it is probable that they had closely approached long run cost levels by 1840 [5]. Fares at 4*d* per mile 'inside' and 2½*d* per mile 'outside' were described as slightly 'over the mark' by a parliamentary Select Committee in the 1840s but they were accepted as accurate by the Royal Commission of the 1860s [6]. In a sixfold increase of scale without technical change, the most likely movement of the long run cost curve is upwards as such items as road maintenance become more burdensome. If fares of 4*d* and 2½*d* are slightly high, the excess will probably do no more than make some contribution to such cost increases.

The Royal Commission of the 1860s introduced a further coaching cost. It compared first class rail travel with 'posting', roughly, the running of an individual coach between any two points changing the horses at prearranged 'posts' on the route. The cost of such travel was estimated by the Royal Commission at 24*d* per passenger-mile. The Royal Commission compared second class rail travel with inside coach travel, and the lower classes of rail travel with outside coach travel.

Such a comparison implies that the travel that actually took place in 1865 would have cost £60.3 million had coaches been required to supply it, instead of the £12.5 million that railways charged for its provision. The saving of £47.9 million was 5.8 per cent of the U.K. national income in 1865.

For railways in the 1840s, however, Lardner adopted a different standard of comparison for personal travel [7]. He compared first class rail travel with inside coach travel, and all other classes of rail travel with outside coach travel. With this comparison, the alternative cost of the actual travel of 1865 would be £25.5 million, and the saving of £13.1 million represents 1.6 per cent of the U.K. national income.

The reason for the different comparisons adopted by Lardner and the Royal Commission is probably the increased comfort of railway travel between the 1840s and 1865. Lardner's comparison dates from the early 1840s. Lardner lived outside England in the late 1840s and his treatment (and my following of it [8]) may have been dated even by 1850. It was in 1844 that Laing wrote,

> Thus each train had a first class, corresponding to the inside of the old stage coach; and a second class, in the absence of cushions, stuffings, and other comforts, and in the exposure, or partial exposure to the weather, corresponding to the outside. [9]

The legislation of 1844 required the 'parliamentary' trains to be covered and the third class accommodation improved as most companies soon ceased to distinguish between the 'parliamentary' and third classes. Competition between companies also led to an improvement in the facilities for passenger travel in all classes, an improvement that can be traced in the descriptions of the rolling stock used for this service. The Royal Commision's comparison is certainly compatible with this evidence. Only in one respect is its comparison unfavourable to coach travel. Posting gives more flexibility to a travel schedule than does first class rail travel. Provided horses were available at each post, the traveller by posting was not tied to any timetable at all. Rail travel in England and Wales, even in 1865, was facilitated by a frequent train service, especially in the first and second classes, but it could not compete on flexibility alone with posting. However. the speed and comfort of first class travel by rail would outweigh the loss of flexibility when a passenger was considering the non-price comparison of the two means of travel.

Railways provided travel with various degrees of comfort and in

1865 the economy could have provided the same services only at the cost of a diversion to passenger travel of nearly 6 per cent of the U.K. national income [10].

III

Two related points about this calculation deserve emphasis. Firstly the calculation is in principle a very simple one. The passenger-mileage figure is calculated from records of receipts and prices and, except for some minor complications reported more fully in *Railways and Economic Growth*, its construction requires no further estimation. The alternative cost figures rest on contemporary estimation and an assumption about the cost structure of coach travel. No other substantive assumptions are required. In particular, nothing has been said about the elasticity of demand for rail travel. The problem as constructed – its mathematical or logical nature – does not require any such assumption. The problem is complete because we have specified that the actual passenger traffic of 1865 is to be sustained. This is not a problem that many historians have explicity considered, nor is it a problem that many economists would encounter in, for example, a cost-benefit study of a projected investment outlay [11]. But there is surely no reason why economic historians should not ask questions different from those asked by scholars in the parent disciplines.

  Secondly, a considerable part of the cost to the economy of maintaining the passenger traffic of 1865 without the services of railways can be attributed to the relative comfort of rail travel. If the 1865 traffic could have been accommodated by outside coach travel, the alternative cost would have been £23.2 million and the additional cost only 1.3 per cent of the U.K. national income. But this calculation is relevant to a quite different problem. It is relevant to the question, 'At what cost could the economy of economy of 1865 have sustained the passenger traffic of that year if it were deprived of railways and if it were allowed to accommodate that passenger traffic on markedly inferior facilities?' As in mathematical thinking, the changing of the assumptions involves turning from one problem to another. An economic historian might be interested in the problem just defined. He would first have to define the degree of inferiority of facilities to be tolerated and if this were done in terms of outside coach travel, he would obtain the answer of £23.2 million. It is difficult to see what historical interest the calculation would have. The railway did produce a commodity that the economy could have by other means at a certain cost, but, deprived of railways, it could have had a poorer commodity at less cost. If when assessing an innovation we are first to deprive it of some of its advantages, then we shall always obtain a low assessment of its value.

IV

There is, however, no reason why we should not ask different questions about railway passenger traffic. We might like to ask how the economy *would* have reacted to a cessation of railway services for passenger travel. Clearly, this would be a very difficult question, but we might think some progress would be possible by dividing it into constituent parts. We might begin by asking how far the travel by railway in various degrees of comfort would have been replaced by travel without the equivalent comfort.

To anwer this question, we need to know the shape and position of the demand curve for comfort in travel. If, for example, we could assume that this demand curve was of a constant-elasticity type

$$D = AP^e$$

then by postulating various levels of the price elasticity of demand, *e*, we could determine the extent to which such comfort would have been demanded as its price increased to make profitable its provision by transport services other than railways [12]. We could then state to what extent the economy would have reacted to its deprivation of railways by using higher cost travelling comfort and to what extent it would have substituted travel without comfort to avoid the extra cost. We could then go on to a study of the comparable substitution between travel without comfort and other commodities, and even perhaps to issues of consumers' surplus. If we are interested only in exercises of logic and arithmetic, there are no insuperable obstacles.

If, however, we wish to use logic and arithmetic to establish something about the economy of 1865, then the assumptions we use must be those that are appropriate for that situation. We need to know, for example, whether the demand curve for transport in comfort in 1865 was of constant-elasticity type. This is a material consideration because we can obtain different results by employing constant slope demand curves. For example, when considering the purchase of travel in first class rail comfort, we know that a point on the demand curve is

368.5 million passenger-miles purchases at a price of 1.1*d* (the difference between the fares for first and third classes) [13]. But this is insufficient to establish the form of the demand curve. As shown in Figure 2, we can construct suitable assumptions to imply any consumer reaction at all. Precisely the same is true of travel in second class comfort.

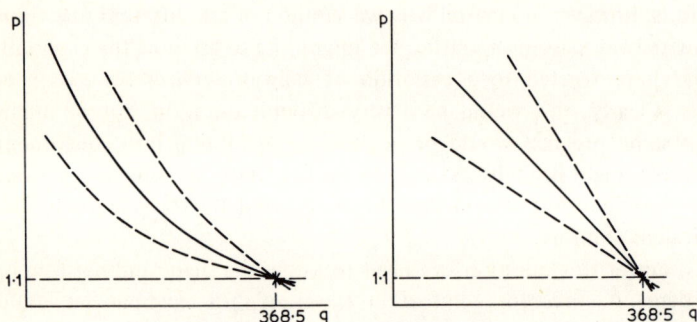

Figure 1   Demand for travel in first class comfort.

The empirical evidence is not, however, limited to the national aggregates. We can use the information in the Railway Returns for each individual railway company in an attempt to identify more points on the national demand curve.

The absolute quantity of travel with different degrees of comfort demanded from individual companies will clearly not be immediately comparable with the national demand curve. The simple size of the individual company contrasted with the size of the railway system as a whole will clearly affect the figures. But, if we are correct in postulating a relationship between the price of comfort and the amount of it demanded at a national level, we can expect at the level of the individual company some relationship between the price of comfort and the proportion of that company's total passenger output that is accompanied by comfort. We can expect a relationship between the difference between the first and third class fares of each company and the ratio of first class passenger-miles to total passenger-miles supplied by that company. An analagous expectation would be held for second class travel. We would expect the form of the curves so constructed to be the same as the curve appropriate for the national average.

The empirical results are shown in Figures 2 and 3. If we look at the demand for travel in first class comfort we might think that the demand curve is of constant-slope of about 1, but there is clearly a great dispersion about any regression line. Even if we confine our attention to large companies, those supplying over 10 million passenger-miles in total (indicated by a ring in the diagram), there is clearly marked dispersion about any average. Figure 3 shows that the position with travel in second class comfort is equally unhelpful. In this case, the curve might be one of constant but very low elasticity or one of very low slope, but the more obvious characteristic is the difference in behaviour of the customers of different railways.

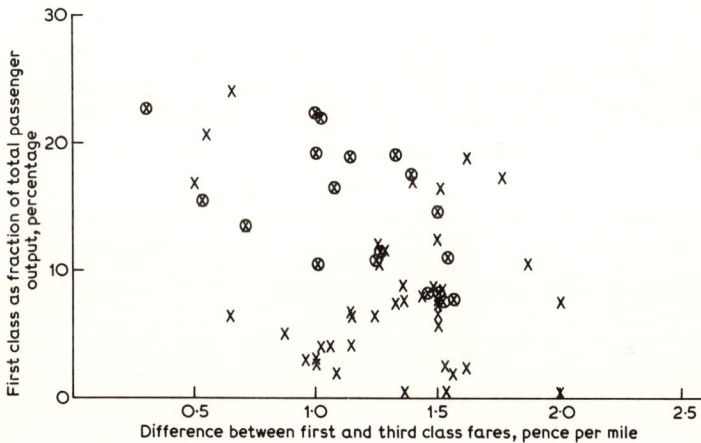

Figure 2 Demand for travel in first class comfort: railways in England and Wales 1865.
Source: Railway Returns.

When we turn our attention from trying to estimate the amount of travel in comfort that would have been demanded in the absence of railways to trying to estimate what loss of consumers' surplus would have resulted from the removal of railways, Figures 2 and 3 reveal a conceptual rather than statistical difficulty. If we have two different markets for a commodity, only when they are correctly aggregated will an accurate measurement of consumers' surplus be made. If two different demand curves are averages, the measurement of consumers' surplus will be inaccurate.

376

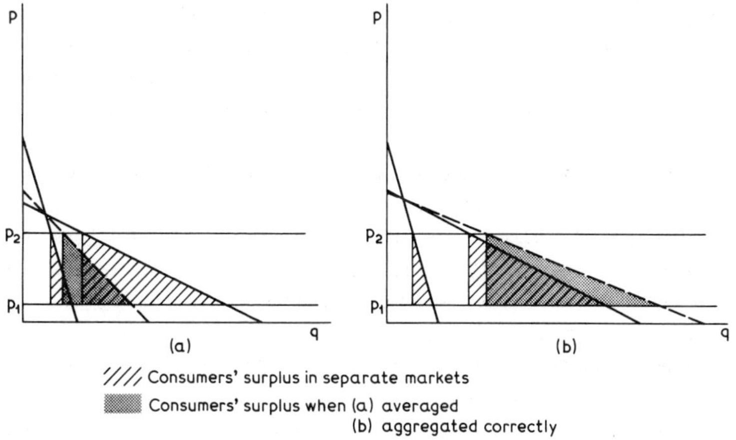

Figure 4   Aggregation errors and consumers' surplus.

It is only too obvious from Figures 2 and 3 that such an error would be possible if we attempted to form any average demand curve. As expected, any attempt to say what the economy would have done in response to a removal of railways proves to be difficult.

V

Our difficulty in relating the demand for the various railway services to price is twofold. At the aggregate level, price was not the main determinant of demand. And the demand for railway services was probably different for different companies, or approximately equivalent, the demand varied in the different regions of England and Wales.

We could have derived the first result more simply from the various time series relating to England and Wales as a whole. The price of third class travel was largely fixed by the legislative requirement that a train must be provided offering travel at 1*d* per passenger-mile over all railway routes. The thrid class fare of approximately 1*d* per passenger-mile remained fixed from the mid-1850s to 1865. The average fare for first class railway passenger traffic declined slightly between 1853 and

Figure 3   Demand for travel in second class comfort: railways in England and Wales 1865.
Source: Railway Returns.

1865, and the average fare of second class travel remained nearly constant [14]. The charge for the travel in comfort must therefore have declined. The proportion of third class to all passenger traffic, however, increased [15]. Any effect of price must have been overwhelmed by other influences.

One such other influence was the average length of a journey. From 15 to 16 miles in the late 1840s, this had declined to about 10 miles in 1870 [16]. Furthermore, on most railways the average third class journey was less than the average journey in the higher classes. The passenger output of railways increased at least partly through attracting shorter distance traffic especially in the third class. An economist is tempted to relate this immediately to increases in income, but anybody who has resided in England would be reluctant to rule out the possibility that it took many years before the opposition of conservatism was overcome and people accepted that rail traffic for short distances by 'common folk' was 'proper'. In economist's language, it is probable that a change of taste as well as a change of income over many years was involved.

It might be thought that different patterns of behaviour with respect to the length of a journey between the customers of different railway companies might illuminate the differences in the reaction to price identified in Section IV above. Unfortunately, this does not prove to be the case. Figure 5 shows the percentage of non-third class passengers who chose to travel in the first class related to the average length of the non-third class journey. A point is plotted for each railway company in England and Wales in 1865. No consistent pattern of behaviour can be discerned. Figure 6 shows that no consistency is evident in the way in which the choice between second and third class travel was related to the average journey in those classes.

One can see *a priori* arguments for both an increase and a decrease in the proportion of passengers who choose greater comfort for a longer journey. It is readily comprehensible that a certain amount of discomfort would be tolerable for a short journey but not for a long journey; that is that the proportion of passengers choosing the greater comfort would increase as the average journey increased. On the other hand, we could postulate a fixed sum of money available for travel; for a short journey a higher class could be afforded but for a longer journey the lower class must be chosen. The opposite relationship between length of journey and the choice of class would then be implied. The

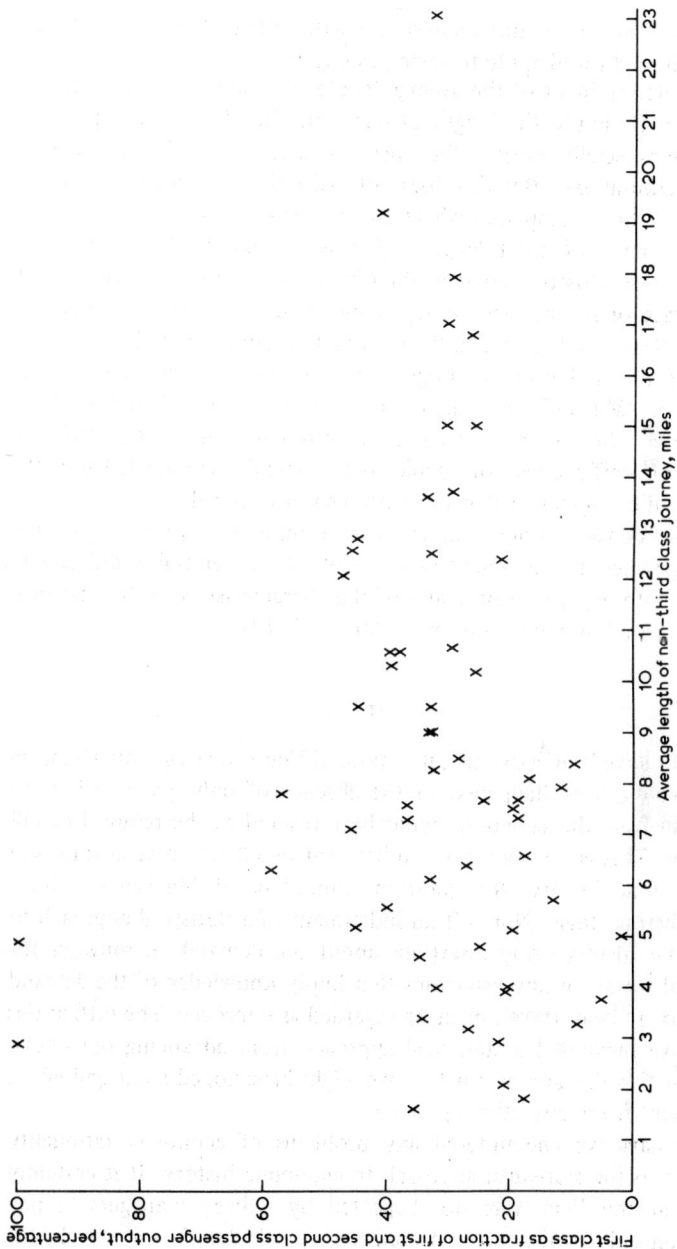

Figure 5 First class comfort and length of journey: railways in England and Wales 1865.
Source: Railway Returns.

empirical evidence is not inconsistent with either of these hypotheses and both might well apply to some passengers.

One determinant of the average length of a journey on a particular company is simply the length of line controlled by that company. In Figure 6 especially, most of the large companies lie on the upper part of the horizontal axis. But this does not make the evidence any easier to interpret; those companies where the average journey was short include a wide range of total lengths. Nor is it easy to find any other classification closely related to the division between those with a high percentage of second class journeys and those with a low percentage of second class travel. Those in the upper left quadrant include companies in the south and north of England just as do those in the lower left quadrant. 'Mineral' and 'agricultural' railways are found in both quadrants. The length of journey on different companies in different classes of traffic does not enable us to extend our knowledge of the pattern of consumers' behaviour with respect to travel.

It was considerations such as those in this and the preceding section that provoked the comment in my book, 'It is regrettably difficult to discuss with any precision many of the characteristics of the passenger traffic carried by railways in the 1860s. . . .' [17]

VI

As might have been expected, it is more difficult to answer questions on what would have happened in the absence of railways than it is to ascertain how the economy could have reacted to the removal of rail facilities. This is, of course, no indictment of a mathematical approach to economic history; the questions cannot be distinguished without some abstract logic. Nor is it an indictment of a statistical approach to economic history. Any assertions about the demand on railways for personal travel, or any assertions that imply knowledge of the demand curve for railway travel, must be regarded as unproven. The difficulties that have prevented a statistical approach from advancing our knowledge of this demand as much as we might have hoped are disguised in, not absent from, any other approach.

Nor have we encountered any problems of economic rationality peculiar to the statistical approach to economic history. It is certainly true that travellers were not expected by railway managers to pay attention only to the price charged for a particular class of travel. One

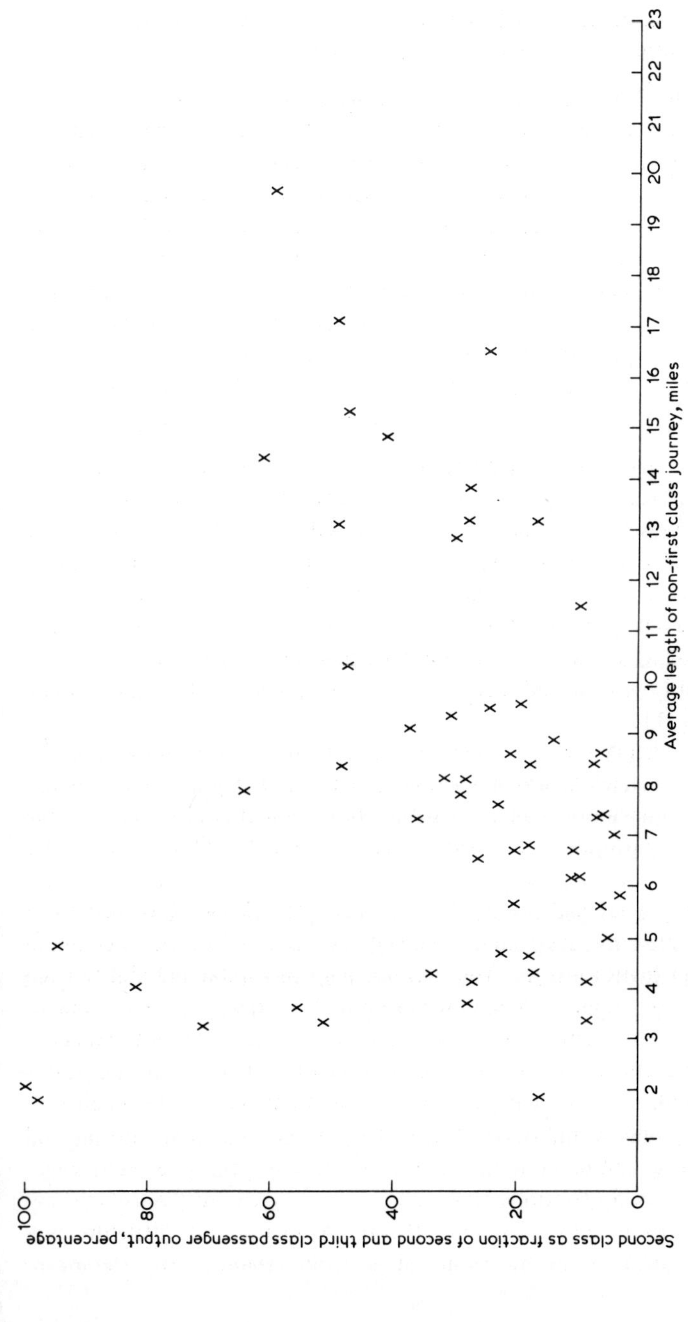

Figure 6 Second class comfort and length of journey: railways in England and Wales 1865.
Source: Railway Returns.

manager explicitly stated that he expected a passenger's choice of class
to be determined by his status in the community

> Our district is full of men who have risen by their own industry
> and energy, but their economy is such, although they occupy a
> respectable position in life, that if third-class carriages were put on
> every train they would avail themselves of them. I think that many
> persons who take advantage of the third-class trains ought not to do
> it, and it would not be a boon to the public in that respect.
>
> When you say they ought not take advantage of the third-class
> trains, it is not a mere matter of choice with a man whether he will
> submit to rougher company and more imperfect accommodation? –
>
> Yes: but still we think that when a man has amassed a fortune it is
> natural to expect that he would travel second or first class. [18]

Another manager complained bitterly of the use of cheaper trains
provided for the poorer classes by gentry families for moving their
establishments to London for the social season [19]. A company
chairman complained that people 'actually write' to the railway
company asking when a cheap train would be run before deciding on
their travelling plans [20]. It seems that it was only Irish railways
whose managers were more confident that the company to be found in
the third class would keep respectable people in their appropriate
classes [21].

The existence of the complaints of English managers shows that the
expected behaviour was not always practised, that prices did influence
some people more than their social status. But it is probable that the
expected patterns of behaviour were adhered to in most cases. The
managers were speaking in 1865 of what they expected in that year, not
lamenting what had occurred in the past. The incidence of behaviour
not directed to maximizing financial returns is, of course, a common
theme in British history. The 'haemorrhage of capital and ability from
industry and trade into landownership and politics' [22] is just one of
several such themes. Railway managers clearly did not expect a
traveller's choice of class to be determined by financial considerations
alone. Indeed, even at the present day, and not only in the nineteenth
century, one would have doubts before asserting that custom and
tradition would be overcome by the influence of price or even by wider
economic considerations. But this is not a great difficulty for any
attempt to employ economic theory. Normally, the difficulty will
become apparent as the result of such an attempt. An attempt to

calculate an elasticity of demand will discover from the poor statistical 'fit' the presence of variables not included in the elementary economic model. Intelligent scrutiny of an attempt to fit a demand curve will see evidence of regional variations within the territory being considered. It would be poor workmanship in any approach to economic history to overlook divergences from the assumptions of the standard economic theory. Economics provides ideas that must be adapted for any particular empirical study.

It should be apparent that I do not see the role of mathematical techniques in British economic history as the rapid discovery of new historical truths by an easy acquisition of some mathematician's quick solution to all puzzles and its immediate application to an historical situation. Nor do I see it as merely the acquisition by historians of more arithmetical ability. Rather, I see the role of mathematical thinking primarily in terms of its usefulness in precisely defining the question under discussion. Alternatively stated, I see the role of mathematical thinking as isolating the different assumptions underlying different arguments. There is a tremendous scope in British economic history for such thinking [23]. In determining what assumptions are appropriate to a particular historical situation, the traditional documentary skills will be required, but statistical evidence and statistical techniques may permit more compelling and even conclusive arguments to be erected. In a constant interchange of hypothesis and statistical material, I would expect British economic history to be greatly enriched.

NOTES

[1] G. R. Hawke, *Railways and Economic Growth in England and Wales, 1840-1870* (Oxford, Clarendon Press, 1970).

[2] J. D. Gould, 'Hypothetical history', *Economic History Review*, 2nd series, XXII, 1969, p. 198.

[3] e.g. D. Lardner, *Railway Economy* (Newton Abbot, 1968 – a reprinting of the 1855 American edition of a book originally published in London in 1850), pp. 162–5, R. D. Baxter, 'Railway extension and its results', *Journal Stat. Soc.*, XXIX, 1866, reprinted in E. M. Carus-Wilson (ed.), *Essays in Economic History*, vol. III (London, 1962), p. 39; *Edinburgh Review*, CXLIII, April 1867, pp. 358–60.

[4] Cited in Baxter, op. cit., p. 39.

[5] H. W. Hart, 'Some notes on coach travel, 1750-1848', *Journal. Trans. Hist.*, IV, 1959-60, pp. 146–50.

[6] *Fifth Report of Select Committee on Railways, Appendix No. 2 by S. Laing*, P.P. 1844, XI, p. 605; *Report of Royal Commission on Railways*, P.P. 1867, XXXVIII, pt. 1, p. 53; see also W. T. Jackman, *The Development of Transportation in Modern England* (London, 1962).

[7] Lardner, op. cit., p. 164.

[8] *Railways and Economic Growth*, pp. 52–3

[9] *Fifth Report of Select Committee on Railways, Appendix No. 2*, p. 605.

[10] No further allowance for speed is made because of the short average distance of a rail journey in 1865. Cf. Section V below, and for a more complete discussion, cf. *Railways and Economic Growth*, p. 191.

[11] But cf. New Zealand Monetary and Economic Council, *Report No. 19, New Zealand and an Enlarged E.E.C.* (Wellington, 1970), pp. 38–9.

[12] We could be more sophisticated and include income as an argument in the demand function, and then investigate whether the loss of railways would result in a loss of income as well as a higher price. If we assume a perfectly competitive economy, no such problem would arise for a small shift of resources, but perfect competition is compatible with few historical problems.

[13] *Railways and Economic Growth*, p. 43.

[14] *Railway Returns*, 1853-9; *Railways and Economic Growth*, p. 43.

[15] Lardner, *Railway Economy*, p. 153; *Railway Returns*, 1853-9; Table 1 above; cf. also *Railways and Economic Growth*, pp. 35–40.

[16] *Railways and Economic Growth*, p. 51. Dr Bagwell is in error when he writes 'The steady percentage which through passenger receipts bore to total passenger receipts disguised both an absolute increase in the number of persons booking through and an increase in the average length of rail journey.' (P. S. Bagwell, *The Railway Clearing House in the British Economy, 1842-1922* (London, Allen & Unwin, 1968), p. 61). The ratio with which Bagwell is concerned can be expressed as

$$\frac{P_t \cdot f_t \cdot d_t}{P \cdot f \cdot d}$$

where P = number of passengers
      f = average fare per mile
      d = average distance

and the same symbols with the subscript, $_t$, represent the same concepts but only for passengers 'booked through' – i.e. through the Clearing House. Clearly, an increase in P_t and d is neither a necessary nor a sufficient condition of constancy of the fraction as a whole. In particular, such constancy is quite consistent with the decline in d reported in the text.

[17] *Railways and Economic Growth*, p. 51.

[18] Royal Commission on Railways, *Minutes of Evidence* (Smithells), qq. 12996-7.

[19] Ibid. (Grierson), q. 13298.

[20] Ibid. (Gooch), q. 17488.

[21] Ibid. (Barrington), qq. 7110-3, and (Murland) qq. 4911-3.

[22] H. J. Habakkuk, *American and British Technology in the Nineteenth Century* (Cambridge, Cambridge University Press, 1962), pp. 190–1.

[23] To offer only one example, one might consider the differences between studies of the implications of pricing policies adopted by railways in the nineteenth century and studies of the perpetuation of those policies in the twentieth century. At what point of the argument does an assumption about the failure of managers to recognize changes in the environment become necessary? Or can an inappropriate policy be blamed on earlier managers? cf. D. H. Aldcroft, *British Railways in Transition* (London, Macmillan, 1968), pp. 18–22, 59–68.

Chairman: P. Mathias

Prepared comments: C. Feinstein

Feinstein: It seemed that there were two main issues in the paper. The first is the question of how much it would have cost to carry on alternative modes the 2200 million passenger-miles that the railways carried in 1865. One estimate makes the assumptions that first class passengers on the railways would have travelled by posting, second class would have travelled inside ordinary coaches, and third class outside. The treatment of first class passengers is critical because posting cost 2*s* per passenger-mile at the time, whereas ordinary inside coach travel cost only 4*d*. Given this assumption, Hawke finds that passenger travel by coach would have cost £60 million in 1865, as against the actual cost on the railways of £12 million, yielding a social saving of £48 million (6 per cent of national income). The alternative estimate abandons the possibility of posting and yields a social saving of £11 or £13 million. Now it is not entirely clear what significance is to be attached to these estimates. The issue is how large the decrease in the productive capacity of the economy would have been had passengers in 1865 been compelled to suffer long and dusty coach rides. Does the estimate assuming posting really imply that national income would have been, as it suggests, 6 per cent lower?

The second question treated in the paper is that of whether there is any relationship between the price of first class comfort on the railways and its price. The results are negative, which is not really surprising: Englishmen were perfectly aware of which class of travel they should choose, namely, the class corresponding to their social class.

Hawke: He agreed with Feinstein that the choice of travel class was dominated by social class. American work on this subject has found that there was indeed a relationship between the difference in prices and the ratio of first to second class travel, but in England the social distinctions in travel were apparently more powerful. The estimate of social saving is part of a larger study of the social saving of all forms of railway traffic. Feinstein brings up the interesting issue of to what degree passenger travel can be considered a productive input, but it proved impossible in the larger study to give any concrete meaning to the common assertions about how much passenger travel was for work and how much for pleasure.

Trace: The combination of coaching with sea travel would be a viable alternative, given the geographical character of England. Was the cost of this alternative calculated?

Hawke: He had done some calculations, very rough ones, and they did not give strikingly different results. A sea journey took longer, which offsets its lower cost per mile. Aside from this similarity of results, the other reason for concentrating on the coaching alternative is that it is the one on which contemporaries concentrated. They apparently believed that sea and coach travel were not good substitutes.

Temin: The time spent travelling does not play a major role in the paper. Was posting slower?

Hawke: It was indeed slower. The neglect of the time-saving, however, is reasonable because the average distance travelled by rail at this time was only 10 miles: the time gained or lost by choosing one mode over another was trivial.

Hunt: It was not outside coach travel that was the relevant alternative for third class travel, but travelling on the carts. In the 1850s there were complaints by the poorer people that it was dearer to travel on the parliamentary trains at a penny a mile than on the carts, and that the carts were being put out of business by the competition of railways for freight transport.

Hawke: He did not know how common carts were. There was always the possibility, of course, of walking.

Mathias: There were supplemental costs of meals, tips and so forth on those modes of travel that took a longer time.

Hawke: The costs of meals were not really supplemental. After all, one had to eat whether travelling or not. The cost of hotels, of course, were indeed supplemental, but, again, they are not important because of the very short distances travelled.

Vamplew: The actual distance travelled by road need not have been the same as that travelled by railway, because of different routing between the two points.

Hawke: This was a problem. For goods traffic he had found that goods travelling by canal, even in the north of England, had to go about one fifth more miles than goods travelling by rail. But the difference could not have been very great for passenger travel.

Pollard: Hawke's calculation answers the question, 'How much would it have cost to replace rail passenger travel by coaches?' It does not answer the broader question, 'What would have happened if railways had not existed?' Some people would have walked and many would have stayed at home.

Hawke: He agreed. Literary historians have been prone to make unsubstantiated generalizations about the answer to the second question, without realizing that even answering the first is difficult.

McCloskey: It should be emphasized that Hawke's calculations give only an upper bound on the answer to the second, more interesting question, because the calculation imposes constraints on how the economy would have adjusted, constraints that raise the estimate above the cost of the alternative that the economy would actually have taken. What, then, is the significance of Hawke's large estimate of the social saving? The American studies of social saving found it to be low. Hawke finds that it is 6 per cent of national income for passenger traffic alone. But given that it is an upper bound, this finding does not really refute the position that one might take on the basis of the American experience – namely, that it was in fact low.

Feinstein: Fishlow had specifically excluded the value of comfort from his calculation. Most of Hawke's high estimate comes from that fact.

McClelland: It came from both comfort and speed. Fishlow assumes that all time lost is to be taken out of consumption, not out of production. Feinstein is right, then, in suggesting that one cannot say that Hawke's number is large by comparison with the American findings, because they are not calculated in a comparable way.

Floud: Was it reasonable to assume that the cost of short coach journeys would make it possible to use them as an alternative to the 10 mile average journey by rail? The mix of length of journeys would have been different in the coach alternative.

Hawke: There were many short, regular coach journeys in the 1830s and 1840s. It is difficult to get information on the cost structure of coaching by length of journey. A suggestive piece of evidence that the cost per mile was constant for any length of journey is that contemporaries spoke of the cost per mile without reference to the length of journey.

Mathias: An expansion of coach travel would have required large expenditures on roads, the cost of which is not reflected in the calculation as it stands.

Hawke: This was a problem. The inclusion of tolls on toll-roads makes up for some of it, but not all.

Hunt: Might the excess of first over second class comfort on the railways have varied from one region to another, obscuring what might be a somewhat more rational pattern of variation than Hawke found in the relationship between the percentage class travellers and the price of first class travel?

Hawke: He had tried to allow for what information there was on this point – the railways of the Midlands had a reputation for comfort, for example – but it did not improve the fit.

Feinstein: He was puzzled by the assertion in the paper that no assumption about the elasticity of demand need be made to make the calculation of social saving. Is this true?

Hawke: For his calculation none was necessary, because he was asking directly what the cost of carrying the 1865 passengers by coach would have been, not what it would have cost to carry those passengers that would have travelled had the railway not existed.

McCloskey: He found this response peculiar. The interesting question concerning the impact of railways on British economic growth is transformed into an uninteresting question concerning the properties of some statistics on coach and rail costs, avoiding criticism of the implicit assumption of perfectly inelastic demand for transport by saying that the question is the second, less interesting one.

Hawke: He had started with the broader question, but had found it impossible to estimate the elasticity of demand. The point is simply that the broader question cannot be answered with the information we have now.

McClelland: One does know that zero elasticity is a lower bound on the true elasticity. As McCloskey suggested earlier, the usefulness of this fact depends on the case you are making. If your object is to prove that railways were unimportant, you can use this knowledge that the elasticity is greater than zero to produce an upper bound estimate of social saving, which, if it is small, will prove your case. If it is to prove that railways were unimportant, or if the estimate produced is large, then, of course, you cannot make the case without knowing more about the elasticity of demand. And the question remains, what is important and what is unimportant?

Falkus: The issue of how to gauge importance was similar to the one involved in the papers on entrepreneurial performance. One cannot say that performance in Britain was bad without introducing some standard of comparison.

Hawke: The estimates of Fogel and Fishlow for the United States are the implicit standard involved. If one can build up a number of such estimates for many different countries, the issue of importance can be settled in a relative way.

General discussion on the performance of the late Victorian economy

Hughes: He wanted to turn the discussion to the more general underlying issue. Economic historians his age or older had been raised to believe in a 'Great Depression' of the late nineteenth century. A student of his, William Kennedy, had found that there was a good deal to be said for turning the idea on its head. One would expect a developed industrial economy like Britain to stop expanding its pig iron and coal output at some point and start expanding its tertiary industries. This is exactly what the British were doing before 1914: Britain serviced the world then as New York City services the Midwest of the United States now. What went wrong was not anything British businessmen did, but World War I. Had it not been for the war and the resulting destruction of the international economy, they would have gone ahead selling manufactured products to the tropics, as New York sells light manufactures to Chicago, and would have concentrated still more on foreign investment, banking, insurance and shipping. The discussion of the period is based on the premise that everything the British did was wrong and stupid. This is an unreasonable premise. An alternative and more favourable view flows from what the men of the late nineteenth century themselves, such as Wicksell, wrote about their times.

Harley: It seemed that the case Hughes is making is precisely the direction in which American research on Britain is going. This conclusion is emerging, for example, from the papers at this conference. He himself was currently working on a notion that in Victorian Britain one can find a Leontief Paradox, which explains some of the peculiarities of trade patterns that most scholars have called 'irrationalities'.

Lindert: It is one thing to take a pessimistic view of how the British economy performed in this period, but quite another to say that 'stupidities' or 'irrationalities' were perpetrated. There is much literature that suggests that things were going badly for Britain, but not that Britain was herself causing these things to go badly.

McCloskey: In response to Lindert, one did not have to read economic historians to form an impression that the late Victorians were to blame for their own situation: whether correctly or incorrectly, many of the late Victorians believed it themselves.

Feinstein: Two separate issues were being confused in the discussion.

The first is the issue of fact, whether or not there was a 'climacteric' in the growth of output per man and whether or not growth was slower in Britain than elsewhere. The second is an issue of explanation, whether the failures of growth were caused by irrational decisions by British entrepreneurs or by objective circumstance. It is not right to say that everyone has said that British behaviour was 'stupid'.

Hughes: The discussion by historians of foreign investment after 1870 was a good case of the charge of irrational behaviour. Thomas, among others, has argued that Britain lost many opportunities when it did not bring this investment home after the Great Depression. He himself, on the contrary, thought the British decision may well have been quite rational, foreseeing a world in which Britain specialized in international commercial and investing services. And, in any case, why should Britain have gone on growing at a fantastic rate?

Thomas: He wanted to state as precisely as he could where he agreed and where he disagreed with Hughes's argument on foreign investment. Up to 1900, there is no question that foreign investment by Englishmen paid, because it made possible the flow of cheap imports. Under these circumstances it is idle to ask what private investors would have done had they been responding to marginal social, rather than private, return. After 1900, however, the circumstances changed. The export of capital from 1902 to 1913 was phenomenally large, larger in proportion to national income than at any other time or in any other country. As Schumpeter pointed out, at precisely the time that foreign investment was taking such a large proportion of the total savings of the country, there appeared the crucial innovations in chemicals, electricity and engineering that required massive investment to bring them to fruition. There was no need by 1900 to build further infrastructure abroad to get the imports. After 1900, then, it is not by any means idle to ask whether the continued adherence to the private market signals in the distribution of investment was in the long run interest of the British economy. And the most likely answer is that it was not.

Supple: On the matter of growth rates, was Hughes saying that if World War I had not occurred the rate of growth would have been as high in the 1920s as it could have been, even though lower than it had been in the past?

Hughes: It would probably have been higher. Some deceleration was to be expected. After all, the American rate of growth has slowed down: why should the British rate have continued indefinitely at the high levels of the nineteenth century?

Pollard: There was still no excuse for the out-of-date equipment that characterized the key British export industries — cotton textiles, iron, and so forth. Charles Wilson has made a persuasive case that a great deal of superior entrepreneurship was shown in the small consumer goods industries, chocolates, books and the like, which do not usually find their way into the statistics. Nevertheless, one cannot ignore the entrepreneurial failures in motor cars, chemicals, electrical engineering and many others.

McCloskey: It remains to be seen that there were in fact entrepreneurial failures even in the old industries. Lars Sandberg has cast doubt on this premise in cotton textiles and he himself has done it for iron and steel: a convincing case can be made that there was no failure. Moreover, one cannot play the game of picking only those industries in which England's performance was poor. The aggregate statistics tell a more balanced story. In fact, the rate of total productivity change in the United Kingdom was as fast as in the United States up to 1900, during the very decades in which Englishmen were becoming convinced of their own failures. The game of examples, moreover, can be played both ways: German agriculture in this period, for example, was certainly not progressive.

Saul: Several other economic historians, including himself, had tried to make a point similar to that of Hughes. Kindleberger's book, *Economic Growth in France and Britain 1851-1950,* was one key source of the opposite view. Kindleberger is one who argues most explicitly that Britain ought to have known before 1913 that she could not go on selling cotton and iron and that she should instead have moved to newer industries. Whether this was so or not in 1913, one can see in retrospect that Britain had to face at some time an enormous problem of transition from the old to the new, and was ill prepared in terms of the training and education needed to make the transition smoothly.

Hughes: Historians a century from now might look back on the United States, as they do now on England, and proclaim the failure of entrepreneurship, simply because the United States is beginning to lose its comparative advantage in, say, automobiles. He agreed with Saul that there may have existed rigidities that made the move from one pattern of comparative advantage to another difficult, but a continuation of conditions before 1913 may well have shown the Victorians' decision to choose the one pattern had been correct.

Sandberg: For the cotton industry many have argued that in 1913 the managers should have known that Britain's world market was narrowing. In the nineteenth century Britain lost one market after another, only to be saved by new markets opening up, especially more and more of India. Perhaps in 1913 they should have foreseen the closure and competition of Japan, India, Europe and Latin America and shifted their money to other industries. As easy as this case is to make in retrospect, it is rather much to expect them to have seen it clearly then. They made decisions intelligently on the basis of the information at their disposal. Their reluctance to adopt the automatic loom, for example, for all the criticism it has inspired, was wise under the reasonable assumption in 1913 that conditions would stay as they were. In the event, it was fortunate they did not install them for the bottom dropped out of their markets.

Edelstein: The cotton textile companies did in fact shift their money to other industries before the war, which Sandberg argues was too much to expect of them. They held securities of local as well as foreign enterprises, and in one case, he believed it was the Thornton Company, these were as high as 75 per cent of their assets.

David: One aspect of the discussion remains most confusing. It seems to slip back and forth between market imperfection and poor entrepreneurial performance on the one hand and market failure on the other. There are some things that even perfectly competitive markets cannot be expected to achieve. An individual cotton textile merchant cannot be expected do always what is best for the industry or the nation as a whole: that he cannot is a market failure. It is important, then, to distinguish two standards of performance. One is the standard of previous performance in the existing market economy and the other is that in a perfect world in which market failures are corrected. Which one is being discussed?

Tyce: The question of the standard of performance is an important one. A common standard, perhaps more common than performance either in the past or in a hypothetical perfect world, is that of foreign performance at the time.

Hughes: He was asked to conclude the discussion by summarizing his case. The best summary, he thought, would be a concrete example. Courtaulds was not an especially dynamic company after the war, but it was able to skirt the brink over which other companies went in 1914 because of American interests in its ownership, which lasted until 1941. Had the war not occurred, there would have been many more such cases of success.

12

Some thoughts on the papers and discussion on the performance of the late Victorian economy

S. BERRICK SAUL

Five of the papers at this conference were concerned directly with the question of the response of different sectors of the British economy to the opportunities and challenges offered by technological and institutional change in the second half of the nineteenth century. It may therefore be useful to comment briefly on the implications of these pieces of research for our interpretation of the performance of the British economy at and since that time. With the exception of Floud, none of the writers concerned himself with evaluating absolute levels of achievement. For the others, the question was: Given the objective conditions facing them, did British farmers, financiers and industrialists behave rationally in an economic sense, or could they have done better with more initiative, knowledge and capital? In general the answer was that they could not. The arguments are not entirely conclusive; it is possible that what McCloskey has proved is that, despite their use of the latest technical devices, the overall performance of the American steel industry never exceeded the mediocre level of the British before 1914. We need a similar comparison with the German steel industry, at least, before it can be said that the argument is convincing. As for coal, the conference did not come to grips with what seems to be one of Arthur Taylor's most telling points. This is that the industry suffered from the existence of numerous small and inefficient enterprises, which moved into production during periods of high prices, shut down during less profitable periods, and effectively hindered rationalization of the industry, both as regards the optimum size of productive units and the most efficient coalfields.

Nevertheless, a powerful case was made out and the entrepreneurial explanation of Britain's weaknesses took quite a beating. Sometimes it was overdone; in discussion it was argued that Sandberg's work showed that cotton manufacturers were rational in not introducing ring spinning and automatic looms before 1914, even though they were sorely missed after World War I. Yet it was also suggested that they did possess enough foresight of future troubles rationally to remove their capital from the industry. But you cannot have it both ways: in fact capital was invested outside the industry only in the context of a unique method of company finance. Huge amounts of new capital moved into the industry during the mill building boom up to 1907. In addition, it must be noted that the papers were concerned almost entirely with the diffusion of technologies. Almost nothing was said about the ability of British industry to *originate* new products and processes; after all, this is where Britain had established such pre-eminence in the Industrial Revolution and it was to be the main way in which American industry overcame its factor price disadvantages in invading world markets. It is significant, too, that it was a man of German extraction and training who first introduced the Solvay process in Britain and that weaknesses of enterprise and education were confirmed as explaining some, at least, of Britain's backwardness in the coal-tar dye industry. Nevertheless, the discussion of the Lindert and Trace paper showed that, as regards replacement of existing plant, the Leblanc makers were justified in holding to their ways, not only while the royalty payments existed but also right on to the mid-1890s, if one makes the correct comparison of variable costs of the old with the fixed and variable costs of the new. Whether or not they would have been justified in increasing total capacity by building more new Solvay plant in addition to that at Fleetwood was not shown in the paper. We would need to estimate what effect this would have had on the price of soda and on the investment plans of Brunner Mond.

As regards the future of the argument for and against British entrepreneurs, we can ignore the rather tendentious argument about where the burden of proof now lies, but we cannot ignore the problem of measurement. How do we show that entrepreneurs were doing badly? Accepting Floud's calculations for Greenwood & Batley, one still has to say: is 2.3 per cent per annum big or little? Floud seems satisfied with it, but at what point would he be disappointed? The answer may lie in a series of international comparisons, but we would face all the time the dictum, given by Lindert and Trace, that the comparisons must reflect the conditions — especially the price relationships — faced by the individuals or firms whose performance is being judged. The usual comparisons of the growth of output or exports tell us nothing here. Aggregate measures of total productivity are very valuable, though a lot of questions remain unanswered, too. It would have strengthened McCloskey's argument, for example, had he been able to show what British steel makers did when they came to create *new* capacity over this period. Alternatively, we might take the Solvay/Leblanc type of comparison further and analyse deviations from best practice in particular industries. Technical journals certainly provide much relevant information on this point.

Assuming that a strong case exists against the entrepreneurial explanation, we are then faced with a new series of problems. The British did as well as could be expected; their businessmen behaved intelligently and rationally but still objective conditions prevented the economy from doing as well as those of other industrializing countries. Whatever measure one takes and whether one sees the problem originating around 1870 or 1900, there is something to be explained. Precisely what were those conditions? This is what David with his field patterns and McCloskey with his geological problems were seeking to establish. This was the burden of the heritage of existing plant in the soda industry. Temin and I have seen the market as such a handicap, too. Now it becomes important to analyse responses under different objective conditions. David has shown that East Lothian farmers had field patterns better suited than most to the introduction of mechanical reaping and that they were in fact way above average in introducing reapers. Unfortunately, this still leaves us with the kind of problem posed by Lindert and Trace early in their paper. Maybe this was due in part anyway to the renowned farming skills of Lothian men, who were in demand as farm managers over the length and breadth of the kingdom. In another context it is pertinent to ask if coal mines in Britain with better geological conditions employed more advanced techniques and were in a position to increase their relative output to a degree that this objective superiority warranted.

But there are other aspects of this general question. We can accept Edelstein's analysis of the effectiveness of the capital market, but the question of externalities that he raises in his last paragraph may cover a wide range of issues. For example, historical factors gave the commercial banks in Britain a limited role in the finance of industry, but strictly from the narrow point of view of raising capital for their own use, the absence of the facilities offered by the investment banks on the continent caused British industry no serious problems. But investment banks had other benefits to offer. In their turn they financed major investment projects and could stipulate that their associated manufacturing concerns should supply the equipment. Undoubtedly the German electrical engineering industry benefited extensively from such arrangements.

A more far-reaching issue was raised by McCloskey's assertion, flatly denied by Landes, that with a free flow of technical knowledge one must normally assume that if a gap began to appear between, say, British and U.S. technologies, which offered substantial financial gains to British entrepreneurs, they would quickly take the new ideas up. Landes's view was that differences in cultural patterns between countries made it most likely that such gaps would persist rather than be closed. It is a pity that the chairman (myself) had to stop discussion of this point because of time difficulties. My feeling is that the current inability of branch plants of American firms operating in Britain to reap the full benefit of their lower labour costs, a baffling phenomenon that they do not themselves understand, indicates that the problem is more complex than McCloskey allows. There is, of course, a fundamental difference between objective irremovable handicaps such as geology and sunk costs, and cultural and institutional patterns. If we are not careful, consideration of the latter will quickly take us back to the vague wonderland of good and bad business men. But it ought to be possible to make a more rational attack on some of these cultural issues. Take the problem of labour. Precisely how, if at all, did restrictive practices by unions hinder the adoption of new technologies? We read that emigrants from Lancashire cotton mills hated the pace of work in American mills and often went back home for that reason. What were the facts and could Lancashire mills with advantage have run at a faster pace? A recent report has shown that fatal accidents in American industry are three times as high per worker as in Britain. Such social costs might be evaluated. Alternatively, we might look to specific industrial problems. Taylor argued, for example, that fierce safety regulations hindered the introduction of electricity into British mines. Was he right, and what were the economic consequences? A close study might tell us how responsive British workers were to wage adjustment and how easy it was to bring about such adjustments.

The conference papers were restricted to discussion of the older industries; even Floud's machine tool firm was definitely not of the newer generation. What of the newer industries? It is still possible to argue that British manufacturers were wholly rational in sticking to making steam engines and textile machinery, and yet be able to see that there were elements derived from early nineteenth-century experience in technical education, labour skills, markets and so forth that were to be inimical to change when it became essential. This seems to be the strong question mark that must be put against Hughes's assertion that Britain's troubles were mostly due to wars. In their absence, Britain would have had time to adjust gradually and would have thrown off the burden of the past easily enough, an argument that gathers force from the adjustments that were actually achieved during the 1930s. But then another war came to hinder adjustment again. It needs careful study, for wars helped as well as hindered, but we need something to explain why the disadvantages of an early start in the first industrial revolution do not yet appear to have been converted into the advantages of a late start in the second.

In the last resort, however, maybe we ought to rethink the whole nature of Britain's development over the last two centuries. Possibly we must come round to accepting that the upsurge of the first two-thirds of the nineteenth century was the unique feature in British economic development. Maybe some of those objective factors that we were all discussing have determined that the long run British rate of growth be well below that of many continental European countries and of the U.S.A. Something like 2 per cent per annum is the natural rate determined by historical and natural conditions. We can always be trying to do better, but should not be too surprised if we fail.

V The Future of the New Economic History in Britain

13

Is the new economic history an export product?

JONATHAN R. T. HUGHES

I will not begin by questioning the legitimacy of this conference. It would not only be ill mannered of me, but an outrage against common sense. We have all gone to considerable trouble to be here, and one must suppose there are sufficient reasons. As I understand it, the purpose of these meetings is the encouragement of quantitative economic history in the United Kingdom. We do not ask whether we think there is enough there now, or whether more would be a good thing. Is the object to 'export' our New Economic History to Britain? I am going to ask if such an exportation is possible. This is going to be a curious paper as I intend to discuss the 'history' of the new economic history and argue that both as an intellectual and a real phenomenon, this particular permutation of economic history is based upon institutional factors that probably cannot be duplicated elsewhere.

I

It ought to be perfectly obvious to anyone who reads the learned journals that there is now, and always has been, plenty of quantitative work of high quality in the British literature. In fact, the quantitative tradition is a great and well developed one in Britain, stretching all the way back to the seventeenth century [1], and it is absurd generally to say that the literature in Britain is in some way deficient; that important historiographical turning points have not hung on quantitative discoveries. Such is just not so. On the basis of the work of individual scholars, the journals contain admirable pieces of every sort of quantitative study of British economic history [2]. No young British scholar could possibly lack for a model, if he were interested in quantitative work. The question is something else. Why are the techniques of modern quantitative work so little used by the 'mainstream' *economic historians* who work and teach in universities in the United Kingdom, compared to the situation here? It has to be a matter of choice, and the vote has apparently gone against computers, economic theory, econometrics and all the rest.

Even if one supposed that British interest were confined to the works of economic historians carrying British passports, how else does one explain how so much of the response to the new ideas that started up with the work of British authors was developed (innovated) on this side of the Atlantic? When some of the greybeards here today were much younger, back in 1953, the Matthews [3] book appeared at the Cambridge Press with its extensive model-building, constructions of intricate hypothetical historical alternatives, data inputs established by complicated estimations of relevant magnitudes from all sorts of evidence, and even a simple regression analysis [4]. What influence did these ideas have in Britain? Certainly no 'movement' comparable to the new economic history has appeared in Britain. Although, I repeat, there have been notable individual exceptions [5]. Over here, the ideas were embraced with alacrity and were developed among the basic techniques which have become bread and butter fare. The same was even more true of the Habakkuk book, now eight years in print. The theses advanced by Habakkuk [6] on Anglo-American technological development in the nineteenth century gave rise to powerful and provocative contributions from this side of the Atlantic, and a vigorous and ongoing debate. Where was the British response? How much of the lack of response is due to active resistance to the use of quantitative techniques among British economic historians? Where is the British part of the new economic history? Why is this movement so largely confined to this side of the Atlantic?

The phenomenon known over here as the 'New Economic History' is most readily understood in terms of its own history, and I think that history is the key to any possibility of its becoming an export product. The truth of the matter is that quantitative economic history here became a real 'movement', which, thus far, has grown like a snowball rolling downhill. That there should be disagreement among scholars about the significance of this body of work is not surprising. But that there should be fear of the work is something else. The idea that the new economic history constitutes a 'threat' to some hypothetical 'establishment' of British historians is a curiosity [7]. What could such a fear mean? How, except on the narrowest possible restrictions regarding the legitimacy of tools of thought, can any sort of historical research be considered a threat to scholars interested in the pursuit of truth for its own sake? For one thing, we should remind ourselves that Americans, too, have written British economic history [8]. British economic history does not belong to Her Majesty's subjects any more than does our history belong to holders of American passports. The most popular research methods of the new economic history were never considered here to be limitationist principles. Those involved wanted to introduce a new range of intellectual aids to research in economic history, not to eliminate the tradition we all built upon and hoped to extend. What happened afterward showed that the new economic history was an idea whose time had come.

Why should its time have come in the U.S.A. and not in the U.K.? Here, I believe, lies the heart of the problem. It is not the case, after all, in economics, that technical advances are circumscribed by national boundaries. The great British economists are ours, too, as are the French, the Dutch, the Swedes, the Germans, Norwegians, Danes, Russians, Japanese, etc. New ideas in the field produce responses in the journals on both sides of the Atlantic, and it makes no difference in which city in the Atlantic community, or elsewhere, the journals are published. Why should it be different in the single case of this particular kind of economic history? Apart from overt professional resistance in Britain, the answer may well be that the conditions of professional development in economic history are too different in Britain and the U.S.A. for our development to be repeated in the U.K., and I suspect that will be apparent in what follows. With your leave, I will speak now as one whose good fortune it was to participate, however modestly, in the growth of the movement over here, and as one who observed the whole thing with the greatest interest.

II

A good deal of modern quantitative work and some celebrated papers appeared before the quantitative movement that came to be called the new economic history gained momentum. When we held the first meetings of what is now the defunct Purdue 'Cliometrics Society' in 1960, we wanted to bring together for discussions those doing quantitative work of any kind in economic history or related fields in the U.S.A. and Canada. The idea was to discuss and criticize each other's ideas and to see how extensive the field was. The first group was small indeed – a dozen or so. We felt the need to meet for mutual support partly because of the evident decline of interest in economic history in economics departments. In several important departments economic history was in danger of becoming extinct in the catalogue offerings. We had to combat that, to try to reunify [9] economic history and economics in undergraduate and graduate education.

I have discussed elsewhere [10] what I think were the reasons for that particular problem over here. The remedy was to introduce into research in economic history at least the *standard* methods of quantitative work then current in economics. It was not at all clear what were the implications of that for the future. But we all felt that the effort had to be made.

The first Purdue meetings proved to us that the prospects were bright. What happened next was something of a surprise, but perhaps should not have been. We discovered that 'demand' for work in economic history among graduate students was there, once it was demonstrated that they need not abandon their interests in modern economics, or their status as economists in that booming market, in order to do historical work. Very quickly the problem of organizing the Purdue meetings on a limited budget became one of rationing out invitations among the tens, and then the scores of young scholars who wanted to attend. From the beginning we had straight theorists, statisticians, historians and econometricians at the meetings to give advice and criticism. Once again, I emphasize that no limitationist principles were used to restrict interest. Soon enough we had international observers at the meetings, some of whom are here today.

I would not go so far as to say that the effort 'saved' economic history from extinction in economics departments, although that contrafactual history is easily constructed. I do agree with Gerschenkron that the effort to apply 'economic analysis and generous use of quantitative tools' is 'far and away the best thing that has happened to the discipline in generations' [11].

Others agreed, too, and demand from economics departments for our young men finally began to rise. The demand was usually specific, for 'Purdue Seminar type' scholars. We found that we could get good jobs for our good students in economics departments. Because new blood had been recruited on a nationwide basis, the jobs could be filled, while the 'pan was hot', as it were. Because our product was in fact economics and added a new dimension to studies of economics at both the undergraduate and graduate levels, the expansion has continued. By the Yale meetings of the Economic History Association in 1964, Ph.D. theses using modern quantitative techniques and computery [12] appeared on the first sessions of that organization devoted to discussion of new Ph.D. dissertations. Such dissertations are now, of course, commonplace.

That the new economic history is primarily an intellectual movement cannot be stressed too much. To this day there had been no organizational structure to the new economic history, no officers, no journal. We did not consider ourselves to be a splinter group. There was no 'direction' of the work, apart from the internal evidence, of how the field would develop. The Purdue meetings of the group called, *for fun*, the Cliometrics Society [13] (now, in its Wisconsin avatar, 'Cliometrics Society International'), served as a focal point only. Invitations were determined informally by soliciting former participants for suggestions. Always the emphasis was upon finding *new recruits*. We wanted to encourage expansion. Money came from Purdue funds, at first under a Ford Foundation grant, and then, on a matching basis, a leading member (Fogel) has diverted funds from our present host, the Mathematical Social Science Board, to keep the meetings propped up, for the 'common good'. It has been a singular movement, and I wonder when there was anything else quite like it in academia. Without a common interest and without willing, and generous, voluntary coopera-tion by all, the Cliometrics meetings could never have succeeded.

The conference participants came from every corner of the United States, from Canada, and from abroad. The impact of the work has been wide indeed, and now the learned journals contain papers representing work far in advance, technically, of those that occasionally startled editors back in the 1950s [14]. This is as it should be, after all. In a healthy profession the old hands should find it increasingly strenuous to keep up with what the younger men are doing.

That the development was a 'natural' one in the American context is explicable by two primary considerations. (1) Even counting the original members, it was the Ph.D. training received in American departments of economics that set (and still sets) the tone of the new economic history. Although, considering the training of the late 1940s and the early 1950s, a lot of the original participants were largely self-educated. Advances in theory and statistics and related 'tools' came directly into the field from the graduate schools. This is a part of being in the economics profession, however, baffling to the superannuated 'founding fathers', already largely in their forties – some nearly out of them. (2) The demand emanating from departments of economics, internationally, for representatives of the new economic history was terribly important. Enthusiasm easily runs high in lucrative professions. Partly the demand is based upon genuine interest in the new work. Partly, though, it must be said that continued demand is due to the good reputations the young men have earned for themselves as teachers in general courses in economics, including straight theory and statistics, as well as in economic history.

Although I do not believe that supply necessarily creates its own demand, it was striking the way the demand for the subject matter from new graduate students made a supply of quantitative economic historians available when demand for them developed. From the straight careerist point of view, the whole enterprise became a gratifying success, and one that was all the more striking compared to conditions of recruitment and placement in the 1950s. We hoped such would be so, we thought it might be, but there were doubts. If I may quote from an appeal we made at the meetings of the Economic History Association at their Philadelphia meetings in 1959:

> We are not suggesting in this paper that there is to be a 'new' economic history which will render non-quantitative economic historians technologically unemployed. It should be obvious that we regard ideas from statistics and data processing as natural aspects of problems of historical study. It should also be obvious that the historian's special knowledge and viewpoint is essential to the useful employment of quantitative methods. Our main point is that modern statistical techniques and computing equipment make possible the intensive exploitation of a vein of historical materials that was perforce only little worked in the past; and that if even a few economic historians would take the time to learn even a little of these new techniques, the 1960s could easily prove the most productive years in the history of the discipline. On the other hand, if the discipline chooses to remain completely in the literary tradition, we can see small hope for anything but a continual rehashing of the already existing sources and a continuation of the century-long cleavage between economics and economic history − a cleavage that should soon disappear if the economic historian is able to provide the economists with new data and new interpretations of the process of economic life. [15]

I think it is clear that the hopes of 1959 were realized and the fears were not. Now then, how good is the product as economic history? Admittedly, we have suffered through some papers that were unique combinations of intellectual stagnation combined with technical escalation. It is no advance in historical knowledge if differential topology or category theory are employed to make trivial points about foolish questions. Some of this sort of thing was to be expected if we were to experiment and to discover how best to use quantitative methods in historical research. We were always aware of the dangers of technocracy, but all were and are economic historians first and foremost, and were constantly reminded that either the object was new light on economic history or else we should be in other fields. Technique alone was never considered to be a primary value in and of itself. Put more baldly, there was a lively awareness that, in the end, either we would be talking to the economic history profession at large, or to ourselves alone.

I think we were most fortunate in the quality of the economic historians who first brought in the new techniques, especially the econometric historians. At the first meeting one expected almost anything. We knew generally about the work of those present that was in print. But econometric history was a surprise. Econometric history was a phrase we did not know of. The attitude was one of complete catholicity as regarded method, though, we were all there to learn. When Fogel [16] was introduced it soon became clear that the new work was going to have a dimension we knew little or nothing about previously. It was not the econometrics that impressed us, but the great patience and care involved in the historical research that lay behind Fogel's numbers. It was clear then that solid historical work of the most arduous kind could be combined with standard econometric techniques to produce unique results. Since then, that standard has had a powerful effect upon the econometric work, always pointing to major economic problems in history. The new recruits who came to successive early meetings at Purdue included, among others, Fishlow, David and Temin, and it was clear that the side would not be let down.

Since the development of the new economic history was so much a matter of mutual support as well as of group criticism, and since the present prosperity of the movement seems so imposing, I think it is worth emphasizing again, in terms of the history of the movement, that there never was a narrowness of direction. This was true in spite of the spectacular success of econometric history, which quickly pulled ahead of some other ideas we were developing. Most of those whose work has fallen under the rubric *The New Economic History* continued their own directions and made the total effort a broadly based one. Materials in monographs, texts, books of readings and articles made it possible to enrich old undergraduate courses and to develop new ones, and the publishers promise more in the immediate future [17]. The tradition of

American economic history was not overthrown, but was enlarged, embellished, sometimes corrected, and many times greatly enriched by this effort. Acceptance of the work by the profession, not without vigorous and heavy criticism, is evidence that the movement *has* made a difference. New questions were raised, old theses revised, and a greater understanding of the past produced.

III

Now I return to the original point. I do not question the premise of these meetings – that it is desirable to encourage this kind of work in the U.K. beyond the individual efforts that have long existed there. How would it be done? Let me underscore certain basic facts about the development of this work over here.

(1)   The guardians of the 'traditional view' did not in most cases attempt to 'legislate' against us. They considered the new work no threat, but as an interesting departure worth studying. Their fair and scholarly attitudes were usually exemplary – and I hope we remember then when our turn to be the 'old' economic history comes, as surely it will. The paper I quoted from earlier was given in the autumn of 1959 to the meeting of the parent body, the Economic History Association, at its invitation. Professor Carter Goodrich personally extended the invitation to us. If we could prove the value of the work, they would accept it. We were spared the miseries of becoming a separatist movement.

(2)   The Ph.D. training as economists of most of the initial members and virtually all the new members infused into the whole movement not only the techniques of quantitative research, but the open attitude of mind of *experiment*. The object of the work was to find the road to truth by intellectual processes that could be checked, work that could be repeated with different data. It was understood that error was an inevitable and no doubt necessary part of the work, and that the detection and correction of error advanced knowledge. Conclusions from deductive processes were not considered to be doctrine or holy writ. This attitude, which comes naturally from modern training in economics, is utterly foreign to those who view history through normative lenses as a platform for political propaganda, or as a field in which certain kinds of research methods, and not others, should be used. I repeat once more, methodological legislation has been foreign to the spirit of the new economic history.

(3)   Not only could new blood be recruited from Ph.D. training programmes in departments of economics, those departments became the places of employment of virtually all of the young 'Cliometricians', and their students, in turn, are already upon us.

There obviously is no 'magic' associated with the great success of the new economic history here. No research techniques used here are unknown in Britain. The differences between what is possible given the structure of the profession in the U.K. and over here may be illuminated for our British guests by the foregoing discussion, and by this question: Could this 'history' have occurred in the U.K.? I would prefer not to answer this question myself. Is there a reasonable alternative 'future history' of the new economic history in Britain? The diversity, breadth and richness of the new economic history in this country is a consequence of easy access to other disciplines. We realized crucial external economies from our involvement in economics departments. How is this, or a substitute for it, to be achieved in Britain?

Others here know far more than do I about the answers to my questions. My own limited experience with economic history in Britain makes me doubt the possibilities there of any extensive development that parallels the way the new economic history grew up here. Some other way would have to be found. Will resistance to quantitative techniques based upon fear of professional obsolescence disappear? Who will *train* the recruits in the methods of modern theory and quantitative analysis? Who will employ them? It would be presumptuous of me to be more specific in the presence of the British economists, historians and economic historians with us here today.

I, for one, would welcome a really extensive movement, backed by sufficient resources, to stimulate quantitative work in Britain. One can easily imagine big payoffs. For the nineteenth century alone the possibilities are dazzling. Mayhew's London could be put on punchcards. It is the equivalent, after all, of a small manuscript census. A vast knowledge of that part of the Victorian world could be made accessible. The same could be done to the Booth volumes for London at the end of the century, and a wealth of comparative information about urban development adduced. The old problem of the lack of *internal* British price indices in the nineteenth century could be solved; using the computer, the declared values and quantities of British exports could be made to yield up price indices for things like hats, shoes, shirts, tinware, china, etc. Interest-yield series for many qualities of securities could be generated from current price quotations. Pure exchange rates between London and her major trading partners could be constructed. One could easily point to a score or more of places where modern quantitative methods could yield really imposing results.

In the event, though, the future of quantitative work in economic history in Britain must be determined within an institutional framework far different from any we have known over here. And only those who live and work within that framework can find that future – if, indeed, there is one to be found.

NOTES

[1] An extensive survey on this point by the present author extending to the early 1960s is in print ('Measuring British Economic Growth', *Journal of Economic History*, March 1964) and need not be repeated here.

[2] Some of it a considerable time ago. For an example of econometric techniques, J. S. Pesmazoglu, 'A note of the cyclical fluctuations of British home investment, 1870-1913', *Oxford Economic Papers*, February 1951. I think the question we are dealing with is the lack of critical reaction by economic historians to such papers in the U.K.

[3] R. C. O. Matthews, *A Study of Trade Cycle History* (Cambridge, Cambridge University Press, 1953).

[4] Ibid., p. 175; consider also the analysis of exports in ch. VI, the discussion and construction of the 'income balance', pp. 99–105, the 'most likely' railway construction pattern, pp. 122–125, and the calculation of the value of cotton output, pp. 148–151.

[5] G. N. von Tunzelmann, 'On a thesis by Matthews', *The Economic History Review*, December 1967.

[6] H. J. Habakkuk, *American and British Technology in the 19th Century* (Cambridge, Cambridge University Press, 1962). Followed by Peter Temin, 'Labor scarcity and the problem of American industrial efficiency in the 1850s, *Journal of Economic History*, September 1966; Robert Fogel, 'The specification problem in economic history', *Journal of Economic History*, September 1967; Ian Drummond, 'Labour scarcity and the problem of American industrial efficiency in the 1850s', *Journal of Economic History*, September 1967; Edward Ames and Nathan Rosenberg, 'The Enfield arsenal in theory and history', *Economic Journal*, December 1968. There are others, including at least one Ph.D. thesis largely stimulated by Habakkuk's book, Paul Uselding, *Studies in the Technological Development of the American Economy During the First Half of the Nineteenth Century* (Northwestern University, 1970).

[7] This attitude has been expressed to several representatives of the new economic history movement by British economic historians in recent years. It was apparent in the note of scarcely restrained hysteria in the critical reviews of Lawrence Stone's book *Crisis of the Aristocracy* (Oxford, Clarendon Press), in which Professor Stone was pilloried for employing a statistician as consultant to help him out with difficult data problems. *Times Literary Supplement*, 7 April 1966, p. 288: '. . . Scholars should welcome statistics, but they must explain fully how estimates and series are constructed and the nature of their limitations as evidence. All this is

tedious and may be abused as a means of evading the duty of attempting meaningful conclusions, however, provisional. But such duties are not discharged by calculating standard deviations and calling in a professional statistician as advisor.' In other words, 'experts need not apply'. The imagination is staggered by such obscurantism. An implied threat of modern techniques appeared at the end of Barry Supple's generous review of *Purdue Faculty Essays in Economic History*, 'Part of our equipment as historians continues under threat of technological obsolescence', *Economica*, August 1968, p. 340. So far as I know, nothing in the new economic history is a methodological substitute for honest scholarship. New techniques strengthen the old, they do not threaten them. I presume that Supple *personally* agrees with me about this view, judging from the broad approaches used in his own work.

[8] And been published in Britain by British presses and enthusiastic and critical British editors. It would be easy to produce a long list of such papers. It can hardly be argued that the professional journals in Britain have been hostile to the new economic history. Such has manifestly not been the case.

[9] Hence the title of Fogel's paper, 'The reunification of economic history with economic theory', *American Economic Review, Papers and Proceedings*, May 1965. The dangers of ignoring theory in the research and writing of American economic history has long been noted of course. Such crimes were blasted by Douglass North, then an editor of the *Journal of Economic History*, before the meetings of the American Economic Association in December 1964, 'The state of economic history', *American Economic Review, Papers and Proceedings*, May 1965.

[10] 'Fact and theory in economic history', *Explorations in Entrepreneurial History*, 2nd Series, Vol. 3, No. 2, 1966. I believe the division of the fields that existed by the 1950s was mainly attributable to changes in economics that occurred with the Keynesian Revolution and the rise of mathematical economics and econometrics after World War II.

[11] Alexander Gerschenkron, *Europe in the Russian Mirror* (Cambridge, Cambridge University Press, 1970), p. 106.

[12] The thesis abstracts are published in 'The tasks of economic history', *The Journal of Economic History*, December 1965.

[13] As a minor historical note, the origin of 'Cliometrics' is described in *Explorations in Entrepreneurial History*, Winter 1965. The inventor of this word was Professor Stanley Reiter.

[14] The paper by Lance Davis, 'The New England textile mills and the capital markets: a study of industrial borrowing, 1840-60', *The Journal of Economic History*, March 1960, raised eyebrows among those who managed the journal in the late 1950s, and temporary limitationist resistance caused a minor *cause célèbre* at the time. Comparison of the quantitative apparatus in that paper with the sorts of things that now commonly appear in that journal will indicate how times have changed.

[15] Lance E. Davis, J. R. T. Hughes and Stanley Reiter, 'Aspects of quantitative research in economic history', *Journal of Economic History*, December 1960, p. 547.

[16] I have tried to stay away from invidious references to individual substantive contributions in the text. But Fogel's 1960 paper was a real watershed. It took hours to read and was called 'The social savings attributable to American railroads in the inter-regional distribution of agricultural products in 1890: an application of mathematical models to a problem of history'.

Many of the results he discussed there appeared later in his book, *Railroads and American Economic Growth* (Baltimore, Johns Hopkins Press, 1964). One reason the paper took so long to read was the intense and almost tortuous grilling Fogel underwent at the hands of the other participants in defending his work. Observation of that process was convincing in a way the published results could never be. Such 'question periods' continue to be the main feature at the Cliometrics meetings.

[17] The new economic history has had unusual publicity almost from the start because its adherents were (are) extraordinarily voluble and prolific. They seized every occasion to proselytize. Of the many summaries, surveys, critiques and methodological works I would suggest: Robert W. Fogel, 'The new economic history: its findings and methods', *The Economic History Review*, December 1966; Lance E. Davis, 'And it will never be literature: the new economic history: a critique', *Explorations in Entrepreneurial History*, 1968, reprinted along with several other papers on methodology and criticism in Ralph Andreano (ed.), *The New Economic History, Recent Papers on Methodology* (New York, John Wiley, 1970). Several papers on specific topics contain general bibliographical information; e.g. P. A. David, 'Transport innovation and economic growth: Professor Fogel on and off the rails', *Economic History Review*, December 1969. At one point, several years ago, Peter Temin entered a mild demurrer in the middle of a famous series on new methods in historical research and writing, *The Times Literary Supplement*, July 28 1966, a demurrer that brought more comment and had the paradoxical effect that it gave the new economic history added publicity in Britain. Many of the papers written using quantitative techniques are well known, but doubtless the most famous paper of all was A. H. Conrad and J. R. Meyer, 'The economics of slavery in the ante-bellum South', *Journal of Political Economy*, April 1958. Probably the best-known monographs in the genre have been, in order of publication, Douglass North, *The Economic Growth of the United States: 1790-1960* (Englewood Cliffs, New Jersey, Prentice Hall, 1961); Robert Fogel, *Railroads and American Economic Growth* (Baltimore, Johns Hopkins Press, 1964); Peter Temin, *Iron and Steel in Nineteenth Century America* (Cambridge, Mass., M.I.T. Press, 1964); Alfred Conrad and John Meyer, *The Economics of Slavery and Other Studies in Econometric History* (Chicago, Aldine, 1964); Albert Fishlow, *American Railroads and the Transformation of the Ante-Bellum Economy* (Cambridge, Mass., Harvard University Press, 1965); Douglass North, *Growth and Welfare in the American Past* (Englewood Cliffs, New Jersey, Prentice Hall, 1966); and Peter Temin, *The Jacksonian Economy* (New York, Norton, 1969). There is a textbook, which has lived into its third edition, L. E. Davis, J. R. T. Hughes and D. McDougall, *American Economic History* (Homewood, Ill., Irwin, 1961, 1965, 1969). There are books of readings: Ralph Andreano (ed.), *New Views on American Economic Development* (Cambridge, Mass., Shenkman Publishing Company, 1965), and more recently *The New Economic History*, cited above. Apparently more collections of readings from various editors and publishers will appear soon. An acidly entertaining roundup and critique by Louis M. Hacker is found in the first chapter, and here and there throughout, in his new book, *The Course of American Economic Growth and Development* (New York, Wiley, 1970). An excellent and fair comprehensive critical paper is G. N. von Tunzelmann, 'The new economic history: an econometric appraisal', *Explorations in Entrepreneurial History*, Winter 1968, also reprinted in *The New Economic History*, cited above.

14

Is the new economic history an export product?
A comment on J. R. T. Hughes

R. M. HARTWELL

I

Why does the new economic history flourish in the U.S.A. and not in Britain? Why, in spite of a distinguished tradition of counting from Thomas Tooke to Colin Clark, in spite also of a long association between economics and history from W. Cunningham (the runner-up when Marshall got his chair in Cambridge) and Clapham (once professor of economics at Leeds) to B. Thomas and A. Lewis, are the economic historians of Britain today so different, in training, work and outlook, from those of the U.S.A.? Posing the difference in terms of persons and their writing highlights the contrast: the difference between the work of R. Fogel, D. North, R. Easterlin, L. Davis, A. Fishlow and R. Gallman (to take a representative senior sample from the U.S.A.) and the work of D. Joslin, J. Fisher, P. Mathias, D. Coleman, B. Saul and S. Pollard (to take a similar senior sample from Great Britain). I am not here arguing that the former write better economic history than the latter, only that there is a world of difference between the type of work they do, the problems they attack and the methods they use, which cannot be explained by a cultural gap measured by the width of the Atlantic. J. R. T. Hughes, as a new economic historian should, explains these differences by the use of economic theory, by an exercise in market analysis. He examines the market for economic history in the U.S.A., concentrating on the demand side, and argues that the growth of new economic history there has been largely demand-induced: new economic history expanded because of the increasing demand for economically orientated economic history or historically orientated economics by an increasing number of graduate students in economics; this demand also induced a growth of faculty, and thus created a beneficial spiral of expanding new economic history. By implication rather than by explicit statement, Hughes infers that the same demand (i.e. the same expanding graduate demand) did not exist in Britain, and that there was, in consequence, no comparable expansion there of new economic history. While agreeing with much of what Hughes says, I would nevertheless give a different explanation for Britain's failure, an explanation that is also market orientated but concentrates on the supply side of the market for economic history, and an explanation that is institutional rather than economic in character. And, perhaps, this concentration on an institutional explanation mirrors the difference between the discipline in our two countries, the one strong in theory and statistics, the other in the traditional studies of the history of politics and of social and economic institutions?

But first let me list my agreements with Hughes:

(1)   Neither of us is concerned with useless discussion about what 'new economic history' is (I would define it, without methodological subtlety, as (*a*) the sophisticated use of theory and statistics, (*b*) the explicit formulation of hypotheses, and (*c*) the careful testing of hypotheses). But we both recognize the importance of the new economic history, agreeing with Gerschenkron that the effort to apply 'economic analysis and generous use of quantitative tools' is 'far and away the best thing that has happened to the discipline in generations'.

(2)   We have no doubts about the expansion of new economic history in the U.S.A. and the lack of expansion in Britain. Although good quantitative analytical history is written in Britain, and has been for a long time, its impact on the research methods of the economic history profession has been small, and 'mainstream economic historians' in Britain are not new economic historians. However, not only has there been no spin-off in Britain from the British quantitative work; there has been none from the new economic history of the U.S.A., even when the Americans have been writing about British history.

(3)   In the development of new economic history in the U.S.A. the Purdue meetings (with mutual support and group criticism) were important in launching and sustaining the subject academically. At the same time the external economies for economic history by being associated with economics and statistics were great, and help to explain the different techniques of the American compared with the British historians.

(4)   Finally, we both agree that there is a great potential payoff for British new economic history of the modern period because of the wealth of Britain's source materials. There is, at present, a gold mine but diggers without tools.

I disagree with Hughes on the following points:

(1)   I argue that the new economic history in Britain does now constitute, if not a threat, certainly a challenge, to the existing economic history establishment; this is a consequence of *not* believing, as Hughes does, that there are no possibilities for the development of new economic history in Britain that would parallel its development in the U.S.A.

(3)   I cannot agree that the new economic history in the U.S.A. flourished as a 'strictly intellectual movement' and that 'organizational structure' was unimportant for its development. It is not proven, to me, that the expansion of new economic history in the U.S.A. was entirely demand-induced, and that supply conditions for its expansion were unimportant.

These agreements and disagreements lead to my own explanation of Britain's culture-lag in new economic history. Briefly, the explanation is institutional, that the organizational structure of economic history in the universities of Britain has successfully prevented the expansion of new economic history. I would argue, further, that, partly by a delayed demonstration effect, but also for other reasons, there are now the beginnings of a new economic history movement in Britain. This move comes mostly, but not entirely, from young economists and economic historians, and, certainly, the absence of Purdue-like meetings to focus and encourage research and discussion has made the process of change a slow one. However, even senior economic historians are now coming to terms with new economic history; articles on it have appeared in *The Economic History Review* and papers on it have been given to the annual conference of the Economic History Society; and there is a move to form an association of new economic historians with regular meetings in mind. Therefore, it seems to me, the revolution is coming, and the next decade will see both a considerable literature of new economic history, and a successful challenging of the establishment and its methods. To give background to these contentions let me give a brief history of economic history in Britain.

II

In 1956 when I arrived in Oxford from Australia there were in British universities only six chairs of economic history — Oxford, Cambridge, Birmingham and Manchester with one each, and London with two — and even fewer readers. Now there are more than twenty-five; indeed a university in Britain today without a professor of economic history is a rarity. And as professors have multiplied, so have departments and supporting staff, so that there is now in Britain a large group of professional economic historians, labelled as such, working in departments of economic history (or departments of economic and social history). Much of this remarkable expansion has come without effort on the part of the economic historians, first as a result of the general expansion of universities, and second as a result of the rapid expansion of the social sciences with which economic history has been identified. As a result of this latter identification, economic history has grown disproportionately. The association of economic history with the social sciences, a main growth sector in British scholarship and academic training, has been, for the purposes of expansion, entirely beneficial to economic history. Yet, to a large extent, this association has been historical, without a comparable association in method and techniques. That the institutional association now exists between economic history and the social sciences cannot be doubted: in most British universities economic history is taught in a separate department, either in an economics faculty, or in a faculty of social sciences; in some universities it is a separate department in an arts faculty (e.g. at Nottingham) and in some it is with the department of history (but only, as far as I know, in Dundee, Manchester, Reading and Southampton). This institutional association, also, has been recognized by the Social Science Research Council (the important body for graduate grants), which includes economic and social history as an appropriate social science within its jurisdiction.

But this recent history of economic history can be understood only in the context of a longer historical background. As a subject, economic history developed in the late nineteenth century, as a branch of economics rather than of history, in hostility to the then deductive basis of economic theory, in hostility also to the policy conclusions to which economic theory seemed to lead (e.g. free trade), and as a natural development from a broadening interest in both economics and history. As a separate discipline it owed most, perhaps, to Cunningham, who urged its claims at a critical period in the history of British universities, just as economics was being integrated into degree courses. Later, largely as a result of the work of historians like Tawney and the Hammonds, who were particularly interested in the social ills of industrial society, economic history was increasingly associated with social history, very often in the same department. The consequence was that economic history became, even before the present great expansion, the only branch or aspect of history to be generally institutionalized in its own department. It is true that there are lecturers (even professors) in legal history, social history, religious history, history of philosophy and history of science, but none of these branches of history has the uniquely privileged position that economic history now occupies in universities. It is significant, for example, that most of the many new universities have departments of economic history, and degree courses in economic history.

I have suggested that the reason for economic history's fortunate strength has owed most to its association first with economics and later with the social sciences. It owes much also to its association with social history and social criticism, and especially with that great surge of social and historical analysis that began in the 1880s and has continued to the present day. Although this analysis was inspired by contemporary problems, it associated these problems with industrial and urban society, and traced their history back to the beginnings of the Industrial Revolution. The result was a literature full of feeling and even passion, of great 'social relevance', and of great influence. And, important for economic history, it was firmly associated with economic history, to the extent indeed that economic history in this country has come to be thought of as 'social and economic history', even if the shorthand 'economic history' is usually used to describe a department, or 'economic historian' to describe an individual.

But the survival of any discipline depends not only on the institutional arrangements for its teaching and research, however favourable they might be, but also on its personnel, both student and teaching, and on the attraction of its subject matter. On personnel economic history has been particularly fortunate. Economic history in Britain has attracted an impressive array of formidable talents. A list of important British historians of the twentieth century would certainly include many economic historians (e.g. Cunningham, Unwin, Clapham, Tawney, Ashton), and in any pecking-order of modern British historians Tawney must come close to the top, not only because of what he wrote, but because of his remarkable influence. The influential economic historians fall into two groups: one group, including the Webbs, the Hammonds and, above all, Tawney, were in the tradition of the great European liberal historians, capable of 'a comprehensive view of human nature' and of human society, who were motivated as much by a feeling for their fellow-man as by a passion for history; they were great historians at the same time as being formidable critics of contemporary society. The other group, including Unwin, Clapham and Ashton, were the great professionals, improving techniques of writing economic history and giving tighter standards to the discipline, and less liable to confuse indignation about the world in which they lived with understanding of the world of the past. It was because of the efforts of both groups that *The Economic History Review* was founded in 1927, and that economic history enjoyed such prestige in the 1930s.

The expansion of economic history, however, depended also on its subject matter. Economic history expanded, particularly between the wars, because it gave precision and prestige to history at a time when its claims were being deflated. In particular, it gave to history explanatory tools; it made it seem scientific. Moreover, all historians fell, to some extent, to the economic interpretation of history: this can be seen in their increasing fondness for explanations in terms, for example, of class interests, and in their use of broad explanatory concepts like feudalism, mercantilism and capitalism. All historians believed increasingly that the economic motive was perhaps the most important factor in historical change. This combination of doctrine and technique undoubtedly gave history a much needed boost. This was important for two reasons. There had been in the twentieth century a general decline in the prestige of history, both as a discipline and also as serious literature. The professionalization of history had certainly been accompanied by a decline in the belief of the utility of history, and by a decline also in the readability of history. By 1930 history was often seen neither as instructive nor artistic, qualities both assumed to be characteristic of history in the nineteenth century. For a long time the historian had regarded his subject as both pleasant and useful; it was reckoned that historical inquiry would yield insights of general application to social processes. The precise mechanism whereby the historian achieved his general insights was uncertain; but there was confidence that history somehow helped the understanding of the present. History was assumed to be an appropriate training for men of affairs, for businessmen as well as for politicians. Hence the general use of such phrases as 'history proves . . .', 'the verdict of history . . .' and 'history tells us . . .', and the training of most men of affairs in classical or modern history. History was past experience and lessons were to be learnt from history that would benefit the man of present affairs.

Since the beginning of the century, however, there had been the development of the social sciences, with techniques of inquiry and methods for testing hypotheses that were far more effective than any the historian had ever possessed. These new subjects not only robbed history of much of its traditional subject matter, but also posed difficult questions about the appropriateness of the historian's method. Thus history was made to appear amateurish and descriptive and without proper tools of analysis. The only rationale left for history seemed to be its entertainment value. However, the development of economic history, with some of the techniques and precision of the social sciences, certainly helped to rescue history from the entertainment industry, and to give it new importance and a new lease of life as a serious subject. Hence the great attraction and importance of economic history to the historians; it combined the traditional values of a humane study with the skills of the new social engineering subjects, especially economics. Hence the popularity of economic and social history with the historians. History as a university discipline was undoubtedly strengthened and expanded by an increasing concentration on economic and social topics, so that today there are in all history departments people who could be described as economic historians, and in all history courses much that could be described as economic history. If, for example, we consider the historical commitment — in research and teaching — to 'the rise of the gentry' theme (which stemmed directly from Tawney's *The Agrarian Problem in the Sixteenth Century*), this point becomes obvious.

III

But if economic history has been important to the historians, it has not been very important, until recently, to the economists. It is true that most economics courses in Britain have included courses in economic history, but the development of economics has not depended, in any significant way, on economic history. Except for Cunningham, a historicist, no economic historian or economist has argued about the prime importance of economic history for economics. Only recently, with universal interest in growth, has the economist turned to economic history for information and guidance. It is fair to say, I think, that generally they have been disappointed in what they have found. Economic history has not been concerned with the analysis of problems in such a way as to interest the economists. This is the main reason, I think, why the economists, when they have become interested in historical problems, have written their own economic history.

Instead of what one might expect, the economic historians turning increasingly to economics to strengthen their discipline, it is rather that the economists have written their own history. And so there exist now in Britain two quite distinct literatures – *economists' economic history,* written by economists, largely for economists, and *historians' economic history,* written by economic historians and historians. *Economists' economic history* is what in the U.S.A. is called new economic history. Generally speaking, it has had less than its deserved impact on *historians' economic history,* both because it is often more technical than either the economic competence or the historical taste of the economic historian can tolerate, and also because it is concerned with subjects that do not particularly interest the economic historian. However as yet there has not been a *Methodenstreit.* There has been, so far, little proselytizing by the economists for new economic history, no serious methodological questioning by economists of traditional economic history, and only the beginnings of an institutional threat to departments of economic history (for example, by economics departments recruiting their own economic historians).

To further understand economic history in Britain today, let me examine staff recruitment in economic history departments and the content of economic history degrees. First, on staff recruitment. Most of the professors in economic history departments are either graduates in 'economic history or history; very rare, if ever, is the graduate in economics. This is not to say that these historians did not do some economics in their degree training, or have not learnt economics since graduation. I am making the point that the background of British economic historians is not in economics. In contrast, the American economic historians, who are best known as new economic historians, have all had their main undergraduate and graduate training in economics (Fogel, North, Fishlow, Davis, Hughes, Gallman, Easterlin) and are, generally speaking, professors of economics in economics departments and faculties.

As with professors, so with supporting staff. Recruitment to economic history departments is rarely from economics graduates. In my own experience, for example, of the more than ten Nuffield students who hold lectureships in economic history in British universities, only one was trained as an economist (and not in Britain), and more than half had their first degree in history; most of them had a first degree either quite devoid of economics or with little economics, backed with a research degree in economic or social history, and it has been the research degree (not graduate courses in economics) that established their claims to be appointed as economic historians in departments of economic history. I know that many departments of economic history have been attempting recently to recruit economists; I know, also, that these efforts have been, generally, unsuccessful. And while economic history remains institutionalized in its own department, it will continue to be difficult to recruit economists to such departments. When, as in the U.S.A., there are departments of economics in Britain that recruit economists to economic history, there will be more new economic historians. To my way of thinking, therefore, it has been a disservice to the technical development of economic history to have had economic history institutionalized mainly in departments of economic history. It would have been better to have had a pluralist system: historians in history departments teaching economic history, as historians; economists in economics departments teaching economic history, as economists; and economic historians in economic history departments teaching economic history, as economic historians. There is a need both for *economists' economic history* and *historians' economic history*. The trouble in Britain today is that economic history is taught generally by historians and rarely, if ever, by economists.

Second, as regards courses. Courses reflect staff, and the predominant pattern of degree courses in economic history in Britain is non-economic. Many courses include economics, sometimes as a compulsory subject, more often as one of a variety of options; but not one course I know has advanced statistics and econometrics as compulsory subjects. Not one course I know assumes that the proper training of an economic historian should include advanced analytical and quantitative techniques for handling historical data. The usual degree course in economic history is historical in character, with various courses in the economic history of Britain and other countries, with special subjects (also historical courses on industries, social movements or themes). Indeed there is a remarkable, and to my mind an unfortunate similarity about the degree courses in economic history throughout Britain, whether at Edinburgh or Canterbury, Exeter or Hull. And the dilution of economic content is much increased by the coverage, which most degree courses in economic history give, of social history.

IV

What of the future? I would argue that, in spite of the relative neglect of economics in economic history departments, and of economic history in economics departments, there is sufficient change to be reasonably optimistic. There is, now, new economic history being written in Britain that exposes much of the traditional economic history for what it is, 'the unsystematic and unscientific marshalling of unreliable data'. Increasingly, especially by younger economic historians, there is realization that, while it is obviously absurd to condemn wholesale the vast range of the literature of traditional economic history, much of that literature is concerned with material that is amenable to sophisticated statistical and economic analysis, and would certainly have been better if better techniques had been used. It is realized, also, that better theory and statistics will enable the new economic historian to identify and analyse problems with which the traditional economic historian cannot cope. Gradually the distinguished work of British economists on British economic history is forcing all economic historians to come to terms, not only with the conclusions of this research, but also with its methods. Already, for example, the influence of A. K. Cairncross, R. Matthews and E. H. Phelps-Brown is being felt in the syllabuses of economic history courses and in the writing of economic history; no doubt, in time, more also will be heard of economists like Brinley Thomas, J. Parry Lewis and G. T. Jones. Also important has been a recent move to enable those interested in new economic history to meet regularly to discuss and criticize their work and methods. And, most important, there are now economics departments that are seeking economists to teach economic history, away from the departments of economic history, and without regard of the traditional course structure of economic history departments.

Finally, I would like to suggest that the best thing for British economic history would be a large scale interest in British economic history by those graduates referred to by Hughes. If we had a stream of technical papers of high standard about British economic history, which challenged traditional theories of how the British economy developed and changed, then there would be a fruitful confrontation. In the first place, therefore, rather than encourage British economic historians to write new economic history, I would like to encourage American economic historians to write British new economic history. That, it seems to me, would be a most beneficial activity for the future health of economic history in Britain.

15

Can the new economic history become an import substitute?

BARRY SUPPLE

The departure point for this paper is Hughes's analysis of the export
prospects (from the American viewpoint) of the new economic history.
My aim is to elaborate some of the points he made about the
institutional setting, which may, or may not, explain the British
reaction to and acceptance of the new economic history – and,
incidentally, to attempt to give some sort of response to the questions
about the counterfactual past and the hypothetical future, which, with
unnecessary modesty, he declines to answer.

There is, I hope, no need for me to say anything in detail about the
recent evolution of econometric and allied sorts of history: their
progress and typology have already been well and frequently charted.
But it is perhaps relevant to confirm a symptomatically important point.
which Hughes made about the first Purdue Conference on Cliometrics
in 1960. It is that the Conference had a genuinely innovating air.
Admittedly, the Meyer-Conrad article on slavery had appeared two
years earlier. But the Purdue Conference was the first gathering of
like-minded practitioners (as well as of a few astonished observers), and
it exemplified that dramatic specification of the counterfactual
hypothesis together with the manipulation of models and quantitative
data, which have become hallmarks of the new *genre*. As a result there
was, indeed, a sudden flush of emotion – optimism, excitement,
anxiety, scepticism – as those attending sensed that new questions were
being put and provocative anwers were being derived.

> Bliss was it in that dawn to be alive,
> But to be young [and numerate] was very heaven!

They were, indeed, times

> When Reason seemed the most to assert her rights,
> When most intent on making of herself
> A prime Enchantress – to assist the work
> Which then was going forward in her name!

Now I make this point not in order to imply that there has been a
subsequent disillusionment comparable to the liberal reaction against

the French Revolution – although it is tempting to see some of the recent hatchet work as the academic equivalent of a Reign of Terror, and to see the modern parallels to a nationalistic reaction to the invasion of revolutionary armies. Rather, it seems to me important to emphasize the sense of vivid radicalism that surrounded those discussions in order to suggest that there *was* a fundamental novelty about the development and prospects of econometric/quantitative history – a novelty that was not the less important for having been partly anticipated (what social movement has not been anticipated?), by the quantitative tradition in economic history or by the more recent history of statistics and econometrics. In other, and more banal, words, the new economic history *was* genuinely new.

In retrospect, the vast proliferation and the considerable achievements of the last ten years, have, I think, justified the enthusiastic response of those few of us who had to be dragged away from Purdue's magnificent underground bowling alley in order to admire – in that hypnotized way that non-statisticians will admire the difficult and the incomprehensible – what was to us a new methodology. But if the product is so good and exciting (or even if it merely appears to be good and exciting) why is it relatively little used in Britain? Even more important, will it ever become significantly *more* used?

I do not think that there can be any doubt that Hughes is right when he suggests institutional reasons for the relative failure of new techniques to change the pattern of British economic history so far. The structure of the profession has been against it in two important and related ways. First (and this was certainly even more so ten years ago), the training of most economic historians in Britain has simply not fitted them to deploy, or in many cases even to *understand*, econometric or statistical or highly theoretical techniques. On the whole, those American economic historians who have absorbed and developed the new methods (as distinct from that large number of Americans who still challenge and reject them) were trained as economists – that is, they secured postgraduate qualifications in economics. What is more, those qualifications (again in contrast to the situation in Britain) frequently presuppose a systematic and 'professional' study of economics and statistics and econometrics. In Britain the tradition – albeit a changing one? – has been quite different: postgraduate students are not given a 'professional' training, and economic historians are produced much more frequently by specialized departments or by departments of history. This, in fact, raises the second point – namely the continuing,

Barry Supple 425

indeed the increasing, structural division between economic history and economics. Over the last generation or so British economic history has come of age in terms of academic structures, by being awarded (and sometimes even earning) separate departmental status. This development has in many respects been beneficial to the discipline, since it has enabled it to operate independently, to move on from a subordinate, instrumental position, and to strengthen its respectability and standing. Yet, in spite of such advantages, independence has also meant continued and even intensified academic compartmentalization. In fact, of course, the growth of separate economic history departments has largely been a matter of differentiating the subject from history. At the same time, however, it has also meant drawing, or at least confirming the existence of, boundaries between economic history and economics. As a result old barriers to methodological communication have tended to remain (although, as I shall argue later, they have been more frequently and more interestingly surmounted than they used to be) and to make it difficult for economic historians to consider new analytical techniques as equal alternatives to the tradition of literary and arithmetical-quantitative evidence in which they were reared.

Yet, as economic and social historians in the literary tradition well know, the relationship between institutional structures and ideologies is a complicated one. While the structure of economic history in Britain – as Hughes implies – makes it difficult to train or employ 'new' economic historians, the historical attitude towards what constituted training for and the nature of economic history obviously helped determine the institutional structures within which training and academic employment are located. In other words we are dealing with a vicious, or a virtuous (depending on your standpoint), circle.

However, none of this gets us very far in understanding the nature of the problem, which is some respects worse and in some respects better than I have implied; nor does it provide the basis for answering the question about the scenario of the new economic history's future in Britain.

To understand the differential development of the new techniques in the United States and in Britain we should, I think, examine the various reactions to it. Now it is true that in America the application of econometric techniques or the use of counterfactual methodology has produced some protests and even an occasional cry of outrage. But on the whole, as Hughes has pointed out, the mainstream of economic history accepted and absorbed the new methods. In Britain, by contrast, the suspicion of them is, perhaps, somewhat more virulent than one might deduce from the printed word. There is, undoubtedly, a good deal to be suspicious of, and aspects of the methodology as well as some of its practitioners are by no means above criticism. But the fact remains that some of the British reaction seems to be based more on the fear of the unknown and the unknowable than on a reasoned critique of the imperfect and the inapplicable.

In his paper Hughes expresses surprise that the new economic history could be considered a 'threat' to British economic history and asks, with a commendable flourish, how any sort of historical research can be considered a threat to scholars interested in the pursuit of truth for its own sake. The answer, alas, lies in the attitude of the members of any profession to the claim that a new range of skills (methodologically very different from any that they have known and, let us assume for the sake of argument, probably beyond their ability to learn) will not only add to the fund of knowledge, but is a critical and perhaps essential way of securing answers to questions that it is his professional responsibility to ask. There is all the difference in the world between an invention that is complementary to existing skills, thus making them more useful, and one that at least threatens to displace them.

I am not, of course, arguing that the new economic history will in fact prove a supreme highroad to truth — merely, that if, and as far as, its claims are valid, then it would hardly be possible to say anything very useful about the profitability of slavery, or the economic importance of railroads, or about a wide variety of other economic problems with quantitive dimensions, without having appropriate qualifications — qualifications which to many British historians are extremely, and perhaps hopelessly, 'technical'. It is this that could pose a threat — not to the monopoly of British economic history by holders of British passports but to those who cannot contemplate with any equanimity the prospect of an intellectual retooling [1]. What we really have to ask — and I hope you will forgive the crudity with which I phrase the question — is whether we are in danger of going through a phase of academic Luddism? For although it is true that new techniques *can* strengthen the old, it is not true, as Hughes implicitly claims, that they invariably do so. Sometimes new techniques *do* threaten the old ones. And I myself feel that whether the intellectual future of new economic history be bright or bleak, and whether it has much or little to say, it is not entirely respectable to offer any rejection or large criticism of its approach that is not also based upon a prior grasp of its techniques. I appreciate that this is a provocative sort of assertion to make, and I can certainly imagine categories of criticism on methodological or philosophical grounds that do not presuppose an understanding of the statistical or econometric tools being used. All I would add is that such criticisms would have to be examined very carefully indeed.

So far, then, I have tended to agree with Hughes about the institutional causes of Britain's having failed to innovate (or quickly imitate) in the field of the new economic history – although I take more seriously than he does the overtones of ideology and threat that have accompanied the discussion of the new economic history in its pioneer years. His own answer to his first question – 'Could this "history" have occurred in the U.K.?' – is implicit in his own paper. It is 'No, because the British beast is reared in a different sort of zoo.' I agree with this judgement, adding only that that is the sort of zoo the beast likes, and that he gets a bit restless (and even dangerous) if disturbed too abruptly.

But all this is past history. What about Hughes's other question: 'Is there a reasonable alternative "future history" of the new economic history in Britain?' And here I think that there are other, and more varied and even optimistic, factors at work that there were a decade ago.

In this respect the first point needing emphasis is the obvious one that if those who called themselves economic historians were not accustomed to using complex statistical and econometric and model-building techniques in the study of the past – those who call themselves economists were! Hughes cited the example of R. C. O. Matthews and, of course, there are many others who could be named in the same category. Moreover (and before I am accused of drawing artificial distinctions), just as one would be hard put to specify why Phelps-Brown, Matthews, Thomas or Feinstein should not be called economic historians, so a good deal of recent work by those whose continued specialist occupation it will be to teach economic history is in fact imbued with both the spirit and the techniques of the new economic history. Slowly and fragmentarily (again because of the institutional handicaps – but not any insurmountable obstacles), a future history is already beginning to emerge. Nor is this because of any slavish imitativeness or idle fashion. It is, I think, because of the nature of the subject-matter and the questions that are beginning to attract research workers. In the past the best examples or anticipations of new economic history in Britain came from the pens, or calculating machines, of economists precisely because they were concerned with problems of economic performance in a historical context. By the same token, as soon as economic historians begin to concern themselves with new sorts of questions, or new ways of phrasing old questions, we may expect that their research methodology will (perforce) grow more 'sophisticated'. Nor, indeed, is it always a matter of any very fundamental methodological novelty. As some of the pioneers of the new economic history pointed out a decade ago, 'Some kinds of historical problems are by nature data-processing problems. In the past they have too often been neglected [or, one might interpolate, tackled imperfectly] simply because too much labour was involved. Today, with the purely mechanical computational problems much reduced, economic historians have the means to study these questions' [2].

We are, in other words, back with a cliché of the social sciences: the fact is that in economic history as in other disciplines your choice of subject matter and the type of questions you ask determine the methods you use (as well as the answers you get). And it is for this reason that I am more optimistic about the future of new economic history in Britain than my earlier view of entrenched attitudes might suggest. For as long as the tide of interest in British economic history is running in the direction of what (for want of a better phrase) can be called 'analytical-economic' topics and questions, the appropriate methodological adjustment will follow as night follows the day — albeit in a more uncertain and lagged fashion as befits the unreliable British climate. As Hughes pointed out, there have never been any national frontiers between the United States and the United Kingdom in the methodology of economic *theory* — and this is because there have never been any national frontiers in the subject matter. So, one might argue, as British historians begin to concern themselves with the type of subject matter — and notably the asking of questions shaped by an awareness of economic theory — exemplified in recent American work, so the 'new' economic history will take root.

To this extent, of course, the implication of the argument is that market mechanisms will be reasonably effective in supplying the new economic history if only the demand (measured in terms of the desire of economic historians to tackle certain sort of problems) is strong enough. On the other hand, however, the ease and efficiency with which these can be achieved and, indeed, the readiness of economic historians to focus attention on relevant issues, are in part functions of the institutional situation. Hence, although I feel that there is an increasingly effective incentive for British historians – especially those in the early stages of an academic career –to follow the trails blazed by American pioneers, it may still be possible to expedite the process, and to stimulate them to ask the newer sorts of questions.

If we turn back to this question of the institutional framework, two aspects stand out as being susceptible to some social engineering. They are those that Hughes had in mind when he asked 'Who will *train* the recruits in the methods of modern theory and quantitative analysis? Who will *employ* them?'

The first of these questions really concerns our *system* of post-graduate education. For just as the first generation of American econometric historians did not receive their *technical* training from economic historians, so in Britain the communication of statistical and analytical skills can be the task of specialist statisticians and economists – or, at least, of specialist statisticians and economists who have an interest in historical problems.

The really important difficulty is not the supply of teachers (although there *are* considerable problems in the teaching of statistics by statisticians to non-specialists) – but, rather, the restructuring of graduate education along more 'professional' and systematic lines.

Indeed, in this respect, and quite apart from the question of new economic history, there are strong arguments in favour of precisely such a restructuring – arguments that are in part being acknowledged by the recent rise of course-work M.A.s. After all, letting an individual loose on his own on a bundle of original sources, while a vital aid to his development as an economic historian, is an inadequate preparation for a professional career in a social science. And for this reason it seems essential that we should pay more attention to the advantages, as well as the vices, of the American Ph.D. system. In the course of that examination we shall no doubt encounter all sorts of structural obstacles in the form of a large number of institutions attempting overambitious tasks with inadequate resources, of the diseconomies of the small-scale production of graduate students, of teaching methods and technology. No doubt, too, there will have to be partial or temporary answers in the form of cooperative work between universities, of short courses at central institutions, and so on. But I do not see how we can continue in our present haphazard way much longer – and, of course, where universities are sufficiently large or lively, individual groups *are* no longer continuing in a haphazard way.

Secondly, as to who would employ new economic historians in

Britain, I myself do not think this is very much of a problem. For one thing, the American experience shows that new-style historians are not the less able to teach good old-fashioned economic history, and that, in any case, undergraduates are keen to confront the demands and excitement of new-style work. In addition (and this is also a lesson of the American experience), there is every reason to expect that new-style economic historians would not only be useful, but would actually be *welcome,* members of economics departments.

In fact, as many of us are now aware, it is the supply of, rather than the demand for, new economic historians that is deficient in British universities. The willingness on the part of individual departments to employ them is patently obvious. It is, however, difficult to track down and capture the beast.

Yet it seems that this situation will and must change. The new techniques will be institutionalized, and perhaps civilized, in one arm of British economic history. For in the last resort they reflect a range of analytical concerns that cannot be ignored.

NOTES

[1] This is what I meant by my comment (quoted by Hughes in a footnote to his paper) that 'Part of our equipment as historians continues under threat of technological obsolescence': *Economica,* August 1968, p. 340. I was in fact arguing that the reaction to the new methods might be obscurantist — although by no means sharing in it.

[2] Lance E. Davis, Jonathan R. T. Hughes and Stanley Reiter, 'Aspects of quantitative research in economic history'. *Journal of Economic History,* XX, 4, December 1960, p. 543.

16

The new economic history in Britain: A comment on the papers by Hughes, Hartwell and Supple
R. C. O. MATTHEWS

This note is not intended to register dissent from the three stimulating papers that have been circulated. Its intention is to add certain supplementary points, relating particularly to the appeal, or rather lack of it, offered by economic history to young British economics graduates.

The major premise of my argument is that work in the style of the new economic history is generally bound in the nature of things to come from those whose original training was in economics rather than history; and from those, moreover, whose original training in economics was carried to quite an advanced level. The reason for this is not that the theoretical or statistical techniques used by the new economic historians are particularly abstruse or advanced. It is more a matter of attitude of mind. Alain Enthoven once remarked that in recruiting economists for the Department of Defense it was necessary to engage Ph.D.s, not because the techniques used were those taught in advanced graduate programmes but because students had not internalized the concepts taught to them in their sophomore years until they had finished their Ph.D.s [1]. The same applies in economic history. The acquisition of the techniques of economic theory and statistics by those originally trained as historians is not impossible, as distinguished examples prove; but it is difficult, and it is not in general likely to be an adequate substitute for indoctrination in these techniques from an early and formative age.

The slow development of the new economic history in Great Britain must therefore be traced to the failure of young economics graduate students to turn to economic history in sufficient numbers. This has not been because of a lack of demand for their services. As Max Hartwell says, many British universities have wanted to recruit such people in recent years but have not been able to find them. What is the reason? And why has the experience been different from that of the United States? I think there are a number of answers, which partly overlap each other.

(1)   British economists are less willing to make a lifetime commitment to a particular 'field' than are American ones. This was true at the

time when Sargent wrote his famous article [2], and it is still true today, though to a rather less extent. The reason lies no doubt partly in the British tradition of the gentlemanly generalist; it is also partly because of the smaller academic job market, which is liable to place at a disadvantage an individual whose skills are highly specific. A graduate student who devotes a major part of his attention to economic history is making a fuller and more irrevocable commitment to a particular field than he would be doing if he were to work on, say, money or public finance. This is because he requires to make a bigger investment in background study and also because he is likely to be drawn into an economic history department from which it may be difficult for him to return to the mainstream of economics.

(2)   A smaller proportion, I think, of British graduate students than of American ones intend from the first to have an academic career. Many of them are considering jobs in government, business or international organizations, or at least want to reserve the option of moving in that direction. For that kind of employment economic history is obviously not the most suitable specialism.

(3)   Everyone naturally tends first to think of doing work on his own country. For the British student, there is in any case not much choice: one can obviously not compete with Americans on American economic history, and economists do not know foreign languages. But there is a feeling, unjustified no doubt, yet still containing an element of truth, that the economic history of Great Britain is a thrice-told tale. It appears less attractive on intellectual grounds than mathematical economics and less attractive on grounds of social utility than development or the present day problems of the British economy — these being the fields that are most popular.

(4)   The mere difference in scale between the American and British academic communities means that even a small proportion of American economics graduate students turning to economic history provides an absolute number sufficiently large to generate *esprit de corps* and other external economies, whereas the same is not true in Great Britain.

These considerations are not likely to change very quickly. Hence it seems to me unlikely that there will be a big flow in the near future of well qualified young economists into economic history.

The best prospect of encouraging the writing of good economists' economic history in Britain at the present time seems to be to persuade economists that economic history is something they can respectably and profitably work on without necessarily committing themselves to be economic historians for life. This approach is not in all respects ideal: I do not mean to suggest that history is something anyone can turn his hand to at a moment's notice, whereas economics requires years of arduous training. Brief incursions by economists into economic history do involve the danger that the practitioners will be insufficiently acquainted with the general historical background of their studies (though there is no reason at all why they should not acquire a proper scholarly knowledge of the material, quantitative and non-quantitative, in their own particular area of research). However, there is compensation, not only in the application of the ways of thought of the economist to economic history, but also in the acquisition by some economists of a historical attitude useful in applied economics generally. Both sides have something to learn.

There will, I am sure, not be lacking at the conference those who will question whether the new economic history is really something we want to encourage as much as all that after all, and who will feel that British economic historians are being urged to replace their no doubt antiquated intellectual equipment with equipment that is itself on the verge of obsolescence. Certainly some topics of economic history − for example, cycles of money, or the balance of payments are more amenable to treatment solely by means of quantitive economic techniques than are others, such as changes over time in the growth rate of productivity. There is perhaps a paradox that we should at the same time urge a more interdisciplinary approach upon economists and urge historians to be more narrowly economic. But one step is better than none, even though two steps may really be needed. An interdisciplinary approach may be the best, but a single-disciplinary approach is better than an approach that is not disciplinary at all.

NOTES

[1] Alain C. Enthoven, 'Economic analysis in the Department of Defense', *American Economic Review, Papers and Proceedings*, May 1963, pp. 413−23.
[2] J. R. Sargent, 'Are American economists better?', *Oxford Economic Papers*, March 1963, pp. 1−7.

General discussion on the future of the new economic history in Britain

Chairman: B. Supple

Hughes: Someone had suggested to him that his paper was somewhat out of date, and he hoped this was true. On the basis of the sample at the conference, the pessimism in the paper may have been unwarranted. Nonetheless, Matthews is right to stress the need in Britain for graduate training in economics. It is not clear where the substitute for the American programme in theory and statistics is to come from.

Feinstein: He agreed with Hughes. A number of people, by no means economic historians alone, were concerned with this lack and are doing something about it. Cambridge, for example, was initiating a pro-gramme for graduate students, but it would of course take several years to produce any sort of output. One can only hope that out of these a certain proportion will be attracted to economic history.

Mathias: There does not appear to be a conspiracy on the part of existing institutions to suppress the new economic history. It was more a lag in supply: the demand for the new practitioners was now running ahead of supply and none would have a warmer welcome at British universities than those who could make up this shortfall. There is a group of adequate minimum size to take-off from the position as it is now. The problem of graduate training, as a precondition for the take-off, is likely to be solved in a decade, perhaps sooner in view of the formal instructional programmes at graduate level breaking out on all sides, leading to a merging of the streams of graduates in economics, economic history and history.

Saul: Demand was definitely not the problem. It is true, though, that the United States was fortunate in its entrepreneurs – Fogel, for example. Moreover, the enormous demand for economists in the last ten years or so for jobs outside universities, given the rigidities of academic pay scales in Britain, has made it difficult for the universities to compete. The suggestion at the end of Hartwell's paper that when the competition is overcome there should be economic historians in each of the separate departments of economics, history and economic history is not, however a good one. Economic history as a discipline is but a part of total history: its true function of contributing to the formation of a broad, balanced picture of history would be lost in such a compartmentalization.

Pollard: He emphasized the distinction between a 'new economic history', a movement separated from economic history in general by inverted commas, and the use of economic and statistical methods. Hughes argues that in the United States there was a fear that economic history as a topic taught in economics departments was on its way out. In Britain, with its separate and strong economic history departments, there is not an equivalent fear of the demise of the field, and consequently there is less incentive to label the work in some distinctive fashion. The opportunity to use econometrics and the new resources for calculation are present in both countries, and there is no reason not to seize the opportunity. On the other hand, there is no need to call it something in inverted commas. When Keynesian economics came into economic history, a revolution of sorts, nobody called it anything in particular, and it flourished without taking a separate identity.

Thomas: One test of the progress of the new economic history was the extent of penetration of the *Economic History Review*. Hughes observes that the new economic history had no formal organization or journal, but it is still true that the 'capture' of the American *Journal of Economic History* was important to its success, permitting many of the articles in the new work to appear. There is, then, an objective test: when will the *Economic History Review* reflect the new work? The *Review* has been eager to publish it, but there is a shortage. Still, this conference demonstrates the promise for the future, in departments of both economic history and economics. Economic history in the new style certainly complements the objectives of both. Economics departments, for example, spend a great deal of time teaching economic growth: in this field and others economic history has a most useful part to play in teaching economics, yet many departments neglect it.

Hughes: It should be emphasized that at the time of the 'capture' of the *Journal of Economic History* there was no general opposition among the establishment of the *Journal* to the new work.

Hunt: Until recently Max Hartwell was one of the editors of the *Economic History Review* and there are few men in Britain more enthusiastic about the new economic history than he. The problem, again, is not one of demand, but supply.

Falkus: There is a more general point. Given the intensive nature of the undergraduate degree in Britain, it might make more sense to teach people to ride the bicycle as undergraduates rather than as graduates. It is desirable for an economic historian to know about the agrarian problem in the sixteenth century as well as multiple correlation techniques, and the question then becomes: how to divide the available time among them?

Supple: The answer to Falkus's question lay in giving up the pretence that the British three-year undergraduate degree is a professional training in any of the social sciences, no more in economics than in economic history. The rare exception aside, at the end of three years you have given the student a rough idea of what it is to do work in his field, but have not produced an economist or an economic historian. In history itself there is no longer the time to give a student a training in the whole field, from classical to modern history. Any other goal than introducing the student to the general lines of the discipline and to a few topics and periods in the study of the past is bound to lead only to frustration.

Trace: It was his own experience that an undergraduate training in history followed by graduate training in theory and statistics is less efficient than the reverse order, if one's goal is to produce new economic historians. That is where the British system needs revision, for undergraduate degrees in economic history do not usually require a deep study of economics. Unfortunately, during the next five years or so the critical constraint is going to be money for intensive graduate training of economic historians who have missed the opportunity as undergraduates. It does not look as though the University Grants Committee and the various research councils are going to give the money to make feasible the scale of graduate programmes discussed here.

Lindert: Was there an underlying assumption in the discussion that the more strictly narrative material was more easily obtained on one's own than the theory?

Supple: The narrative material does not have the sequential nature of economic theory and statistics. One does not have to do A before one does Z.

Temin: It was true as an empirical proposition that it was easier to teach an economist history than a historian economics.

Landes: It was a mistake to characterize either shift as easy. There are historical habits of mind that an economist finds very difficult to acquire and it is difficult, too, for historians to acquire the quantitative methods and theoretical simplifications that economists take for granted. It is not surprising that great economists like Keynes have stumbled when they ventured into history.

Feinstein: He agreed with Temin. It is not strictly relevant to compare the typical economist and the typical historian, for it is atypical men who move from one field to the other. The move from economics to history is probably easier.

Temin: He agreed with Landes's point that each discipline had characteristic habits of mind. One of the striking features of the new economic history is precisely its dependence on the economists' simplifications. People who have acquired this habit of mind will do better work in the new economic history.

Maier: It was true that the economic techniques were acquired cumulatively. On the other hand, learning the historian's craft required a long training, too, learning to see the relevance of a broad range of facts to a particular problem. The papers at the conference had focused on the problem of development and growth, but to a historian, especially a twentieth-century historian, the tools applied do not seem relevant to the equally important and more complex questions of income distribution – the incidence of taxes and social services, the burden of the German inflation, and so on.

Roth: Who were the new economic historians writing for? It seems that in the United States it is primarily for economists, but the question is, then, *why* do they write economic history for economists? Do they expect to bring something new into economics itself by writing history using economics?

McCloskey: The question is in part that asked by the German historical school. The promise then of contributing to economics through the study of history was never fulfilled.

Landes: A related question was: do the new economic historians expect to communicate with historians? An occupational sociologist examining the field now would probably conclude they do not: their reference group is economics and they wish to gain the respect of their fellow economists for themselves and for the field of economic history, which economists have tended recently to look down on. Economists have thought of history as something to dabble in when they are too old to do serious work. There is, then, a serious problem of translating the new economic history into terms useful to the general historian. Moreover, there is a deeper problem of how useful it will be once translated.

Supple: He was not entirely satisfied with the formulation that new economic historians write for economists. At this conference, for example, they have addressed themselves to the question of British entrepreneurial failure, a question that could not be more pertinent to the interests of economic historians. They are not merely exhibiting their ingenious applications of economics for the amusement of economists. It is true, as Landes suggests, that much more remains to be done once the crude economic aspects of the question are examined. But everything can come at its proper time: first things first.

Tyce: It was not useful to emphasize so much the market for which a new economic historian writes. Milton Friedman and Anna Schwartz had no particular market of historians or economists in mind when they wrote *A Monetary History of the United States, 1867-1960*. And every historian interested in its subject, whatever his training, has no doubt read it.

Hughes: The influence of economic history on economics was by no means negligible. The influence worked more through students taking economic history courses, and developing new economic theory in the courses to handle historical problems, than through mature economists, but it was there nonetheless. The students become more sophisticated economists for their chance to apply the tools they have learned to important problems, albeit past problems, and their new awareness that the economic world they see before them is a historical artefact.

Floud: One problem that *is* one of the market is that, in Britain especially, one is teaching undergraduates, not graduates. For this group the problem of translating the new economic history is quite serious. Indeed, this may be one reason the development of it in Britain has not been so rapid as it has been in America. Another difficulty is that Britain has had a longer history and consequently its study is more diffused. The result is that it is more difficult than in America to build up a group of sufficient size with sufficient common knowledge to have the type of discussions we have had at this conference.